GLOBALIZED FATHERHOOD

Fertility, Reproduction and Sexuality

GENERAL EDITORS:

Soraya Tremayne, Founding Director, Fertility and Reproduction Studies Group, and Research Associate, Institute of Social and Cultural Anthropology, University of Oxford
Marcia C. Inhorn, William K. Lanman, Jr. Professor of Anthropology and International Affairs, Yale University
David Parkin, Fellow of All Souls College, University of Oxford
Philip Kreager, Director, Fertility and Reproduction Studies Group, and Research Associate, Institute of Social and Cultural Anthropology and Institute of Human Sciences, University of Oxford

GLOBALIZED FATHERHOOD

Edited by

Marcia C. Inhorn, Wendy Chavkin, and José-Alberto Navarro

berghahn

NEW YORK · OXFORD

www.berghahnbooks.com

Published by

Berghahn Books

www.berghahnbooks.com

Library of Congress Cataloging-in-Publication Data

Globalized fatherhood / edited by Marcia C. Inhorn, Wendy Chavkin,
and José-Alberto Navarro.
    pages cm. -- (Fertility, reproduction and sexuality ; volume 27)
    ISBN 978-1-78238-437-3 (hardback : alk. paper) -- ISBN 978-1-
78238-438-0 (ebook)
    1. Fatherhood. 2. Infertility I. Inhorn, Marcia Claire, 1957- II.
Chavkin, Wendy.. III. Navarro, José-Alberto.
    HQ756.G554 2014
    306.874'2--dc23
                                                           2014016237

British Library Cataloguing in Publication Data

A catalogue record for this book is available from the British Library.

Printed on acid-free paper

ISBN 978-1-78238-437-3 hardback
ISBN 978-1-78238-438-0 ebook

CONTENTS

Tables and Figures

ACKNOWLEDGMENTS

This edited volume represents an intellectual companion to *The Globalization of Motherhood: Deconstructions and Reconstructions of Biology and Care*, edited by Wendy Chavkin and JaneMaree Maher (Routledge 2010). We believe that this current volume is unique. To our knowledge, it represents the first collection of studies on fatherhood by scholars working in a variety of sites around the globe. As a result, all of the chapters in this volume can be said to be original, timely, and cutting edge, capturing the rapidly evolving forms of emergent fatherhood now present in the second decade of the new millennium. This book attempts to carefully theorize and precisely portray these emergent fatherhood forms in every chapter, rendering a rich conceptual vocabulary for consideration. This vocabulary is summarized in the book's introduction, with the hope that this "table of tropes" will prove intellectually fruitful for future scholars of fatherhood as they embark on their own research projects in the twenty-first century.

This volume would not have been possible without the support of a number of institutions and individuals. First, we would like to acknowledge the tremendous support of Yale University, particularly The Whitney and Betty MacMillan Center for International and Area Studies, and the MacMillan Center's Council on Middle East Studies (CMES). The Edward J. and Dorothy Clarke Kempf Memorial Fund of the MacMillan Center provided generous support. We especially want to thank Ian Shapiro, Sterling Professor of Political Science and the Henry R. Luce Director of the MacMillan Center, who provided us with Kempf funding, and to Richard Bribiescas, Chair of Yale's Department of Anthropology, who provided us with the beautiful cover image for this book. We also want to acknowledge the exceptional work of CMES staff members, Lora LeMosy and Amaar Al-Hayder. Special thanks go to Bonnie Rose Schulman, copy editor *extraordinaire,* who brought this collection together through her fine editing skills and her attention to detail. Her role was absolutely crucial in completing a volume with so many parts in a timely and professional fashion. Final thanks go to the brilliant Mira Vale for constructing the index, and Jennifer DeChello, whose faculty support in the Yale Department of Anthropology is invaluable.

Marcia C. Inhorn, Yale University
Wendy Chavkin, Columbia University
José-Alberto Navarro, HEC Paris

Introduction

GLOBALIZED FATHERHOOD

EMERGENT FORMS AND POSSIBILITIES IN THE NEW MILLENNIUM

Marcia C. Inhorn, Wendy Chavkin, and José-Alberto Navarro

Introduction

One of the key insights of 1970s second-wave Western feminism was that paternal participation in childrearing was necessary for gender equity (Chodorow 1999). Yet, even today, there persists a widely held (although largely untested) assumption in feminist, social science, population policy, and lay circles that men remain disinterested and disengaged in matters of human reproduction, childrearing, and the intimate domains of fatherhood and family life.

Is this true? Are men really so removed from the realms of reproduction and fatherhood? In *Reconceiving the Second Sex: Men, Masculinity, and Reproduction*, Marcia C. Inhorn and a group of Danish colleagues (Inhorn et al. 2009) challenged this assumption, drawing inspiration from Simone de Beauvoir's (1949 [2011]) classic feminist treatise, *The Second Sex*. Arguing that men have been relegated as "the second sex" in the scholarship on reproduction, Inhorn and colleagues issued a call to arms to bring men back into the reproductive imaginary as progenitors, partners, decision makers, lovers,

nurturers, fathers, and sentient human beings. Men not only contribute their gametes to human procreation, but are often heavily
involved and invested in most aspects of the reproductive process,
from impregnation to parenting. Furthermore, men have their own
reproductive issues and concerns, which may be connected to, but
also separate from, women's reproductive health and well-being.
Thus, men need to be reconceived as reproductive in their own right,
and men's reproductive "rights" need to be acknowledged along with
women's.

The present volume is intended to further this first volume's aims
by focusing attention on men *as fathers*. A number of volumes—including Faye Ginsburg and Rayna Rapp's (1995) seminal volume,
Conceiving the New World Order: The Global Politics of Reproduction, Barbara Ehrenreich and Arlie Hochschild's (2004) *Global Woman: Nannies, Maids, and Sex Workers in the New Economy,* and Wendy Chavkin
and JaneMaree Maher's (2010) more recent volume, *The Globalization of Motherhood: Deconstructions and Reconstructions of Biology and
Care*—explore new versions and new vicissitudes of motherhood
around the globe, including the ways in which mothers in the Global
North depend upon the mother-care of women from the Global
South. However, nothing comparable has ever been published about
fatherhood in the era of globalization. Indeed, to our knowledge,
this is the first volume devoted mainly to social science research on
fatherhood outside of the West. It includes new work by anthropologists, sociologists, political scientists, and geographers on fatherhood in a wide variety of global locations, ranging from Peru to
India to Vietnam. It also offers an entirely new conceptual vocabulary through which to understand men's experiences and expectations of fatherhood at the dawn of the twenty-first century.

Fatherhood: The State of the Art

This is not to say that fatherhood and its global variations have been
entirely absent from the scholarly imagination. In fact, the literature
on fatherhood has been growing and evolving in recent decades, as
we will describe. However, this research is neither diverse nor comprehensive, particularly when compared to the research on women
as mothers and caretakers. Furthermore, fathers who have been
studied fall largely into two categories: namely, white, American,
middle-class men in monogamous marriages, who are the biological
fathers of children with whom they live, and, in contrast, men who

have sired biological children but have failed to enact the role of fatherhood for the most part. Other forms of "unconventional" fatherhood have been largely ignored. These would include different manifestations of paternity among adoptive fathers, non-biological fathers, non-resident fathers, non-white fathers, mentally disabled fathers, economically disadvantaged fathers, homosexual fathers, and unmarried/separated fathers, including their enactments of fatherhood in various regions of the world.

Fortunately, emerging research on fatherhood is beginning to include such nontraditional study populations. Much of this research is occurring within the three interrelated fields of developmental psychology, human development, and family studies. Topics now included in this growing body of research include the changing relationships between fathers and children; the role of fathers during the distinct stages of child development; adolescent fatherhood; the male single parent; cultural differences in father-child relationships; the ramifications of paternal absence; fathers of children with special needs; and the effects of divorce and custodial arrangements on paternal relationships with children. Particularly significant within this literature are a number of edited volumes by the renowned social and developmental psychologist, Michael E. Lamb. His books include *The Role of the Father in Child Development* (Lamb 1976), *Fatherhood and Family Policy* (Lamb and Sagi 1983), *The Father's Role: Cross-Cultural Perspectives* (Lamb 1987), and *Fathers in Cultural Context* (Shwalb, Shwalb, and Lamb 2013). The contributors to these volumes discuss the ways in which sociocultural influences across time, distinct trends within societies, and established social policies shape and influence notions of fatherhood and the men who enact these roles. These works provide innovative perspectives into the ways in which fatherhood and its many implications are negotiated in various diverse communities and societies.

Historians have also analyzed the ways in which notions of paternity have been socially constructed over time. In what is generally regarded as the first major historical analysis of fatherhood, Robert L. Griswold (1993) suggests that a variety of social and economic forces rooted in the Industrial Revolution generated a "new fatherhood" in the United States, in which men sought to develop more emotionally invested relationships with their children. Furthermore, he argues that this emergent manifestation of fatherhood not only stems from men's longing to be closer to their children, but also from their desire to validate their masculine utilitarian value within the changing family structure. However, Griswold's study focuses primarily on white, middle-class, American men, and thus cannot be said to be representative of fathers from different social, racial/ethnic, cultural, and economic backgrounds within the United States.

An emerging corrective on minority fatherhood in America can be found in public health scholarship, which tends to rely heavily on large, national data sets. Focusing primarily on African-American men, various public health studies have been conducted on how notions of fatherhood in African-American communities can be employed as part of comprehensive HIV prevention strategies, primarily among heterosexual black men and within the context of American welfare policy (Frye and Bonner et al. 2012; Frye and Williams et al. 2012; Geva 2011). Much of this research focuses on non-resident African-American fathers, suggesting that the level of father involvement greatly decreases when a relationship between unmarried parents ends (Edin et al. 2009; Edin and Nelson 2013). Furthermore, these scholars argue that decreases in father involvement are greatest when children are younger. As a result, public health interventions to reconnect non-resident fathers with their adolescent children take on added importance in African-American communities, according to researchers (Caldwell et al. 2004).

Outside of America, development economists have been interested in fatherhood within the context of economic development processes, particularly the ways in which economic and cultural factors shape power hierarchies and resource allocation within the family unit. For example, P. J. W. Bartle (1978) suggests that urbanization, industrialization, and modernization in Ghana have, in many instances, resulted in the increasing subordination of wives and mothers, increasing men's power as fathers, husbands, and uncles. Some scholars explore the implications of different child preferences and the bargaining power of mothers versus fathers, including their effects on offspring. For example, Nancy Qian (2008) argues that in tea-growing agricultural communities in China, the different levels of bargaining power and relative preferences among mothers and fathers ultimately affect the survival rates and levels of educational attainment for both male and female offspring. These data indicate that increasing mothers' income has a positive effect on girls' survival rates and also increasing educational attainment for both boys and girls. However, increasing fathers' income decreases educational attainment for girls and has no effect on the level of educational attainment for boys.

Research in anthropology has differed from these other disciplines in its decidedly global scope across broader expanses of human history. Anthropological studies have demonstrated the many ways in which fathers contribute to raising their children, even though the level of paternal involvement appears to vary dramatically within and between cultures (Hewlett 1991). Biological anthropologists in particular have explored the origins of human fatherhood and paternal involvement from an evolutionary perspective (Gray and Anderson 2010). They have revealed cross-cultural differences in fertility patterns and the involvement of men as both fathers and stepfathers. They have also documented men's concerns over paternity (un)certainty, and how changes in male sexuality and testosterone levels are, in fact, attributable to men's roles as fathers (Bribiescas 2008).

From a somewhat different angle, cultural anthropologists have explored the ways in which the rights, duties, responsibilities, and statuses of fathers are socially constructed and determined, varying considerably across cultures. In recent years, important anthropological research has been conducted on fatherhood in the context of emergent masculinities (Inhorn 2012). For example, in his seminal volume, *The Meanings of Macho: Being a Man in Mexico City,* Matthew Gutmann (2006) explores fatherhood in a social location typically associated with machismo and other vilifying masculine stereotypes. Gutmann's ethnographic study of working-class Mexican men provides insight into the nuanced ways in which various cultural and economic transformations are also transforming the ways in which Mexican men engage in parenting and conceive of their role as fathers.

Turning to the United States, Nicholas Townsend's (2002) book, *Package Deal: Marriage, Work, and Fatherhood in Men's Lives,* takes an innovative ethnographic approach to examining gender and fatherhood within contemporary, middle-class American society. Through a feminist lens, Townsend argues that fatherhood is both an evolving institution and an experience, and he explores the ways in which men's acceptance (or rejection) of "dominant cultural values" influence how they negotiate their roles as fathers.

Several anthropologists have also been interested in men's participation in childbirth, both within and outside America. In *Birthing Fathers: The Transformation of Men in American Rites of Birth,* Richard Reed (2005) explores childbirth from the perspectives of fathers themselves, showing men's emerging desires to participate in birth rituals with their wives, despite ongoing constraints within the American hospital settings where most births take place. Similarly, in *Embodying Culture: Pregnancy in Japan and Israel,* medical anthropologist Tsipy Ivry (2009) highlights and questions men's near total exclusion from childbirth in Japan, as well as the tensions and conflicts she observes when Israeli men attempt to "share" the pregnancy and childbirth experiences of their wives. As she points out, paradoxically, men's participation in childbirth may conflict with women's best interests, especially when birth is highly medicalized and under the control of mostly male physicians.

Although certainly not a comprehensive review of all of the existing literature on fatherhood, this brief examination of major themes sheds light on the ways in which scholars from diverse disciplines are approaching fatherhood across space and time. To be truly comprehensive, the next generation of research on fatherhood must be interdisciplinary and global in nature. Understanding how men's roles and identities as fathers are constructed, negotiated, and enacted is increasingly important in today's world, with its pressing global concerns including economic insecurity, political violence, population movement, and fertility decline in many "aging" societies. As of now, much of the existing research still ignores the ways in which fatherhood is being transformed by cultural, social, political, and economic processes, many of which are global in nature. Yet, global forces are transforming not only fatherhood, but family structures as well. Thus, the chapters in this present volume are intended to interrogate the intersection of globalization and fatherhood, a topic that seems timely, even urgent, at this current moment in twenty-first-century history.

Fatherhood: A New Vocabulary

Given the above, this volume is devoted to "globalized fatherhood," a term that we use to highlight the globally emergent, transnationally inflected transformations in fathering and fatherhood in the twenty-first century. Namely, the convergence of widespread female employment and dramatic declines in birth rates worldwide, with the rise of unprecedented global movements of people, capital, and information, the new global hegemony of neoliberal economic policies, and the continuous invention and dissemination of a host of new reproductive technologies, have led to profound changes in—and new potentialities for—fatherhood across the globe. Whereas nations in the Global North face challenges surrounding declining fertility, aging populations, and shrinking labor markets, many nations in the Global South face challenges around un- and under-employment, the consequent migration of male labor to other countries, and the loss of state institutions in the wake of neoliberal privatization. These intersecting trends in the context of a rapidly globalizing world make men's labor, and their lives in general, more fluid, transitory, stressful, and transnational. The question remains as to how men manage to balance their roles as progenitors, fathers, and nurturers amid these global transformations.

The chapters in this volume suggest that men are responding to globalization in creative and unprecedented ways *as fathers*. We offer the term "emergent fatherhood" to capture the creativity, hybridity, and transformations abundantly apparent in both the discourses and practices of fatherhood in the twenty-first century, not only in the West, but in numerous global locations. Indeed, the focus of most of the chapters of this volume is on emergence: those practices of fatherhood that appear new and transformative. Our notion of emergent fatherhood extends from the earlier work of Inhorn (this volume) on "emergent masculinities" (see also Inhorn and Wentzell 2011; Inhorn 2012). Drawing upon the definition of "emergent" offered by Marxist scholar Raymond Williams (1978)—as "new meanings and values, new practices, new relationships and kinds of relationship [that] are continually being created"—the concept of emergent masculinities focuses attention on the ongoing, relational, and embodied processes of change in the ways that men enact masculinity. In other words, manly selfhood is not a thing, nor a constant; rather, it is an act ever in progress. Men enact manhood in different ways from moment to moment as they move through the different social contexts that form their daily lives. Individual masculinities also change in response to larger life changes; these may include health problems such as infertility, job change, marriage, and fatherhood. Importantly, men live out all of these changes in bodies that are also ever-changing; these changes include aging, becoming ill, or being altered through medical treatment, exercise, or neglect. In other words, the understanding of masculine practice must account for the emergence of change, physically and socially, over the male life course, over the generations, and over the course of social history.

Such emergent masculinities are clearly manifest in emergent fatherhood, or the new ways in which men around the world are thinking about and enacting their fatherhood. As seen in this volume, emergent fatherhood entails new forms of fatherly affect and caretaking, often within the parameters of busy work lives, strict corporate work cultures, and lingering conservative gender norms. Emergent fatherhood also involves a fundamental questioning of paternal labor, as some men make conscious shifts out of the formal work force to raise and care for their children as stay-at-home dads, while others do so out of necessity. Fathers now also include gay men, who increasingly achieve their fatherhood desires through the contributions of egg donors,[1] commercial gestational surrogates, reproductive technologies, and social media sites. Indeed, reproductive technologies have enabled both heteronormative and queer fatherhood, leading to the birth of children for men who would otherwise have remained sterile, childless, or both.

Emergent fatherhood today includes new ways of controlling the timing and spacing of reproduction; new styles of co-parenting that enhance father-child intimacies; new family formations that involve two dads, single dads, stepdads, and dads-at-a-distance; and new forms of fatherly support, including men's reliance on wives' wages, encouragement of wives' careers, and facilitation of daughters' education. All of these fatherhood practices are, in fact, emerging around the world, but are rarely noticed by scholars and media pundits.

Indeed, this book's major intervention is to broadly expand the conceptual vocabulary for theorizing fatherhood in the twenty-first century. Virtually all of the chapters in this volume contribute new tropes, new ways of thinking and talking about fatherhood, and new working vocabularies. In Table 0.1, we highlight these new terms and their definitions, pointing readers to the particular authors and to the global locations in which they carry out their empirical research.

TABLE 0.1. Emergent Fatherhood and Masculinities: A New Vocabulary

Term	Author(s)	Countries	Definition
Activist fathering	Rudrappa (Ch. 12)	India, Australia, and United States	Fathers who work to safeguard the community of children born to gay men through international commercial surrogacy; they serve as active role models and references for other potential gay fathers
Ambivalent fatherhood	Smith (Ch. 13)	Nigeria	Modern fatherhood as characterized by significant contradictions and ambivalence, particularly in relation to expectations of masculinity and men's on-going desires to retain patriarchal authority
Assumed fatherhood	Gürtin (Ch. 9)	Turkey	An assumption of fatherhood that forms a central life-course expectation and can be disrupted by involuntary childlessness

Term	Author(s)	Countries	Definition
Caring communities	Rudrappa (Ch. 12)	India, Australia, and United States	The real and fictive kinship networks that gay fathers create for themselves and their children in order to be accepted without prejudice, especially after transnational commercial gestational surrogacy in India
Composite masculinities	Wentzell (Ch. 7)	Mexico	Contingent and fluid constellations of acts, attitudes, relationships, and physicalities that men weave together into coherent masculine selfhoods through a variety of bodily and social practices, including modeling good parenting practices
Controlling fatherhood	Tremayne (Ch. 14)	Iran	In the midst of social change, the need for men to reassert their paternal authority through resort to strategies of control; four types of controlling fatherhood emerge: 1) resourceful fathers who foresee and pre-empt children's disobedience, 2) resilient fathers who flexibly adjust their approaches to retain control over their children, 3) alienated fathers who become isolated and lose connectivity with their children, and 4) violent fathers, who use physical force against their children to counteract any form of disobedience
Emergent fatherhood	Inhorn, Chavkin, and Navarro (Introduction)		Men are responding to the global forces in creative and unprecedented ways *as fathers*; the focus on *emergence* foregrounds those practices of fatherhood that appear new and transformative, thereby capturing the creativity, hybridity, and transformations abundantly apparent in both the discourses and practices of fatherhood in the twenty-first century, not only in the West, but in numerous global locations; this term derives from "emergent masculinities" (see below)
Emergent masculinities	Inhorn (Ch. 10)	Arab countries of the Middle East	New understandings and practices of manhood, involving change over the male life course, generations, and social history, and

Term	Author(s)	Countries	Definition
			involving men in a variety of transformative social processes, including emergent forms of fatherhood
Excess masculinity	Greenhalgh (Ch. 15)	China	Surplus men, or potential non-fathers, who are unable to find mates and father children because of skewed, male-heavy sex ratios, the result of the one-child policy and discrimination against girls
Expressive fatherhood	Birenbaum-Carmeli, Diamand, and Abu Yaman (Ch. 6)	Gaza Strip and Israel	Complete immersion in the fatherhood caring role, fulfilled wholeheartedly, with open expressions of affection toward one's children
Father-as-provider	Leinaweaver (Ch. 3)	Peru and Spain	The long standing primary social role of fatherhood being equated with economic provision, and encoded transnationally in migration policy and remittance practices
Father-carers	Lam and Yeoh (Ch. 4)	Indonesia and Philippines	Fathers who are in charge of buying food, managing finances, earning money, attending school events, disciplining, and undertaking the intimate and mundane aspects of care work in relation to their children
Forbidden fatherhood	Gürtin (Ch. 9)	Turkey	The pursuit of fatherhood beyond acceptable parameters, thereby forcing men to act as "moral pioneers"; an example entails the use of donor sperm, which is legally banned in most Muslim countries
Globalized fatherhood	Inhorn, Chavkin, and Navarro (Introduction)		Globally emergent, transnationally inflected transformations in fathering and fatherhood in the 21st century; in the context of a rapidly globalizing world, men's lives and labor are more fluid, transitory, stressful, and transnational; thus men must balance their roles as fathers and nurturers amidst these global transformations
Hidden fatherhood	North (Ch. 2)	Japan	Male caregivers who keep a low profile in the workplace to maintain the façade of "corporate warrior-hood," even though they may desire increased parental leave and more time with their children

Term	Author(s)	Countries	Definition
High-tech homunculus	Kahn and Chavkin (Ch. 8)	United States (as global donor sperm exporter)	The ongoing primacy accorded the male gamete in the high-tech field of assisted reproduction, with implications for the health and well-being of infertile fathers, sperm donors, women, and their offspring
Ikumen	North (Ch. 2)	Japan	Men who enjoy raising children and "grow themselves" in the process; a new attempt to connect involved fathering with fashionable masculinity
Promised fatherhood	Gürtin (Ch. 9)	Turkey	The promise of fatherhood held out by technological advancements in the treatment of male infertility, even when most of these technologies are not highly successful
Relational fatherhood	Browne (Ch. 1)	United Kingdom	A very basic condition of fatherhood involving time spent personally interacting with children, physical caring, playing, emotional engagement, and education
Relational fatherhood work	Dempsey (Ch. 11)	Australia and United States	Time spent by fathers reflecting on and enacting relationships that is sensitive to concerns about children's future sense of identity; it involves processes of emotional labor and communicative effort to secure children's sense of kinship, belonging, and connectedness
Silent fathers	Leinaweaver (Ch. 3)	Peru	Men who are "silent" because they do not fulfill the "father-as-provider" model; these men let their wives and children emigrate while they stay behind, or give up their biological children to overseas adoptive families
Stay-at-home fathers	Thao (Ch. 5)	Vietnam	Men who stay at home to care for their children while their wives migrate for work; these men enact "emotion work" through their housework and involved childcare
Toxic fatherhood	Kilshaw (Ch. 16)	United Kingdom	Men's fears that their toxic exposures are contagious and that they will pass on the disability or illness to their offspring; this form of fatherhood is toxic in that it impacts family life as a whole

Fatherhood: Key Themes

This volume is intended as both a corrective and a beginning for future discussions of emergent fatherhood around the globe. It is organized around five key themes, which highlight some of the most salient aspects of emergent fatherhood around the globe. These themes include: (1) work, (2) migration, (3) care, (4) reproduction, and (5) family formation.

Fatherhood and Work

In the countries of the Global North, progress toward gender equity in both employment and domestic responsibilities is certainly not complete, but has nonetheless transformed men's roles and responsibilities in family life. These include the various policies and laws that affect men as fathers, including their ability to work for meaningful family wages, to take leave upon the birth of children or the disability of family members, to balance work with family life, and to migrate for work, under laws that facilitate or limit these various practices.

Fatherhood and Migration

In the countries of the Global South, where economies may be unable to support the well-being of breadwinning fathers and their families, the dynamics of fatherhood may include solo labor migration of men to many other countries, a process that often disassociates men from their wives and children for long periods of time. How men construct their notion of "fatherhood at a distance" requires interrogation. This includes fathers whose primary motivations for labor migration are to provide a better life for their children back home. Increasingly, fathers are left at home tending to children as their wives head into global labor markets. Men's responses to childcare responsibilities, and their relationships with both their children and migrant wives, require careful scholarly analysis.

Fatherhood and Care

Increasingly, men around the world are assuming new roles as carers, giving care to their wives and children and taking care of themselves for the sake of their families. Today, fatherly care assumes many forms, from feeding and bathing young children, to assisting with homework and attending parent-teacher conferences. Men's caretaking may also occur in situations of uncertainty and duress, for example, during periods of childhood illness, when fathers may be called upon to manage medical emergencies and provide direct health care services to their children. Caretaking may also assume other forms, including providing care and support to female partners during periods of reproductive crisis and child loss.

Fatherhood and Reproduction

Fatherhood is intimately tied to reproduction. Yet, this basic insight is generally taken for granted and remains unexamined. In the new millennium, reproduction has been transformed, with paths to fatherhood emerging through a variety of forms and techniques of assisted reproduction. In many cases, men who never would have produced biological children are now able to do so. In other cases, social fatherhood is being achieved through new global markets in sperm, transnational adoption, and commercial gestational surrogacy, catering to both heterosexual couples and gay men.

Fatherhood and Family Formation

Indeed, if there is one strong thematic running through this volume it is that fathers come in many forms. This volume highlights a variety of new forms, including gay men fathering children who have been born through the paid services of egg donors and gestational surrogates, left-behind fathers who are raising their children while their wives work—and live—elsewhere, and single men who may sire hundreds of biological children through their work as commercial sperm donors. This "brave new world" of fatherhood is brought to light in numerous chapters in this volume, suggesting that today fatherhood may or may not involve: (1) direct parenting of one's biological children, (2) co-residence with wives and children, (3) participation of wives or other women as co-parents, and (4) assumptions of heteronormativity in fatherhood. Gay dads are creating communities of care for their children, who are conceived through a variety of means, often transnationally. Many different family configurations are emerging around the globe, and men are participating in these families as fathers in diverse ways.

Fatherhood: Future Challenges and Possibilities

Finally, it is important to emphasize that the focus on emergence and new forms of fatherhood does not imply that all that is new is necessarily positive, nor that fatherhood everywhere is changing for the better. There are still serious challenges confronting fatherhood around the globe. Some of these challenges are structural and relate to poverty, lack of employment opportunities, and unforgiving work environments and policies (Edin and Nelson 2013). Other challenges are demographic, reflecting increasing pressures on men in the absence of marriageable women—for example, in several countries of Southeast Asia with male-heavy sex ratios, or in the so-called "barren" states of Europe and East Asia, where fertility rates have fallen so low that concerns about future social reproduction are real. Finally, some challenges are related to shifting gender dynamics and the unremitting persistence of patriarchy in many societies. As women pursue education, employment, and gender equality, men are likely to lose some of their masculine privilege and patriarchal authority. In some cases, men may be unwilling to relinquish their hegemonic roles as family breadwinners and authoritarian fathers. As shown in some of the chapters, how men deal with the decline of patriarchy around the globe is variable. In some cases, men amplify their efforts to control wives and children, while in other cases, men make attempts to accommodate increasing gender equality by ceding patriarchal control.

Social and political change is never linear and clean, as we know well from historical examination of efforts toward racial integration, religious tolerance, improved working conditions, rights of minorities, and so on. Those with power and privilege do not cede them easily, and their retention is sometimes aided even by those disadvantaged who may experience the cultural manifestations of the inequitable status quo to be normative and entwined with identity. Nowhere is this more apparent than in the most intimate sphere of gender roles and selfhood, reproduction and family.

The patriarchal familial norm (with variations) accords power and participation in the public domain to the wage-earning husband/ father and assigns biological and social reproduction to women. Indeed, the globally subordinate status of women has been explained by their relegation to the domestic sphere (Ortner 1972). Yet, female employment outside the home increased dramatically during the twentieth century without toppling women's requirement to reproduce, biologically and socially. For example, after the Russian Revolution, the Soviet government attempted to change the status and role of women and the family. However, shortly thereafter, the Stalinist government replaced these initial efforts toward gender equality with policies designed instead to enable women to combine gendered family responsibilities with their newly expanded educational and employment options (Lapidus 1978). Similar patterns prevailed in the Western capitalist countries where varied public programs facilitated women's newfound engagement in the labor market with their traditional responsibilities for rearing children and maintaining life at home.

A host of scholars have concluded that women found the burden of responsibilities in these dual spheres to be unsustainable and that this has led to the dramatic declines in birthrates that began in the highly developed world in the last third of the twentieth century and have now spread everywhere but sub-Saharan Africa (Castles 2003; McDonald 2000). Thus, at the beginning of the new millennium, the Organization for Economic Development (2005) and the United Nations Development Programme (2003) have concluded that policies need to promote paternal participation in the domestic sphere and to support men and women in combining work and family responsibilities. Such shifts in social roles require structural underpinning in order to be feasible on a population level.

The Nordic countries led the way in crafting such policies beginning in the 1970s but soon found that men did not take as much leave as expected. Further analysis revealed that occupational gender and wage divisions persisted with women concentrated in the lower paying public sector and men in the higher paying private sector. The private sector discouraged use of extended leave provision, and the wage disparity between men and women meant that it would be disadvantageous economically for a couple to forgo the man's wages. In recent years, several Nordic countries have stipulated that specified portions of the extensive leave available must be taken by fathers ("use it or lose it") (Gornick and Schmitt 2010; Haataja 2009). Sweden also launched a public relations campaign to shake up cultural assumptions, showing stereotypic "Viking" men holding babies and crowing that "half (of leave) is ours" (Klinth 2008). Men's use of parental leave in these countries has increased significantly, whereas it has not in France, a country that has policies to help women accomplish their double load, but does not address male workers as fathers.

Of course, in order for policy to be effective, given the staying power of old modes and tropes, it must be based on accurate diagnosis of the underlying driving forces. The Swedish efforts did not redress gender segregation at work and the accompanying wage gaps that perpetuate the primacy of the male higher wage. China's sex ratio imbalance is reportedly driven by peoples' belief that sons will care for aged parents and thus, if allowed only one child, Chinese parents consider it imperative to have sons, and achieve this by relinquishing baby girls or aborting female fetuses. Establishing pensions may thus be a far more relevant policy intervention than prohibition of sex-selective abortion. China is now piloting pensions for rural farmers (Ying 2012). While some work-family policies in the Global North allow for care of elder parents or family members other than children, data regarding whether new fathers are undertaking this increasingly needed aspect of care is as yet unavailable.

Given the historic weight and internalized salience of gender-associated familial roles and male privilege and power, it is not surprising that expressions of change in the behaviors of fathers are uneven, complicated, and contradictory. The conflation of female reproductive capacity with social assignment for childrearing and maintenance of domestic life remains the determinative factor underlying job segregation by gender and the associated gender wage gap in developed economies, and with female mortality and economic and sociopolitical deprivation in developing ones. Individuals maneuver within all of these contexts simultaneously (Spar 2013). Thus, in this volume, we see accounts of some men who are pioneers in melding new technologically assisted bio-possibilities with new paternal roles in social reproduction, while not questioning the old hierarchies of gender, colonial relationships, and race that enable them to do so. It should come as no surprise, therefore, that the emergence of new forms of fatherhood is uneven and replete with contradictions. What is amazing is the rapidity of these changes and the fact that they are occurring in so many settings, as amply demonstrated in the chapters of this volume.

Fatherhood: The Chapters

This volume comprises sixteen chapters, most of them based on original ethnographic research undertaken by anthropologists, human geographers, and sociologists. But the volume is also explicitly interdisciplinary, drawing upon perspectives from public health and medicine, public policy, political science, and demography. The chapters have been organized in pairs, based less along disciplinary lines than on topical resonances. Furthermore, they are organized to highlight the connections between the eight different sections. Brief descriptions of the chapters are as follows:

Corporate Fatherhood

Chapter 1, "The Corporate Father," by Jude Browne, considers the shortcomings of contemporary parental leave policy in the context of European corporate work. It introduces the concept of "relational fatherhood" to think about how best to design policies aimed at working fathers and gender equality. In particular, Browne, a political scientist and gender scholar, focuses on the ways in which current approaches to gender equality lack the necessary focus or mechanisms for addressing structural constraints at the institutional level. By way of a future direction for policy design, Browne explores the arguments of political philosophers Gheaus and Robeyns's (2011) work on default policy and concludes with recommendations aimed at both corporate and state policy makers.

In Chapter 2, "Hiding Fatherhood in Corporate Japan," Scott North examines the stereotypical portrayal of Japanese fathers as stern, distant, and minimally involved at home. However, recent demographic challenges and rapid transformation of the labor market and employment practices have created conditions in which men's attitudes toward fathering and their actual fathering behavior are obviously changing. This chapter takes stock of how the interplay of changing gender roles, economic conditions, and state policies is transforming fatherhood in contemporary Japan. Current efforts to stimulate and support increased paternal involvement in family work at the grassroots, governmental, and corporate levels are visible, including in new social media campaigns. However, the author finds that Japanese men must continue to "hide" their fatherhood in the corporate workplace, including use of officially sanctioned paternity leave. Although emergent forms of fatherhood are increasingly valorized in contemporary Japan, corporate culture continues to inhibit parental involvement, resisting changing fatherhood.

Transnational Fatherhood

In Chapter 3, "Transnational Fathers, Good Providers, and the Silences of Adoption," Jessaca Leinaweaver uses two case studies to examine the different parenting tools available to adoptive and migrant fathers. Peruvian children who are adopted by Spanish fathers may, as a result of their adoption, enter Spain as Spanish citizens, and grow up there with the caring guidance of their co-resident parents. Peruvian children whose Peruvian fathers have migrated to Spain for work, by contrast, often must remain in Peru—in part because Spanish policies of family reunification preclude their entry and preclude that of other family members, with the result that there are no extended kin in Spain able to care for them while the father works. As a consequence, Spanish-resident Peruvian fathers separated from their children by an ocean engage in certain fathering practices; Spanish fathers who have brought their children across that ocean via adoption engage in others. This chapter examines the similarities and differences between what these fathers want, and attempt to do, for their Peruvian-origin children. Contrasting the parenting work that these two groups of fathers do reveals certain globalized inequalities that underlie contemporary fatherhood, including many silences surrounding transnational adoption of children from the Global South. Leinaweaver shows that a model of father-as-provider shapes the parenting work both of migrant fathers (whose fathering is discursively limited to sending remittances) and of adoptive fathers (who are prohibited from mentioning their work as providers by a powerful adoption language ideology, and thus lack a key tool to construct themselves as legitimate and real fathers to their children).

In Chapter 4, "Long-Distance Fathers, Left-Behind Fathers, and Returnee Fathers: Changing Fathering Practices in Indonesia and the Philippines," Theodora Lam and Brenda S. A. Yeoh argue that one of the key structural causes leading to emergent transformations in fathering practices in Southeast Asia is the feminization of labor migration. In response to the increasing demand for domestic and care workers in gender-segmented global labor markets, house-holding strategies are being reformulated at the Southernmost end of the global care chain when women-as-mothers rewrite their roles (but often not their identities) through labor migration. Women can now be seen as productive workers, who contribute to the well-being of their children through financial remittances and "long-distance mothering." The burgeoning scholarship on transnational forms of motherhood and mothering has in turn put the spotlight on the corresponding role of fathers, both in terms of the transnational equivalent of the "long-distance father" as well as the localized figure of the "left-behind father." Using interview material with household members in source communities in Indonesia and the Philippines experiencing considerable pressures from labor migration, this chapter explores communication practices, the provision of care, and the construction of intimacies in three contrasting modes of house-holding—the "father-migrant, mother-carer" household, the "mother-migrant, father-carer" household, and the "mother-resident, father-returnee" household—giving emphasis to the way fatherhood is affirmed, vilified, and negotiated, even as fathering practices adapt to the realities of globalized mobilities.

Primary Care Fatherhood

Chapter 5, "When the Pillar of the Home is Shaking: Female Labor Migration and Stay-at-Home Fathers in Vietnam," by Vu Thi Thao, focuses on the increasing numbers of rural female migrants moving to urban areas of Vietnam in search of employment since the economic reforms of the early 1990s, known as Doi Moi. While women's responsibilities for reproduction and fathers' role as the "pillar of the home" retain their significance in contemporary Vietnam, this chapter explores the implications of female labor migration for fathering and fatherhood. More specifically, Thao examines the performance of fathering in families where mothers migrate, as well as how stay-at-home fathers reconstruct their roles as breadwinners and heads of families. Using interviews with stay-at-home fathers, migrant wives, and their children, the chapter shows that fathers accept their new responsibilities as primary caregivers, while simultaneously strongly opposing changing gender relations. They struggle to maintain their role—as the pillar of the home—even though children's and wives' perceptions of fathers' status and role are changing.

Chapter 6, "On Fatherhood in a Conflict Zone: Gaza Fathers and Their Children's Cancer Treatments," by Daphna Birenbaum-Carmeli, Yana Diamand, and Maram Abu Yaman, is a poignant account of Palestinian men from Gaza, who must seek cross-border treatment for their sick children in Israeli pediatric oncology wards. While attending to sick children has traditionally been a woman's responsibility, the chapter shows how an international political conflict has prompted a profound change in gender roles in this caring sphere. Due to the obstacles that Israel presents to medical patients at every border crossing from the Gaza Strip into Israel, Israeli oncologists must keep children with cancer hospitalized until they have completed their full treatment course. The extended hospitalization requires many mothers to remain at home in order to care for their other children. Thus, it is the unemployed Gaza father who often accompanies a sick child during long months of severe illness, and is then isolated in the foreign country that is largely responsible for the very need to seek treatment abroad, and for the restrictions that prevent him and his child from going back home on treatment breaks. The chapter reveals that despite the hardships of exile, this group of Gaza fathers manages not only to fulfill the instrumental tasks, but to transcend traditional gender roles and images. These men tend to their children; invent ways to overcome their boredom, loneliness, and suffering; and express emotional warmth openly. The chapter reflects on this form of caring, expressive fatherhood in the context of violent conflict.

Clinical Fatherhood

In Chapter 7, "Enhancing Fathering through Medical Research Participation in Mexico," Emily Wentzell shows that some Mexican men of child-rearing age strive to be different kinds of men and parents than the fathers they see as problematically traditional. The chapter investigates men's enactment of these self-consciously "modern" masculinities through participation in an international, longitudinal study of human papillomavirus (HPV) transmission in males. Study participants undergo biannual testing for this common (and commonly asymptomatic) sexually transmitted infection, including collection of biological samples and sexual and health behavior data over a period of five years. This frequent engagement, plus the additional enrollment of female partners, makes participation in the study likely to have a significant impact on these men's lives. While the study organizers conceive of their research as focusing narrowly on sexually transmitted infection, this group of Mexican men appears to be using their participation in this international project as a way to enact "progressive" masculinity and fatherhood. They understand their participation in relationship to local discourses about global modernity, which often entail calls for enactment of "modern" masculinity through good parenting. These participants voice and strive to enact a holistic vision of health that includes progressive fathering. Thus, they see their participation as enabling self-care that physically ensures their fitness to father, modeling socially positive behavior for their children, and enhancing Mexico's "modernity" on the world stage.

In Chapter 8, "The High-Tech Homunculus: New Science, Old Constructs," Linda G. Kahn and Wendy Chavkin address new forms of fatherhood via technologically assisted reproduction. As they note, the ability of women to reproduce via artificial insemination—once the stuff of feminist fiction—has brought to the fore a number of questions relating to the notion of fatherhood and the role of fathers in the high-tech, globalized economy. While we may no longer believe in the theory of the homunculus—the little man inside the sperm that contributed all of the material necessary to grow a child in the passive female womb—hints of the enduring primacy accorded the male gamete range from the aggressive marketing of frozen sperm in the United States to the very strict and particular rules governing use of third-party sperm elsewhere around the globe, to the burgeoning use of intracytoplasmic sperm injection (ICSI). There is now a lively—and profitable—international market for sperm, influenced by both cultural and regulatory factors. However, the rapid development of the market in sperm and normalization of ICSI have outpaced the ability of governments to deal with the ethical and legal implications, much less the impact on individual and public health. This chapter poses a number of questions about the use of purchased or donor sperm and the use of ICSI to facilitate fatherhood, focusing on the medical and public health implications. While some countries have begun to deal with these issues in a variety of ways, few have matched their support for assisted reproductive technologies that resolve male infertility with corresponding support for fathers once the children have been born.

Infertile Fatherhood

In Chapter 9, "Assumed, Promised, Forbidden: Infertility, IVF, and Fatherhood in Turkey," Zeynep B. Gürtin examines fatherhood in Turkey, where it is so central to men's life expectations that most men automatically assume that they will become fathers. In this strongly pronatalist country, infertile men turn to in vitro fertilization and other assisted reproductive technologies, which deliver the promise of fatherhood. However, some forms of technological assistance are forbidden, including all forms of third-party reproductive assistance (i.e., donor eggs, donor sperm, donor embryos, and gestational surrogacy), which have been illegal in Turkey since the introduction of a law to regulate assisted reproductive technologies (ARTs) in 1987. Moreover, the taboo, particularly on the use of third-party sperm, reflects and is enforced by both the moralities of the local religion of Sunni Islam and by cultural ideals about procreation, family, and lineage. Thus, men with intractable infertility face an extremely difficult decision: a childless life or recourse to forbidden ARTs. While most Turkish men opt for the former, the chapter shows that there are a few Turkish men who accept others' sperm and have engaged in cross-border reproductive care with their wives for this purpose.

Chapter 10, "New Arab Fatherhood: Emergent Masculinities and Assisted Reproduction," by Marcia C. Inhorn, presents a humanizing portrayal of ordinary Arab men as they struggle to overcome their infertility and become loving fathers. Contrary to popular expectations, male infertility is more common than female infertility in the Middle East, and many Middle Eastern men are engaged in high-tech forms of assisted reproduction. Through in-depth ethnography undertaken in ART clinics in four countries, the chapter captures the marital commitments and fatherhood desires of infertile Arab men as they engage with ARTs, often across transnational borders. Emerging technologies—particularly ICSI to overcome male infertility—are changing Middle Eastern men's hopes for fatherhood. However, these "ICSI quests" are also fraught with material and moral challenges. For example, because of low ICSI success rates, some men become "reproductive tourists," searching globally for efficacious ARTs. Furthermore, ICSI may perpetuate genetic disorders into the next generation, especially among male offspring. As Middle Eastern men engage with these globalizing ARTs, they are self-consciously rethinking fatherhood, masculinity, and marriage. Indeed, in the twenty-first century, emergent masculinities in the Middle East involve the questioning of many taken-for-granted assumptions about Arab men *as* men and fathers in an era of emerging science and technology.

Gay/Surrogate Fatherhood

Chapter 11, "Relating across International Borders: Gay Men Forming Families through Overseas Surrogacy," by Deborah Dempsey, shows that intentionally planned parenthood by gay male couples through commercial surrogacy in the United States and India is gaining momentum in Australia. Very little is known about the relational considerations of men forming families through sperm provision, egg purchase, and internationally sourced surrogate mothers. This chapter uses data from a self-selected small sample of gay men to consider the meaning and management of biogenetic and gestational maternity in the creation of these men's family relationships. The choice as to who provides the egg and who serves as the surrogate reveals a range of strategic considerations related to beliefs in children's entitlement to knowledge about their biological heritage, and the maintenance of parent-child and extended family relationships, as well as unexamined assumptions about race and class. The chapter also considers the status of relationships with egg providers and surrogates as family relationships, in the context of an ongoing debate in Australia about whether international commercial surrogacy constitutes an exploitative and unacceptable commodification of women's reproductive services.

In Chapter 12, "Conceiving Fatherhood: Gay Men and Indian Surrogate Mothers," Sharmila Rudrappa examines the fathering practices of gay men in the United States and Australia who have achieved paternity through cross-border reproductive care. Because of a plethora of reasons, including homophobia, these men have turned to Indian surrogate mothers to achieve fatherhood. Rudrappa addresses two questions on globalized fatherhood. First, how do intended fathers living in Australia and the United States create familial bonds to the not-yet-born fetuses in India, and subsequently to the newborn babies once they arrive? Second, what sorts of caring labor do the fathers engage in once the babies arrive into their social worlds back home? Along with the considerable caring labors the commissioning fathers engage in before and after the surrogate-born infants arrive, these gay men narrate thick stories regarding their fatherhood practices. These narratives are central to nurturing what Rudrappa calls "caring communities," within which gay fathers raise these almost always biracial babies who were born to Third World surrogate mothers halfway across the world. Caring communities are the real and fictive kinship networks that the fathers create for themselves and for their children. Caring communities not only support the gay fathers in their family-building efforts, but also provide safe spaces within which these children can securely grow. However, Rudrappa demonstrates how these First World men may sideline the labor of and risks to the Third World surrogate mothers who are so central to their attainment of fatherhood. The marginalization of the mothers' efforts reflects the structure of the global market in surrogacy, as well as how fatherhood itself is constituted for these gay men.

Ambivalent Fatherhood

In Chapter 13, "Fatherhood, Companionate Marriage, and the Contradictions of Masculinity in Nigeria," Daniel Jordan Smith describes how siring children and providing for one's family are the most important markers of manhood in southeastern Nigeria. Yet, even as having children continues to be the ultimate measuring stick for successful masculinity, changes in economic, social, and domestic life are reconfiguring men's expectations and experiences of fatherhood. For modern Nigerian men, contradictions abound. Messages from ever more popular Pentecostal churches that exhort men to embrace monogamy and fidelity compete with male peer pressure to prove their rising economic status by spending money on young mistresses. The emergence of globally influenced ideals of romantic love and marital intimacy—and, to an increasing extent, gender equality—frequently come into conflict with the enduring conviction that a man must be the king of his castle. Pressures to have fewer children and invest in them educationally and emotionally contend with still salient notions of children as a form of wealth and fatherhood as characterized by paternal authority, distance, and emotional reserve. This chapter examines changes in the experience of fatherhood among men married in the last twenty years or so—arguably the population in Nigeria most affected by these transformations and the contradictions they produce. In particular, new patterns of fathering are analyzed in the context of the intersection of notions of masculinity with changing marriage practices, lower fertility, and increasingly nuclear household composition in a society that still valorizes extended kinship ties and male privilege. These patterns—and their contradictions—create uncertainties and ambivalence about modern fatherhood in Nigeria.

Chapter 14, "The Four Faces of Iranian Fatherhood," by Soraya Tremayne, examines contemporary fatherhood in the Islamic Republic of Iran. State-sponsored population policies and increasing education have led to a major reduction in the average size of the family, which is still declining. The total fertility rate is similar to that of western Europe, below the level needed for population replacement. With fewer children in the household, the assumption is that children are more cherished, perceived as more precious, and thus receive better care. While these observations may be correct, they remain true of a limited sector of Iranian society, that which is predominantly secular, well educated, and affluent. Unfortunately, abundant evidence exists of ongoing family violence in Iran, including toward children. This chapter examines the understanding of what constitutes fatherhood in a predominantly patrilineal and patriarchal society among men who are caught at the crossroads between modernity and the fight to preserve their identities and privileges. For many men in Iran, being in control of their children is still central to normative notions of fatherhood. Thus, many men are willing to assert themselves, including violently, in order to "save face" when their children question their authority in the household.

Imperiled Fatherhood

Chapter 15, "'Bare Sticks' and Other Dangers to the Social Body: Assembling Fatherhood in China," by Susan Greenhalgh, analyzes China's aggressive policies to limit fertility in order to spur economic development and its rise as a global power. Greenhalgh argues that these policies transpired against the backdrop of longstanding assumptions about male superiority and the need for sons to carry out filial duties, with the consequent loss of girls. Now, thirty years later, China has a surplus of men unable to find brides or reproduce. This chapter explores how the one-child policy, introduced in the feverish political context of post-Mao China, inadvertently produced this group of men; the strategies the men, known in Chinese as "bare sticks" (*guanggun*), are using in response to their reproductive plight; and the ethical and political consequences of denying fatherhood to some 10 percent of China's adult male population.

The final chapter, Chapter 16, "Paternity Poisoned: The Impact of Gulf War Syndrome on Fatherhood," by Susie Kilshaw, explores militarism and fatherhood with a focus on Gulf War veterans. In particular, it investigates the ways in which these military men experience themselves as damaged fathers as a result of their military service, and their subsequent fight for recognition of their condition. Gulf War Syndrome is reported to affect the core of a sufferer's masculinity, with veterans' narratives focusing on physical symptoms affecting sexuality and reproduction. Furthermore, veterans consider their illness to be contagious and believe that they themselves may be toxic and may put family members at risk. They see fatherhood as impaired through symptoms that make fatherhood difficult to attain (problems in conceiving, miscarriages, low libido, and burning semen) and problematic once attained. One of the challenges these men face is their need to present as ill, wounded, and vulnerable in order to fight for recognition of their illness. Yet, this sick role means that Gulf War veterans are often unable to fulfill familial roles such as breadwinning and caring for their children as fathers.

Together, these chapters provide a rich overview of new and complex developments in fathering at the beginning of the twenty-first century. They present us with evidence of profound shifts in gendered behaviors toward children, while at the same time demonstrating the persistence of hierarchically based assumptions about men's and women's roles in the world. These apparent contradictions are to be expected, as are uneven rates of adaptation to new economic, social, and technologically fueled possibilities. However, the rapidity of the profound alterations in such intimately experienced domains as reproduction and parenthood is dramatic and noteworthy and requires ongoing scrutiny and analysis. Which norms and behaviors have been amenable to change and under which circumstances? What sorts of structural or policy shifts support new forms of parental and domestic arrangements, and which components appear resistant? This volume suggests that we must continue to pay close attention to the varied, multidirectional, emerging versions of fatherhood around the world, and probe their underlying dynamics. Only then can we hope to design empirically based policies and structural supports for fathers and mothers to nurture children within equitable gender relationships.

Notes

1. Although the term "donor" is commonly used, it is important to emphasize that most egg and sperm donors are paid for their services.

References

Bartle, P. J. W. 1978. "Modernization and the Decline in Women's Status: An Example from a Matrilineal Akan Community." *Proceedings of the Seminar of Ghanaian Women in Development* 2: 737–65.
Bribiescas, Richard. 2008. *Men: Evolutionary and Life History.* Cambridge: Harvard University Press.
Caldwell, Cleopatra H., Joan C. Wright, Marc A. Zimmerman, Katrina M. Walsemann, Deborah Williams, and Patrick A. C. Isichei. 2004. "Enhancing Adolescent Health Behaviors through Strengthening Non-resident Father–Son Relationships: A Model for Intervention with African-American Families." *Health Education Research* 19, no. 6: 644–56.
Castles, Francis. 2003. "The World Turned Upside Down: Below Replacement Fertility, Changing Preferences and Family Friendly Public Policy in 21 OECD Countries." *Journal of European Social Policy* 13: 209–27.
Chavkin, Wendy, and JaneMaree Maher, eds. 2010. *The Globalization of Motherhood: Deconstructions and Reconstructions of Biology and Care.* New York: Routledge.
Chodorow, Nancy J. 1999. *The Reproduction of Mothering: Psychoanalysis and the Sociology of Gender.* Revised Edition. New York: Penguin.
De Beauvoir, Simone. [1949] 2011. *The Second Sex.* New York: Vintage.
Edin, Kathryn, Laura Tach, and Ronald Mincy. 2009. "Claiming Fatherhood: Race and Dynamics of Paternal Involvement among Unmarried Men." *The Annals of the American Academy of Political and Social Science* 621, no. 1: 149–77.
Edin, Kathryn, and Timothy J. Nelson. 2013. *Doing the Best I Can: Fatherhood in the Inner City.* Berkeley: University of California Press.
Ehrenreich, Barbara, and Arlie Hochschild. 2004. *Global Woman: Nannies, Maids, and Sex Workers in the New Economy.* New York: Holt.
Frye, Victoria, Kim Williams, Keosha T. Bond, Kirk Henny, Malik Cupid, Linda Weiss, Debbie Lucy, and Beryl A. Koblin. 2012. "Condom Use and Concurrent Partnering among Heterosexually Active, African American

Men: A Qualitative Report." *Journal of Urban Health:* Bulletin of the New York Academy of Medicine.

Frye, Victoria, Sebastian Bonner, Kim Williams, Kirk Henny, Keosha Bond, Debbie Lucy, Malik Cupid, Stephen Smith, and Beryl A. Koblin. 2012. "Straight Talk: HIV Prevention for African-American Heterosexual Men: Theoretical Bases and Intervention Design." *AIDS Education and Prevention* 24, no. 5: 389–407.

Geva, Dorit. 2011. "Not Just Maternalism: Marriage and Fatherhood in American Welfare Policy." *Social Politics* 18, no. 1: 24–51.

Gheaus, Anca, and Ingrid Robeyns. 2011. "Equality—Promoting Parental Leave." *Journal of Social Philosophy* 42, no. 2: 173–91.

Ginsburg, Faye, and Rayna Rapp, eds. 1995. *Conceiving the New World Order: The Global Politics of Reproduction.* Berkeley: University of California Press.

Gornick, Ray R., and J. C. Schmitt. 2010. "Who Cares? Assessing Generosity and Gender Equality in Parental Leave Policy Designs in 21 Countries." *Journal of European Social Policy* 20, no. 3: 196–216.

Gray, Peter B., and Kermyt G. Anderson. 2010. *Fatherhood: Evolution and Human Paternal Behavior.* Cambridge: Harvard University Press.

Griswold, Robert L. 1993. *Fatherhood in America: A History.* New York: Basic Books.

Gutmann, Matthew C. 2006. *The Meanings of Macho: Being a Man in Mexico City.* Berkeley: University of California Press.

Haataja, A. 2009. "Father's Use of Paternity and Parental Leave in the Nordic Countries." Working Paper. Helskini: The Social Insurance Institution of Finland.

Hewlett, B. S. 1991. *Intimate Fathers.* Ann Arbor: University of Michigan Press.

Inhorn, Marcia C. 2012. *The New Arab Man: Emergent Masculinities, Technologies, and Islam in the Middle East.* Princeton: Princeton University Press.

Inhorn, Marcia C., and Emily A. Wentzell. 2011. "Embodying Emergent Masculinities: Reproductive and Sexual Health Technologies in the Middle East and Mexico." *American Ethnologist* 38, no. 4: 801–15.

Inhorn, Marcia C., Tine Tjørnhøj-Thomsen, Helene Goldberg, and Maruska la Cour Mosegaard, eds. 2009. *Reconceiving the Second Sex: Men, Masculinity, and Reproduction.* New York; Oxford: Berghahn Books.

Ivry, Tsipy. 2009. *Embodying Culture: Pregnancy in Japan and Israel.* New Brunswick, NJ: Rutgers University Press.

Klinth, R. 2008. "The Best of Both Worlds? Fatherhood and Gender Equality in Swedish Paternity Leave Campaigns, 1976-2006." *Fathering* 6, no. 1: 20–38.

Lamb, Michael E. 1976. *The Role of the Father in Child Development.* New York: Wiley.

Lamb, Michael E., ed. 1987. *The Father's Role: Cross-cultural Perspectives.* Hillsdale, NJ: Lawrence Erlbaum Associates.

Lamb, Michael E., and Abraham Sagi. 1983. *Fatherhood and Family Policy.* Hillsdale, NJ: Lawrence Erlbaum Associates.

Lapidus, Gail W. 1978. *Women in Soviet Society: Equality, Development and Social Change.* Berkeley: University of California Press.

Marsiglio, W., M. Lohan, and L. Culley. 2013. "Framing Men's Experience in the Procreative Realm." *Journal of Family Issues* 34, no. 8: 1011–36.

McDonald, Peter. 2000. *The Toolbox of Public Policies to Impact on Fertility— A Global View of Low Fertility, Families, and Public Policies.* Sevilla, Spain: European Observatory on Family Matters. Organization for Economic Development.

Organization for Economic Development. 2005. *Babies and Bosses: Balancing Work and Family Life.* Policy Brief. Paris: OECD.

Ortner, Sherry. 1972. "Is Female to Male as Nature is to Culture?" *Feminist Studies* 1: 5–31.

Qian, Nancy. 2008. "Missing Women and the Price of Tea in China: The Effect of Sex-Specific Earnings on Sex Imbalance." *The Quarterly Journal of Economics* 123, no 3: 1251–85.

Reed, Richard K. 2005. *Birthing Fathers: The Transformation of Men in American Rites of Birth.* New Brunswick, NJ: Rutgers University Press.

Shwalb, David W., Barbara J. Shwalb, and Michael E. Lamb. 2013. *Fathers in Cultural Context.* New York: Routledge.

Spar, Debora L. 2013. *Wonder Women: Sex, Power, and the Quest for Perfection.* New York: Sarah Crichton Books.

Townsend, Nicholas W. 2002. *The Package Deal: Marriage, Work, and Fatherhood in Men's Lives.* Philadelphia: Temple University Press.

United Nations Development Programme. 2003. *Partnership and Reproductive Behaviors in Low Fertility Countries.* New York: United Nations Department of Social and Economic Affairs.

Williams, Raymond. 1978. *Marxism and Literature.* Oxford: Oxford University Press.

Ying, Heijing. 2012. "Fulfilling Promises: China is Beginning to Face Up to Its Pension Problems." *The Economist.* 11 August.

Part I

CORPORATE FATHERHOOD

Chapter 1

THE CORPORATE FATHER

Jude Browne

Introduction

What does a political commitment to gender equality mean in the context of fatherhood? In what ways should the state support or compel fathers so as to effect greater gender equality? If there is any consensus on these questions in the gender literature, then it is that existing family leave policy—even the most progressive—falls short of a satisfactory answer. Typically, this failure is understood either in economic terms—that policy provision is simply inadequate in scale—or in terms of individual preferences that should be encouraged to change. Indeed, both of these approaches are intended to incentivize men to take up more caring duties—a theme that has become central to the politics of gender equality (Gornick and Meyers 2008; Haas and Rostgaard 2011; Hobson 2002; Kamerman and Moss 2009).

Some scholars, such as Berit Brandth and Elin Kvande (2009a), Linda Haas (2003), and myself (Browne 2006), have conducted large-scale empirical studies of employing institutions and the particular problems therein associated with gender equality and associated policies, such as parental leave. From these detailed studies, it seems clear that effective policy must be built upon a nuanced picture of how fathers are not only limited by economic considerations or driven by individual aspirations but are also constrained by a complex range of structural and institutional factors. My argument in this chapter is that, despite gender equality being a fundamental right of all European citizens, existing approaches fail to address such crucial structural and institutional factors and little has been offered in these empirical studies by way of a new direction. To this end I turn to the "default model" of political philosophers Anca Gheaus and Ingrid Robeyns (2011) and consider its merits as a state-level approach to gender equality.

What follows is divided into three main sections. The first is intended to provide some context for the arguments presented in subsequent sections. I begin by introducing the concept of "relational fatherhood," which I find useful for thinking about the efficacy of policy models aimed at working parents and gender equality ideals. I go on to illustrate the shortcomings of existing parental leave provisions, focusing on two very different European models. On the one hand, I set out the U.K. approach, which offers relatively low levels of provision to parents, and on the other, I consider the Nordic approach, using Sweden and Norway as examples. These Nordic states (along with Finland and Iceland) are widely considered as having developed the most effective public policy for facilitating the combination of parenting duties and employment. Nonetheless Nordic policies have been criticized in recent debates as failing to deliver sufficient gender equality. In order to think about how these criticisms might inform ideal policy design, I analyze, in the second section, a proposal by political philosophers Gheaus and Robeyns that employs "the normative power of defaults" (174). While I consider this model appealing, I argue that its key objective—to motivate fathers to take on greater primary-carer roles—should not be the primary basis on which to design parental leave policy. Instead, as I set out in the third section, I focus on the more structural constraints facing relational fatherhood. To contextualize this view, I present a series of responses from qualitative interviews with a number of corporate leaders based in Britain with responsibility for a great many employees (often worldwide). While I do not claim a representative account, these particular insights nevertheless indicate how the choices made by fathers cannot be reduced simply to the particular aspirations of the individuals in question or corollaries of economic facts, but are formed by a range of expectations, pressures, and restrictions that are part of the institutional fabric itself. I argue that current state approaches to gender equality lack the necessary focus or mechanisms for addressing these structural constraints at the institutional level and that a reinterpretation of Gheaus and Robeyns's default model has much to offer by way of solution.

Fatherhood Shaped

There are of course many types of father: genetic, step, adoptive, legally designated. Perhaps the father is partnered to the genetic mother, with a non-related partner, is single, or is one of two gay fathers. He might be a long-distance father, estranged, absent, or even unknown. Irrespective of the various biological and legal characteristics and circumstances, the central feature of fatherhood is the way in which a father relates to his child.[1] In this chapter I focus less on those aspects of fatherhood that concern the economic or symbolic relationships between father and child, although these are important. Rather, I concentrate on what I call "relational fatherhood." This concept is intended to capture a basic condition of parenting—*time* spent personally interacting with a child—physically caring, playing, emotionally engaging, and educating, etc., and is a crucial theme of gender politics. The most concentrated form of relational fatherhood is the primary-carer father, who takes (even if only for a relatively short period) the primary responsibility for childcare. One of the aims of this chapter is to contribute to current debates on the power dynamics between institutions and (gendered) individuals through a consideration of how relational fatherhood and, in particular, fathers who wish to become primary-carer fathers are restricted from doing so by current governmental approaches to gender equality, existing policy design, and institutional structures.

While the facilitation of relational fatherhood is not an explicit political goal for most European states, the promotion of gender equality is. My argument, however, is that any society in which relational fatherhood is substantially limited is intrinsically unequal in the key respect of how fathers and mothers are able to relate to their children. Scholars in this area are all too familiar with the ways in which limitations of this kind result from policy design that is inadequate or underfunded, such as that of the United Kingdom and, moreover, that even generously funded provisions, such as those often found in the Nordic states, also result in more gendered outcomes than might have been hoped for (see for example, Brandth and Kvande 2009b; Haas and Rostgaard 2011). Some critics have used this observation to refocus discussion away from economic incentives onto a broader conception of how individual behavior might be changed (e.g., Gheaus and Robeyns 2011). My argument is that these analyses underplay the structural constraints on relational fatherhood and in particular the power relations between individuals and institutions. First, however, I set out the U.K. approach, the shortcomings of which show the fundamental importance of economic incentives to policy outcomes. This will be followed by examples of the latest provisions in the Nordic states of Sweden and Norway.

U.K. Approach

The Conservative–Liberal Democrat coalition government of the United Kingdom is split in its opinion on the merits of extending parental leave beyond the most basic of provisions. David Cameron, the Conservative Prime Minister, has labeled this as nothing more than "political correctness,"[2] while Liberal Democrat Deputy Prime Minister Nick Clegg described earlier policy as "Edwardian" and championed reform.[3] These reforms, however, fall far short of the substantive changes needed, and strong economic incentives against relational fatherhood persist.

As a full member state of the European Union, the United Kingdom is directly subject to a wide range of laws, social policy objectives, and principles that are set and monitored at the supranational EU level, including by the European Court of Justice and European Court of Human Rights. One such example is the Principle of Equal Treatment, which is a foundational principle of all EU equality and anti-discrimination law widely considered the most sophisticated equality legislation in the world. The Principle of Equal Treatment is the legal requirement that individuals who are alike in relevant and specified respects be treated equally.[4] The question that immediately follows, in the context of parental leave, is: What are the relevant respects in which a father and a mother can be alike and thus be treated equally?

Under the Principle of Equal Treatment, pregnancy is a specific condition that qualifies mothers as being in an exclusive category. Fathers, then, cannot be like mothers "in the relevant respect" and therefore are lawfully excluded from maternity leave. As EU law sets out: "Maternity leave ... is intended to protect a woman's biological condition and the special relationship between a woman and her child over the period which follows pregnancy and childbirth, by preventing that relationship from being disturbed by the multiple burdens which would result from the simultaneous pursuit of employment" (Case C-366/99 Griesmar [2001] ECR I-9383, paragraph 43). Accordingly, maternity, paternity, and parental leave can be provided as distinct forms of leave. This is the case in the United Kingdom, where Statutory Maternity Leave from employment is available for a total of fifty-two weeks and is paid for a maximum of thirty-nine weeks—six weeks of which are paid at 90 percent of average gross weekly earnings and the remaining thirty-three weeks at the current rate of £136.78 per week (or 90 percent of average gross weekly earnings if lower).[5] Paternity leave is available to the father (or partner of the mother) for two weeks and is paid at the same rate as the lower standard of Statutory Maternity Pay (£136.78 per week). Since 2011, up to nineteen weeks paid leave (at the same rate of £136.78) has been available if a child's parents decide to extend the father's paternity leave, but only if the mother has already returned to work and has left the required amount of her leave unused so as to transfer it to the father or co-parent. The father or co-parent may only take this additional paternity leave after the first twenty weeks of the child's life and before the child is twelve months old. Finally, under the European Union's Revised Framework Agreement on Parental Leave Directive (2010/18/EU) citizens of the United Kingdom can apply for four months' leave, including at least one month's entitlement exclusively for the father or co-parent. The European Union introduced the Parental Leave Directive to "encourage men to assume an equal share of family responsibilities."[6] However, the United Kingdom has interpreted this leave entitlement as unpaid (a choice entirely at the EU member state's discretion).

The most recent U.K. Equality and Human Rights Commission (EHRC) report (Equality and Human Rights Commission 2009), based on interviews with 4,500 parents, states that the take-up rate of paternity provision (set at the statutory rate) is around 55 percent. For context, the average male wage in U.K. is £556 per week (United Kingdom 2013), and it is easy to see how many working families would struggle to decrease one family income by circa 75 percent (to £136.78 per week). The ECHR reports that of the 45 percent who did not take up this paternity leave, 88 percent said they would have liked to but were unable to do so. Reasons given included unsupportive employers and work commitments (19 percent) while a further 49 percent said they could not afford to take the leave at its current level of pay (Equality and Human Rights Commission 2009: 18). Moreover, 54 percent of fathers with children under the age of one year stated that they felt they spent too little time with their children, and 53 percent of parents reported that their current arrangements were by "necessity rather than choice" (17).

As "additional paternity leave" legislation only came into force in the United Kingdom in 2011, there is as yet insufficient data on the take-up rates, but the likelihood is that the restriction of paternity leave to the statutory rate means it will be low. The EHRC (Equality and Human Rights Commission 2009) reports that overall 60 percent of parents think fathers are unable to spend as much time as they need with their children due to working arrangements and conclude that "modern mothers and fathers defy the Fifties stereotype of stay-at-home mums and breadwinner dads. They aspire to approach parenting as a team effort, shared between mothers, fathers, partners and other carers."

U.K. policy inhibits relational fatherhood. The limitations and in particular the low levels of pay offered in these provisions tend to herd parents into unequal caring roles along stereotypically gendered lines, irrespective of preferences. Aspirations of more equal parenting are, in general, outweighed by the economic implications of current policy that makes no serious attempt to facilitate relational fatherhood and in so doing compounds gender inequality. This seems nonsensical and contrary to what we might think the Principle of Equal Treatment ought to be about.[7]

Nordic Approach

As many of us interested in gender politics have come to expect, the Nordic states provide particularly generous options for working parents.[8] Indeed it is always the Nordic states that compete for first place in rankings of equality and socially progressive policy design reported by, for example, the World Economic Forum's Global Gender Gap Report (Hausmann et al. 2012) and the United Nations Development Programme's (2011) Human Development Report. In this section I briefly set out the provisions of Sweden and Norway as examples of Nordic parental leave entitlements. Unlike the U.K,, each offers a period of well-paid non-transferable leave to both the mother and the father ("use it or lose it" parent-specific quotas), as well as similarly well-paid longer periods of leave, which can be taken by either parent. In both cases, the state and employer share the cost of parental allowance, which is taxed like other income and counts toward pensions.

Sweden is presently governed by a coalition of the Moderate Party, the Liberal Party, the Centre Party and the Christian Democrats.[9] Sweden is a full member state of the European Union (like the United Kingdom) but has a longstanding history of family and employment policy provision that, like all other Nordic states, far exceeds the current EU interpretation of the Principle of Equal Treatment. In addition to a period of two weeks' maternity leave and ten days' paternity leave, working parents are provided with 240 working days each of paid parental leave per child. (Swedish leave is purposefully calculated in days rather than weeks or months so as to encourage more flexible use of leave entitlement.) Of these 480 days, 390 are paid at 80 percent of earnings to a ceiling of SEK424,000 (£38,896) per year and the remaining ninety days are paid at a standardized set rate of SEK180 (£16.50) per day. Sixty days of paid parental leave are reserved for each parent while the rest can be transferred to either parent. In 2010 fathers took virtually all of their paternity leave (97 percent) but only 23 percent of all parental leave days (Haas et al. 2011). The Swedish government also provides a "gender equality bonus," which is a tax reduction for the parent who has stayed at home the longest when he or she returns to work if the other parent uses the parental leave for more than his or her sixty-day quota period (Sweden 2012; for further details also see Haas et al. 2011).

The current Norwegian government is a coalition of the Labor Party, the Socialist Left Party, and the Center Party. It is a member of the European Economic Area and is renowned for offering the most generous parental leave provisions, despite not being a member of the European Union. In addition to nine weeks' maternity leave and ten weeks' "use it or lose it" fathers' (or co-parents') quota, working parents are provided with paid parental leave of up to fifty-six weeks at 80 percent of earnings or forty-six weeks at 100 percent up to a ceiling of NOK437,286 (£46,055) per year (Brandth and Kvande 2011), which can be taken by either parent. In 2008, 90 percent of fathers took their full fathers' quota, but only 16.5 percent of fathers elected to extend their leave beyond the reserved ten weeks (Norway 2012).

Many scholars have written on the positive benefits of these Nordic provisions of leave with a particular focus on increased gender equality in both the workplace and the domestic sphere (see for example Hobson 2002; Kamerman and Moss 2009). Many commentators in countries other than those of the Nordic region see these models as almost utopian. Gheaus and Robeyns (2011) make this point in particular comparison to the United States, which has no federal provision of paid maternity, paternity, or parental leave at all.[10]

However, recent debate on Nordic parental leave policies has taken a different direction. Despite seemingly ideal policies in Sweden and Norway, which provide substantial periods of well-paid leave for both parents and evidence to suggest that changes in those policies (in particular increasing quota periods for fathers' leave) do lead to greatly increased take-up rates by fathers (see for example, Brandth and Kvande 2009a, 2009b; Haas and Rostgaard 2011), several feminists nevertheless argue that these policies do not go far enough in terms of gender equality. Their argument is focused on the fact that mothers tend to take the majority of leave available to either parent (as set out in the Nordic policy provisions above) and call for longer periods of non-transferable leave or, in some cases, that all leave should be split completely equally between mothers and fathers as non-transferable ("use it or lose it"). This sort of argument has, for example, been developed by Janet C. Gornick and Marcia K. Meyers (2008). Their "gender-equalizing" family leave policy model requires that all employed parents be granted the right to take six months non-transferable leave with full job protection paid at 100 percent of earnings with a ceiling cap. (Single parents would be entitled to nine months under the gender-equalizing model.) This policy model, they suggest, "substantially increases incentives for father's participation" (324), thereby increasing gender equality.

The problem with such an approach, however, is that it is overly prescriptive. It seems unfair on the family unit, and in particular on the child, that there is so little flexibility in how and by whom the leave is taken. In effect, if one or other parent does not feel they can or does not want to take the full extensive period of leave under this model then the family will receive no further provision. While the two Nordic states discussed here have successfully increased fathers' take-up rates of relatively short periods of leave with "use it or lose it" policies, it seems overly interventionist to demand that parents split all of the leave entitlement equally in the pursuit of greater gender equality, irrespective of personal circumstances and preferences.

Fatherhood and Ideal Policy

So what sort of approach would be ideal? Here I turn to the "default model," developed by political philosophers, Gheaus and Robeyns (2011). Like Gornick and Meyers, Gheaus and Robeyns are concerned that even in the most socially progressive countries such as Norway, as many as 83.5 percent of men do not take leave beyond the fathers' non-transferable quota of ten weeks, as described above. Unsatisfied with the overly prescriptive gender-equalizing model, however, Gheaus and Robeyns ask: "Is there something more we can do to motivate fathers to take leave than only making it paid rather than unpaid, and making it entirely non-transferable?" (183).

Their solution is the default model. In a similar vein to the gender-equalizing model, the default model requires six months well-paid parental leave for both parents (allowing four weeks simultaneous leave around the birth of the baby). Gheaus and Robeyns argue: "This will strongly encourage [the father] to learn the necessary hands-on caring skills for the new-borns which, in turn, may have long-term egalitarian effects on the gender division of labor within the family" (185).

However, where the default model crucially differs from the gender-equalizing approach is that the equal split of leave between mothers and fathers is set only as a default with the option to transfer leave to the other parent. By "default," Gheaus and Robeyns mean the provision mothers and fathers would automatically receive unless either decided to opt out. Rather than the total non-transferable approach proposed by Gornick and Meyers, behavior is guided rather than strictly prescribed (or constrained).

Gheaus and Robeyns suggest we look to the example of organ donation as an illustration of how successful default policy models can be in guiding behavior. Certainly, analysis of the recent work of Anne-Maree Farrell et al. (2011), and in particular by Salla Lötjönen and Nils H. Persson (2011), supports Gheaus and Robeyns's claims. Their work on organ donation policy shows that Nordic countries have the highest rate of deceased donor organ transplantation in the world with attendant low rates of deaths related to lack of donor organs. These successes are principally due to the fact that there is a national scheme of presumed consent, whereby all deceased citizens are deemed to be organ donors unless they have formally registered to opt out of the scheme or their close family members object to organ donation at the point of death. Accordingly, the majority of Norwegians remain donors, which is considered by many to be a national and moral duty. Alternatively the United Kingdom's "opt-in" scheme, in which each individual must register to become a donor, has resulted in one of the lowest organ donation rates in Europe, despite high levels of public support for organ donation in general (Farrell et al. 2011). The higher death rates (currently one thousand a year) due to lack of available organs is unsurprising.[11]

Gheaus and Robeyns offer persuasive arguments for why their default model would yield a more desirable outcome for gender equality than existing models or the gender-equalizing model proposed by Gornick and Meyers. The first is that to make a decision other than the set default has unattractive costs, such as taking the time and effort to opt out formally and also to acquire the relevant information to do so. This, in turn, leads to the second argument, which is that there is a normative element to the default position suggesting assurance that the policy provisions have been thoroughly investigated and have been approved by both government experts and also by society as "the right" decision. By applying these characteristics to parental leave policy, Gheaus and Robeyns believe that fathers will be maneuvered into fuller primary-carer roles with subsequent positive social outcomes.

While the Gheaus and Robeyns default model is the most appealing to date, I suggest that they put too strong an emphasis on motivating men to take up primary-carer leave. My description of their work above quotes several examples—another follows: "Those who would 'opt-out' of default will also have to directly face the loss of the opportunity to spend crucial months with their children at home and will, therefore, have to be more reflective about their parenting choices" (Gheaus and Robeyns 2011: 183).

To assume that all men need to be motivated into taking responsibility for primary-care whereupon they will become good at it, is, in many cases, a misrepresentation and certainly should not be the main assumption behind parental policy design. This sort of perspective on fatherhood fails to appreciate that many men find themselves constrained by national policy, the nature of their contractual employment, and the culture of their employing institutions, communities, and society. This is not to suggest that some men do not have negative views about becoming primary-carers or gender equality, more generally, but we can know as little about the various and conflicted preferences of men from their take-up rates of parental leave as we can know about women's lifestyle preferences from their wage packets (Browne 2006). Inferences of this kind recall rational-choice-based understandings of preferences (see for example Becker 1991; Hakim 2007) and can lead to circular and unhelpful reasoning: "How do we know men don't want to be primary-carers? Because there are low take-up rates of parental leave entitlement. Why are there low take-up rates? Because men don't want to be primary-carers."

Rather than focus debate at the individual level by asking fathers to reflect on their choices or presume to know their attitudes and preferences, I argue that we should give much more consideration to how those choices—and how the potential for relational fatherhood—are not simply economically but also structurally and institutionally constrained.[12] Decision making is seldom, if ever, the product of a simple calculus of costs and benefits to the individual but rather the complex outcome of a whole host of social, cultural, and political structures in which we are embedded. Gheaus and Robeyns seem to underappreciate the structural nature of hierarchical employment pressures to which individuals often find themselves subject.

A further consideration is that Gheaus and Robeyns's model would seem to lose something of the very clear successes of "use it or lose it" fathers' quotas, demonstrated by the empirical work of Linda Haas and Tine Rostgaard (2011), for example. In addition to changing the premise on which the default policy would be based, an even more effective model might be a combination of these quotas for a relatively short period (e.g., ten weeks as in Norway), and establishing the default policy model for the remaining leave, which would be split equally between parents, as a statutory right, with an opt-out clause. This combination, through an insistence on some non-transferable leave, would strengthen the norm for fathers to have the opportunity to become and experience being primary carers, but at the same time, through the establishment of an additional default period of equally split leave, it would fundamentally challenge the myriad structural factors which, even in the most progressive Nordic countries, consistently result in unfavorable equality outcomes.

Primary-Carer Fatherhood and Structural Constraints

In calling for greater engagement with the structural level,[13] a number of factors regarding structural constraints associated with modern parenting are overlooked by approaches focused on the individual. First, there are the cultural norms and, in particular, specific interpretations of fatherhood embedded in political approaches, institutional practices, and social structures that greatly constrain relational fatherhood. This is not in any way to suggest that these factors should be tolerated or ignored, but merely that they must first be understood if they are to be overcome in the struggle for genuine equality. Second, although these conceptions of fatherhood are unconsciously shaped and naturalized by the routinized actions of numerous individuals and institutions—indeed, resulting not necessarily from design but as unintended consequences—they are nonetheless the results of human actions and are therefore alterable social constructs. It is imperative, if we are to effect substantive change, that we do not fall into the trap of thinking of these constraints as natural, fixed, or insurmountable, for to do so is to turn a blind eye to structures in our society that are a very real source of constraint and injustice (Young 2011).

Taking a more structural approach to these issues helps us to move beyond a narrow conception based on essentialist assumptions and/or individual preferences and onto a broad understanding of the manifold relationships between individuals, institutions, and society. If we think of how policy might facilitate relational fatherhood through a structural approach, the focus shifts away from the need to encourage fathers to take up parenting roles and instead moves to the ways in which people experience considerable obstacles resulting from the actions of others through institutional traditions, practices, and norms.

In order to illustrate these points in a particular context, I now turn to some extracts of interviews I recently conducted with corporate leaders. An important point to be made here is that the sorts of constraints and injustices that come about as a product of market and cultural structures are not the sort captured by anti-discrimination laws. It is not necessarily the case that any individual or even corporation has acted inappropriately or broken a law and therefore cannot be identified as acting illegally. It is rather that many individual and institutional practices combined generate unintended constraints and injustices that can only be challenged effectively through policy coordinated by government at the macro level.

The Corporate Father

I was recently given the rare opportunity to interview a number of heads of some of Britain's largest employing corporations (many of them global institutions) on the topic of their own working lives and their opinions of present and future corporate working conditions. As part of these interviews, I discussed the topic of working parents in the corporate culture. These discussions proved very helpful for thinking about relational fatherhood and the demands of modern-day working.

The method of "elite interviews" (Aberbach and Rockman 2002; Harvey 2010; Moyser and Wagstaffe 1987) is in many ways opposite to conventional qualitative research in that sample selection is focused on persuading a particular individual to participate rather than targeting groups or random samples. With such an approach, the researcher is attempting to capture a specific person's view rather than to glean a representative overview of the attitudes of a given population. Typically, elite interviewees, whether they be, for example, heads of state, famous celebrities, or high-powered business leaders, are notoriously difficult to access. I was fortunate in that ten heads (chairmen and chief executive officers) of some of Britain's most influential companies, with very large numbers of employees, agreed to speak with me.[14]

To date, little research has been conducted at the most senior levels of corporations on the topic of this essay. Methodologically, elite interviewing is of particular value regarding corporate structures that are, by definition, hierarchical. Of course, this is not to say that attitudes at the top necessarily filter all the way down, but it does suggest that an important part of analysis is at the highest level within those hierarchies, and a crucial element of policy design must reflect how the hierarchical structure replicates and reinforces views of corporate leaders. As the head of one of the world's biggest financial services companies, employing over one hundred and forty thousand people worldwide,[15] explains: "One thing that has never ceased to amaze me is the crucial difference that the identity of the top person makes. ... When the guard changes, everything changes—it is quite extraordinary how everything percolates down from the leadership of that individual."

The first topic of discussion relevant to this chapter is that of a state-administered well-paid parental leave policy along the lines of the revised default model described above. I presented this approach as having the potential to enable twenty-first-century families to cope with the ever-increasing "time poverty" associated with the demands of modern labor market employment. In particular, I stressed the potential such a policy would have for fathers to facili-. tate their social function as primary carers of their children and the likely consequences for greater equality between men and women. The quotes below illustrate two common responses. The first was shared by nearly all the respondents who thought that, ultimately, women were more likely to be primary carers.[16] (Often when I spoke of "parents," respondents answered with specific references to women.) "I think it's fine for your person who is going to just make his way in life... but I have to say that if you want to get to the top and really have ambition, one of you is going to have to do it and be selfish. ... You ask me if the men can drop out to look after children... but I think the DNA of how it all works that the more natural person, dare I say, is the woman for dropping out, fairly or unfairly. ... I'm afraid the 'corporate father' doesn't do that much fathering. (Head of a global manufacturing corporation)."[17] The second theme was more focused on a sense that such a policy might impede a worker's contributions to the organization's competitiveness. As the head of a global financial services corporation[18] responded: "I'm not recoiling against the idea as an outrageous idea. I'm just not sure what the unintended consequences are. It's a merciless law, the 'twenty-first-century Law of Unintended Consequences.' So many things are done for a good purpose but then the system gapes. ... It is jolly difficult. If you operate in a competitive market and some-one is out there who is prepared to do 'it' and you're not prepared to do 'it,' they have the marginal advantage." During my discussions with these institutional leaders, the "corporate father" emerged as a standardized global male worker. He was not from any particular country, nor of any particular nationality—as one director of a global private equity trust[19] explained, "The talent pool is international—the larger corporations can afford to employ the best people from all over the world." If serious about his position in the organization or sector, the corporate father would not contemplate taking a sub-stantial period of leave to adopt a primary-carer role. As the head of a publishing company and a board member of an international me-dia conglomerate[20] explained, "It would never be explicitly said, but the salary is presumed to offset any inconveniences to family life—no-one would ever take six months parental leave—end of story."

Here we can think back to the European Court of Justice's im-plication that the mother needs to be protected in law from "un-desirable pressures to return to work prematurely" after childbirth but that this does not apply to the father (Case C-366/99 Griesmar [2001] ECR I-9383, paragraph 43). It is of course, also the case that many jobs do not offer as high a salary as corporate employment, but even without this sort of "compensation," the assumption remains that a substantial period of parental leave for fathers is inappropriate.

As fathers, all interviewees were sympathetic to the difficulties of younger generations of workers who attempt corporate working in conjunction with maintaining family life. When I asked, "What advice would you give the younger generation coming up behind you in the business?" the following quotes demonstrate a recurring theme of time poverty: "The pressure on family life is immense. What would I wish for the next generation? A lifestyle which was more balanced" (head of a global publishing corporation).[21] "Take more time to reflect on what's really important to you—that is my biggest regret" (head of an international media group).[22]

Finally, I discussed how the state's legislative framing was per-haps the only way in which some of the drives of the market might be tempered in the interest of social relationships, such as father-hood: "Well, I certainly don't think the private sector will play a major part. [Perhaps] funds for specific charitable endeavors, for ex-ample, training unemployed youth but no, companies are not going to pay for that sort of thing (enhanced parental leave). It wouldn't fit with the philanthropic (corporate social responsibility) projects. More structural things are the government's area—it would make a lot of difference. (Head of a global manufacturing corporation)."[23] "If the state doesn't demand it then the corporate sector won't do it unless they see a market advantage. Social policies only ever come in from the state—once they *are* in things start to change slowly" (head of a publishing company and board member of an international media conglomerate).[24]

These comments indicate that it is unrealistic to expect any substantive change regarding parental leave to emerge spontaneously from the corporate sector. The dominant imperatives of market competition and the pursuit of the marginal advantage, coupled with the fear of unintended consequences and a version of accountability that extends only so far as maximizing shareholder value, do not provide a promising basis from which to generate a macro perspective on the well-being of citizens and families. Only under exceptional circumstances, when progressive family-friendly policies are a form of marginal advantage, might one see a voluntary move on the part of corporations. But for the majority, the nature of those relationships between and within corporate institutions will tend to reinforce and exacerbate these structural constraints. As these two last quotes suggest, the state (or a collective international body such as the European Union) must ensure a reasonable balance between familial and labor relationships. As a mechanism for achieving this, a reinterpretation of Gheaus and Robeyns's default model has considerable appeal. Not only does it provide much greater independence for families to make their own decisions about their working and care arrangements but also, crucially, it alters the relationship between the employee and the employing institution. By setting a default whereby fathers are expected to take equal amounts of paid primary care leave to mothers (with a "use it or lose it" quota followed by an opt-out clause along the lines discussed above), this approach fundamentally shifts the power dynamics between individual and institution and enables the government to achieve substantive gender equality objectives. This would contrast dramatically with existing policy whereby the individual employee is required to negotiate with the employer for anything exceeding the current statutory minimum leave. The default approach does not mean that families would be disempowered to make complex arrangements regarding their preferred leave patterns (including arrangements where the father will take only a short period of leave or none at all). Rather, it ensures that the starting position (the default), which would likely become a cultural norm as a standard policy provision, is strongly oriented toward relational fatherhood and greater freedom of choice for both men and women.

Conclusion

In this essay, I argue that a relational interpretation of fatherhood is crucial for good policy design. The nature of this relationship may take many forms and is codependent with the other relationships (within families, communities, employing institutions, and governments, etc.) that make up daily life. In contrast, current Western liberal policies tend to define fatherhood in terms of rigid categories (biological or legal) that serve to strengthen unhelpful perceptions of essential sex differences.

Perhaps unsurprisingly, the Nordic states, propelled by a strong commitment to greater gender equality, have come closest to designing policies that not only provide the option for fathers to be primary-carers in the early stages of a child's life, but also set cultural norms within which and through people and institutions orient their priorities. The policy provisions found in Sweden and Norway escape the charge leveled at other countries (such as the United Kingdom) that state provision is too inadequate financially to enable families to make genuine choices. Moreover, the evidence is abundantly clear that "use it or lose it" fathers' quotas increase the take-up rates of fathers who then, by virtue of becoming primary-carers, contribute to greater gender equality.

Yet, despite the substantial levels of paid leave on offer beyond the "use it or lose it" quota period in Nordic states, fathers regularly take substantially shorter periods of leave than mothers overall. I suggest that critics who represent these low take-up rates of fathers as evidence of revealed preferences fail to consider the full institutional and cultural context in which these fathers' decisions are made and do not give sufficient weight to the constraints that institutions may place upon them as individuals. Indeed, such criticisms recall—somewhat ironically—feminist critiques of rational choice and preference theories (Browne 2006).

While there are merits in keeping some period of the "use it or lose it" father quotas so as to strengthen the opportunity for men to become and experience being a primary-carer, to extend this non-transferable model to the full extent of leave for both parents (as Gornick and Meyers's gender-equalizing model does) is too prescriptive and inflexible. I suggest that a revised version of Gheaus and Robeyns's default parental leave model is a productive way forward. In addition to reorienting its aims from the individual to the structural, I have suggested that a better model would be to combine the "use it or lose it" father (or co-parent) quota followed by an extensive period equally split between parents (with an "opt-out" element). Such a proposal reflects the structural nature of gender politics and has real potential for *changing institutional norms*.

As shown by the statements of a number of corporate leaders, such a policy is unlikely to emerge spontaneously from corporations themselves and could only be effectively administered at the macro level. While a state like Norway, with a longstanding and serious commitment to gender equality, might well be attracted to a version of the default parental policy model presented here, it is unlikely that the U.K., under its current administration at least, would be similarly inclined. Indeed the Prime Minister, David Cameron, has called for a renegotiation of the U.K.'s membership of the European Union precisely[25] because his party wishes to see legal powers relating to, for example, employment conditions and gender equality (including maternity and parental leave) repatriated to Westminster. Cameron's objective would seem to be to take back greater powers to deregulate in the United Kingdom in order to reduce obstacles to private sector competitiveness.

One of the major reasons for having collective minimum standards across the European Union is to ensure that economic competition among members states will not be based on low employment standards and will not override the ideals of gender equality. But the imperatives of economic competition and the structural nature of the constraints on relational parenthood are two sides of the same coin in a state like the U. K. in which political discourse has become ever more corporate. In calling for a revised version of the Gheaus and Robeyns's default model, I argue for greater state-based intervention to address the power dynamics that constrain relational fatherhood and with it twenty-first-century gender equality. As one previous head of a European Conservative Political Party and now corporate leader[26] told me: "Look, this goes against my politics, but it's true that if you really want something to happen—*legislate*."

Acknowledgments

I am extremely grateful to Umar Salam for his comments on various drafts of this article and likewise to Marcia Inhorn, Wendy Chavkin,

José-Alberto Navarro, and Bonnie Rose Schulman, as well as all the participants of the 2012 Globalized Fatherhood Conference at Yale University.

Notes

A longer version of this article ("The Default Model: Gender Equality, Fatherhood, and Structural Constraint") first appeared in *Politics & Gender* 9, no. 02: 152–73. © 2013 The Women and Politics Research Section of the American Political Science Association. Reprinted with the permission of Cambridge University Press.

 1. This interpretation of fatherhood chimes with the work of psychologists Susan Golombok (2000) and Michael E. Lamb (2010).
 2. See BBC news, 17 January 2011: http://www.bbc.co.uk/news/uk-politics-12204079.
 3. See Deputy Prime Minister Nick Clegg's "Parenting Speech" of 17 January 2011: http://www.dpm.cabinetoffice.gov.uk/news/parenting-speech.
 4. The EU Principle of Equal Treatment, for example, requires that all people, and in the context of the workplace all workers, have the right to receive the same treatment and will not be discriminated against on the basis of criteria such as sex, age, disability, nationality, race, or religion. "Equality between women and men is a fundamental principle, under Article 2 and Article 3(2) of the EC Treaty and the case-law of the European Court of Justice. These Treaty provisions proclaim equality between women and men as a 'task' and an 'aim' of the Community and impose a positive obligation to 'promote' it in all its activities" (Directive 2002/73/EC of the European Parliament and of the Council of 23 September 2002 amending Council Directive 76/207/EEC).
 5. These policies are administered by the central government, from which employers can recover between 92 and 100 percent of employee leave paid (see http://www.direct.gov.uk).
 6. Point 8 of the Preamble to the Framework Agreement on Parental Leave annexed to EC Parental Leave Directive 96/34/EC.
 7. See also Case C-184/83 [1984] ECR 3047, paragraph 25; Case C-222/84 [1986] ECR 1651, paragraph 44; Case C-312/86 [1988] ECR 6315, paragraph 13; Case C-285/98 [2000] ECR I-69, paragraph 30.
 8. See, e.g., Gislason and Eydal (2011). There is, of course, great international variation in terms of policies relating to economic activity and childcare, see for example Moss (2011). For various typologies of European welfare regimes see Esping-Andersen (1990); Lewis (1992); Galvez-Munoz et al. (2011).
 9. Although, in the context of Nordic coalitions, this is a center-right government, which campaigns for higher tax cuts, for example, it nevertheless operates within the Nordic approach, which is based on a highly developed welfare state, a strong commitment to social equality, and

powerful trade unions. In the context of non-Nordic member states of the European Union (including the United Kingdom), the Swedish coalition policies still appear left of center.

10. The U.S. Family and Medical Leave Act requires employers of over fifty employees to provide up to twelve weeks of unpaid leave. Five states provide Temporary Disability Insurance programs, which provide parental leave for up to twelve weeks (there is no distinction between maternity and paternity) at the following proportions of average salary to various ceilings of benefit: California (55–60 percent); New Jersey (66 percent); New York (50 percent); Hawaii (58 percent); and Rhode Island (85 percent). Minnesota, Montana, New Mexico, and Washington have also put in place some minimal provisions for parents (DelPo and Guerin 2011: 206; also see Kamerman and Waldfogel 2011).

11. The most recent statistics produced by the National Health Service show that "more than 10,000 people in the United Kingdom currently need a transplant. Of these, 1000 each year—that's three a day—will die waiting as there are not enough organs available." (See the home page of the National Health Services Blood and Transplant organ donation web site: http://www.organdonation.nhs.uk/ukt/.)

12. It is also a limitation of Gheaus and Robeyns's (2011) default model that the issue of non-nuclear families beyond the single-parent family is not considered. Many gay male couples wish to procure the services of a surrogate, for example. However, surrogacy in Norway and Sweden is a criminal offense. In the United Kingdom, where altruistic surrogacy is permitted, the intended parents are not entitled to any paid leave. In a similar vein, divorced fathers are not automatically entitled to paid leave—their entitlement can be usurped by the new partner of the mother and cannot be shared between what are considered two fathers. These examples serve to illustrate further the structural constraints on the relational interpretation of fatherhood irrespective of technical characteristics. One solution is simply to open up the leave provision (after opting out of the default described above) to multiple designated carers to be agreed on by the gestational mother.

13. Here I am particularly influenced by Iris Marion Young's (2011) conception of structural injustice.

14. Even when elite interviewees are in communication with the researcher, they are often unwilling to be interviewed face-to-face without prepepared questions and answers lest something unscripted does not quite hit the right note, or is taken out of context by the researcher. Here, as George Moyser and Margaret Wagstaffe's (1987) work suggests, it is imperative that there be a sense of trust in the researcher's credentials, previous work, and contacts through which communication was originally arranged. Certainly in these interviews, which were not prepepared but face-to-face using semi-structured aide-mémoires, the promise of anonymity was key. While I indicate the sorts of companies each of these men lead, I am careful not to disclose any infor-

mation that might identify the individuals. Interviews were conducted in person in London or Cambridge or by telephone in 2011 and 2012. I use data from seven of the ten interviews, which were most relevant to this essay. Each of the interviewees was generous with his time, and I am extremely grateful to them for their insights and highly engaging discussions.

15. Corporation revenue of approximately £30 billion; interview October 2011.
16. All respondents were fathers themselves, and all but one described their own lives as working fathers as "traditional," whereby their wives had been primarily responsible for their children while young. A typical day of a corporate leader is 7:00 A.M. to 7:00 P.M., often followed by an evening event or dinner.
17. Head of global manufacturing corporation employing over thirty-five thousand people across the world, with annual turnover of £10,000 million; interview January 2012.
18. See note 15.
19. Trust asset management of over £16 billion; interview August 2011.
20. Corporation employing over thirty-five thousand people worldwide with revenue of almost £600 million; interview April 2012.
21. Business with revenue of over £1 billion; interview June 2011.
22. Business with revenue of over £750 million; interview July 2011.
23. See note 17.
24. See note 20.
25. As indicated, for example, by Prime Minister David Cameron's "EU Speech at Bloomberg" on 23 January 2013: http://www.number10.gov.uk/news/eu-speech-at-bloomberg/.
26. Global business services corporation with revenue of approximately £405 million; interview January 2011.

References

Aberbach, Joel D., and Bert A. Rockman. 2002. "Conducting and Coding Elite Interviews." *PS: Political Science and Politics* 35, no. 4: 673–76.
Becker, Gary. 1991. *A Treatise on the Family.* Cambridge: Harvard University Press.
Brandth, Berit, and Elin Kvande. 2009a. "Gendered or Gender-Neutral Care Politics for Fathers?" *The Annals of the American Academy of Political and Social Science* 642, no. 1: 177–89.
Brandth, Berit, and Elin Kvande. 2009b. "Norway: The Making of the Father's Quota." In *The Politics of Parental Leave Policies: Children, Parenting, Gender and the Labour Market,* ed. Sheila Kamerman and Peter Moss. Bristol: The Policy Press.
Brandth, Berit, and Elin Kvande. 2011. "Norway." In *International Review of Leave Policies and Related Research 2011,* ed. Peter Moss. International Net-

work on Leave Policies and Research. London: Institute of Education, University of London.

Browne, Jude. 2006. *Sex Segregation and Inequality in the Modern Labour Market*. Bristol: The Policy Press.

Case C-184/83 [1984] ECR 3047. *Hofmann v. Barmer Ersatzkasse.*

Case C-222/84 [1986] ECR 1651. *Johnston v. Chief Constable of the Royal Ulster Constabulary.*

Case C-285/98 [2000] ECR I-69. *Kreil v. Germany.*

Case C-312/86 [1988] ECR 6315. *Commission of the European Communities v. France.*

Case C-366/99 [2001] ECR I-9383. *Griesmar v. Ministre de l'Economie, des Finances et de l'Industrie et Ministre de la Fonction publique, de la Réforme de l'Etat et de la Décentralisation [Griesmar v. Minister for the Economy, Finance, and Industry and Minister for Civil Service, State Reform, and Decentralization].*

DelPo, Amy, and Lisa Guerin. 2011. *The Manager's Legal Handbook.* 6th Edition. Berkeley, CA: NOLO Press.

Directive 2002/73/EC of the European Parliament and of the Council of 23 September 2002 amending Council Directive 76/207/EEC. http://eurlex.europa.eu/LexUriServ/LexUriServ.do?uri=CELEX:32002L0073:EN:HTML.

Equality and Human Rights Commission. 2009. "Working Better Report Summary." London. http://www.equalityhumanrights.com/news/commission-calls-for-radical-approach-to-parental-leave/.

Esping-Andersen, Gøsta. 1990. *The Three Worlds of Welfare Capitalism.* Princeton: Princeton University Press.

Farrell, Anne-Maree, David Price, and Muireann Quigley. 2011. "A Principled and Pragmatic Approach to Organ Shortage." In *Organ Shortage: Ethics, Laws and Pragmatism,* ed. Anne-Maree Farrell, David Price, and Muireann Quigley. Cambridge: Cambridge University Press.

Galvez-Munoz, Lina, Paula Rodriguez-Modrono, and Monica Dominguez-Serrano. 2011. "Work and Time Use by Gender: A New Clustering of European Welfare Systems." *Feminist Economics* 17, no. 4: 125–57.

Gheaus, Anca, and Ingrid Robeyns. 2011. "Equality—Promoting Parental Leave." *Journal of Social Philosophy* 42, no. 2: 173–91.

Gislason, Ingólfur V., and Guðný Björk Eydal, eds. 2011. *Parental Leave, Childcare and Gender Equality in the Nordic Countries.* Copenhagen: TemaNord, Nordic Council of Ministers.

Golombok, Susan. 2000. *Parenting: What Really Counts?* London: Routledge.

Gornick, Janet C., and Marcia K. Meyers. 2008. "Creating Gender Egalitarian Societies: An Agenda for Reform." *Politics and Society* 36, no. 3: 313–49.

Haas, Linda. 2003. "Parental Leave and Gender Equality: Lessons from the European Union." *Review of Policy Research* 20, no. 1: 89–114.

Haas, Linda, and Tine Rostgaard. 2011. "Father's Rights to Paid Parental Leave in the Nordic Countries: Consequences for Gendered Division of Leave." *Community, Work and Family* 14, no. 2: 177–95.

Haas, Linda, Ann-Zofie Duvander, and Anders Chronholm. 2011. "Sweden." In *International Review of Leave Policies and Related Research 2011,* ed.

Peter Moss. International Network on Leave Policies and Research. London: Institute of Education, University of London.

Hakim, Catherine. 2007. "The Politics of Female Diversity in the Twenty-First Century." In *the Future of Gender,* ed. Jude Browne. Cambridge: Cambridge University Press.

Harvey, William S. 2010. "Methodological Approaches for Interviewing Elites." *Geography Compass* 4/3: 193–205.

Hausmann, Ricardo, Laura D. Dyson, and Saadia Zahidi. 2012. "Global Gender Gap Report." World Economic Forum.

Hobson, Barbara, ed. 2002. *Making Men into Fathers: Men, Masculinities and the Social Politics of Fatherhood.* Cambridge: Cambridge University Press.

Kamerman, Sheila, and Peter Moss, eds. 2009. *The Politics of Parental Leave Policies: Children, Parenting, Gender and the Labour Market.* Bristol: The Policy Press.

Kamerman, Sheila, and Jane Waldfogel. 2011. "United States." In *International Review of Leave Policies and Related Research 2011,* ed. Peter Moss. International Network on Leave Policies and Research. London: Institute of Education, University of London.

Lamb, Michael E. 2010. *The Role of the Father in Child Development.* 5th Edition. Hoboken, NJ: John Wiley & Sons.

Lewis, Jane. 1992. "Gender and the Development of Welfare Regimes." *Journal of European Social Policy* 2, no. 3: 159–73.

Lötjönen, Salla, and Nils H. Persson. 2011. "Kidney Donation: Lessons from the Nordic Countries." In *Organ Shortage: Ethics, Laws and Pragmatism,* ed. Anne-Maree Farrell, David Price, and Muireann Quigley. Cambridge: Cambridge University Press.

Moss, Peter, ed. 2011. *International Review of Leave Policies and Related Research 2011.* International Network on Leave Policies and Research. London: Institute of Education, University of London.

Moyser, George, and Margaret Wagstaffe. 1987. *Research Methods for Elite Studies.* London: Allen & Unwin.

Norway. 2012. "Parents and Paternity Leave." Norway's official web site in the United Kingdom: http://www.norway.org.uk/aboutnorway/society/welfare/benefits/.

Sweden. 2012. "Parental Benefit." http://www.forsakringskassan.se/wps/wcm/connect/28f32b72-c3fd-43a9-9c33-038fdad53c00/foraldrapenning_eng.pdf?MOD=AJPERES.

United Kingdom. 2013. "2013 Annual Survey of Hours and Earnings" http://www.ons.gov.uk/ons/rel/ashe/annual-survey-of-hours-and-earnings/2013-provisional-results/stb-ashe-statistical-bulletin-2013.html#tab-Weekly-earnings.

United Nations Development Programme. 2011. "Human Development Report."

Young, Iris Marion. 2011. *Responsibility for Justice.* Oxford: Oxford University Press.

Chapter 2

HIDING FATHERHOOD
IN CORPORATE JAPAN

Scott North

Introduction

Theories of family change in industrial nations posit complex linkages between the market economy and the interpersonal emotional economy at home and at work (Chafetz 1996; Goode 1963; Hochschild and Machung 1989). Although most research has focused on motherhood, modernity's undeniable transformative effects on twentieth-century fatherhood are equally significant (LaRossa 1997). Locally, family changes and gender roles are influenced by historically derived, durable, and more or less habitually deployed cultural strategies of social action (Swidler 1986). Normative practices in most societies limit fathers' caregiving, but close examination reveals various innovations in fathers' responses to the dual-career, postindustrial division of labor and rising economic uncertainty associated with today's increasingly globalized mode of production.

Guided by these two theoretical premises about the effects of postindustrial modernity on family life and the importance of local culture in social change, this chapter explores contemporary Japanese fatherhood, focusing on parental leave-taking. The Japanese example of modern fatherhood sheds light on powerful work-family

conflicts arising between fathers' increased desire for family involvement, inadequate national policy provisions, and market-driven,
corporate practices.

Although the reality of fathering lags behind the rhetoric (Nakatani 2006), caring fatherhood and paternity leave are promoted in
Japan's recent family policy reforms. Moreover, they are acquiring
cachet among working Japanese women, who want husbands to be
partners in parenting as well as breadwinning, Male willingness and
ability to do family work is becoming social capital readily convertible in Japan's marriage market, just as in Europe (Breen and Cooke
2005). But Japanese fathers' practices in the current economic-legal
context reflect continued constraints on the time that men can de-
vote to care. This knowledge is important for advancing research on
gender, work, and family as "interlinked social systems" (Haas and
O'Brien 2010: 271) and for illustrating regional variation in global
fatherhood trends.

Studying Fathers in Japan

The worlds of Japanese men are often closed to outsiders (Hamabata
1991), leaving large gaps in understanding of their private lives
(Shwalb et al. 1987). This chapter first contextualizes men's work
and parenting in Japan's recent economic history. I then use Japanese government policy statements, white papers, and population
surveys, as well as vernacular newspaper stories and first-person
accounts from two cohorts of paternity leave-takers to characterize
recent changes in fatherhood, especially childcare leave-taking practices. The primary source on the first cohort (1992–99) of pioneer
leave-takers is a book-length collection of father-authored newspaper columns (*Asahi Shinbun* 2000). After 2000, active government
promotion of fathering somewhat increased the volume and range
of source materials, including fathers' self-submitted statements of
involved fathering published on the Ministry of Health, Labour, and
Welfare's (MHLW) *Ikumen* website and new survey data. As discussed below, these sources are not ideal. Persistent associations between care and femininity, and the possibility of backlash, make
many Japanese hesitant to speak or write frankly about being involved fathers. Nevertheless, the available evidence suggests that
latent desires for new fatherhood are hiding behind provider role
obligations and corporate structures of time and career.

The Bubble Economy as a Turning Point
for Japanese Fatherhood

Japan's so-called "bubble economy" was a period (roughly from 1985 to 1990) of speculation, rapid asset inflation, and currency appreciation. The frenzy of highly leveraged investing drove land and stock prices to unprecedented levels. The yen strengthened from more than 250 to a dollar to less than 100. Japan was predicted to overtake the United States as the world's largest economy. Purchases of luxury goods, art works, Pebble Beach Golf Course, and Rockefeller Center symbolized the legitimacy of Japan's triumphal, and seemingly unstoppable, rise. But Iraq's 1990 invasion of Kuwait sent oil-dependent Japanese markets crashing. After the speculative bubble collapsed, companies gradually restructured. Employment security was a notable casualty of this cost-cutting. Cracks appeared in Japan's mass middle-class consciousness as gaps grew between "winners," with regular, permanent employment, and "losers," with irregular, term-limited employment. Although Japan remained indisputably rich, postbubble employment structures diminished workers' hopes for egalitarian sharing of that wealth.

Employment reforms mattered to fatherhood because Japan's known history of work and parenting emphasized masculine provider ideals. The Japanese character for man (男), composed of parts meaning rice paddies (田) and power (力), prescribed the historical male role: source of household sustenance. Until 1946, male household heads held legal and customary authority over family members and resources. Fathers were called *daikokubashira,* the massive beam supporting the roof in the traditional architecture of multigenerational agricultural households. Declining use of that term, and the simultaneous rise of mass-produced dwellings for "salaryman" nuclear families, illustrate how rapid industrialization transformed family structures and fathers' roles.

Although some upper-class Japanese fathers took charge of children's education (Fuess 1997), postwar reconstruction and subsequent high-speed economic expansion caused men to become so absorbed in work that families could be characterized as fatherless (Doi 1973). Organization-man fathers of the 1960s and 1970s were ridiculed as weak or pathetic (Buruma 1984), but critique of the absence thesis argued convincingly that, even if fathers were not at home physically, they provided a psychological presence that mothers evoked to support their own authority (Ishii-Kuntz 1993). Work as men's *ikigai*, the thing that makes life worth living (Hidaka 2010; Mathews 1996), complemented wives' self-effacing commitment to family and children as basic architectural principles of Japanese social structure (Rohlen 1974). Following the collapse of the bubble economy, however, salarymen's devotion to work became increasingly synonymous with unpaid overtime, burnout, depression, suicide, and *karoshi*, death or permanent impairment caused by overwork (Weathers 2009).

After 1990, the remarkable comradeship born of Japanese management's enterprise-centered orientation (Dore 1973) was gradually supplanted by a market-centered management orientation. Increased work intensity followed as Japanese managers purposefully intensified competition between workers by melding neoliberal management strategies, such as performance-based wages, with existing corporate warrior traditions of hierarchical deference and unquestioning obedience (Matanle and Lunsing 2006). Labor market deregulation allowed increased use of low-paid, irregular employees. Their presence was a constant reminder to regular workers of changing employment patterns. The threat of being "restructured" put ever more pressure on workers to perform (Meyer-Ohle 2009).

In the wake of the bubble's collapse, even firms listed on the elite First Section of the Tokyo Stock Exchange declared bankruptcy. These shocking failures marked the point where Japan's corporate "culture of security" (Brinton 2011: 18–19) became a culture of risk, in which the prebubble bargain of loyal service for stable employment might not be honored.

Between 1990 and 2013, the number of irregular employees tripled, reaching nearly 40 percent of the workforce (Ministry of Health, Labour, and Welfare 2013). Many of the regular jobs eliminated belonged to men. Economic contraction prompted political support for labor deregulation; regular workers' wages did not rise, bonuses were cut, and youth unemployment rose (Sparks 2004). Lacking secure employment to support stable family life, young singles delayed or abandoned marriage. Married couples coped by sending wives out to work, mostly in irregular, low-wage jobs. Dual-income households became the majority in 2005 (Ministry of Health, Labour, and Welfare 2009).

The changing structure and intensity of work were manifest in work hours. Ostensible postbubble declines in Japan's average annual work hours resulted primarily from increased part-time (female) employment. The percentage working sixty or more hours a week (nearly all men) held steady (Morioka 2007). Men aged twenty to fifty-nine, those most likely to be fathers, reported annual hours averaging 2,625 in 1990, rising to 2,703 in 2000 (Mouer and Kawanishi 2005: 74–75). Furthermore, unpaid overtime, averaging 247 hours in 2007, exceeded the average 161 hours of paid overtime (Morioka 2008). Such behavior was consistent with Japanese society's weak tradition of self-determination with regard to time use. Historian Thomas Smith (1986) found that Japanese conceptions of work connote subordination and obligation: the ideal worker was like a son or a serf, bound by traditional loyalties and lacking agency. In this idealized hierarchy, workers' time was a collective resource rather than a personal possession. Obligations to workmates and employers, plus a weak sense of entitlement regarding the disposition of one's time, explained Japan's long hours and low rates of paid leave use, which fell from its early 1980s peak of roughly 60 percent (Cole 1992) to less than 50 percent recently (Japan Institute for Labour Policy and Training 2010).

Early-twentieth-century gender role prescriptions supported Japanese imperial expansion (Garon 2010) and, although female employment declined through the 1970s (Danjo Kyodo Sangaku Kaigi 2005: 6), the social division of labor was considered fair. Self-abnegation for family and hardship in childrearing remained the ideal path to female fulfillment (Sasakawa 2006: 131). Nevertheless, after 1970, Western-style feminist discourse gained traction, and hopes for gender equality rose among some women and men (Yamaguchi 1995). In many corporations, institutionalized discrimination was a bulwark against women's increased education and aspirations, but the slow increase in career-minded women posed troubling existential questions for corporate warriors. Meanwhile, an undercurrent of feminist discourse and foreign family life images (e.g., the movie *Kramer vs. Kramer*) stimulated some men to reconsider gender-segregated lifestyles. One well-regarded scholar-activist (Ito 1996) predicted a possible 1990s consciousness revolution: discovering the pathos of their corporate-centered lives, men would pursue liberation. But the majority could not take even half their paid leave. Multiyear transfers to distant posts sans family *(tanshinfunin)* were common for salarymen, but being away from work for family reasons was nearly unthinkable.

The foregoing sketch of pre- and postbubble gendered employment practices and family roles outlines how fathers' options were constrained by the dominant conception of man as ideal worker. But policy was important, too. Japan's rapid economic growth brought foreign complaints about Japan's trade surpluses and domestic initiatives to distribute the fruits of prosperity more evenly. In response, late 1980s blue-ribbon Japanese government panels advised reduced work hours, more leisure, and improved work-life balance to create a *seikatsu taikoku*, a lifestyle superpower, worthy of Japan's economic preeminence. Under government guidance, Japanese citizens would enjoy lives with leisure befitting an advanced industrial nation (Leheny 2003), a *yutori no aru shakai*: a society that gives people "time and space to do their own thing" (McCormack 2001: 85). Japan's sensitivity regarding its international image was matched by apprehension about falling birth rates, population aging, and future labor and tax shortages. Japanese men's very low rank in international comparisons of housework and childcare (Ishii-Kuntz 2008) were suspected of combining with workplace gender discrimination and weak welfare supports to thwart women's investment in family life and reproduction (Usui 2005). Thus the need for caring fatherhood gradually became obvious.

In sum, Japan's 1990 asset bubble collapse initiated twenty years of relative economic stagnation,[2] a period marked by deflation, falling wages, and increasing employment instability. Amid promises of "time and space to do their own thing," many Japanese worked increasingly hard to preserve what they had. Japan resembled other postindustrial powers that sought policy solutions to conflicts between the increasingly globalized mode of production and maintenance of local economies, social relations, and reproduction.

Paternity Leave and Leave-Takers in Japan, 1992–99 and 2000–11

Laws promoting gender equality were among countermeasures passed to cope with the population panic and economic concerns.[3] Support for fathering was a novel component of the legislation. But we need to note that Japanese civil law is frequently more suggestive than substantial. It has been compared to an ornamental samurai sword, a symbol of authority that should not be used (Haley 1991). Lacking resources to easily enforce civil statutes directly, Japanese authorities instead rely on administrative guidance and moral suasion. Combined with gradual implementation of new statutes, purposeful inclusion of loopholes, and trifling or nonexistent penalties for noncompliance, informal enforcement has weakened the effect of Japanese laws regulating industrial pollution, civil rights, and worker health and welfare (Upham 1987).

Policy Reform

The case in point here is the Child Care and Family Leave Law, part of Japan's comprehensive legislative effort to address demographic issues (Roberts 2002). While care leave for women became law in 1972, amendments supporting paid leave of up to one year for newborn child (or elder) care for both male and female regular employees (those without employment term limits) were passed in 1992. These provisions were incorporated into the Child Care and Family Leave Law in 1995, but knowledge of the law and corporate compliance were slow to spread because most women quit work upon becoming pregnant. A few high-profile examples, however, sparked widespread female leave use (Japan Institute of Labour 2003).

The law's provisions expanded incrementally. In 1995, the leave allowance was set at 25 percent of preleave pay, and exemptions from night work and limits on overtime for parents with young children were added. Smaller firms (with fewer than thirty employees) were initially exempt, but in 1995 all companies were required to comply. Revisions in 2001 prohibited disadvantageous treatment of those who applied for or took leave, and leave allowance was raised to 40 percent of normal salary to encourage men, whose salaries tend to be higher, to take leave. Further revisions in 2002 and 2005 limited overtime work for new parents, raised the ages of children eligible for care leave or reduced work hours, eased limits on the number of leaves that could be taken, and enjoined employers to consider employees' parental status when making transfers. In 2005 irregular workers also became eligible for leave. Moreover, a certification system was introduced, in which government recognition was bestowed upon companies that had at least one man take leave. Amendments in 2008 helped small- and medium-sized enterprises to provide leave, reiterated the prohibition on discriminating against leave-takers, and extended maximum leave to eighteen months. In 2010 the effective leave allowance for parents who returned to work for at least six months became 50 percent of regular salary (Ministry of Health, Labour, and Welfare 2009).

Fatherhood Images and the "Flexibility Stigma"

With gradually increased legal support, maternal childcare leave expanded quickly. Controversy over the landmark 1999 MHLW campaign promoting caring fatherhood, however, exposed social fault lines (Roberts 2002: 76–82). The ponytailed dancer husband of a famous female pop singer symbolized caring fatherhood's new ideal on posters and television advertisements. Beside a photo of him holding his laughing, infant son, the posters declared, "Men who do not raise children will not be called dad," noting also that the average Japanese father spent only seventeen minutes a day with his children. Conservatives, who defined fatherhood by bloodline, attacked the campaign as bureaucratic meddling in venerable family traditions (Kageyama 1999). The ruling Liberal Democratic Party, whose welfare philosophy was based on women caring for children, objected to reforming a division of labor that had served Japan well for over a century by freeing men for economic combat and keeping government welfare burdens light. Gender-equality activists, on the other hand, said the campaign failed to address obstacles to caring fathering and women's careers.

Few employers were eager to establish paternity leave as a norm (Roberts 2002: 68). Rising unpaid overtime, declining use of holidays, and increasing health problems accompanying men's struggles to maintain regular employment all suggested that fathers did not dare slack off amid diminishing employment stability. Surveys showed, however, that most men acknowledged the importance of family work, with 30 percent expressing interest in taking some childcare leave (Ministry of Health, Labour, and Welfare 2009: 19). Younger (20- to 40-year-old) married men with preschool-aged children were the most likely to desire childcare leave and feel very strongly about it (Sakai 2007). Younger men's budding interest in paternity leave in the late 1990s correlated with growing disenchantment with paid work (French 2002; Ishii-Kuntz 1996). These trends were depicted in newspaper comic strips featuring fathers (Yasumoto and LaRossa 2010). Moreover, young wives increasingly rejected marriage traditions that justified husbands' absences from family life and regretted making such marriages (*Asahi Shinbun* 1998).

Despite the surveys showing increasing concern for male domesticity, postbubble fathers use of reformed childcare leave policies was burdened by a "flexibility stigma," the notion that workplace flexibility policies are female accommodations (Williams et al. 2013). As in the United States, leave-taking conflicted with male, "ideal worker" norms, characterized by single-minded devotion to corporate goals (Hochschild 1997). Thus tainted, leave-taking Japanese fathers generally kept a low profile. Who they were and how many, their motives, and the effect of policy changes on the challenges of taking leave were represented by testimonials from a handful of articulate men who did not hide fatherhood behind a corporate warrior façade.

Corporations were required to establish family care leave systems only in 1999, at the same time that the Equal Employment Opportunity Law was strengthened. Until then, companies simply had a "duty to make efforts" to promote family-friendly policies (Roberts 2002: 75). The year 2000 marked the point after which fathers' leave-taking and other forms of gender-equal family work participation should have become easier (Kashima 2003). Comparing pre- and post-2000 cohorts of fathers allows evaluation of policy prescriptions as antidotes to flexibility stigma.

Paternity Leave Pioneers: 1992–99

Two months before the 1992 revisions to the leave law took effect, Ota Mutsumi, a managerial-level research engineer at a large electronics firm, began three months' leave to care for his infant daughter. Only 0.02 percent of newborns' fathers took paternal leave that year. In the run-up to the introduction of the reformed law, the media treated him like a rare species. "You'd think I was a panda or something," he wrote in retrospect (Ota 1999: 84).

Thereafter, despite expanding several fold from this tiny base, paternal leave-taking remained rare. Thanks to changes in law and policy driven by the population panic, maternal leave became almost universal. Yet notwithstanding the equal legal right to paternal leave, fewer than 3 percent of eligible fathers took leave in any year (see Table 2.1). Parental leave became thoroughly feminized.

TABLE 2.1. Percent of Eligible Parents Taking Childcare Leave (1996–2012)

	Mothers	Fathers
1996	49.1	0.12
1999	56.4	0.42
2002	64.0	0.33
2004	70.6	0.56
2005	72.3	0.50
2007	89.7	1.56
2008	90.6	1.23
2009	85.6	1.72
2010	83.7	1.38
2011	87.8	2.63
2012	83.6	1.89

Source: Asahi Shinbun 2013; Ministry of Health, Labour, and Welfare 2012a.

Analyzing detailed narratives by six paternity leave pioneers who wrote weekly newspaper columns about their experiences (*Asahi Shinbun* 2000) showed that paternity leave depended on (1) company policy toward leave-taking; (2) reactions of bosses, co-workers, and parents; (3) structural obstacles to leave in the organization of work; (4) the power of gender-role expectations; (5) leave-takers' occupation and rank; and (6) anticipated postleave workplace prospects. These factors represented constraints that kept fatherhood hidden. How did the pioneers overcome them?

In contrast to the typical Japanese worker (a woman without a university degree, working part-time in a firm of less than thirty employees that has no union (Sugimoto 2010: 1–2)), the pioneers were professionals and managers. Their long leaves (between three and six months) were enabled by rank and by virtue of so-called lifetime employment in large Japanese firms (three men), government offices (two men), or a large foreign company (one man). Large enterprises (500 or more workers) employ less than 10 percent of the labor force (Mouer and Kawanishi 2005: 119). Offering the best working conditions, large companies had childcare leave plans that supported or even encouraged leave-taking. Nevertheless, each of the six pioneers was the first in his office to take paternity leave. Four of the men's wives had the same employer, occupation, rank, salary, and benefits as their husbands (the other wives were a graduate student and a self-employed translator), eliminating the family income penalty usually accompanying male leave-taking. All the men took leave on the heels of their wives' maternity leave, timing it to create the smallest possible disruption at work, and ending leave just as their children were eligible (at one year of age) to enter public childcare. Paternity leave was part of couples' strategy for preserving wives' careers and for negotiating Japan's inadequate childcare system, with its limited infant care capacity and complex admission rules. The leave-taking fathers and their wives generally lacked relatives nearby who could help, or they preferred to be self-reliant.

Some grandparents opposed the pioneers' leave-taking on the grounds that infant care was not suitable for men. The mother of one wife apologized to her son-in-law for "trouble caused by my poor childrearing," meaning a daughter so selfishly absorbed in her career that he would have to take childcare leave (*Asahi Shinbun* 2000: 91), but family opposition was a minor constraint compared to concern for human relations at work. Employers created leave systems on paper to fulfill MHLW requirements, but to take leave fathers had to set precedents, which change-averse Japanese organizations resisted. The pioneers described months-long processes of nervous meetings in which they first requested leave, submitted applications, reconfirmed their intentions, and then negotiated arrangements with bosses and colleagues. The foreign company employee received excellent support from his American male boss: "This is a wonderful idea for you and your family," and that man's American female supervisor: "Although surprised by your application, we want to support your decision because we want to encourage the kind of reflection and determination it reveals and we expect the childcare experience will be a growth experience for you, too" (91–92). At Japanese firms the responses from colleagues varied. The only male full-time public daycare center worker in his prefecture received strong co-worker support. But others endured prickly questions about how "such a long vacation" would be spent (senior research engineer), or whether he was "really serious" (i.e., crazy). A trading company customer accounts manager was chided, "Throwing away your career, are you?" (211). Sensitivity to colleagues' feelings and fear of repercussions stemming from having caused inconvenience (*meiwaku*) to others were the most commonly mentioned impediments to fathers' leave.

To minimize ruptures to workplace harmony, the pioneers combined two strategies. Some (research engineer, manager at materials manufacturer, trading company accounts manager, construction ministry office manager) emphasized arranging leave to coincide with annual personnel movements or the completion of major projects to minimize workload increases for colleagues. Others (electrical engineer, daycare center worker) inoculated against disapproval through consensus building talk with colleagues about the benefits of paternity leave for families, workers, companies, and society.

The trading company employee had the most trouble. Trading companies are bastions of corporate warrior traditionalism. The company did not want customers to know that it had permitted an employee to take extended leave. Although this father was permitted to talk about his experience on television and in lectures, he was forbidden to mention his employer's name (213–14). When he returned to work, co-workers grumbled that he was "rather lacking in responsibility" or "concerned only with rights and had no sense of balance" (234). He, however, justified his behavior as a way of meeting his responsibilities to his wife and family (216) and countered his firm's company-centric male traditionalism by declaring that in the future only "socially responsible firms" would attract the best talent and prosper (234).

In print, the father-authors reflected that taking leave helped them see life differently. Ota, the research engineer, stopped working unnecessary overtime. He and three others reported being sought out by parenting groups. All pioneers increased involvement in their communities due to contact with other parents at children's schools. As outspoken examples of caring fathering, they challenged the flexibility stigma. Their newspaper columns urged men to be in the delivery room to share the miracle of birth, to acquire house-keeping skills, and to realize that childrearing is a gender-neutral activity. They emphasized how hands-on fathering helped them see children as people (127). These fathers were, from the start, inclined toward relatively egalitarian marriages and the idea of taking leave originated with them, but through leave they gained appreciation for the simple pleasures, isolation, and boredom of daytime society outside work, for the fleeting nature of childhood, and for how it feels to care, which helped them comprehend a "fair" and "equal" division of labor (85). They were uniformly grateful to their firms for the support they received, and all returned to their former posts after their leave.

It is also significant that these leave-takers' wives were pioneers in busting the pervasive "myth of the three-year-old": that until age three, only mother's love is good enough (Ohinata 2000). Although detailed discussion is beyond the scope of this chapter, wives' career orientation and acceptance of involved fatherhood were import-ant in shaping family strategies and husbands' attitudes, perhaps as much as the husbands' resistance to ideal worker norms. The wives, too, faced stigma, in the form of disapprobation from tradi-tionalist, non-working women. When fathers failed to perform up to standard on female-typed tasks, such as making box lunches or embroidering children's nursery school futon covers, the mother's reputation was at stake (*Asahi Shinbun* 2000).

One pioneer (the electrical engineer) gathered data on other early leave-taking fathers through an Internet survey. Twenty-three men submitted replies to his online questionnaire in 1999. Sum-marized on a web site (Wakita 2000), the results supported the pic-ture of leave-takers found in the *Asahi* volume. About half of the respondents were public officials, occupations most likely to have and support the use of gender-equality policies. Seventeen fathers were between ages thirty and forty, when men become established in their posts. Fifteen of the twenty-three worked in large orga-nizations of more than one thousand workers. Most had children between five and eleven months old when leave began, and leave

generally ended when children reached the one-year age requirement for public nursery entrance, confirming that paternity leave
was generally an extension in support of working mothers. All but
one man received favorable reaction to taking leave, suggesting that
their working wives were willing to endure the stigma of a caregiving father. Thirty-five percent of the respondents mentioned unease
or opposition from parents, but this diminished; only 22 percent
faced opposition when leave ended. All but one man expressed satisfaction with taking leave. Four fathers faced discrimination from
their bosses before taking leave, and three said it persisted after they
returned to work. Most (57 percent) were not penalized in annual
evaluations for taking leave, but four men said leave was scored as
a "blank," one was given a low rating without reason, and five others either did not know how leave was regarded or received some
other treatment with regard to leave. Returning to work, 35 percent said the seniority-based component of their salary rose as if no
leave had been taken, but 26 percent saw salary increases reduced
by the prorated length of their leave. Eighty percent reported no
long-term effects of taking leave, but twelve of the twenty-three indicated varying degrees of impact on being promoted. All were able
to return to previous positions or posts acceptable to them.

The generally positive paternal leave experiences of these self-
selected survey respondents and the pioneer leave-takers in the
Asahi volume contrasted with the views of mainstream fatherhood
advocates. They argued that men should contribute just enough at
home to enable women to work for wages and care for family. This
conservative, neo-Parsonian, gender-role discourse was exemplified
by a special edition on fathering in the magazine *Tōdai* (1999), in
which fathers, notable academics, and other public figures emphasized father involvement with older children, stressing discipline,
play, and provision of experiences in nature. The magazine justified
gender-segregating parenting by cherry-picking from the work of
experts, for instance Jon Gottman, who maintained that the father
should be a "heart coach," responsible for emotional intelligence
(36). Chuo University professor Fukuda Masaaki wrote that a father's job is to help children transition away from their mother, noting, "Even a little bit of help shows you love your wife. Until the
age of three, your job is to help. After that, your role is to open children's eyes to society" (38–39). In addition to "helping" mothers, fathers were assigned the traditional roles of enforcing peace between
squabbling siblings and impressing upon children morality and the
need to study. As designated disciplinarians, fathers assumed some

of the burden from wives so that mothers' frustrations did not interfere with performance of their affective roles. All of this agreed well
with the neopatriarchal views expressed in psychologist Hayashi
Yoshimichi's (1996) bestseller, *The Restoration of Fatherhood,* which
symbolized opposition to the egalitarian paternal involvement represented by paternity leave pioneers.

Resistance to Paternity Leave: 2000–11

Despite legal reforms, gender-equity promotion, and Ministry man-
dates for companies to draft family-friendly policies, implementation
was slow and uneven because of gender conservatism. Summarizing
Japan's housework and childcare gender gap, Masako Ishii-Kuntz
(2008: 5) found childcare sharing less likely: (1) in three-generation
households; (2) when mothers did not work; (3) when fathers' work
hours or commutes were long; (4) when spouses held traditional
gender ideas; and (5) when men's employers were traditionalists or
hostile toward family-friendly policies. Although dual-income households became the majority following the bubble's collapse, international comparisons still showed Japanese fathers much less involved
in housework and childcare than those in other industrialized countries. In 2005, married Japanese fathers with a child under age six
averaged forty-eight minutes per day of family work (twenty-five
minutes on childrearing), versus more than three hours a day in
Sweden, Germany, or the United States (roughly one hour on childrearing) (Ministry of Health, Labour, and Welfare 2006). Analysis
of spouses' housework in thirty-four countries (Knudsen 2008) found
Japanese men's two and a half hours of housework per week (childcare was not measured) the least by far of any nation studied.

Even a decade after passage of the Child Care and Family Leave
Law some paternity leave-takers were demoted and others dismissed
just for daring to apply (Wijers-Hasegawa 2002). Revision of the law
in 2002 prohibited treating leave-takers disadvantageously, but employer backlash persisted, and the norm of childcare as women's
work kept leave-taking fathers' numbers low (Sakai 2007). By 2004
the percentage of eligible fathers taking paternity leave edged up to
0.56 percent, far short of the 10 percent target. Reasons included:
(1) ignorance about the leave law applying to men; (2) childcare
being seen as women's role; (3) resistance from colleagues; (4) in-
dispensability within workplace systems; (5) fears about promotion;
and (6) lost income (Sato and Takeishi 2004). The stigma attached
to incomplete devotion to company and career constrained fathers'
leave-taking.

Meanwhile, MHLW reports accentuated instances of compliance with the law, such as companies' plans for leave. In 2009, 68 percent of firms with five or more workers had such plans. With thirty or more employees the rate stood at 89 percent (Ministry of Health, Labour, and Welfare 2010a). Other desired accommodations, such as shorter hours for parents (47.6 percent), flextime for childrearing (13.9 percent), adjustable starting and quitting times (31.8 percent), overtime exemptions (40.8 percent), in-company nurseries (2.5 percent), and financial assistance for childrearing (6.3 percent) all expanded over 2006 (2010a). Moreover, additional reforms were in the pipeline. By July 2012 companies with more than one hundred workers (roughly 30 percent of the labor force) were obliged to provide parents with children under age three a short, six-hour workday, and fathers taking childcare leave within eight weeks of birth could take additional leave later on. The requirement that leave-taking fathers have a working spouse was also abolished from 2012 (Ministry of Health, Labour, and Welfare 2010b).

Ministry optimism about incremental progress toward policy compliance dissolving barriers to paternity leave was, however, not supported by observed workplace realities. In 2009 Japan's main business daily conducted a national poll of 4,395 eligible fathers who did not take childcare leave and found their reasons (multiple responses were permitted) almost unchanged from 2004: reluctance to cause *meiwaku* (inconvenience for others) at work (35 percent); too busy (30 percent); no precedent (23 percent); atmosphere at work not conducive (20 percent); income loss (20 percent); never thought of taking leave (18 percent); and wife quit work due to birth (14 percent) (*Nihon Keizai Shinbun* 2010). The survey confirmed the estimated $300,000 cost of raising a child through college as the biggest risk associated with children. Small wonder, then, that careers trumped childcare leave as demonstrations of fatherly responsibility.

Moreover, the Japanese phrase *dansei no ikuji kyūgyō* (men's childcare leave) carried self-contradictory implications. A family tragedy or sudden illness could justify burdens imposed temporarily on co-workers by a man's brief absence, but a lengthy absence to care for children was inconceivable as long as their mother was alive. Being absent from work when others were not (*kaisha wo yasumu*) connoted dereliction of duty akin to being AWOL (Morita 2008).

Promoting Cool Fatherhood: The Ikumen Project

In mid 2010, just as 2009's (then) record high paternity leave statistic of 1.72 percent was announced, the MHLW launched the *Ikumen*

Project (Ministry of Health, Labour, and Welfare 2012b). Defined as "men who enjoy raising children and grow themselves in the process," *ikumen* (childrearing men) was a play on the word *ikemen*, trendy slang for a man with a perfect face. To native Japanese speakers, this connection between fathering and fashionable masculinity was obvious. The project homepage noted that one-third of men wanted to take childcare leave. This exceeded the official goals of 10 percent by 2017 and 13 percent by 2020, targets intended to put Japanese fathers' leave-taking on rough par with Britain. The expressed purpose of the *Ikumen* Project was to "change families so society will shift" (Ministry of Health, Labour, and Welfare 2012b), and build a virtual safe space for paternal consciousness-raising where fathers could come out of hiding and contribute to a new social consensus. It resembled other social engineering projects in which Japan's bureaucrats tapped latent public sentiment to bolster the limited power of law to influence the pace of social change (Upham 1987).

The images of celebrities, academics, and corporate leaders on the *Ikumen* Promotion Team lent the project legitimacy. The website displayed pages of "Declarations of *Ikumen*," where men publically (though anonymously) expressed determination to take leave or become caring fathers. The site emphasized fatherhood education, especially the advantages of fathers' presence at home for children and for mothers' careers. The site included links to a work-life balance handbook, information about the revised leave law, answers to common questions about how to take leave, descriptions of how some leading companies supported caring parenting, and an *ikumen* theme song. The centerpiece was fathers' self-submitted declarations and testimonials about childcare and fathering.

As data, these brief testimonials left much to be desired. The authors were usually identified by nicknames and ages given in ten-year blocks. Eleven percent were fathers-to-be, 55 percent had one child, 33 percent had two or three, and the rest had four or more, but unless they were forthcoming in their statements, their occupations (most just said "company employee"), their ranks, and the sizes of their firms were missing. Also missing were what their wives did or thought, what the family financial situation was, how their colleagues or bosses reacted to paternal leave, how much leave they took, and other important details that would enable controlled comparison of the *ikumen* with the pioneers. Against these shortcomings, the *ikumen* declaration database was easy to access and keyword searchable. In August 2011 just over four hundred fathers had posted declarations on the site. As of September 2013 there were posts from 1,684 fathers, 62.5 percent in their thirties. About half included a thumbnail photograph of father and/or children. All forty-seven prefectures were represented, though *ikumen* in many rural prefectures were in the single digits. About half of the total were in the metropolitan Tokyo area.

As the following examples show, *ikumen* were keen to explain the sincerity of their motives.

> "I want to be a father who is loved by his daughter." (Kitamura Yumei, thirties, one child)

> "Children are Japan's treasure. I want to contribute to the national spread of *ikumen* and easily take what could not be taken before' [childcare leave]." (Kawaman, twenties, one child)

> "I want to think about how spousal relations can be repaired." (Sarasara, forties, three children)

> "From now on I will make family and children the center of my lifestyle." (Y. K., thirties, father-to-be)

> "Let's take two weeks of childcare leave. Surely we can arrange to miss two weeks at work! Think of it as a long honeymoon or absence due to flu!" (Murata Ryuichi, thirties, one child)

> "The joy of childrearing can change your life. Pouring love into our children, human ties are born. What mothers teach children, fathers can teach, too. There is more to life than earning money. In parents' smiling faces, children can see the future. Let's do our best!" (Taki, thirties, two children)

Some inspirational submissions were singled out by the MHLW as "Stars of Ikumen." A few are paraphrased below:

Mr. Ochi (Twenties)

This company employee and father of two worked nightly overtime, but when the second child came, he took two months of childcare leave, using the time to consider deeply with his wife what was really important. After returning to work he made use of the short-hours option so he could share housework and childcare with his employed wife. He learned to make simple foods that his children loved and felt he was growing because he was doing more than wage work.

Mr. Horikawa (Twenties)

Although he was curious about taking leave when his first son was born, he did not. Those regrets, and his wife's job, pushed him to take a three-month leave after his wife's leave, following the birth of their second son. He enjoyed pushing baby in the stroller, attending classes for "new mothers," and reconsidering the value of family ties. After returning to work, he changed from sales to the work-life balance promotion section. The less demanding position allowed him to drop off and pick up his children at daycare, prepare dinner, bathe them, and put them to bed. Each day he searched for better ways to harmonize work and family, saying there was no joy greater than helping build a society where men can take leave. He wanted to reinvent carework as a way for men to express love.

Mr. Nomura (Twenties)

Mr. Nomura's boss congratulated him and readily agreed to let him take six months' leave when he announced that his wife was pregnant. However, before his leave began, he was asked repeatedly if it was really necessary and this made him hesitate. People he thought were on his side turned out to be critical, asking him if leave was really the best way to support his family. He worried about interrupting his career, but seeing his wife's belly swell, he wanted to share the burden. He felt fortunate that his comfortable circumstances afforded him the opportunity to learn and grow, and he thought it would not be so easy otherwise. Still, he hoped most men could share this "hard" experience.

Mr. Kitahashi (Twenties)

Mr. Kitahashi, a disabled man who was an accountant in an elder care facility, and his wife, both needed to work to make ends meet. His boss kindly suggested that he take leave and work a modified schedule upon restarting work. He was grateful to this supervisor, for children do not know night from day: they cry when they feel like it regardless of parents' needs for sleep. Thanks to his accommodating workplace, he found time to make his son smile every day. He said that in this era of dual-income families and recession, even if the husband's income was less than his wife's, there was little awareness and understanding of paternity leave, but it would be good if such notions were incorporated in the re-creation of society.

Ikumen accounts could not be verified, but their consistency and generally modest tone gave them credibility. Factors enabling successful caring fatherhood included getting off the fast track, declining to work overtime, having a considerate boss, and enduring some level of self-doubt and questioning from others. Crucially missing were other spouses' information and workplace details, but despite those limitations, the *ikumen* testimonials symbolized trends among a growing minority of fathers, varied in their willingness to be visible, but modestly proud to be conscious agents of social change.

Indeed, *ikumen* may be the tip of an iceberg. A nationally representative survey (1,030 married, regularly employed fathers aged twenty and older, with a child less than eighteen months old) conducted by Fathering Japan (2011), a MHLW-connected non-profit organization, revealed that many fathers (46.6 percent of those surveyed) took "hidden childcare leave." That is, they used some annual paid leave to support their wives just after childbirth or to provide childcare rather than using the family care leave system. About 50 percent of the men took three days of hidden leave and nearly all kept it under a week, although they wished to take between ten days and one month.[4]

Taking annual paid leave was comparatively simple procedure for workers and helped companies meet MHLW calls to boost low leave use rates, while showing sympathy toward employee needs. Fathers who hid childcare leave behind annual paid leave avoided the flexibility stigma that attends "men's childcare leave." A short, hidden care leave demonstrated maturity: the ability to keep *honne*, real feelings, subordinated behind *tatemae*, façades of appropriate behavior that maintain social harmony. That the desired leave period was far short of what the law allows suggests the continuing strength of workplace constraints on Japanese fatherhood.

Conclusion: Toward Fatherhood as Care

Recent Japanese fatherhood practices, and parental leave use in particular, reflect the combined effects of economic stagnation and rising demands for men's care filtered through local cultural strategies. While the collapse of the late-1980s bubble economy made employment more precarious and demanding, Japanese family policy sought to simultaneously stem falling birthrates and boost female labor force participation. The time and care fathers could contribute at home, however, was limited by globalized market forces and corporate warrior role demands at work and the gendered emotional economy of the dual-income household division of labor.

State promotion of involved fathering consisted primarily of guidelines enforced by administrative guidance. Although consistent with Japanese consensus-building practices, such incrementalism could not counter the stigma that associated men's use of flexibility policies with selfish disregard for co-workers and corporate goals.

The lack of real penalties for violations of the law (Koyama 2008) and the low level of financial support for leave-taking established a legal framework that guaranteed the feminization of leave. Maintaining the gendered social status quo and division of labor restrains emergent patterns of fatherhood. Even when the object is family care, insisting on one's legal rights is not necessarily taken as a sign of mature manhood. The case of paternity leave shows how gender and relationship norms rooted in employment structures compel many young fathers to conceal their desire to realize new fatherhood ideals within a brief period of regular paid leave.

The symbolically significant men who dared to take long paternity leaves and the statistically significant group taking short periods of regular leave point out the comparatively limited role of social policy in increasing Japanese fathers' care contributions. The cases of the paternity leave pioneers highlight how key variables in enabling longer leaves are beyond the reach of legislation. The men taking leave were solidly established in permanent positions in government offices, large firms, or foreign companies that were better able to be father-leave friendly. They were additionally sheltered by their wives' high-paying careers, which had long-term prospects that compensated for fathers' short-term income loss. Their examples show that supportive bosses and co-workers matter a great deal because successful postleave return to the workplace depends on those human relationships as well as on notions of legal rights.

The pioneers of 1992–99 enjoyed a milder economic climate than the men who followed in 2000–11. The 1990–94 postbubble recession was believed to be no more than a cyclical downturn. But it dragged on, and after major bankruptcies in 1997 and the "Lehman Shock" of 2008, hiring fell sharply and the risks of being restructured loomed large. Proliferating temporary and other irregular, low-paid workers are constant reminders for men with children to be cautious. Because they have the most at stake, they often work the longest hours.

The unfortunate situation in Japan today is that extended paternity leave providing sustained time for father-child bonding is still so rare that it can be stigmatized. The practice of taking short, hidden leaves does not add new strategies to the cultural toolkit of Japanese masculinity so much as it reproduces the norm of work and family as separate, gendered spheres. By not requesting paternity leave, fathers avoid causing *meiwaku* and the flexibility stigma, but this does not advance family men's shared interests, nor those of workers in general. The MHLW is dedicated to making Japan a better place to live and work, and efforts are underway to build the adequate child-care facilities called for in the national vision for childrearing (*Japan Times* 2010). But it is tough to balance health and welfare with labor, because short-term business concerns trump longer-term welfare and demographic agendas. Thus arises the curious situation in which paternity leave systems are now nearly universal in Japan, but today's fathers are only slightly more likely to use them than the 1990s pioneers. The enormous physical and economic disruption caused by the Great Tohoku Earthquake of 2011, as well as Japan's enormous public debt, will almost certainly keep the creation of gender-blind, family-friendly workplace regimes hidden far down on the list of priorities.

Notes

1. Unless otherwise noted, translations of Japanese sources are my own.
2. By official statistics, the period from January 2002 to October 2007 was Japan's longest postwar period of sustained economic expansion. This growth was, however, based on exports and confined largely to gross national product. It failed to trickle down into workers' wages, and domestic demand was weak (Koji Ito 2009).
3. In Japanese documents, "gender equality" is rendered *danjo kyōdō sangaku*, a phrase that implies mutual participation but distinctly lacks the explicit mention of equality found in government English translations. The Japanese term for equality, *byodo*, appeared in early drafts, but was replaced by *kyodo* in the final bill.
4. The surprising prevalence of hidden childcare leave is consistent with anecdotal evidence that young urban fathers are spending more time with infants and children. Especially on weekends, one now sees unaccompanied fathers and children, often infants in slings or strollers, out in public. Especially in urban Japan, the reality of caring fathering may be outrunning the research.

References

Asahi Shinbun. 1998. "Majority of Wives Regret Marriage" [In Japanese]. 17 October: 19.

2013. "Ikkukyū Shutokuritsu, Danjotomo 2 Nenburi Genshō [Childcare leave use rate falls for first time in 2 years]." 5 July. http://www.asahi.com/national/update/0704/TKY201307040464.html.

Asahi Shinbun, ed. 2000. *Ikukyū otōsan no seichō nisshi* [Paternity leave fathers' growth logbook]. Tokyo: Asahi Shinbunsha.

Breen, Richard, and Lynn P. Cooke. 2005. "The Persistence of the Gendered Division of Domestic Labour." *European Sociological Review* 21, no. 1: 43–57.

Brinton, Mary. 2011. *Lost in Transition: Youth, Work, and Instability in Postindustrial Japan.* Cambridge: Cambridge University Press.

Buruma, Ian. 1984. *A Japanese Mirror: Heroes and Villains of Japanese Culture.* London: Jonathan Cape.

Chafetz, Janet, and Jacqueline Hagen. 1996. "The Gender Division of Labor and Family Change in Industrial Societies: A Theoretical Accounting." *Journal of Comparative Family Studies* 27, no. 2: 187–219.

Cole, Robert E. 1992. "Work and Leisure in Japan." *California Management Review* 34, no. 3: 52–63.

Danjo Kyodou Sangaku Kaigi. 2005. *International Comparison of Social Environments Concerning Gender Equality and Low Birthrates.* Tokyo: Government of Japan.

Doi, Takeo. 1973. *The Anatomy of Dependence.* Tokyo: Kodansha International.

Dore, Ronald P. 1973. *British Factory, Japanese Factory: The Origins of National Diversity in Industrial Relations.* Berkeley: University of California Press.

Fathering Japan. 2011. *Sankyū papa purojekuto* [Paternal leave project]. http://www.fathering.jp/sankyu/pdf/kakureikukyu2.pdf.

French, Howard. 2002. "Teaching Japan's Salarymen to Be their Own Men." *The New York Times.* 27 November.

Fuess, Harald. 1997. "A Golden Age of Fatherhood? Parent-Child Relations in Japanese Historiography." *Monumenta Nipponica* 52: 381–98.

Garon, Sheldon. 2010. "State and Family in Modern Japan: A Historical Perspective." *Economy and Society* 39, no. 3: 317–36.

Goode, William. 1963. *World Revolution and Family Patterns.* New York: The Free Press.

Haas, Linda, and Margaret O'Brien. 2010. "New Observations on How Fathers Work and Care: Introduction to the Special Issue—Men, Work and Parenting—Part I." *Fathering* 8, no. 3: 271–75.

Haley, John O. 1991. *Authority without Power: Law and the Japanese Paradox.* New York: Oxford University Press.

Hamabata, Matthews M. 1991. *Crested Kimono: Power and Love in the Japanese Business Family.* Ithaca, NY: Cornell University Press.

Hayashi, Yoshimichi. 1996. *Fusei no fukken* [The restoration of fatherhood]. Tokyo: Chuo Koronsha.

Hidaka, Tomoko. 2010. *Salaryman Masculinity: The Continuity of and Change in the Hegemonic Masculinity in Japan.* Leiden: Brill.

Hochschild, Arlie R. 1997. *The Time Bind: When Home Becomes Work and Work Becomes Home.* New York: Metropolitan Books.

Hochschild, Arlie R., and Anne Machung. 1989. *The Second Shift: Working Parents and the Revolution at Home.* New York: Owl Books.

Ishii-Kuntz, Masako. 1993. "Japanese Fathers: Work Demands and Family Roles." In *Men, Work, and Family,* ed. Jane Hood. Beverly Hills: Sage.

————. 1996. "A Perspective on Changes in Men's Work and Fatherhood in Japan." *Asian Cultural Studies* 22: 91–107.

————. 2008. "Sharing of Housework and Childcare in Contemporary Japan." Geneva: United Nations, Division for the Advancement of Women.

Ito, Kimio. 1996. *Danseigaku nyūmon* [Introduction to men's studies]. Tokyo: Sakuhinsha.

Ito, Koji. 2009. "Japan's Post-Crisis External Economic Policies." Research Institute of Economy, Trade, and Industry.

Japan Institute for Labour Policy and Training. 2010. *Japanese Working Life Profile 2009/2010: Labor Statistics.* Tokyo: Japan Institute for Labour Policy and Training.

Japan Institute of Labour. 2003. "Research Report on the Child-Care Leave System: Findings of a 'Study of Women's Work and Family Life.'" Research Report No. 157, July. Tokyo: Japan Institute of Labour.

Japan Times. 2010. "National Vision for Child-Rearing." 23 February.

Kageyama, Yuri. 1999. "Japan Says Dads Should Help out More." *San Francisco Chronicle,* 24 April: A14.

Kashima, Takashi. 2003. *Danjo kyōdō sangakushaki no jidai* [The age of gender equality]. Tokyo: Iwanami Shoten.

Knudsen, Knud, and Kari Wareness. 2008. "National Context and Spouses' Housework in 34 Countries." *European Sociological Review* 24, no. 1: 97–113.

Koyama, K. 2008. *Chichi no ikukyū: shokuba kakumei ga hitsuyō* [Promoting fathers' childcare leave requires a workplace revolution]. *Yomiuri Shinbun,* 3 July: 3.

LaRossa, Ralph. 1997. *The Modernization of Fatherhood: A Social and Political History.* Chicago: University of Chicago Press.

Leheny, David. 2003. *The Rules of Play: National Identity and the Shaping of Japanese Leisure.* Ithaca, NY: Cornell University Press.

Matanle, Peter, and Wim Lunsing. 2006. *Perspectives on Work, Employment and Society in Japan.* New York: Palgrave Macmillan.

Mathews, Gordon. 1996. *What Makes Life Worth Living? How Japanese and Americans Make Sense of their Worlds.* Berkeley: University of California Press.

McCormack, Gavan. 2001. *The Emptiness of Japanese Affluence.* Revised Edition. Armonk, NY: M. E. Sharpe.

Meyer-Ohle, Hendrik. 2009. *Japanese Workplaces in Transition: Employee Perceptions.* New York: Palgrave Macmillan.

Ministry of Health, Labour, and Welfare. 2006. *Heisei 18 nendo shoshika shakai hakusho* [2005 Declining birthrate society white paper]. Tokyo: Government of Japan.

————. 2009. *Introduction to the Revised Child Care and Family Leave Law.* Tokyo: Government of Japan.

————. 2010a. *Heisei 21 nendo koyō kintō kihon chōsa kekka gaiyō* [Results summary of the 2009 employment equality survey]. Tokyo: Government of Japan.

———. 2010b. *Ikuji, kaigo kyūgyō tō ni kansuru kisoku no kiteirei* [Examples of regulations relating to child and elder care leave]. Tokyo: Government of Japan.

———. 2012a. *Heisei 23 nendo koyō kintō kihon chōsa kekka gaiyō* [Results summary of the 2011 employment equality survey]. Tokyo: Government of Japan.

———. 2012b. *Ikumen purojekutto* [*Ikumen* Project]. Tokyo: Government of Japan. http://ikumen-project.jp/index.html.

———. 2013. *Rōdōryoku Chōsa* [Labor Force Survey]. Tokyo: Government of Japan. http://www/stat.go.jp/data/roudou/sokuhou/4hanki/dt/index.ht.

Morioka, Koji. 2007. "Atarashī hatarakisugi to howaito karā eguzenpushon" [The new overwork and the white-collar exemption]. In *Kakusa shakai no kouzō: gurōbaru shihon shugi no dansō,* ed. Morioka Koji. Tokyo: Sakurai Shoten.

———. 2008. *Rōdō konpuraiansu to sābisu zangyō* [Labor compliance and unpaid overtime]. Report presented to Hatarakikatanet Osaka, 10 April.

Morita, Misa. 2008. *Chichioya ha ikuji kyūgyō ha toritai no ka* [Do fathers want to take paternity leave?]. In *Otoko no ikukyū, onna no ikukyū* [Men's childcare leave, women's childcare leave], ed. Yamato Reiko, Onode Setsuko, and Kiwaki Nachiko. Tokyo: Showado.

Mouer, Ross, and Hiroshi Kawanishi. 2005. *A Sociology of Work in Japan.* Cambridge: Cambridge University Press.

Nakatani, Ayami. 2006. "The Emergence of Nurturing Fathers." In *The Changing Japanese Family,* ed. Markus Rebick and Ayumi Takenaka. London: Routledge.

Nihon Keizai Shinbun. 2010. *Dansei no ikukyū ni kakei no kabe* [Household budget barrier to men's care leave]. 28 July: A11.

Ohinata, Masami. 2000. *Boseiai shinwa no wana* [The trap of the myths of motherhood]. Tokyo: Nihon Yoronsha.

Ota, Mutsumi. 1999. "Dad Takes Child-Care Leave." Trans. Michael Hoffman. *Japan Quarterly* 46, no. 1: 83–99.

Roberts, Glenda S. 2002. "Pinning Hopes on Angels: Reflections from an Aging Japan's Urban Landscape." In *Family and Social Policy in Japan,* ed. Roger Goodman. Cambridge: Cambridge University Press.

Rohlen, Thomas P. 1974. *For Harmony and Strength: Japanese White Collar Organization in Anthropological Perspective.* Berkeley: University of California Press.

Sakai, K. 2007. *Shokuba ni okeru dansei no shigoto to ikuji no ryōritsu shiensaku no genjō to ikuji kyūgyō shutoku kibouritsu no bunseki* [Analysis of current workplace supports for male childrearing and desire to take childcare leave]. In *Shigoto to seikatsu.* Tokyo: Dokuritsu Gyōeihōjin Rōdō Seisaku Kenkyū Kenshū Kikō.

Sasakawa, Ayumi. 2006. "Mother-Rearing: The Social World of Mothers in a Japanese Suburb." In *The Changing Japanese Family,* ed. M. Rebick and A. Takenaka. London: Routledge.

Sato, Hiroshi, and Emiko Takeishi. 2004. *Dansei no ikuji kyūgyō: shain no niizu, kaisha no meritto* [Men's childcare leave: employee needs, company benefits]. Tokyo: Chukoshinsho.

Shwalb, David W., Nobuto Imaizumi, and Jun Nakazawa. 1987. "The Modern Japanese Father: Roles and Problems in a Changing Society." In *The Father's Role: Cross-Cultural Perspectives,* ed. Michael E. Lamb. London: Lawrence Erlbaum Associates.

Smith, Thomas. 1986. "Peasant Time and Factory Time in Japan." *Past and Present* 111, no. 1: 165–97.

Sparks, Chris. 2004. "Changes in Japanese Wage Structure and the Effect on Wage Growth since 1990." Tokyo: Japan Institute of Labour.

Sugimoto, Yoshio. 2010. *An Introduction to Japanese Society.* 3rd Edition. Cambridge: Cambridge University Press.

Swidler, Ann. 1986. "Culture in Action: Symbols and Strategies." *American Sociological Review* 51, no. 2: 273–86.

Tōdai. 1999. *Tokushū: chichi koso dekiru koto* [Special: What fathers can do]. No. 470 (November): 28–41.

Upham, Frank K. 1987. *Law and Social Change in Postwar Japan.* Cambridge: Harvard University Press.

Usui, Chikako. 2005. "Japan's Frozen Future: Why Are Women Withholding Their Investment in Work and Family?" In *Japanese Women: Lineage and Legacies,* ed. Amy Thernstrom. Washington, DC: Woodrow Wilson International Center for Scholars: 57–68.

Wakita, Yoshihiro. 2000. *Ikukyū tōsan anketto shūkei hyō* [Paternity leave survey results]. http://www.eqg.org/~wakita/ikukyu/resulttable.html.

Weathers, Charles, and Scott North. 2009. "Overtime Activists Take on Corporate Titans: Toyota, McDonald's and Japan's Work Hour Controversy." *Pacific Affairs* 82, no. 4: 615–36.

Wijers-Hasegawa, Yumi. 2002. "Dads Take Child-Care Leave at Own Risk." *The Japan Times,* 4 January.

Williams, Joan C., Mary Blair-Loy, and Jennifer Berdahl. 2013. "Cultural Schemas, Social Class, and the Flexibility Stigma." *The Journal of Social Issues* 69, no. 2: 209–34.

Yamaguchi, Masanori. 1995. "Men on the Threshold of Change." In *Japanese Women: New Feminist Perspectives on the Past, Present, and Future,* ed. Kumiko Fujimura-Faneslow and Atsuko Kameda. New York: The Feminist Press.

Yasumoto, Saori, and Ralph LaRossa. 2010. "The Culture of Fatherhood in Japanese Comic Strips: A Historical Analysis." *Journal of Comparative Family Studies* 41, no. 4: 611–27.

Part II

Transnational Fatherhood

Chapter 3

TRANSNATIONAL FATHERS, GOOD PROVIDERS, AND THE SILENCES OF ADOPTION

Jessaca Leinaweaver

Introduction

Across generations and across cultures, the role of social father is often equated with that of economic provider. Father-as-provider is a familiar model, as Nick Townsend (1997: 77) shows in the U.S. context: for middle-class men in California, fatherhood involves providing economically for one's family and owning a home in a good neighborhood, two features that are then reinterpreted as emotional closeness.[1] This model has also been identified as one shared by men and women in Spain (Luxán et al. 1999; Brandes 1975; Gilmore 1998) and in Peru (Fuller 2003). Feminist scholars have shown how this model is inadequate in a variety of ways, noting, for example, the very ordinariness of migrant women who mother their children from afar. In this chapter, I consider some of the further implications of this model for a globalized fatherhood.

Drawing on case studies of fathers residing in Madrid, Spain, I develop the contrast between migrant men who leave their children and adoptive fathers who cause their children to migrate via international adoption. I show how global trends of adoption and migration shape men's abilities to define themselves and their relationships with their children using a model of father-as-provider. Specifically, I argue that when the migrant is an adopted child, as opposed to a transnational parent, the notion of father-as-provider comes under fire from unexpected quarters. One consequence is that adoptive fathers are much more limited in their ability to draw upon the model of father-as-provider than are transnational fathers, something that has paradoxical implications for adoptive fatherhood and, perhaps, for the success of international adoption itself.

Research Setting and Methodological Approach

At the turn of the twenty-first century, international adoption was taken up rapidly in Spain (Howell and Marre 2006; Marre 2007; Marre and Bestard 2004), a nation with a birth rate well below replacement and a well-developed fertility industry despite prohibiting surrogacy (Bergmann 2011). Between 1998 and 2004, global numbers of international adoptions rose by 42 percent, and in Spain they rose by a full 273 percent (Selman 2009: 578). In the past fifteen years over forty thousand children from over thirty-five countries have been adopted by Spanish parents and moved to Spain (Giró 2012). Although numbers of adoptions have fallen since 2004, as Laura Briggs (2012: 5) notes, "[A]doption, while a practice that affects a small and shrinking number of people, has been important to national and international politics out of all proportion to its numerical significance."

My research examined adoptions of Peruvian children. A full two-thirds of the children adopted internationally to Spain in 1997 were Latin American (Selman 2009: 581–82). Latin America was initially seen as an important continent for Spanish adoptions because of both linguistic and cultural affinity, and because of existing connections with Spanish clergy in Latin America who could facilitate adoptions (Marre 2009).

However, due in part to legal changes within Peru aimed at achieving greater transparency and regularity (changes that were mirrored in other Latin American countries), by 2000 the number of children adopted from Peru to Spain dropped below one hundred and it has not surpassed that figure since. For the four most recent years for which data is available (2008–11 inclusive), an average of twenty-five Peruvian children have been adopted to Spain per year, significantly fewer than to the top destination of Italy and around the same number as to the United States (Ministerio de la Mujer y Poblaciones Vulnerables 2012). Meanwhile, the figures from other countries were skyrocketing. In 2002 the annual number of children adopted from China topped 1,000, and in 2003 so did the annual number from Russia. Latin American countries typically demanded that adoptive parents spend one to three months in the country, but "express adoption" was available in China, with nine-month wait times and one-week stays in the country (Marre 2009).

It is important to note that transnational adoption from Peru to Spain is usually also transracial adoption. Outsiders and family members alike identified adopted children's phenotypes as different from those of their parents. At the beginning of international adoption in Spain, this observable difference meant that young children of color were easily identifiable as adopted. The alternative, which has appeared more recently as adoptees have aged into adolescence and beyond and as international migration to Spain has grown impressively, is that adoptees may be "mis-identified" as immigrants (see Hübinette and Tigervall 2009: 344). As U.S. immigration policy tightened in the 2000s, Spain, Italy, and Japan encouraged labor migration and received the bulk of migrants from Peru (Takenaka et al. 2010: 6; see also Escrivá 2005). Spain is the nation with the third largest number of Peruvian migrants overall, and the city of Madrid is home to a full 8.6 percent of all Peruvian migrants globally, second only to Buenos Aires (Cooperación Interinstitucional INEI-DI-GEMIN-OIM 2010). At the close of 2011, almost 20 percent of the population of the Community of Madrid was made up of migrants, 40 percent of them from the Americas (El País 2012).

Since 2009 I have conducted qualitative fieldwork with adopted and migrant Peruvians in Madrid, Spain. The purpose of the study was to ethnographically chart the connections between migration and adoption (Leinaweaver 2013). Scholars typically treat migration and adoption separately. Migration scholars who study transnational parenting may study migrant fathers who leave their children behind and send remittances to contribute to the child's upkeep (Dreby 2006; Dreby and Adkins 2012; Lamb and Bougher 2009; Parreñas 2005; see also Thao, this volume; Lam and Yeoh, this volume). Meanwhile, kinship scholars who study international adoption may contrast adoptive fathers with their peers who have reproduced in other, more biological fashions, including the new reproductive technologies (Howell and Melhuus 2007; Lewin 2005). By comparing transnational migrant parents with internationally adoptive parents, I found unexpected similarities in their parenting practices, as well as challenges these parents face that would otherwise remain invisible without the revelatory power of comparison.

As an anthropologist I prize depth over representativeness, and as such this chapter offers an in-depth exploration based on a small but diverse set of data, collected over the course of eight months spread over four years (2009–12). I carried out over twenty intensive interviews (when feasible, following up for additional interviews in later years) with adoptive families, migrant families, and professionals residing in Madrid, and recorded field notes based on participant-observation. The families were selected opportunistically using snowball sampling, with the aim of attaining thematic saturation and recording a diverse range of experiences (such as transnational parenting, family reunification migration, adopting an older child, or adopting as a single parent).

This chapter presents two case studies of men who live in Madrid, Spain, and parent children born in Peru. The similarities end there. César, a Peruvian labor migrant, sends remittances to his 6-year-old daughter, who resides in Peru. Sergio is the Spanish adoptive father of a teenage son who was born in Peru. My material for this chapter is drawn mainly from two recorded interviews conducted in Spanish (lasting half an hour for César's and over one hour for Sergio's), additional visits made to César's home, observations of informational meetings about international adoption and educational presentations to adoptive parents, and publicly available materials, such as international websites, national legal documents, and international conventions regulating adoption and migration. Prior to beginning this study in Spain, I conducted over two years of research on adoption and fostering in Peru (Leinaweaver 2008), and my understanding of Peruvian and international adoption policy is grounded in that work.

By focusing on fathers in this chapter, I do not mean to overlook the role of women as migrant mothers and as adoptive mothers, nor as mothers who stay in Peru and raise the children of migrant men, nor indeed as the women who give birth to the children who are later adopted by fathers overseas. Family-making in contemporary Western countries is gendered feminine and adoption is overwhelmingly the work of women (mothers as well as professional social workers, psychologists, and lawyers). The literature on adoption rarely focuses directly on fathers (but see Herrera 2013; Lewin 2005). Furthermore, 53 percent of Peruvian migrants living in Spain are women, many of them mothers, which shapes parental debates over whether, and when, a migrant should bring his or her children to Spain. The gender difference among migrants and their desires for their children is significant: as Rhacel Salazar Parreñas (2005: 127) argues with regard to the Philippines, children of migrant mothers feel abandoned because mothering is thought to be performed through presence, while children of migrant fathers do not have that sense, because fathers can perform fathering through financial support, i.e., sending remittances (see also Ansión et al. 2009: 37; Horton 2009; Madianou and Miller 2011). But it is precisely because both adoption research and studies of transnational parenting so often emphasize women's roles that it is important to consider men's stories. In making this contrast between adoption and migration, we learn from migration about the silences that adoptive fathers must maintain.

Father as Provider?

Father-as-provider is encoded in migration policy and remittance practice (Leinaweaver 2011). In Spain, legal migrants have been granted the "right to a family life" (Jefatura del Estado 2000 Cap II, Art 16.1),[2] a phrase that is carefully limited to include only spouses, unmarried minor children (or legal dependents who are disabled) of whom the migrant has custody, and parents over the age of sixty-five. The right is further limited by a model of provision. The immigrant soliciting family reunification must document sufficient economic resources to cover any reunified family members' needs, as well as "proof of an adequate home to meet the needs of the petitioner and the reunified family member(s)" (Ministerio de la Presidencia 2011, Articles 54–55). This includes the legal right to occupy the home (a title or a contract), the number of rooms, what each room is used for, how many people live there, and the home's conditions of "habitability" and its furnishings. This is partly based on the assumption that children (and other dependents) require economic security in order to thrive. Partly, of course, it is because the Spanish state (especially these days) wants no new dependents of its own. Regardless, the emphasis on economic provision for reunified dependents is clear and present. The state's anxieties about material provision reinforce preexisting notions of what makes a good father, and I do not doubt that the men considering bringing their children to Spain share those ideals of father-as-provider, if not the ideals about the precise steps for realizing them.

This emphasis on economic provision within the legal and policy framework is echoed in migration scholarship. One of the most carefully elaborated arenas of research is on remittances. For example, Verónica Frisancho Robles and R. S. Oropesa (2011: 591) argue that "a substantive emphasis on remittances in the literature" prevents a firm understanding of the effects of parental migration on children. The focus on remittances highlights how parents economically provide for dependents even while separated from them via migration.

Meanwhile, economic provision is also central to the process of becoming eligible to adopt internationally. Adoption eligibility is determined by applying international norms such as the Hague Adoption Convention of 1993, Spanish adoption law, and the requirements of the country the applicant intends to adopt from. Norms for adoption from Peru require that prospective parents document "financial stability and a home suitable to meet the basic needs of the child" (Ministerio de la Mujer y Poblaciones Vulnerables 2013).[3]

Paradoxically, however, that documentation is ideally the last mention of provision in adoption. This is because of anxieties in the adoption world, on the one hand that adoption should not appear in any way as an economic transaction, and on the other hand that adoption should not be done out of a motivation to help a needy child. The history of this latter position draws on discourses that have depicted transnational adoption as philanthropic or humanitarian (Bystrom 2012: 224), a rescue (Dubinsky 2010: 131), or in the framing most commonly seen in Spain, a form of solidarity (Giménez Romero 2008: 110).

The idea that adoption is not about helping a needy child was spelled out in no uncertain terms by Antonio Calles, a legal staff member at Madrid's government adoption office, as he led an information session I attended in 2011. To the forty prospective parents (and one anthropologist) present, he bluntly stated: "Adoption has nothing to do with solidarity. It should be the desire to be parents. Those kids you see on TV who are abandoned, working, living on the street—those aren't the kids being looked after in orphanages. If you want to help [those] children, contribute to a development organization. We only want people who desire to parent a child." Calles was criticizing the subtext of adoption in which Spain is imagined to be intrinsically a better place to raise a child than is Peru (or any other country from which Spaniards adopt). He sketched an extreme version of this sentiment by suggesting that it was better to halt an adoption in the child's country of origin if a prospective parent had serious doubts, than to bring the child to Spain because "you think he'll be better off in an orphanage here," i.e., already anticipating eventually abandoning the child upon return to Spain.

To depict adoption as a "rescue," the sociologist Sara Dorow (2006: 62) argued, sets up parents as morally, socially, and economically superior to their children, an unsustainable representation which could easily backfire (see also Berástegui Pedro-Viejo 2006: 7). Dorow's analysis implies that a parent should not be (or should not admit to being) economically superior to a child. One consequence of a rescue or solidarity framing is that the parent is represented as generous and the child as lucky or grateful (Dubinsky 2010: 3). The idea is that such an unequal representation should be avoided because it is not what is best for the child, since what is best for the child is to be parented by someone who wants only to be a parent. This is a complicated—perhaps circular—construction because, if providing for a child is so central to the concerns of so many (migrant parents, law makers, and scholars, to name a few), then to prevent adoptive parents from speaking in those terms takes away from them one of the tools they might use to construct themselves as legitimate parents.

Transnational adoption is figured potentially as an insecure, questioned, or fragile form of parenting. I argue that one of the features that underlie this insecurity is that parents—and especially fathers—are, essentially, prohibited from drawing on models of opportunity provision to construct their fatherhood. The discourse of adoption professionals prevents parents, who genuinely want to do what is right for their children, from talking in that way (see Frekko et al. n.d.). This is ironic because the grounding of the professionals' discourse is that one has to want to be a parent. By contrasting migrant and adoptive parent approaches, as I do here, it becomes apparent that if and when there is an economic or provision element to being a father, it may be contradictory or self-defeating to instruct adoptive fathers to mute that aspect of their fatherhood.

In migration and adoption policy, then, parenthood is directly tied to a parent's ability to provide economically. It is also worth noting that both transnational migrant fatherhood and adoptive fatherhood are mediated by the state more than are most men's fatherhood experiences. In the remainder of this chapter I turn to my ethnographic material to show the ways in which two fathers living in Spain talk about what fatherhood consists of for them—primarily, the ways in which they talk about their relationships with their children. Migration scholars will not be surprised to see that César, a labor migrant from Peru, talks about the ways he provides for his daughter despite the distance. Kinship scholars will not be surprised to see that Sergio, a Spanish man who (along with his wife) has adopted a son from Peru, talks about emotional support and his attempts to help his son form an identity. The novel part of my argument comes from contrasting these two narratives, holding them together in order to show that it is of great interest that they diverge so strongly, and that this has particular consequences for understandings of contemporary globalized fatherhood. I close by raising the specter of the "silent fathers," men from whom we must not hear if this model of father-as-provider is to remain intact—men who remain in Peru and let their wives and children emigrate, and men who remain in Peru while their biological children are placed overseas in adoptive families.

César and Zoraida: Distanced Fathering

Norma Fuller (2003: 148) has written that fathers in Peru "work and accumulate goods and prestige to provide and care for their families." As Fuller argues, "To be a father is not to procreate but rather to socially assume the bond with a son or a daughter and to dedicate oneself to forging this tie… The father figure is defined as the one who determines the destiny of his children… those who abandon their families condemn their children to poverty" (149; see also Fuller 2000). Abandonment, in Fuller's analysis, does not refer to physical separation but rather to poverty. In this model, a man who resides far from his child can nonetheless be said not to have abandoned his child precisely because (and as long as) he continues to support her economically. Money is convertible in a way that af-fect is not: money substitutes or compensates for co-presence. The social assumption of the fatherhood bond, as Fuller puts it, can be achieved long-distance (see also Leifsen and Tymczuk 2012). This is because it fits well with the model of father-as-provider—to em-igrate and send remittances is precisely a form of economic provi-sion for one's child. In the framework developed by Marsiglio et al. (2013: 1019), emigration is a "non-procreative turning point" in men's lives that nonetheless, if it relates to their ability to provide for their children, can "ultimately influence how men develop and express their procreative consciousness."

As César told me in an interview in 2011, he migrated to Spain legally from Peru in 2006 "for the opportunity to work, for work, my only objective was to get a good job like I have now and to help my family in Peru… my parents, my daughter." Unlike many immi-grants whose work is contractual and limited-term, César is a me-chanic with an "undefined contract" (a form of tenure). Auto repair is a career that is not adversely affected by the economic crisis presently racking Spain: when people are unable to buy new cars they must redouble their efforts to repair their existing ones.

When César came to Spain, he left his daughter Zoraida, age two, in Peru. He had separated from Zoraida's mother and was living with his parents. Zoraida lived with her mother in a room of her maternal grandparents' home, and César visited her on weekends. Although I emphasize César's experiences in this chapter, he would be (and was) the first to remind me that Zoraida's mother plays a central role in the girl's life. As he put it, "Her mom is bringing her along the right road so that she's obedient and does her chores. Of course, it's not that much about me because I'm far away and the little time I speak with her is not the same as being there in person." In this way, the extent to which he is a father to Zoraida is possible only through both his and Zoraida's relationship with her mother.

Zoraida was six and in first grade when I first interviewed César. He told me that he visits Peru for one month every year, during which he spends lots of time with her. In the interim, he speaks with her by phone weekly. "Sometimes it's hard to be far away and to be with her, so I've always tried to be together with her even if it's on the phone, just being with her for a while." I asked him what they talk about, imagining that at six years old it might be tough to sustain a weekly telephone conversation. He replied: "I ask her how it's going in school, how it's going with her mom, 'What do you need?' I ask her. Sometimes I ask her, 'What do you want me to buy you?' I'm always trying to keep up her spirits and so, she tells me yes, she's doing well in school, she has good grades, and she wants a bed or a computer or new clothes, and I tell her, 'I'll get it for you bit by bit.' I'm always talking with her. I ask about her health too, I ask her mother how her health is and how she is, and how she is doing in school. Yes, that's mostly what I ask her."[4] In his description Zoraida's mother acts as the pivot point between daughter and father. It is also clear how César highlights both education and material provision in his conversations with his daughter, instilling in her a correct orientation to the world (cf. Behnke et al. 2008).

Many migrant parents intend to bring their children to join them and take advantage of the opportunities offered in another country. César vehemently did not. He argued that children's experiences of life narrow considerably with migration: "Here the kids don't have the freedom like in our country we do, to go out or visit their cousins. Children are closed up in the apartment all day, as if they're in jail. Or they go to daycare with other kids and they learn bad habits. Spanish kids are already cussing by age five, which is not good.

Here you would be giving your kids another upbringing (*educación*), one that's not—we Peruvians aren't like that." Having his daughter in Peru is something that makes sense on various levels to him. His analysis of child-raising possibilities in Spain and his insistence that Zoraida is better off in Peru are ways in which he takes control of her environment and protects her, not merely providing economically for her.[5] He calls this absence from her an aspect of his responsibility for her.

César's desire to keep his daughter in Peru may have many other practical effects. For example, he is not married to her mother, so if Zoraida were to come to Spain she would be deprived of her mother's care. In other words, he would be the sole caregiver. More provocatively, as I spoke with César, one of his roommates muttered with a laugh that César now has a girlfriend in Spain and is reluctant to return to Peru. Such life-course changes transform hopes of and possibilities for family reunification. What interests me here, though, is that given these other possibilities for explaining César's separation from his daughter, he nonetheless presents things the way he does. I take him at his word that, for him, transnational fathering can include a considered absence from one's child.

At the same time, César wants to provide Zoraida with the opportunity to come to Spain one day if she wants to. He has applied for Spanish citizenship, based on years of permanent residence, and he included Zoraida's name on the application as his minor child. He explained: "For me citizenship is important because it opens so many doors for me and for my daughter. I am going to go back to Peru one day, and if I have Spanish nationality I can come back here for work and I can give my daughter the opportunity to come and stay here if she wants. So more than anything it's for the nationality." Importantly then, father-as-provider has come to encompass not only financial provision, but the provision of opportunity, which in contemporary Peru includes the opportunity that transnational mobility can offer.

Because of César's and Zoraida's positions within the global political economy and the gendered norms of their relationship, because of policies and legislation that overdetermine her as his dependent and him as responsible for her from afar, because of the emphasis within migration scholarship on remittances, and because he is complicit in valuing monetary provision over and above the other forms of care he offers, it can be difficult to see the multiple and layered ways he is a father while focusing solely on how and in what ways he materially provides. César cares for Zoraida in the idiom of money not only because it is normative but because it is a form of caring that transcends transnational boundaries: sending money represents more than money (Leinaweaver 2010). It gives him traction to represent himself as a good father and Zoraida as benefiting from his care.

Sergio and Nelson: Discursive Fathering

For César, talking about the ways that he provides for Zoraida—in terms of materiality (the computer), mobility (Spanish citizenship), and morality (her upbringing in Peru), are all important ways for him to expresses fatherhood. But Sergio and the other adoptive fathers I spoke to rarely, if ever, deploy this common and widespread idiom of provision. This does not mean that social class and economic matters were absent from Sergio's analysis, simply that they were not usually highlighted as such. This is particularly striking given the greater relative reproductive significance that prospective fathers have in adoption processes, as seen in Florencia Herrera's (2013: 1071) research in Chile where "adoption is experienced as a reflective, learning, and preparation process, where men have a legitimate space to participate in decision making."

Sergio and his wife, both Spaniards living in Madrid and employed in professional positions as engineers working for the government, have several children. They adopted their eldest, Nelson, who is now a teenager, from Peru in the late 1990s. Sergio repeatedly told me that adoption is just another way to have a child. As he put it, "We've never told Nelson that his parents were bad people. We have never judged them for abandoning him, we've never talked about whether the family he's in now is better or worse. We didn't rescue him from anywhere, he wasn't in danger. It's just a different way of having kids. That's all it is." In framing transnational adoption as a reproductive strategy, Sergio hints at its similarity to new reproductive technologies, and indeed surrogacy is its closest kin: another woman bears a child who may not be genealogically related to those who have made it happen through paperwork, payments, and plans (see Dempsey, this volume; Rudrappa, this volume). Sergio's emphasis on adoption as having—rather than as rescuing—a child is perfectly in line with what adoption professionals recommend.

Sergio did not, in our 2011 interview, draw attention to the economic and material ways he provided for Nelson. They should not simply be downplayed—they are actually taboo in a sense. Obviously, the economic context of transnational adoption is understood by those who participate in it—it is the elephant in the room. Christine Gailey argues (2010: 121) most pointedly that adoption is a form of class mobility. The countries from which children come are usually poorer than the countries to which they go. Children who are available for adoption are those from the poorest families, and adoptive parents have had to prove they have the resources available to raise a child in a suitable middle-class fashion, own room and all. Laura Briggs (2012: 194) offers a reading of the adoptive memoir of a U.S. parent to an El Salvador–born child, who will receive "clothes, a nice house, and food in exchange for losing people and places one loves; this is the bargain they have to offer, and the naked materialism of that offer shames [the memoir's author]." Peruvian authorities are well aware of the appearance of unequal exchange and of the stark differences that underscore it; the social worker who managed adoptions from the city I worked in during previous research explained to a DJ in a radio interview that foreign adopters were usually from Class B—a widely familiar Peruvian economic category signaling professionals, like doctors. Meanwhile, the adoptable children are usually from "poorer classes: Class E."

Other aspects of the process further index the adoptive parents' class status. For example, Sergio and his wife spent six weeks in Peru at an apartment-hotel recommended by the adoption office. They had to be able to take that much time off of work (or to telecommute, something a mechanic cannot do), as well as the money to travel and reside in Peru for that long and to pay for the steps of the process. Furthermore, Sergio did not frame it as an onerous burden but as travel and adventure. He explained to me that the first step in international adoption is to choose a country, something that must be done thoughtfully and with care. The emphasis on the country meant that for Sergio, becoming a father was entwined with travel, tourism, and the appreciation of another country *as country,* as depersonalized object that one contemplates and reads about. The trip to Peru itself was "the first long trip she [my wife] and I made together," like a honeymoon. An exciting international trip combined with becoming parents meant, as a psychologist warned the couple, that there would be "many emotions… an enormous happiness and joy."

Another way that provision might insinuate itself in Sergio's narrative is in his discussion of the resources he draws upon to make Nelson's life easier. He gestured to bookshelves overflowing with books about adoption and adolescence, and mentioned a psychologist who the couple consults with whenever particular issues come up with their son and his development. He also promised further international travel in Nelson's future. Even though the young man is quite uninterested now, Sergio said that "we want to go back to Peru... because we want him to know his country close up—his country of origin." But in all of these examples Sergio did not come out and say that these were things he was giving to Nelson in his role as a father and provider. They were disconnected objects, instances, suggestions of things that he offers Nelson without any glue of a local theory of parenting that would hold them together.

I argue that the considered absence in Sergio's narrative of a father-as-provider discourse is directly related to the instruction adoptive parents receive on how they are not rescuing needy children and bringing them to a better place. This became particularly clear as Sergio mentioned how his son has become dismissive toward Peru. He explained: "When he sees our photographs of shantytowns and things like that, he says with a laugh, 'Look how poor they are.' I say 'Come on Nelson, Peru's a huge country. Yes, there is a lot of poverty there, but even in their poverty people are happy. You don't see so many of them here in Spain, and even if they do come here to work it's because Spaniards don't want those jobs, and they are willing to work, even at half the pay, because they're used to it.' Anyway, I don't take him seriously, he'll figure this out eventually." Nelson's developing rejection of Peru, in Sergio's view, is part of his own confusion about who and what he is. This attitude is paired with occasional bursts of sensitivity when Nelson asks Sergio to give some coins to the beggar on the street corner.

Perhaps not talking directly about the ways in which life in Spain may be economically better than in Peru makes things hard on Sergio, who cannot draw on the father-as-provider model to ground his role in Nelson's life. But perhaps this discursive absence is also hard for Nelson, who sees images of his country of origin as drenched in poverty and does not yet possess the tools to make sense of what that might mean.[6] The difference between the emphasis on father-as-provider in César's narrative, and the muting of that model in Sergio's, is partly a consequence of the way that a model of father-as-provider is built into migration policy, while adoption policy deliberately deemphasizes economic aspects of the transaction. The fact that migrant and adoptive fathers also align in many cases with working- and middle-class parenting ideals, respectively, is significant too. If other middle-class fathers share Sergio's reluctance to make explicit the ways that their parenting is partly based on provision of economic and social opportunity, they may be missing a key source on which they might be drawing to forge their relational fatherhood (see Browne, this volume).

The Silent Fathers

My analysis of the ways that César and Sergio actualize fatherhood should not obviate a consideration of the silent or absent fathers, those men whose actions or inactions made possible cases like the two I consider. International adoption requires a child who is detached from his or her natal family. This happens for different reasons. Men who refuse responsibility for their children appear in many of the adoption files I reviewed, but so do men who did not want their children to be adopted. Men are silenced in other ways in adoption stories, for as De Graeve and Longman argue, "biological fathers in the metaphorical South who live in poverty are not attributed a similar connection and seem to figure less prominently in the adoptive families' adoption narratives than birth mothers do" (2013:142). Meanwhile, the migration of a parent may involve a myriad of competing claims: new relationships, new children, or parents who refuse to give up custody so that a child can travel to join the migrant parent.

Issues relating to the model of father-as-provider are present whether the "irresponsible" father is a migrant or the natal father of a child to be adopted. The former can be seen in a recent case where a Peruvian residing in Madrid is reportedly soon to become the first to be extradited for not paying child support for his son, now fourteen years old. The Peruvian press referred to the man as "the father who washed his hands of (*se desentendió de*) his son" (El Comercio 2012). The man went to Spain in 2001 and sent remittances at first, but little by little ceased to do so. In 2006 his wife filed suit, in 2010 his extradition was ordered, and in 2012 an international warrant was put out on him. The mother reported the boy as saying that the father "deserved it, because he never did what a father should do. It makes me sad, but he asked for it" (2012). The model of father-as-provider suggests that men who fail to provide for their children, such as migrants who lose their jobs and stop remitting, may have no claim to fatherhood.

For birth parents too, questions about father-as-provider are present even without being overt. Adoptive parents who must prove economic ability to support a child are implicitly contrasted with birth parents who are unable to do so (Briggs 2012). But this is a more uncomfortable area to tread than it is for migrant fathers already steeped in ideologies of provision, because contemporary adoption is structured as diametrically opposed to economic transactions. To legally transfer a child from a poor parent to a well-off parent looks uncomfortably economic, so it is written into Peruvian law that children may not be removed from birth parents on account of poverty. But poverty's many expressions are instead marshaled to buttress a claim that a child is "morally and materially abandoned"—the legal catchphrase required in these cases, and a phrase that notably references material matters. For example, an elderly caretaker, a mentally ill parent, or an extended family that cannot for lack of economic resources "adequately maintain the child" may ground a court's argument that a child's conditions are unsuitable for upbringing (Leinaweaver 2008).

I saw how this worked as I read adoption files in Peru a decade ago. In one case, an elderly, impoverished, rural farmer was at a loss about what to do with his infant daughter after his wife died in childbirth (Leinaweaver 2007). His wife's brother, also a poor farmer, assumed responsibility for the baby with the support of his own grown children. After two months of this arrangement the baby became ill. Her uncle was too poor to pay for medical treatment, so he brought her to the closest place that would care for her temporarily—the local orphanage. According to his testimony, he expected that she would remain in the orphanage until he was able to reclaim her, which he planned to do within a few years' time. When interviewed by state representatives, the two men stated that they were opposed to the baby being placed for adoption. Yet his actions were perceived by state child protection workers as indications that the baby had been abandoned. As I read the file, it seemed painfully obvious to me that if her father and uncle had not cared about her they would not have planned to return to the orphanage to try to reclaim her, they would not have articulated their unwillingness to have her adopted when interviewed by state representatives, and in fact, they would not have tried to find help for her when she first fell ill. But their fathering abilities were questioned because they could not provide materially. This is a drastic example of how in the legal and policy frameworks that constrain men's parenting possibilities, the meaning of fatherhood has been narrowed so that only men's abilities to provide are examined.

Neither César nor Sergio mentioned other potential fathers for their children—a new partner for César's ex-wife, for example, or a birth father for Sergio's son. Sergio told me that Nelson had been abandoned in the hospital by his birth mother, so no natal father was implicated. But deadbeat migrant dads, and poor men who are deemed unable to provide for the children that were born to them, are the tacit backdrop for César's and Sergio's representations of what they do for their children. The difference between those fathers who must let their children go and those fathers who can cause their children to migrate to join them (through family reunification migration or through international adoption) is one expression of class inequities of globalization. The "silent fathers," perhaps unable to provide for their children, may not even be recognized as fathers by a policy that privileges a parent's ability to provide. But they are also written out of a child's past by adoptive parents who argue—as Sergio did—that because Nelson was abandoned in the hospital, "His story begins with us. ... We have to help him to accept that everything begins there." When Sergio told me that adoption is "just a different way of having kids, that's all it is," he acknowledged that Nelson came from somewhere else but did not (and perhaps could not) acknowledge that adoption involves or implicates a process for removing children, too. Such recognition, again, might push the conversation too close to a discussion of economic matters that Sergio knows not to raise.

Conclusion

These fathers' places within legal, procedural, and ideological regimes of masculinity and economy channel their discussions of fatherhood into particular tracks. César, as migrant father, emphasizes the remittances he is able to provide his daughter, but he also speaks about the way that he cheers his daughter up on the phone, spends quality time with her when he visits Peru, and insists that she not come to Spain to be corrupted by Spanish peers. Sergio, as adoptive father, has already passed the test of father-as-provider, the sometimes humiliating submission of paystubs, work contracts, and real estate titles that is required before someone is approved to adopt. Furthermore, he is embedded in a discursive sphere in which it is deemed inappropriate to draw attention to material matters, because that would emphasize the globalized inequalities of adoption and would suggest that adoption itself is built on a ground of inequality and philanthropy that is inherently unstable. In both cases, the model of father-as-provider shapes what can and cannot be said. César must emphasize the material; Sergio must deemphasize it.

These two case studies show the power and persistence of a global model of father-as-provider. On the one hand, the model prevents a full consideration or acknowledgment of other ways in which men like César father across and despite borders. If scholars of migration take this model at face value, highlighting economic support and perhaps expanding this to include provision of opportunity, we may end up taking for granted many other things about the nature of men, as Matthew Gutmann (2007) has argued in the context of men's health. A model of father-as-provider constrains scholarship, inciting us to reproduce it rather than to identify sites at which it might be contestable. It also constrains policy and practice, and the findings of this study suggest that migrant fathers would benefit if immigration law and regulations placed economic provision on a par with, rather than dominant over, other facets of fatherhood in family reunification decisions.

On the other hand, identifying this model of father-as-provider makes it ever more clear what a paradoxical position adoptive fathers like Sergio find themselves in when they cannot explicitly engage with it. Adoptive fathers already fall into a category that incites doubt as to their fathering bona fides, because of ideologies of biological, genealogical kinship that militate against accepting their relationship as unqualified. They also participate in a discursive frame that prevents them from drawing substantially on the father-as-provider model to construct themselves relationally as fathers. The findings of this study suggest that international adoption policy and practice could be more closely aligned with men's and children's actual experiences by permitting a recognition and discussion of the vast class differences between a family of origin and an adoptive family. Such a reorientation could give men like Sergio and youth like Nelson more tools to make sense of their experiences. While a model of father-as-provider still holds sway, an adoption language ideology that prohibits such conversations potentially places adoptive fathers (and their children) at a disadvantage.

Acknowledgments

Thanks to the intrepid Nicole Berry for reading this manuscript in its earliest form, and to Rebecca Carter, Bianca Dahl, Paja Faudree, and Becky Schulthies for reading it early on, as well. Marcia Inhorn and

Wendy Chavkin were wonderful interlocutors and gave very useful suggestions, as did the anonymous reviewer for this volume. I am also grateful to "César," "Sergio," and everyone else who agreed to speak with me in Spain and Peru on this topic. Finally, I am indebted to the National Science Foundation (Grant No. 1026143), the Wenner-Gren Foundation, the Fulbright IIE Program, the Social Sciences and Humanities Research Council of Canada (SSHRC) Standard Research Grant, and the Howard Foundation for external funding of this study. I also thank Brown University for support from the Richard B. Salomon Faculty Research Award; the Faculty Research Fund for the Arts, Humanities, and Social Sciences; the Karen T. Romer Undergraduate Teaching and Research Award for International Summer Research Collaboration; the Center for Latin American and Caribbean Studies; and the Population Studies and Training Center (R24 HD041020).

Notes

1. Men's provider role is also central to romantic relationships in many parts of the world. For example, Mark Hunter (2010: 16) writes eloquently about "provider love" and "provider masculinity," describing the significance of the assistance and gifts that men provide women as a key aspect of male-female relationships in South Africa.
2. The law I cite here has been modified several times since 2000, but this original version contains the actual text discussed. Family reunification was first written into Spain's immigration policy (itself dating from just 1985) in 1996 (Paerregaard 2008: 387). The International Labour Organization, by contrast, does not protect undocumented migrants' rights to family unity (Bosniak 1991: 759 n.38).
3. The current legal requirement is somewhat vague: prospective parents must show the "ability to meet the needs of child rearing, health, and development of the family, particularly the adopted child or adolescent" (Ministerio de la Mujer y del Desarrollo Humano 2005, Article 11.i).
4. He obtains these things by wiring money to Zoraida's mother, who then buys the designated items. For many children, "everyday consumption depends upon remittances from parents" (Dreby 2010: ix).
5. Esben Leifsen and Alexander Tymczuk (2012: 231) suggest that for migrants, "[s]chooling in Spain opens up a much wider world of possibilities for higher education." However, unlike other migrants I met in Spain, César did not value the Spanish educational system over the Peruvian one.
6. See Gailey (2010: 145) on the equation of underdevelopment with a child's origins.

References

Ansión, Juan, Luis Mujica, and Ana María Villacorta. 2009. "Perú: 'En el aeropuerto me djio que cuidara a mi madre' [In the airport he told me to take care of my mother]." In *Más allá de las remesas: familias de migrantes en América Latina*. 1st Edition, ed. Juan Ansión, Rosa Aparicio, and Pedro Nel Medina. Lima: Federación Internacional de Universidades Católicas and Pontificia Universidad Católica del Perú.

Behnke, Andrew O., Brent A. Taylor, and José Ruben Parra-Cardona. 2008. "'I Hardly Understand English, But…': Mexican Origin Fathers Describe their Commitment as Fathers Despite the Challenges of Immigration." *Journal of Comparative Family Studies* 39, no. 2: 187–205.

Berástegui Pedro-Viejo, Ana. 2006. "Adopción internacional: ¿solidaridad con la infancia o reproducción asistida? [International adoption: solidarity with children or assisted reproduction?]" At the *I Forum Internacional de Infancia y Familias 'De Filias y Fobias.' Del parentesco biológico al cultural: la adopción y otras formas de construcción de familias diversas*. Barcelona.

Bergmann, Sven. 2011. "Reproductive Agency and Projects: Germans Searching for Egg Donation in Spain and the Czech Republic." *Reproductive Bio-Medicine Online* 23: 600–608.

Bosniak, Linda S. 1991. "Human Rights, State Sovereignty and the Protection of Undocumented Migrants under the International Migrant Workers Convention." *International Migration Review* 25, no. 4: 737–70.

Brandes, Stanley H. 1975. *Migration, Kinship, and Community: Tradition and Transition in a Spanish Village*. New York: Academic Press.

Briggs, Laura. 2012. *Somebody's Children: The Politics of Transracial and Transnational Adoption*. Durham, NC: Duke University Press.

Bystrom, Kerry. 2012. "On 'Humanitarian' Adoption (Madonna in Malawi)." *Humanity* 2, no. 2: 213–31.

Cooperación Interinstitucional INEI-DIGEMIN-OIM. 2010. "Perú: Estadísticas de la emigración internacional de peruanos e inmigración de extranjeros, 1990-2009 [Peru: Statistics of international emigration of Peruvians and immigration of foreigners, 1990-2009]." Lima: Organización Internacional para las Migraciones (OIM), Instituto Nacional de Estadísticas e Informática (INEI) y Dirección General de Migraciones y Naturalización (DIGEMIN). http://www.inei.gob.pe/BiblioINEIPub/BancoPub/Est/Lib0928/Libro.pdf.

De Graeve, Katrien, and Chia Longman. 2013. "Intensive Mothering of Ethiopian Adoptive Children in Flanders, Belgium." In *Parenting in Global Perspective: Negotiating Ideologies of Kinship, Self and Politics*, ed. Charlotte Faircloth, Diane M. Hoffman and Linda L. Layne. New York, Routledge.

Dorow, Sara K. 2006. *Transnational Adoption: A Cultural Economy of Race, Gender, and Kinship*. New York: New York University Press.

Dreby, Joanna. 2006. "Honor and Virtue: Mexican Parenting in the Transnational Context." *Gender & Society* 20, no. 1: 32–59.

———. 2010. *Divided by Borders: Mexican Migrants and their Children*. Berkeley: University of California Press.

Dreby, Joanna, and Tim Adkins. 2012. "The Strength of Family Ties: How US Migration Shapes Children's Ideas of Family." *Childhood* 19, no. 2: 169–87.

Dubinsky, Karen. 2010. *Babies without Borders: Adoption and Migration across the Americas*. Toronto: University of Toronto Press.

El Comercio. 2012. "Peruano a extraditar por no pagar pensión de alimentos amenaza a su esposa [Peruvian to be extradited for non-payment of child support threatens his wife]." 30 June. http://elcomercio.pe/actualidad/1435321/noticia-peruano-extraditar-no-pagar-pension-alimentos-amenaza-su-esposa.

El País. 2012. "Cae la población inmigrante en Madrid por segundo año consecutive [Immigrant population in Madrid falls for the second year in a row]." 26 March. http://ccaa.elpais.com/ccaa/2012/03/26/madrid/1332763931_227852.html.

Escrivá, Ángeles. 2005. "Peruanos en España: ¿de migrantes a ciudadanos? [Peruvians in Spain: from migrants to citizens?]" In *El quinto suyo, transnacionalidad y formaciones diaspóricas en la migración peruana*, ed. Ulla D. Berg and Karsten Paerregaard. Lima: Instituto de Estudios Peruanos.

Frekko, Susan, Jessaca Leinaweaver, and Diana Marre. n.d. "How (Not) to Talk About Adoption in Spain." Unpublished manuscript.

Frisancho Robles, Verónica, and R. S. Oropesa. 2011. "International Migration and the Education of Children: Evidence from Lima, Peru." *Population Research and Policy Review* 30, no. 4: 591–618.

Fuller, Norma. 2000. "Significados y prácticas de paternidad entre varones urbanos del Perú [Meanings and practices of fatherhood among urban Peruvian men]." In *Paternidades en América Latina*. 1st Edition, ed. Norma Fuller. Lima: Pontifícia Universidad Católica del Perú, Fondo Editorial.

———. 2003. "The Social Constitution of Gender Identity among Peruvian Males." In *Changing Men and Masculinities in Latin America*, ed. Matthew C. Gutmann. Durham, NC: Duke University Press.

Gailey, Christine Ward. 2010. *Blue-Ribbon Babies and Labors of Love: Race, Class, and Gender in U.S. Adoption Practice*. Austin: University of Texas Press.

Gilmore, David D. 1998. *Carnival and Culture: Sex, Symbol, and Status in Spain*. New Haven, CT: Yale University Press.

Giménez Romero, Carlos. 2008. "La imagen social del inmigrante y su influencia en la adaptación de los niños [The social image of the immigrant and its influence on child adaptation]." In *Los retos de la postadopción: balance y perspectivas*, ed. Ana Berástegui Pedro-Viejo and Blanca Gómez Bengoechea. Madrid: Ministerio de Trabajo y Asuntos Sociales.

Giró, Carmen. 2012. "El último reto de la adopción [The last challenge of adoption]." La Vanguardia. 24 June. http://www.magazinedigital.com/reportajes/sociedad/reportaje/cat_id/88.

Gutmann, Matthew C. 2007. *Fixing Men: Sex, Birth Control, and AIDS in Mexico*. Berkeley: University of California Press.

Herrera, Florencia. 2013. "'Men Always Adopt': Infertility and Reproduction from a Male Perspective." *Journal of Family Issues* 34, no. 8: 1059–80.

Horton, Sarah. 2009. "A Mother's Heart is Weighed Down with Stones: A Phenomenological Approach to the Experience of Transnational Motherhood." *Culture, Medicine and Psychiatry* 33, no. 1: 21–40.

Howell, Signe, and Diana Marre. 2006. "To Kin a Transnationally Adopted Child in Norway and Spain: The Achievement of Resemblances and Belonging." *Ethnos* 71, 3 (September): 293–316.

Howell, Signe, and Marit Melhuus. 2007. "Race, Biology and Culture in Contemporary Norway: Identity and Belonging in Adoption, Donor Gametes and Immigration." In *Race, Ethnicity and Nation: Perspectives from Kinship and Genetics*, ed. Peter Wade. New York; Oxford: Berghahn Books.

Hübinette, Tobias, and Carina Tigervall. 2009. "To be Non-White in a Colour-Blind Society: Conversations with Adoptees and Adoptive Parents in Sweden on Everyday Racism." *Journal of Intercultural Studies* 30, no. 4: 335–53.

Hunter, Mark. 2010. *Love in the Time of AIDS: Inequality, Gender, and Rights in South Africa.* Bloomington: Indiana University Press.

Jefatura del Estado. 2000. "Ley Orgánica 4/2000, de 11 de enero, sobre derechos y libertades de los extranjeros en España y su integración social [Law 4/2000, of January 11, on rights and freedoms of foreigners in Spain and their social integration]." Boletín Oficial del Estado. http://www.boe.es/boe/dias/2000/01/12/pdfs/A01139-01150.pdf.

Lamb, M. E., and L. D. Bougher. 2009. "How Does Migration Affect Mothers' and Fathers' Roles Within their Families? Reflections on Some Recent Research." *Sex Roles* 60, no. 7–8: 611–14.

Leifsen, Esben, and Alexander Tymczuk. 2012. "Care at a Distance: Ukrainian and Ecuadorian Transnational Parenthood from Spain." *Journal of Ethnic and Migration Studies* 38, no. 2: 219–36.

Leinaweaver, Jessaca B. 2007. "On Moving Children: The Social Implications of Andean Child Circulation." *American Ethnologist* 34, no. 1: 163–80.

———. 2008. *The Circulation of Children: Adoption, Kinship, and Morality in Andean Peru.* Durham, NC: Duke University Press.

———. 2010. "Outsourcing Care: How Peruvian Migrants Meet Transnational Family Obligations." *Latin American Perspectives* 37, no. 5: 67–87.

———. 2011. "Kinship Paths to and from the New Europe: A Unified Analysis of Peruvian Adoption and Migration." *Journal of Latin American and Caribbean Anthropology* 16, no. 2: 380–400.

———. 2013. *Adoptive Migration: Raising Latinos in Spain.* Durham: Duke University Press.

Lewin, Ellen. 2005. "Family Values: Fatherhood and Gay Men in America." In *Adoptive Families in a Diverse Society*, ed. Katarina Wegar. New Brunswick, NJ: Rutgers University Press.

Luxán, Marta, Pau Miret, and Rocío Treviño. 1999. "Is the Male-Provider Model Still in Place? Partnership Formation in Contemporary Spain." *South European Society and Politics* 4, no. 2: 171–94.

Madianou, Mirca, and Daniel Miller. 2011. "Mobile Phone Parenting: Reconfiguring Relationships between Filipina Migrant Mothers and Their Left-Behind Children." *New Media & Society* 13, no. 3: 457–70.

Marre, Diana. 2007. "'I Want Her to Learn Her Language and Maintain Her Culture': Transnational Adoptive Families' Views of 'Cultural Origins.'" In *Race, Ethnicity and Nation: Perspectives from Kinship and Genetics*, ed. Peter Wade. New York; Oxford: Berghahn Books.

———. 2009. "Coming Back to Latin America." Latin American Studies Association Annual Meeting. Rio de Janeiro, Brazil.

Marre, Diana, and Joan Bestard. 2004. *La adopción y el acogimiento: Presente y perspectivas.* Barcelona: Universitat de Barcelona.

Marsiglio, William, Maria Lohan, and Lorraine Culley. 2013. "Framing Men's Experience in the Procreative Realm." *Journal of Family Issues* 34, no. 8: 1011–36.

Ministerio de la Mujer y del Desarrollo Humano. 2005. MIMDES Decreto Supremo No 010–2005-MIMDES [MIMDES Supreme Decree 010-2005-MIMDES]. Peru. http://www.mimdes.gob.pe/archivossites/daff/compend io/iv normatividad adopciones/Decreto Supremo 010-2005-MIMDES.pdf.

Ministerio de la Mujer y Poblaciones Vulnerables. 2012. "Niñas, niños y adolescentes adoptados según país de procedencia de los/as adoptantes. 2007-2012 [Girls, boys, and adolescents adopted according to the country of the adopters: 2007-2012]." Peru. Document dated November 30. http://www.mimdes.gob.pe/files/direcciones/dga/Adopciones_NNApro cedenciaAdoptantes_30Nov2012.pdf.

———. 2013. "Preguntas Frecuentes [Frequently Asked Questions]." Peru.

Ministerio de la Presidencia. 2011. Real Decreto 557/2011, de 20 de abril, por el que se aprueba el Reglamento de la Ley Orgánica 4/2000, sobre derechos y libertades de los extranjeros en España y su integración social, tras su reforma por Ley Orgánica 2/2009 [Royal Decree 557/2011, of April 20, by which are approved the Regulations of Law 4/2000 on rights and freedoms of foreigners in Spain and their social integration, following its amendment by Law 2/2009]. Spain. Boletín Oficial del Estado (BOE), http://www.boe.es/boe/dias/2011/04/30/pdfs/BOE-A-2011-7703.pdf.

Paerregaard, Karsten. 2008. *Peruvians Dispersed: A Global Ethnography of Migration.* Lanham, MD: Lexington Books.

Parreñas, Rhacel Salazar. 2005. *Children of Global Migration: Transnational Families and Gendered Woes.* Stanford, CA: Stanford University Press.

Selman, Peter. 2009. "The Rise and Fall of Intercountry Adoption in the 21st Century." *International Social Work* 52: 575–94.

Takenaka, Ayumi, Karsten Paerregaard, and Ulla D. Berg. 2010. "Peruvian Migration in a Global Context." *Latin American Perspectives* 37, no. 5: 3–11.

Townsend, Nicholas W. 1997. "Reproduction in Anthropology and Demography." In *Anthropological Demography: Toward a New Synthesis*, ed. David I. Kertzer and Tom Fricke. Chicago: University of Chicago Press.

Chapter 4

LONG-DISTANCE FATHERS, LEFT-BEHIND FATHERS, AND RETURNEE FATHERS

CHANGING FATHERING PRACTICES IN INDONESIA AND THE PHILIPPINES

Theodora Lam and Brenda S. A. Yeoh

Introduction

Increasingly used by many Southeast Asian families as a household livelihood improvement strategy, transnational labor migration bears unforeseen challenges and changes for families in the region. The complex transformations that families undergo when members live in considerably different and distant worlds have been progressively highlighted in the literature on migration and social reproduction over the past decade. We have gained insight into the challenges migrants face on their trajectories away from home, and more recently, also gleaned glimpses into the experiences of those members left behind. The growing scholarship clearly demonstrates that migration dynamics are often most keenly felt at the family level, entailing individuals to constantly rework their roles and responsibilities within the changing framework of their family circumstances.

However, the analytical focus of this research thus far has been trained on the feminization of migration in response to the increasing demand for domestic and care workers in gender-segmented global labor markets. Of considerable interest is the way house-holding strategies are being reformulated in sending countries at the Southernmost end of the global care chain, when women-as-mothers rewrite their roles (but often not their identities) through labor migration as productive workers who contribute to their children's well-being through financial remittances and "long-distance mothering." Lorena Carrasco (2010: 189), when writing of the "impossibility of being" and "emotional dislocation" experienced by migrants, concludes that "[t]his is particularly true for women in transnational motherhood situations for whom the notion of family in one place is painfully disrupted."

Given far less attention in the migration literature is the role of men in social reproduction, largely a consequence of the assumed association of social reproductive work with women and femininity. While there are indications in the research on Southeast Asia that mothers continue to shoulder the burden of caring for the children and household when men-as-fathers migrate to fulfill their bread-winning roles (Parreñas 2005; Scalabrini Migration Center 2004), little is known about whether non-resident fathers remain actively engaged in their families' lives, albeit remotely, and what they contribute in terms of non-material care provisioning for their children. As Nicole Constable (2009) reminds us, men are also involved in reproductive labor and intimate care but these aspects are seldom studied within the field of migration research.

Much of the available research on the implications of gender-differentiated transnational mobility on "left-behind"[1] families also emphasizes the way female labor migration destabilizes traditional gender ideologies and "engenders contradictory and paradoxical positions" (Bunnell et al. 2007: 138). This vein of literature clarifies that such migration implies both "a redefinition of the economic role of women in the society and within their family," as well as a "redefinition of the traditional family" itself (Tobin 2008: 1), but is relatively unspecific on the impact on left-behind men in terms of their roles and identities within the family. Some existing studies indicate that when migrant women shoulder the provider's role, left-behind men take over the absent mothers' task of nurturing and assume more caregiving roles (Asis et al. 2004; Hugo 2005). Other studies emphasize instead the "other mothers" (Hondagneu-Sotelo and Avila 1997: 559), such as female relatives who were solicited to fill the void left by the migrant mother. What is even less explored in the scholarly literature are the implications of changing family roles on men's identities in the context of female labor migration from Southeast Asia. Not only is there a need for more evidence to respond to the question of whether left-behind men are "forced to assume caregiving at home as a result of new care deficits," scholarly attention is also needed to work out whether such shifts in roles "cause further disruption because these roles often contradict cultural understandings of masculinity" (Zimmerman et al. 2006: 14).

In this context, this chapter puts the spotlight on men-as-fathers in Southeast Asia by exploring the previously neglected fathering practices and experiences of father-migrants, left-behind father-carers,[2] and returned-father-migrants. By drawing on both quantitative and qualitative data from source communities in Indonesia and the Philippines with high levels of out-migration, this chapter explores the communication practices, care provisions, and constructions of identities and intimacies in three distinct forms of households: the "father-migrant, mother-carer" household, the "mother-migrant, father-carer" household, and the "mother-resident, father-returnee" household.[3] Emphasis is placed on the ways fatherhood is affirmed, vilified, and negotiated within the realities of globalized mobilities.

In the following sections of the chapter, we first briefly explore the evolution of the scholarly discourses on fatherhood in the context of Indonesia and the Philippines. After describing our methodology, we focus on the way fathering roles and identities are negotiated as relationships that are "co-dependent with other relationships" (Browne, this volume), using the figures of the long-distance father, the left-behind father, and the returned-father-migrant as three distinct points of departure.

Constructing Fatherhood in Indonesia (Java) and the Philippines

Fatherhood is a multifaceted field that has been studied through varying theoretical lenses by different disciplines. It is a highly variegated, unstable, and politicized concept that is also culturally specific and continually being (re)created and reified under the influences of societal changes. Similar to Western discourses on fatherhood, scholarly discourses about Indonesian/Javanese and Filipino fatherhood have also been shifting though some common threads relating to men's/fathers' changing roles and whether fathers are assuming mothers' tasks. A general, though non-representative, portrait of the Javanese[4] man and/or father is encapsulated in this summary gleaned through the eyes of scholars such as Hildred Geertz (1961),[5] and Ratna Megawangi (1997): As heads of family (typically nuclear), Javanese men rarely dominate their households and are mostly physically and emotionally uninvolved in family matters including housework or childcare. An ideal Javanese father is someone who is "patient and dignified with his wife and children [and who] lead[s] them with a gentle though firm hand, not interfering with their petty quarrels, but being always available to give solemn sanction to his wife's punishments of disobedient children" (Geertz 1961: 107).[6] In contrast, Javanese wives are the "household manager[s]" with relatively high status and authority in the household (Megawangi 1997: 3). They exert greater control over family finances and make most of the family decisions thus rendering Javanese men comparatively "functionless" in the matrifocal family system. The "completely dependable" Javanese mothers are also very close to their children but will briefly leave infants with other female relatives when working (Geertz 1961: 106). Javanese men reportedly have an affectionate and warm relationship with their children only when they are between one and five years old, and children learn to distance themselves from their fathers thereafter.

Under Suharto's New Order, the Indonesian family has been reshaped by predominantly masculine interests where men and fathers remain as the benevolent, heterosexual, breadwinning heads of household, deserving of respect and deference (Newberry 2010). Men hold "God-sanctioned" control over their female counterparts—often regarded as servers or reproducers—acting as guardians of their morality and are generally not expected to participate in the household or raise children (Adamson 2007: 20; Sen 1998). Under this regime, Indonesian women are portrayed as men's subordinates; their main roles are to be supportive wives and mothers (Lindawati and Smark 2010). However, Juliette Koning (2004: 234) argues that this "New Order gender ideology is far from being practised by the majority of its citizens," dangerously maneuvering women into narrowly defined roles and "discarding the reality of the often triple roles many women fulfill, in which they might very well be the main provider of livelihood (and not the one who merely supplements it)."

The New Order image of men is further challenged by the increasing feminization of labor migration in recent decades. Though this is an under-researched topic, piecemeal evidence from Graeme Hugo (2005), Rachel Silvey (2006), and Sukamdi et al. (2001) suggests a gradual shift in gender ideologies within the migrant family.

First, many women decided to migrate independently regardless of their spouses' feelings of unhappiness or belittlement. Postmigration, husbands often become more respectful and less dominant over their migrant wives due to their own lower economic status. Realignments of traditional gender roles in the family were observed with fathers taking on more household and caring tasks during their wives' absence. Fathers' efforts were largely bolstered by the kin system and many husbands received help from extended family members in handling these chores. Nonetheless, this change was temporary and the women's role and position did not change drastically upon their return. Instead, most female returnees considered homemaking to be their main role, and only some migrant women improved their social position.

Recent, albeit limited, scholarship on Filipino fatherhood and masculinities also suggests that the country's conventional family dynamics, parenting styles, and gender ideologies are being confronted by globalization and mobilities (Alampay and Jocson 2011).[7] Filipino families are traditionally "patriarchal in authority" with the husbands' breadwinning role (power) taking precedence over the women's position (Castro et al. 2008: 1; Pingol 2001). As household heads, Filipino men are similarly expected to be good providers, protectors, and role models, "virile sex partners, firm and strong fathers," having limited concerns over their children's daily lives (Medina 2001; Pingol 2001: 8). Instead, mothers are heavily involved in childrearing, domestic work, and household management.

Societal changes, modernization, and migratory movements have since presented Filipino men with the chance to undertake a more multifaceted role in their children's upbringing, resulting in more differentiated forms of fathering. Higher educated Filipino households are reportedly leaning toward more "egalitarian gender roles," where parents make joint decisions pertaining to their children and finances (Alampay and Jocson 2011: 166). Studies also find these fathers to be spending more time performing housework and childcare, and engaging in other nurturing activities (Harper 2010). Belen Medina (2001), drawing from numerous studies, reveals active participation of Filipino men (including those from Laguna) in childcare and domestic work, especially when the wives are working. She hints at the gradual acceptance of men's increased participation in the household realm "in consideration of the employed wife" but concedes that husbands will currently not accept "a reversal of roles [to househusband] which runs counter to the traditional 'macho' image of the husband" (152).

The longstanding migration of Filipinas as global care workers means that role reversal of the traditional gender ideology whereby men are the "pillars" while women are the "lights" of the home is becoming increasingly common in Filipino society (Asis et al. 2004). While Joeven Castro et al. (2008) find that the majority of Filipino men still reject and denigrate the notion of househusbands, they would now set aside their pride and perform household tasks for the sake of their family's survival needs. This finding aligns with that of Alicia Pingol's (2001) study whereby Filipino male respondents with migrant wives were found to project themselves as important providers of care, even if they perform care differently from women. In their wives' absence, left-behind husbands took on all domestic tasks including child and animal rearing, cooking, monitoring household items, and marketing, but those with older children or support systems were able to continue working. Pingol's study reveals that while Filipino men may "experience sudden shifting of gears that heavily disorients them" (220), the maintenance of their productive selves keeps them going. They shared that being able to perform the additional caring tasks well "enhances their sense of self worth... [and] gives them pride not only as they view themselves but also as they are looked upon by the community" (221). Left-behind Filipino husbands are thus constantly refashioning their masculine identities by "appealing to broader masculine ideologies of 'being in control' and 'maintaining autonomy'" (McKay and Lucero-Prisno 2012: 23). Nonetheless, Pingol (2001) discovers that left-behind husbands who are completely dependent on their wives' earnings feel intimidated and have lower self-esteem as they are scorned by their in-laws and other men.

Another way in which migration can change fatherhood manifests when the men leave. Compared to the near silence of substantive work on the way migration affects Indonesian fatherhood, a small vein of literature focuses on the relationships between migrant Filipino fathers and their left-behind children. Rhacel Parreñas (2005: 34), for example, argues that "fathering narrows in transnational families" as migrant fathers hold steadfast to their roles as material providers and continue to maintain an authoritative figure even from afar. They do not adjust their fathering practices to accommodate distance and instead "perform a heightened version of conventional fathering," thus creating "gaps" in intimacy and missing opportunities in building emotional ties with their children when "fathering from a distance" (Parreñas 2008: 1058). While "migration enables men to better fulfill the traditional responsibility of breadwinning with their access to greater income earning potential abroad," it "also removes fathers from daily interactions in the family and consequently in their absence further reaffirms the traditional division of labor of a male breadwinner and female homemaker" (1058). Nevertheless, Parreñas (2005; 2008) contends that migrant-fathers are more involved in childcare and housework upon their return compared to left-behind fathers with migrant wives. In observing Filipino seafarers "lament their long separation from family members while onboard… [and trying] to expand their care work when home and deepen their emotional attachment with kids and claim 'good fatherhood,'" Steven McKay (2011) furthers the argument: alongside privileging the "good provider" image, Filipino seafaring fathers do invest in building emotional bonds with their children in building paternal identities as part of a "package deal" approach, as proposed by Nicholas Townsend (2002), to constructing masculinity. He concludes that seafarers are able to appropriate some nontraditional gender practices and contravene gender stereotypes because "their master gender status is that of provider, which does not threaten existing gender relations and allows their 'manhood' to remain unquestioned despite their increased child-centered parenting" (McKay 2011: 15; see also McKay and Lucero-Prisno III 2012).

In terms of discipline, Filipino fathers are said to "discipline their children with their firm voice [while] mothers nurture them with their tenderness" (Pingol 2001: 64). The "strict parental discipline and child obedience" parenting style of Filipino men has also gradually altered to one that is "nurturing, affectionate, protective and at times indulgent" (Harper 2010: 67). Though some researchers observe that the Filipino father's role continues to adhere solely to the provider and disciplinarian model, Medina (2001) suggests that Filipino fathers are also involved in activities such as storytelling, playing with children, helping with homework, and going on outings and walks with their children. She contends that a new role for fathers—as warm and supportive yet authoritative—has emerged.

CHAMPSEA Study and Methodology

This research utilizes both quantitative and qualitative data from the CHAMPSEA study, a mixed-method study investigating the impacts of parental migration on children's health and well-being in Southeast Asia.[8] The quantitative data are derived from surveys conducted in 2008 with 1,034 Indonesian (East and West Java) and another

1,000 Filipino (Laguna and Bulacan) households that contained at least one child in one of two age groups: 3-, 4-, and 5-year-olds (preschool or young children) and 9-, 10-, and 11-year-olds (primary school–aged or older children). These neighboring countries were chosen as they both have considerably high numbers of female emigrants in Southeast Asia and share similar migration patterns and traditions. However, the predominantly Christian Philippines, versus largely Muslim Indonesia, has a longer history of female migration and is likely to have developed more institutional structures to support transnational living. To remove possible biases of any potential family problems from our findings, CHAMPSEA purposely sampled only "intact, heterosexual families," and the exclusion of single-parent or other family types may be its greatest limitation.

The sample from each country comprises transnational and non-migrant households in roughly equal proportions. Further interviews with some sixty-two Indonesians from Tulungagung and Ponorogo (fifty-two carers; eight RMMFC households; two RFMMC households) and fifty-five Filipinos from Laguna (forty-eight carers; five RMMFC households; two RFMMC households) were conducted between 2009 and 2012. Interviews were conducted in native languages and translated into English.

Fathers Near and Far

For the large majority of children living in non-migrant households in Indonesia (90.6 percent) and the Philippines (92.4 percent), their mother was the key person responsible for their daily care. When fathers migrate overseas to work, mothers remain as principal carers of the children (96.5 percent in Indonesia and 91.5 percent in the Philippines). When mothers assume the roles of the overseas breadwinner, the care arrangements for the children featured a more visible proportion of non-parental carers, mainly close relatives such as grandmothers (30.4 percent in Indonesia and 36.2 percent in the Philippines) but also others such as uncles and non-relatives (1.7 percent in Indonesia and 4.3 percent in the Philippines). Nonetheless, the majority were cared for by their fathers (67.9 percent in Indonesia compared to 59.6 percent in the Philippines).

Fathers at Home

For many families in our study, fathers took on the role as main carers of the children (cf. Birenbaum-Carmeli et al. this volume; Thao, this volume) when mothers were away because there was "no other choice" or the sense that "nobody else can help me" care for the family. This sentiment stemmed partly from the unavailability of help from relatives and kin; returned mother-migrant Putrie (thirty-five, Indonesian, RMMFC[9]) shared that her "mother is already old and our relatives were busy with their work. So, only my husband and daughter were able to look after him [the index child or IC]." Furthermore, the sense of "having no choice" was also partly motivated by a strong sense of parental responsibility for their children. Several father-carers spoke of their duty to care for their children, saying, "I don't mind, because for me, it is my duty as a parent to look after my child" (Sadewa, fifty, Indonesian, MMFC). Mawar (thirty-nine, Indonesian, RMMFC), another returned-mother-migrant, expressed the same idea when she was asked about the care of her children during her absence. She said, "The father is the main parent.... All the other persons are just help." Sometimes, parents also felt too embarrassed to seek help from relatives and chose to rely solely on the left-behind parent. Returned-mother-migrant, Sarah (thirty-three, Indonesian, RMMFC) said, "[I felt]...embarrassed.... I felt not good to ask others to look after my child. It's okay if they would not view that as a burden, but what if they do view this as a burden [but do not tell her directly]?"

When mothers migrated, father-carers were more likely to care for an older than young child. In Indonesia, father-carers (56.9 percent) were the key category of primary carers for young children followed by "close female relatives" (41 percent), but they featured more prominently in the case of older children where the percentages were 77.3 percent for father-carers and 20 percent for "close female relatives." In the Philippines, father-carers (50 percent) were the main carers for young children, closely followed by the "close female relatives" category (46.4 percent), while the equivalent percentages in the case of older children were 63.6 percent for father-carers and 31.8 percent for "close female relatives." In the study, most mother-migrants appeared to trust their husbands with the care of their older children (e.g., most did not give their left-behind husbands much advice before departure) while expressing more concern when it came to care arrangements for their young children.

Within transnational households, and compared to mother-carer equivalents, father-carers were more likely to be engaged in paid work outside the home. The majority of father-carers (83.3 percent in Indonesia and 64.3 percent in the Philippines) in the absence of their breadwinning wives reported that they were working even though they were their children's primary carers. In contrast, when fathers migrate for overseas work, fewer mother-carers work outside the home (29.9 percent in Indonesia and 27 percent in the Philippines). This is consistent with Lan Anh Hoang and Brenda S. A. Yeoh's (2011) finding that while Vietnamese left-behind fathers did not shun carework, the large majority persisted in balancing childcare with some form of paid work in order to preserve their masculinity and pride in the face of their migrant wives' increased economic power. They conclude that paid work in the context of left-behind men "serves to ward off potential ridicule arising from men's engagement in 'women's work,' counteracting any demasculinization effects that this new arrangement may bring" (Hoang and Yeoh 2011: 733). This argument also finds some congruency with Michele Gamburd's (2000) observation in Sri Lanka whereby left-behind husbands without regular jobs tended to feel a strong sense of inadequacy, leading them to indulge in "vices" such as drinking, gambling, and womanizing.

As the principal carers of their children, left-behind father-carers spent fewer hours in carework (compared to left-behind mother-carers), possibly given that a larger proportion of them were also engaged in waged work. The mean number of hours spent per day in caregiving was 9.3 hours (Indonesia) and 8.8 hours (the Philippines) for father-carers as compared to 12.7 hours (Indonesia) and 10.7 hours (the Philippines) in the case of mother-carers. In performing carework, father-carers also received more support and help from others. About 60 percent of father-carers (60.1 percent in Indonesia and 60.7 percent in the Philippines) received support from other family members and relatives as compared to lower percentages (49.7 percent in Indonesia and 41.2 percent in the Philippines) for mother-carer equivalents.[10] The father-carer figure that emerges from the CHAMPSEA study is hence one who is engaged in remunerative labor[11] alongside taking primary responsibility for the care of his children while receiving support from others in discharging care duties. In contrast, the left-behind mother-carer's principal responsibility is more likely to be caring for her children without taking on paid work, spending more time in caregiving work and with less recourse to receiving support from others.

Our interview materials allow us to provide a more nuanced picture of the social reproductive work in which father-carers (as compared to mother-carers) engaged.[12] While father-carers were generally in charge of buying food, managing finances, earning money, attending school events, and administering discipline as part of caring, many were also involved in the intimate or mundane aspects of carework in relation to their children. Many left-behind Indonesian fathers were prepared to cook, feed, and bathe the children, do the laundry, and support children in their studies (Hoang et al. 2012). Similarly, as an illustration of what Filipino left-behind father-carers did, Eric (thirty-eight, Filipino, FCMM) shared:

> With regard to making assignments and projects, I'm the one [who helps the IC]. For a project, or for example, as long as I've fixed [the other children] and fed them, bathed them, before sleeping. When they're already in bed, that's the only time I help him with his project. If he can't do it anymore, I let him sleep and I finish his project. I stay up until four in the morning. ... Whatever his mother used to do, that's what I do. I prepare the breakfast; I cook for all of us. I do everything.... I'm the one who takes them to school. After I take them to school, I drive for hire for two hours. Then I go home and cook. After cooking, I go back to the school. If I still have time to drive for hire, I do so. Then I fetch them. Even if for example, I'm feeling cold due to fever ... even when I feel bad, I force myself to get up to be able to take care of their needs.

Left-behind fathers in this study emphasized their adaptability and versatility in assuming the mothering roles vacated by their wives while retaining their identities as fathers. Some confessed that they were initially apprehensive and worried about taking on mothering work that involved caring for their children and doing all the household chores "on top of" their usual paid work and that life was rather hard in the first three months, especially if there were no other kin to rely on for help. Several father-carers reported that they experienced stress and even health problems during their wives' absence.[13] But the majority were able to narrate a story of "victory" over the odds, and felt that with time, they were able provide both emotional and physical care, and be both "father" and "mother" to their children. Sadewa, for example, declared, "I can do male and female jobs. I can cook, I can wash. No problem." In some ways, this was a remarkable turn of affairs as few fathers reported themselves to have helped out actively in household chores or shared in caring duties before their wives' migration. Mothers and children were also quick to affirm the good work of father-carers: "No problem, the husband can play them [be a mother and father]" (Bethari, thirty-three, Indonesian, RMMFC); "[I would still choose *ibu* (mother) to be the migrant] because father can take care of both the house and children (12-year-old son of Hanif, Indonesian, MMFC).

This is not to say that left-behind fathers had no issues with being mothers, as well. Tensions developed, for example, when their adolescent daughters started menstruating. In these cases, father-carers expressed a strong preference for mothers to be present. Matius (forty-five, Indonesian, MMFC) observed, "As her father, I think I am not in the right position to teach her." Puberty was a rite of passage that could turn father-daughter relationships awkward as men exhibited great discomfort dealing with issues such as menstruation. Others lamented the need to spend longer hours at home, thereby sacrificing leisure activities and the freedom to spend an evening out with friends. Sukmo (forty-two, Indonesian, MMFC), for example, complained, "It is hard to be a mother because I have to do everything: cooking... going to the field... go home without rest and then cook and sometimes, washing." Hence, while father-carers in the study seemed to take on their caring duties quite positively, they also expressed considerable relief in having their wives back home: "[When my wife comes back]... my burden is lessened. ... I do not have to cook before I work, so when I work I do not need to think about cooking... have no burden. ... I have more free time" (Soleh, thirty-eight, Indonesian, MMFC). Says Matius, "Yes, I am free now to do what I want to do, but only positive things. I have about 50 percent less burden unlike before."

Pingol (2001) has argued that the key for Filipino men with migrant wives to upholding their masculine identity was to retain "control." In our study, this control was not only manifested in their choices, the roles they assumed and the ways they performed their roles; it was also evident in the way men presented themselves and explained their circumstances. For example, when it comes to using remittances, many father-carers claimed that they themselves decide how to use the money and that the money is mainly meant for their children. Mario (forty-three, Filipino, MMFC) insisted, "Because I'm not like other husbands who would ask money for themselves. With me, I'm used to hardships. What I only ask for, for my children, electricity, and water." Even in cases where the evidence from other sources pointed to the fact that it is their wives who decided that she would migrate, left-behind fathers invariably would assert their power and control over family decisions by placing the emphasis in their narratives on "I", as in "*Me, myself* decided [not to rely on a helper]," "*I* want to take care of the children," and "*I* can get money."

Fathering from Afar

Father-migrants in the CHAMPSEA study appeared to be conscious of the need to fulfill their fathering duties even when physically absent. Overall, the need for fathers to be away as they pursue job opportunities abroad to generate financial remittances for the family was accepted as consistent with their role as provider/breadwinner (see Leinaweaver, this volume). Yet this did not absolve them from the expectation that they continue to fulfill their childcare responsibilities from afar. Interestingly, while the literature thus far offers mixed evidence on the contact patterns between father-migrants and left-behind children (as noted earlier), CHAMPSEA's father-migrants from Indonesia and Philippines demonstrate more frequent contact with their children than mother-migrants (Graham et al. 2012).[14] In fact, a higher proportion of the older children, especially Indonesians, expressed having no contact at all with their migrant-mothers compared with their migrant-fathers.[15]

Also, some father-migrants prioritize communication with their children over communication with their wife. Tikah (thirty-five, Indonesian, FMMC) complained about her migrant husband, "Recently, he talks to the children more frequently.... He talks to me only when there is something important to be talked about. Sometimes, he calls me at midnight to be able to talk with me alone [on urgent matters] while he phones the children at noon." Our findings regarding the quality of communication between migrant fathers and their children contradict the general belief that absent fathers have no interest in communicating with their children (as compared to the image of migrant mothers who communicate with their children as a means of conveying care and affection in validating themselves as "good mothers"). Our interviews reveal that Filipino father-migrants exhibit love and care in their communication with their children, exchanging stories about their respective lives and daily activities, and expressing words of love and encouragement across the distance. For several Filipino families, the quality of the conversations was further enhanced by the ability to see each other through a web camera. Migrant-fathers and their children could personally see how each other was doing and/or changing in the other's absence. Father-migrants often observed with pride how much their children had grown, expressing delight even in seeing their daughters' hair having "grown longer" (in the case of Guia, forty-four, Filipino, FMMC).

Likewise, Indonesian father-migrants tried to convey a genuine interest in their children's welfare, conversing with them mainly about their day and activities, schoolwork and performance, religious practices such as reading the Quran, and health (including height) and diet. And while Indonesian migrant-fathers said that they still attempt to maintain their disciplinarian front by advising and reminding children to behave, heed their carers, and save money, the emotional "gap" between father and child identified in Parreñas's (2008) work was not evident in most cases.

Communication did not only allow father-migrants to perform fathering duties from afar; it also encouraged a certain degree of reciprocity in the father-child relationship by providing the opportunity for their children to tell their fathers how much they miss them, asking them to return home soon. Riyati (thirty, Indonesian, FMMC), for example, revealed that, to her daughter, her migrant-father was an "absent present," and she continued to include her father in her daily activities. In the course of the day, she might "suddenly" decide to speak to her migrant-father, and in so doing, provided the opportunity for their father-daughter bond to be refreshed: "Sometimes [she says], 'Mother, I want to call Father.' Then I will call him right away. Since usually she does not want to. I will miscall him right away, '*Mas*, Jenia wants to talk to you. Phone her after *Maghrib*.' That is what I say to him.... Sometimes, she wants it in a sudden. She wants to talk to her father directly. Well, I leave her in her room, talking.... I suppose [this happens] when she misses her father. [In the course of her normal routine], she misses him." Reciprocity in the father-child relationship was also evident in some cases when children took it upon themselves to remind father-migrants to fulfill their breadwinning responsibilities. Jessica (thirty-two, Filipino, FMMC) said of her son, "When he is bad and hot-headed, sometimes when his father calls he says: 'Send money because we don't have what.' He is like that. I tell him not to say it because he would say: 'Papa, send money; we don't have money anymore. Mama is pitiful. We have no money. We don't have food anymore, we haven't eaten yet.' I dissuade him, [reminding him that] his father is far away."

The communication between Filipino father-migrants and their left-behind children appears more variegated in substance. Similar to Parreñas's (2008) findings, we found that many Filipino father-migrants were expected to play the role of the disciplinarian for their children even from a distance. Left-behind mother-carers would continue to look to their migrant husbands for help and support in disciplining their children, as in the case of Stella (twenty-five, Filipino, FMMC): "Yes, he talked to him [their son about his behavior]. For instance, if I know that he is free at certain hours, I would call him at that very moment. [I tell my husband,] 'You be the one to explain things to your son. I am having a hard time trying to discipline them. Talk to him.' My migrant husband would talk to him...."

They are on speaker phone." In some cases, the question of who is responsible for correcting their children's behavior and exerting control over their activities becomes in itself a terrain of struggle. Ina (forty-nine, Filipino, FMMC), for example, recounted the many times when she told her migrant-husband about their son's misconduct over the phone, only to find that "he will get angry with the kid, he would tell me to 'wake him up' and he would say I don't take care of him." In order to avoid getting blamed for her son's misbehavior, she has since resorted to only reporting "the good things" to her migrant-husband.

Returned Fathers

Migrant fathers who returned after a migration stint abroad were confronted with key issues of adjustment, not least in terms of fitting in with the household routine that had taken shape in their absence. For those who were returning temporarily (in between work contracts) to farming families, making an effort to work the fields at least some of the time was expected of themselves. As left-behind wives observed of their husbands on their temporary sojourn home: "Well, he worked [for two months when he was home] at *ladang* (un-irrigated agricultural field) and *tegalan* (un-irrigated field near the rice fields used for vegetables and other secondary crops). [Or he will be just] relaxing with his children [at home]," said Leteri (thirty-nine, Indonesian, FMMC). Hanura (forty, Indonesian, FMMC) said, "Sometimes, if it is time to grow rice in rice field, he goes to the rice field; if it is not the time, he is just at home. Sometimes he takes us for a walk."

Some wives noticed a newfound sense of responsibility in their husbands upon return which they attributed to the rigors of overseas work. Ina said, "When he was first here [before migration], he was always drinking. When he experienced the hardship in earning a living, he just stayed here most of the time. He wouldn't go out anymore." Others on return after a successful overseas work stint were more willing and able (compared to the premigration period) to help their wives with the household chores. Said Adi (forty-five, Indonesian, RFMMC), "Yes, now I sometimes do household work. Yes, I sweep the floor, sometimes. Sometimes if I have free time, I look after our chickens...clean up the garden. [But I] did not [do this before], especially work days [before migration]. Yes, in my work days. I always worked and went home in the evening, that's it."

Not only were some returned migrant-fathers breaking with gender-role stereotypes and expanding their household duties, what was also evident in the study were the efforts made by CHAMPSEA's returned-father-migrants to reconnect emotionally with their children. Our work supports McKay's (2011) argument that migrant fathers, despite the high priority placed on fulfilling the conventional fatherhood role as providers, are unwilling to assume an "emotionally detached role." In fact, it is precisely their ability to be effective breadwinners that allows them to transcend traditional gender conventions without the danger of stigmatization and expand their gender/household repertoire in building more intimate and personal relationships with their children. It was clear in the interviews that the men tried to make their presence felt as much as possible when they returned for a limited period. They would mainly stay at home, make themselves useful around the house by helping out with various chores, and focus their attention on building bonds with their children, sometimes to the extent of temporarily marginalizing their wives:

> When he is here at home, he really focuses his attention on our child. He gives her as much attention as he can because he is away for a long time and is here only for a short while.... They are close even when he was here.... When he's on vacation they are always together. When I leave them, sometimes they go to town together.... From what I observe, the moment her Daddy arrives she is always beside him and she seems to be very happy that he is here....When he has to go somewhere and Elaine does not have classes, we take her with us.... As much as possible he doesn't like to leave her behind. (Risa, forty-one, Filipino, FMMC)

Says Marvie (forty-two, Filipino, FMMC): "He would help me with household chores and then he would bond with the children through music. They like to sing together. He would also teach my eldest son to play the guitar since he wasn't very good yet then. That is why they are always upstairs. I would not be able to join them. They are always in the room."

Fathers who had returned permanently confront a larger challenge in having to make more sustained adjustments over time. While they came home as "heroes," having triumphantly fulfilled their breadwinning roles, their hard-earned statuses might be fragile and quickly downgraded as they were unlikely to find jobs that would accord them with salaries comparable to what they had earned overseas. In these cases, migrant fathers in our study presented themselves as active agents who engaged in careful strategic planning even before returning to ensure their own continued productivity in their providership roles and to secure the livelihood and well-being of their families. When Adi realized that he could not continue working in the harsh Qatar climate, he made plans for his return by setting aside money to buy a truck and start a business as a coconut supplier. He has been gainfully engaged in his business upon his return, making enough to "cover our daily needs." He acknowledged that he could earn more overseas but was contented: "It's just usual [implying that there is no decline in his family's living standards on his return]. ... The most important is that we have started our business to maintain our life[style] among our society, that's already enough."

In other cases where return inevitably led to a reduction of household income, returned-father-migrants took pains to justify their return as positive, often adding that the reduced income was amply compensated by their observation that their presence actually brought about a beneficial "change" in their children's behavior; for example, returned-fathers noted that their children were happier, healthier, had an improved attitude, and were performing better at school. They also said that they no longer felt "guilty" about being absent when their children were sick and were able to be doubly attentive in making efforts to ensure that their children received better medical care. Sitra's returned-migrant husband (fifty, Indonesian, RFMMC), said simply, "He [IC] is better, his health is also better." In most cases, often with the complicity of their left-behind wives and children, men on their return resumed their positions as heads of households and decision makers, not just expressed in terms of their breadwinning roles but also in the sphere of social reproduction, as seen in the fact that they would proudly attend parent-teacher meetings.

Returned father-migrants in our study were thus able to maintain their self-esteem and masculine identities, as long as they had sufficient reason to validate their worth and physical presence at home. As McKay (2011: 14) argues, while "providership has long been recognized as a defining element of... hegemonic masculinity," masculine practices that uphold fatherhood ideals allow for greater flexibility. While the continuation of breadwinning roles remained a significant concern for return fathers, their value to their masculine identities could in fact be enhanced or supplemented by expanding household work and deepening the ties that bound them to their children in order to claim "good fatherhood" (15).

Conclusion

In the wake of the rapid feminization of labor migration in Southeast Asia, gender ideologies around parenthood remain resilient but flexible at the Southernmost end of the care chain. When care cannot be purchased elsewhere, fathers step up to do what is necessary. Among left-behind father-carers in the CHAMPSEA study, despite claiming to be able to perform mothers' roles, fathers still prefer to migrate as Sadewa shares, "Sometimes, I only have to work ten days in a month [when overseas]. Only ten days in a month but I have to fulfill the household needs every day [when at home in Indonesia]. Every time, the children will ask me for money for their education so it is better to go overseas." Mothers agree and chime in with this view: "I think it is better that it is my husband [and not me] who goes abroad, [where] the child is concerned" (Titik, thirty-five, Indonesian, FMMC). While the preferred parenting model for the respondents of the CHAMPSEA study was to either have both parents present in order to share the work of caring, or have gender-normative arrangements when fathers work abroad while mothers stayed behind, left-behind father-carers in this study appear to have coped well with the changes in gender roles during their wives' absence over the years, and at different life stages. In particular, father-carers expressed a sense of pride when they could claim that their children were doing well under their charge. While "good fatherhood" is strongly anchored on men's ability to be successful providers of material welfare, their strengths in "overcoming the odds" in ensuring that their children were thriving under their watch also feature prominently in their construction of masculine selves. As Pingol (2001) notes, left-behind men do not lose their masculinities but seek to construct and reclaim them in other ways. In the process, they create alternative versions of what constitutes "good fatherhood" to counter hegemonic notions of masculinity that restrict men to breadwinning roles. Accomplishing their caring duties well is considered to be an achievement as long as the work invested in caring does not overwhelm their place (even if this "place" is notional) as men who are actively and substantially contributing to the welfare of their families. Holding on to work that generates an income and having a web of other carers to depend on in looking after their children are hence important dimensions of fathers' ability to provide sustained care for their children. For left-behind father-carers, the knowledge that role-reversal is temporary also helps men cope better.[16]

The "package deal" (McKay 2011) notion of successful father-hood prevalent in the region also encourages father-migrants in the study to prioritize the maintenance of close links with their left-behind families. This has largely been facilitated in the last decade by the availability of cheaper communication technologies such as the cell phone (for calling and texting) to allow frequent and meaning-ful communication between father-migrants and their children back home. On return, the study indicates that father-migrants are eager to pick up the threads with the children where they were left off and to continue in their "disrupted" fathering roles. In the process, he-gemonic masculine identities of being heads of households and de-cision makers responsible for the overall welfare of their families are largely conserved, even as fathering practices—at home, from afar, on return—are constantly readjusted given changing circumstances.

Despite major structural shifts wrought by globalization and the speeding up of mobilities in Southeast Asia, the family as a living ar-rangement underwritten by both the sharing of material resources and ties of intimacy remains relatively resilient if ever-changing. Normative gender practices and identities are in flux as people con-stantly "do" and "un-do" gender in everyday life (cf. Thao, this vol-ume). Within this highly mobile world, fathers, like mothers, are actively adapting their gender practices and identities in small steps, even as broader ideational change progresses more slowly.[17]

Notes

1. While the term "left-behind" is undeniably problematic and carries negative connotations, it is used here as in studies by Nguyen et al. (2006) and Toyota et al. (2007) to simply describe the non-migrating family members and communities who have stayed behind at the des-tination countries.

2. The term "father-carer" (or "caregiver" in American English) is a short-ened phrase to describe fathers who have reported themselves as the primary caregivers of their children during their migrant spouse's ab-sence. It is not used here to imply that fathers outside of this study do not perform care work or that they are the only caregivers. Also, as reviewed in the later sections of the chapter, neither Indonesian nor Filipino men are usually expected to take on the primary caregiving role when their wives are present.

3. "FMMC" refers to father-migrant, mother-carer families; "MMFC" re-fers to mother-migrant, father-carer families; "RFMMC" refers to re-turned-father-migrant, mother-carer families; and "RMMFC" refers to returned-mother-migrant, father-carer families.

4. It must be stressed that Indonesians are notably diverse in class, culture, and ethnicity, and Javanese constitute the largest group.

5. Scholars such as Nina Nurmila (2009) and Ekawati S. Wahyuni (2005) disagree with Geertz (1961). They counter that Javanese women have limited control over their own sexualities or matters inside and outside the household and that their power in the household is derived from men, the real power holders. Women's power is constrained by their small income and lack of land, and women are also largely absent from public and political affairs.

6. Such high expectations placed on fathers limit their freedom to express their emotions (Jay 1969).

7. Filipino fathers have been grossly neglected in existing research, which has focused mainly on Filipino mothers and transnational motherhood. Asis and Marave (2009) attribute the underrepresentation of Filipino fathers to their inaccessibility to researchers which has thus rendered them generally invisible. Fortunately, glimpses of Filipino fatherhood can be gathered from family studies due to the emphasis placed on family life in the Philippines.

8. "CHAMPSEA" stands for "Child Health and Migrant Parents in South-East Asia." Graham and Yeoh (2013) provide more information on the CHAMPSEA study.

9. Pseudonyms are used to ensure the anonymity of respondents.

10. Filipino and Indonesian father-carers received help mainly in babysitting. This support could have, as Pingol (2001) argued, freed them from home confinement and allowed them to take on paid work.

11. Indonesian father-carers are mainly involved in agricultural work while Filipino father-carers work mainly as drivers.

12. In considering Doucet's (2006) three criteria—emotional, communal, and moral—when answering the question, "Do men mother?", most CHAMPSEA Indonesian and Filipino father-carers appear to fit the bill. They, in their own way, exhibit emotional responsibility for their children, assume community responsibility for their children at schools and health centers, and are mindful of their moral responsibility for them.

13. A larger proportion of left-behind fathers felt physical stress as compared to left-behind mothers. The reverse is true for mental stress with a higher percentage of left-behind mothers experiencing more mental stress than their male counterparts.

14. The mobile phone, either for calling or texting, has become the most common mode of communication between CHAMPSEA transnational family members.

15. Differences in communication frequencies between countries and gender can be generally attributed to affordability, poor infrastructure (e.g., Filipinos have more access to computers and the Internet) and restricted opportunity due to occupation types (see Lam et al. 2013). Furthermore, as reflected in McKay and Lucero-Prisno III's (2012: 28)

study on seafarers, Filipino men view calling home as a way of reasserting their masculinities and paternal authority "as responsible breadwinners, husbands and fathers."

16. Migrant mothers in the region are usually circular labor migrants who can return after two-year work contracts.

17. We are grateful to the Wellcome Trust UK for funding the CHAMPSEA project (GR079946/B/06/Z and GR079946/Z/06/Z) and Singapore Ministry of Education Academic Research Fund Tier 1 (R-109-000-156-112) for supporting the work behind the publication of this chapter. We also thank all members of the CHAMPSEA teams in the four study countries involved in data collection and compilation, and especially all our respondents who agreed to participate in this project.

References

Adamson, Clarissa. 2007. "Gendered Anxieties: Islam, Women's Rights, and Moral Hierarchy in Java." *Anthropological Quarterly* 80, no. 1: 5–37.

Alampay, Liane Peña, and Rosanne M. Jocson. 2011. "Attributions and Attitudes of Mothers and Fathers in the Philippines." *Parenting* 11, no. 2/3: 163–76.

Asis, Maruja M. B., Shirlena Huang, and Brenda S. A. Yeoh. 2004. "When the Light of the Home is Abroad: Unskilled Female Migration and the Filipino Family." *Singapore Journal of Tropical Geography* 25, no. 2: 198–215.

Asis, Maruja M. B., and Cecilia Marave. 2009. *CHAMPSEA: Qualitative Study in the Philippines, Laguna Province*. Philippines: Scalabrini Migration Center.

Bunnell, Tim, Lily Kong, and Lisa Law. 2007. "Social and Cultural Geographies of South-East Asia." In *Mapping Worlds: International Perspectives on Social and Cultural Geographies*, ed. R. Kitchin. London: Routledge.

Carrasco, Lorena. 2010. "Transnational Family Life among Peruvian Migrants in Chile: Multiple Commitments and the Role of Social Remittances." *Journal of Comparative Family Studies* 41, no. 2: 187–204.

Castro, Joeven, Fredaline R. Dado, and Catherine I. Tubesa. 2008. "When Dad Becomes Mom: Communication of Househusbands with Breadwinner Wives." *Far Eastern University Communication Journal* 2: 1–11.

Constable, Nicole. 2009. "The Commodification of Intimacy: Marriage, Sex and Reproductive Labour." *The Annual Review of Anthropology* 38: 49–64.

Doucet, Andrea. 2006. *Do Men Mother?: Fathering, Care, and Domestic Responsibility*. Toronto: University of Toronto Press.

Gamburd, Michele. 2000. "Nurture for Sale: Sri Lankan Housemaids and the Work of Mothering." In *Home and Hegemony: Domestic Service and Identity Politics in South and Southeast Asia*, ed. Kathleen M. Adams and Sara Ann Dickey. Ann Arbor: The University of Michigan Press.

Geertz, Hildred. 1961. *The Javanese Family: A Study of Kinship and Socialization*. New York: The Free Press of Glencoe.

Graham, Elspeth, Lucy P. Jordan, Brenda S. A. Yeoh, Theodora Lam, Maruja
    M. B. Asis, and Su-kamdi. 2012. "Transnational Families and the Family
    Nexus: Perspectives of Indonesian and Filipino Children Left Behind by
    Migrant Parent(s)." *Environment and Planning* A 44, no. 4: 793–815.
Graham, Elspeth, and Brenda S. A. Yeoh. 2013. "Introduction: Child Health
    and Migrant Parents in South-East Asia: Risks and Resilience among Pri-
    mary School-Aged Children." *Asian and Pacific Migration Journal* 22, no.
    3: 297-314.
Harper, Scott E. 2010. "Exploring the Role of Filipino Fathers: Paternal Be-
    haviors and Child Outcomes." *Journal of Family Issues* 31, no. 1: 66–89.
Hoang, Lan Anh, and Brenda S. A. Yeoh. 2011. "Breadwinning Wives and
    'Left-Behind' Husbands: Men and Masculinities in the Vietnamese Trans-
    national Family." *Gender and Society* 25, no. 6: 717–39.
Hoang, Lan Anh, Brenda S. A. Yeoh, and Anna M. Wattie. 2012. "Transna-
    tional Labour Migration and the Politics of Care in the Southeast Asian
    Family." *Geoforum* 43, no. 4: 733–40.
Hondagneu-Sotelo, Pierrette, and Ernestine Avila. 1997. "'I'm Here, but I'm
    There'—The Meanings of Latina Transnational Motherhood." *Gender &*
    Society 11, no. 5: 548–71.
Hugo, Graeme. 2005. "Indonesian International Domestic Workers: Con-
    temporary Developments and Issues." In *Asian Women as Transnational
    Domestic Workers*, ed. S. Huang, B. S. A. Yeoh, and N. A. Rahman. Singa-
    pore: Marshall Cavendish.
Jay, Robert R. 1969. *Javanese Villagers: Social Relations in Rural Modjokuto.*
    Cambridge: MIT Press.
Koning, Juliette. 2004. *Generations of Change: Migration, Family Life, and Iden-
    tity Formation in a Javanese Village During the New Order.* Indonesia: Gadjah
    Mada University Press.
Lam, Theodora, Miriam Ee, Lan Anh Hoang, and Brenda S. A. Yeoh. 2013.
    "Securing a Better Living Environment for Left-Behind Children: Impli-
    cations and Challenges for Policies." *Asian and Pacific Migration Journal* 22,
    no. 3: 421-45.
Lindawati, Ang, and Ciorstan Smark. 2010. "Education into Employment?
    Indonesian Women and Moving from Business Education into Profes-
    sional Participation." *e-Journal of Business Education & Scholarship of Teach-
    ing* 4, no. 2: 29–42.
McKay, Steven. 2011. "Re-Masculinizing the Hero: Filipino Migrant Men
    and Gender Privilege." Asia Research Institute Working Paper Series No.
    172.
McKay, Steven, and Don Eliseo Lucero-Prisno, III. 2012. "Masculinities
    Afloat: Filipino Seafarers and the Situational Performances of Manhood."
    In *Men and Masculinities in Southeast Asia*, ed. M. Ford and L. Lyons. Milton
    Park: Routledge.
Medina, Belen. 2001. *The Filipino Family.* Diliman, Quezon City: University
    of the Philippines Press.
Megawangi, Ratna. 1997. "Gender Perspectives in Early Childhood Care

and Development in Indonesia." *The Consultative Group on Early Childhood Care and Development* 20: 1–7.

Newberry, Jan. 2010. "The Global Child and Non-Governmental Governance of the Family in Post-Suharto Indonesia." *Economy and Society* 39, no. 3: 403–26.

Nguyen, Liem, Brenda S. A. Yeoh, and Mika Toyota. 2006. "Migration and the Well-Being of the 'Left Behind' in Asia." *Asian Population Studies* 2, no. 1: 37–44.

Nurmila, Nina. 2009. *Women, Islam and Everyday Life: Renegotiating Polygamy in Indonesia.* Oxon: Routledge.

Parreñas, Rhachel. 2005. *Children of Global Migration: Transnational Families and Gendered Woes.* Stanford, CA: Stanford University Press.

———. 2008. "Transnational Fathering: Gendered Conflicts, Distant Disciplining and Emotional Gaps." *Journal of Ethnic and Migration Studies* 34, no. 7: 1057–72.

Pingol, Alicia. 2001. *Remaking Masculinities: Identity, Power, and Gender Dynamics in Families with Migrant Wives and Househusbands.* Philippines: University Center for Women's Studies.

Scalabrini Migration Center. 2004. *Hearts Apart: Migration in the Eyes of Filipino Children.* Philippines.

Sen, Krishna. 1998. "Indonesian Women at Work: Reframing the Subject." In *Gender and Power in Affluent Asia,* ed. Krishna Sen and M. Stivens. London: Routledge.

Silvey, Rachel. 2006. "Consuming the Transnational Family: Indonesian Migrant Domestic Workers to Saudi Arabia." *Global Networks* 6, no. 1: 23–40.

Sukamdi, Setiadi, Agus Indiyanto, Abdul Haris, and Irwan Abdullah. 2001. "Country Study 2: Indonesia." In *Female Labour Migration in South East Asia: Change and Continuity,* ed. S. Chantavich, C. Wille, K. Angsuthanasombat, M. A. B. Asis, A. Beesey, and Sukamdi. Bangkok: Asian Research Centre for Migration.

Tobin, Vanessa. 2008. *Gender, Migration and Children's Rights.* The International Conference on Gender, Migration and Development: Seizing Opportunities, Upholding Rights. Hotel Sofitel Philippine Plaza Manila, Philippines.

Townsend, Nicholas. 2002. "Cultural Contexts of Father Involvement." In *Handbook of Father Involvement: Multidisciplinary Perspectives,* ed. C. Tamis-LeMonda and N. Cabrera. Mahwah, NJ: Lawrence Erlbaum Associates.

Toyota, Mika, Brenda S. A. Yeoh, and Liem Nguyen. 2007. "Editorial Introduction. Bringing the 'Left Behind' Back into View in Asia: A Framework for Understanding the Migration-Left Behind Nexus." *Population, Space and Place* 13, no. 3: 157–61.

Wahyuni, Ekawati S. 2005. *The Impact of Migration on Family Structure and Functioning: Case Study in Jawa.* International Union for the Scientific Study of Population XXV Conference. Tours, France. 18–23 July.

Zimmerman, Mary K., Jacquelyn S. Litt, and Christine E. Bose. 2006. *Global Dimensions of Gender and Carework.* Stanford, CA: Stanford University Press.

Part III

Primary Care Fatherhood

Chapter 5

WHEN THE PILLAR OF THE HOME IS SHAKING

FEMALE LABOR MIGRATION AND STAY-AT-HOME FATHERS IN VIETNAM

Vu Thi Thao

Introduction

Since the Doi Moi economic reforms of the 1980s, the Vietnamese economy has transitioned from being centrally planned to market-oriented. Vietnam became increasingly integrated into the global economy when it joined the World Trade Organization in 2006, a development that created new employment opportunities in export-oriented manufacturing, trade, and services. However, these jobs are clustered in urban areas and favor women workers. Consequently, the flow of rural women migrants seeking jobs to urban areas is increasing rapidly (General Statistics Office 2010; Ha and Ha 2001; Jensen and Peppard 2003). According to 1989 and 1999 censuses, men predominate in population mobility, yet the participation of women in migration is increasing. The 2009 census shows women migrants slightly dominating all migration flows.[1] Although many of these industrial jobs require low-skilled workers, this sector attracts young and single women who can work long hours (ActionAid 2005). More mature and married women migrants tend to dominate many occupations in the informal sector, such as street vendors, junk pickers, and domestic helpers (Asian Development Bank 2005; General Statistics Office 2006; Jensen and Peppard 2003; Truong et al. 1996). Hence, changes in the labor markets have provided rural families in Vietnam with new ways of pursuing their livelihoods: mothers migrating to cities for employment with fathers and children staying behind in villages.

In much of Asia, the increasing participation of women in labor migration, the so-called "feminization" of migration, has also been observed as a result of global economic restructuring (Nguyen et al. 2006; Yamanaka and Piper 2005: 7–12). The feminization of migration suggests the rise of stay-at-home father/breadwinning mother families. How does the entry of men and women into nontraditional roles affect men's lives as fathers, as well as women's lives as mothers? How do fathers and mothers renegotiate gender norms in parenting in relation to the migration of these mothers? Much research focuses on the experience of women migrants who left their children behind in their hometowns to seek jobs elsewhere (e.g., Asis et al. 2004; Devasahayam et al. 2004; Hondagneu-Sotelo et al. 1997; Pinnawala 2008), and some attention is paid to children left behind (e.g., Asis 2006). However, the current research neglects the lives of stay-at-home fathers in relation to women's migration. Furthermore, gender scholarship in Vietnam primarily focuses on women's lives, while men's lives, attitudes, behaviors, and relationships with other family members remain unaddressed (Harris 1998). Lan A. Hoang and Brenda S. A. Yeoh (2011) also claim that literature on men and masculinity in Vietnam is "both rudimentary and fragmented." This chapter therefore aims to fill in these gaps.

The migration of a family member inevitably has an enormous impact on the family, particularly when the mother takes the responsibility for migration. A mother's absence from home motivates rearrangements in everyday family life and changes her role as carer. Also, being on the move, the mother assumes breadwinner roles traditionally assigned to men. Women's new economic roles as breadwinners and their simultaneous absences from home may push men into becoming stay-at-home fathers. Research shows that the father's role is strongly linked to that of the breadwinner (Dermott 2008: 24–42; Miller 2010: 111–44) and, in Vietnamese culture, to the idea of the head of the family or the pillar of the home (Huou 1991: 39; Pham 1999: 22–42). How do stay-at-home fathers who face challenges to fulfill these gendered expectations experience family life? The goal of this chapter is to explore lived experiences of stay-at-home fathers through their everyday interactions with their migrant wives around childcare, housework, and gender relations and to examine the implications of women's migration for gender inequalities. In so doing, I employ the "doing gender" and "undoing gender" approaches which emphasize a critical focus on everyday interactions as sites of reproducing and diminishing gender inequalities. I pay special attention to the fathers' feelings and how they manage their feelings or work on their emotions, what Arlie R. Hochschild (1979) terms "emotion work," in order to negotiate tensions that arise in their new situations as stay-at-home fathers. According to Hochschild (1979: 561), emotion work refers to "the act of trying to change in degree or quality an emotion or feeling." Emotion work is guided by feeling rules that are culturally constructed and shaped by social norms. In the case of stay-at-home fathers, feeling rules are strongly tied to gender norms and ideologies.

This chapter is based on a case study of stay-at-home fathers from two rural villages in the Red River Delta whose wives migrated to Hanoi, Vietnam, for paid jobs. To better understand stay-at-home fathers' everyday lives, I also analyze migrant mothers, children, and villagers. I first discuss the three sets of literature that inform the analysis: the doing gender and undoing gender perspectives (Deutsch 2007; Risman 2009; West and Zimmerman 1987), the linkage between fatherhood and motherhood, and consequences of women's migration for fatherhood. I then present the Vietnamese case, followed by the methodology and study sites. The analysis examines the involvement of stay-at-home fathers in childcare and housework, and how they (re)construct their role as the pillar of the home, with a focus on their emotion work. In conclusion, I discuss how stay-at-home fathers do and undo gender in response to the migration of mothers, thus influencing gender inequalities.

Doing and Undoing Gender

According to Candace West and Don H. Zimmerman (1987), gender is not something we are but something we do. They write, "Doing gender involves a complex of socially guided perceptual, interactional, and micropolitical activities that cast particular pursuits as expressions of masculine and feminine 'nature'" (126). Hence, individuals act with the awareness that their behaviors will be judged according to normative standards considered appropriate for their sex category. The doing gender approach accounts for the reproduction of gender through everyday interactions and thus emphasizes gender differences and inequalities. West and Sarah Fenstermaker (2002) acknowledge that one may fail to live up to normative conceptions of masculine or feminine behavior under given circumstances but that this particular behavior may lose its relevance to a sex category. It is because gender differences are linked to power and resource differentials that these differences are reinforced through an ongoing process of accountability (West and Zimmerman 1987). As explained by West and Zimmerman (1987), individuals hold themselves accountable for their actions, which are at the risk of gender assessment. Thus, they consciously orient their actions to be seen in accordance with gender norms. "Hence doing gender is unavoidable" (West and Fenstermaker 2002: 50).

The doing gender approach is criticized as a theory of gender maintenance. Drawing on a large research deployed the doing gender perspective, Deutsch (2007) sees the approach as useful in documenting conformity to gendered norms and the persistence of gender inequalities but fails to explain reducing gender inequalities. In a similar vein, Barbara J. Risman (2009: 82) argues that the "ubiquitous usage of 'doing gender' also creates conceptual confusion as we try to study a world that is indeed changing." Thus these scholars suggest that it is possible to undo gender when gender differences are diminished over time. They claim that the linkage between gender inequalities and power and resource differentials may be weakened due to structural changes, such as economic shifts. They therefore propose the "undoing gender" approach that accounts for the resistance to gender inequalities through everyday interactions. Yet they do not reject the doing gender approach; instead they call for a critical focus on everyday interactions that either do or undo gender. Through these doing and undoing gender processes, gender inequalities can be claimed to be reproduced or diminished.

Gender, Fatherhood, and Motherhood

"Around motherhood and fatherhood gender usually sits centre stage" (Miller 2011: 1096). Transformation of women's identity and status as a result of their labor migration may challenge men's roles as fathers and their involvement in family life. As Robert E. Griswold (1993: 220) puts it, "[W]omen's [paid] work has destroyed the old assumptions about fatherhood and required new negotiations of gender relations." Research on fatherhood in industrialized countries shows that fathers are now more involved in childcare and the domestic sphere and value their experiences in these areas (Miller 2011). However, despite this shift, breadwinning is still considered one of the most central aspects to men's fathering identity and commitment to family life (Dermott 2008: 25–42; Wall and Arnold 2007; Williams 2008). As breadwinning is central to fatherhood, the consequence of women's employment for stay-at-home fathers can be profound (Chesley 2011; Doucet and Merla 2007).

Hegemonic masculinity, referring to a set of cultural normative ideals of being a man that permits men's dominance over women to continue (Connell and Messerschmidt 2005), provides insights that inform research on practices of fathering as opportunities to do gender (Chesley 2011: 646) and to undo gender, as well. Reflecting on the concept of hegemonic masculinity, R. W. Connell and James W. Messerschmidt (2005) criticize those who rely on it to imply the social reproduction of gender inequalities. They emphasize that the conceptualization of hegemonic masculinity must acknowledge "the possibilities of democratizing gender relations, of abolishing power differentials, not just of reproducing hierarchy" (853). In doing so, it is important to recognize the agency of subordinated groups as much as dominant groups because gender hierarchy is also influenced by configuration of women's identity and practice. Furthermore, the plurality of masculinities has been increasingly recognized to acknowledge the complexity, fragmentation, and diversity of men's lives (Aboim 2010: 1–61). For instance, "caring masculinities" refers to fathers who "trade cash for care" (Johansson and Klinth 2008).

Studying men's experiences of fatherhood in the United Kingdom, Tina Miller (2011) documents that fathers may perceive and/ or experience being involved in nurturing and childcare as threatening to their masculine identity. They therefore return to traditional gendered norms in which breadwinning is central and highly valued. Men have greater power than women to choose the degree of their involvement in the spheres of paid work and caring because men's agency is supported by the dominance of the breadwinner identity as part of the theoretical framework of hegemonic masculinity (Gatrell 2007; Miller 2010: 44; Vuori 2009; Wall and Arnold 2007). Yet others claim that involvement in fatherhood is not a matter of men's choice—to be a breadwinner or carer—but rather is a consequence of structural circumstances. For example, gender segregation in labor markets has pushed some men into stay-at-home fatherhood (Chesley 2011; Williams 2008).

"To understand fatherhood is possible only by also understanding motherhood" (Dermott 2008: 6). Previous research has shown that mothers' attitudes and behaviors have a considerable impact on fathers' behaviors (Marsiglio and Cohan 2000: 87–88). New fathers or involved fathers who contribute a greater share of childcare may challenge the status of mothers. Mothers may oppose men's interference into their domestic domain if they fear their status as primary caretaker is threatened (Gatrell 2007). Yet some authors find that mothers are collaborative with fathers in parenting work. These mothers welcome fathers' greater contribution to childcare (Miller 2011). In any instance, the close interlinkage of fathering and mothering roles incorporates mothers into the analysis of fatherhood, which is necessary to provide a better understanding of how fathers and mothers are doing gender and undoing gender at the intersection of work and family life.

Women's Migration and Fatherhood

In much of Asia, women outnumber men in migration (Nguyen et al. 2006). Transformation in mothers' identity and status as a result of their labor migration can challenge men's roles as fathers and men's involvement in family life. Supang Chantavich (2001) finds that, in Southeast Asia, stay-at-home fathers may take greater responsibilities in childcare, but that this is not necessarily maintained once the mothers return home. Studying female rural-urban migration in Vietnam, Bernadette P. Resurreccion and Ha Thi Van Khanh (2007) observe a similar pattern. In the Philippines, fathers take on mothers' childcare work with the help of elder children and extended family members (Asis et al. 2004). Yet in other studies, for example in China, fathers oppose engaging in caretaking roles because they see it as a threat to their masculine identity (Fan 2003). The pressure to comply with gender norms impedes fathers' abilities to make greater contributions to emotion work in the absence of mothers (Fan 2003; Parreñas 2005: 92–140).

Migration experiences, in many cases, offer women greater access to financial resources. Research shows that migrant women become the main provider for families and that their remittances contribute significantly to their families' economic sustenance (Asis et al. 2004; Pinnawala 2008). Women's new income is in general highly appreciated by family members and paves the way for enhancing the independence of women, strengthening their decision-making power

within the family. This puts women in a more equal position in relation to their husbands (Silva 2005: 13–46; United Nations Economic
and Social Commission for Asia and the Pacific 2010). However,
the benefits of women's increased economic position do not necessarily carry over onto the home front. Many men oppose wom-
en's new bargaining power as a threat to their masculine identities,
which they either have to rework or reclaim aggressively (Elmhirst
2007).

Gender Ideologies and Practices in Vietnamese Families

Traditionally, the Vietnamese family structure has been characterized by the Confucian model of family hierarchy based on gender,
generation, and age. Fathers, husbands, and sons have authority
over women, and children owe filial debts to their parents even after
their parents' deaths (Pham 1999: 22–43; Hy 2003: 203). A father
is considered to be *trụ cột gia đình,* literally translated as "the pillar
of the home." Responsible for providing material and moral care to
all family members, he makes decisions on all family matters (Huou
1991: 39). In rural families, a father's authority is decisive. Although
women participate in decision-making processes, the fathers have
the final word. Fathers often control household income and large
expenditures. Mothers are assigned caregiving roles but are also expected to contribute to household income (Ashwill and Thai 2005).
Note that some studies find that the traditional Vietnamese family is
also influenced by the Southeast Asian culture, which emphasizes
bilateral kinship and gives a higher status to women (Pham 1999:
40–41).

Although Doi Moi has offered women more economic opportunities, the male-oriented model still applies (Hy 2003; Knodel et
al. 2005). Housework is still considered unsuitable for men (Tran
1996). Yet drawing on statistical data, John Knodel et al. (2005)
find fathers in the Doi Moi era more likely to become involved in
childcare than those in the past. Recent studies on women's migration show that although father's breadwinning roles are replaced,
fathers still hold authority over migrant mothers (Hoang and Yeoh
2011; Resurreccion and Ha 2007). However, little research focuses
on men. Thus little is known about the lives of fathers in the face
of women's increasing participation in labor migration. This chapter
seeks to fill this gap.

Location and Methodology

This chapter draws on a case study of families whose fathers and
children stay in the villages of Binh Ho and Phu Khe (located in the
Red River Delta of Vietnam) while mothers migrate to Hanoi for paid
jobs in the informal sector (see Figure 5.1). As the fastest-growing
city in North Vietnam, Hanoi has become the most attractive destination in the region, drawing an increasing number of female migrants from surrounding provinces. The distance from the villages to
Hanoi is about fifty kilometers, or an hour and a half by car. However, for reasons of cost and time, migrants do not commute daily
but stay in the city on a permanent or semi-permanent basis.

Binh Ho is a medium-sized village with 464 households (1,780
people) at an average level of socioeconomic development, whereas
Phu Khe is much smaller with only 256 households (1,056 people)
and relatively high socioeconomic development. In the two villages,
men and women both migrate, yet women's migration is much more
common (about 60 to 70 percent of migrants are women). Local
people migrate because of land shortages, epidemic animal diseases,
frequent price fluctuations on agricultural products, lack of financial
credit, and few options for off-farm activities in local communities.
Yet women often migrate while men stay behind for the following
reasons: First, more low-skilled jobs are available for women. While

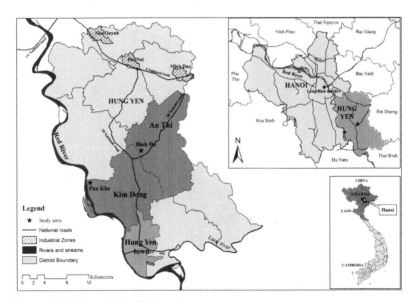

FIGURE 5.1. Map of Study Location.

single women can find jobs in factories nearby, married women end up in a service segment of the Hanoi's informal sector. These service jobs require solicitation skills, which local people believe that women are better able to provide. Second, although women earn less money than men do, they spend considerably less than men on urban living expenses. Therefore, women are able to send greater remittances home.[2] Third, local people believe that young children need more care from mothers but that adolescents should be strictly disciplined, ideally by fathers.

Married women migrants work as fruit- and fish-porters, street vendors, and traders (of chili, ginger, garlic, and limes) in Hanoi. With high urban living costs, these women could not bring their families with them to Hanoi. And even if they could afford to pay the living costs, without Hanoi permanent household registration,[3] their children could not go to school there. Furthermore, a majority of local people consider their lives to be in the village: their kinship and identity are tied to the village. For these reasons, men stay behind to take care of children while women can concentrate on making a living in Hanoi so that the families can have better lifestyles in the villages. The migration of women has brought prosperity to the villages: migrants often build new two- or three-story houses. Inside their houses, one can typically find a big flat-screen television, a refrigerator, fine furniture, a gas cooker, and a flush toilet. In addition to table telephones, migrant families use mobile phones for communication. Some migrant families whose mothers are big wholesale traders even own cars and houses in Hanoi City. (See Figure 5.1.)

The fieldwork was carried out in two periods, totaling eight months, between 2008 and 2010. Out of 121 families[4] randomly selected, thirty-five families had fathers and children who stayed in the villages with mothers migrating to Hanoi. Remittances[5] from the migrant mothers contributed up to 70 percent of total household income. Five out of thirty-five families relied entirely on remittances. I selected all thirty-five families for in-depth interviews. The interviews with the fathers[6] and mothers were conducted separately. The purpose of these interviews was to explore feelings and behaviors of stay-at-home fathers and their migrant wives toward childcare, housework, and gender relations in response to the migration of the wives.

All the interviews were conducted in Vietnamese. Interviews with the stay-at-home fathers were conducted in the villages, while the interviews with migrant mothers were carried out in both Hanoi and the villages. I conducted half of the interviews with stay-at-home fathers (the rest were carried out by a male Vietnamese researcher to reduce gender bias) and all the interviews with migrant mothers. I am aware that my position as an academic Vietnamese woman educated abroad, unmarried, and under the age of thirty posed some barriers in my interviews with stay-at-home fathers, especially since the interviews were related to masculine identity. Some fathers did not open up, which made our conversations brief. However, others were more open and viewed me favorably, as someone concerned with their "troubles." In addition, this chapter draws on data from informal conversations with twenty-four children (ages ten to eighteen) from these thirty-five families. The conversations were conducted in the presence of a child's guardian and agreed to by the parents. Child respondents were included because they would provide further explanations for fathers' feelings and behaviors. I also conducted interviews with six returned migrant mothers. In addition, I held focus group discussions with local villagers to capture local perceptions of family ideals and gender ideologies in the context of the mothers' migration. None of the interviews or discussions were tape recorded. The interviewees' names are pseudonyms.

Before turning to the analysis, I briefly describe the characteristics of these thirty-five families. They are Kinh (Viet) people, the majority ethnic group of Vietnam. The average husband was forty-seven years old, and the average wife was forty-five years old. The fathers had a slightly lower educational level than their wives, seven and eight years of schooling, respectively. Except two returned migrant mothers, all the mothers were current migrants and had been migrating from one to twenty-five years. Almost all of them started migrating after they married and had children. It is common for the mothers to interrupt their migration for childbirth, then migrate again after the child is about two years old. The child remains in the village with the father.

Involvement in Childcare and Housework

Stay-at-Home Fathers

In the absence of their migrant wives, stay-at-home fathers assume caregiving roles. They shop for food, cook, and clean. They are mainly in charge of providing care for children (see also Hoang and Yeoh 2011), looking after them, disciplining them, and helping them do homework. They feed, bathe, and dress small children and take them to kindergarten. Fourteen percent of these families live with a grandparent, from whom a few stay-at-home fathers receive help.

Some stay-at-home fathers also provide care for older grandparents. But grandparents are considered to be soft disciplinarians, and parents fear that their care may lead grandchildren to become bad boys or girls. Many families decide to send their children to kindergarten instead of asking for help from grandparents.

These stay-at-home fathers bear a heavy workload, which affects the quality of care fathers provide to their children. During my focus group interviews, stay-at-home fathers mentioned that they rarely have chances to get together and are unable to keep a close eye on their children because of this workload. Tan, a 30-year-old father, stays with his 14-year-old son and 2-year-old daughter in the village while his wife works in Hanoi as a shop assistant. Tan said, "I work twice as much as before my wife moved to Hanoi because I have to take care of my daughter besides my agricultural and construction work. I have no spare time. My son may help for preparing lunch if he studies in the afternoons." Tan's case is not uncommon. Besides agricultural work, half of all fathers interviewed did or do seasonal sideline production work. However, some of them had to stop or reduce such work in order to take on domestic tasks from their wives. Stay-at-home fathers of families with small children have a much greater workload.

To reduce the workload for stay-at-home fathers, some families purchase modern household facilities, such as a gas stove, electric cooker, and refrigerator. Several families hire domestic help when the children are small. These families, whose mothers are usually wholesale traders, receive considerably larger amounts of remittances to pay for these expenses.

The attitudes of stay-at-home fathers about their new roles are mixed. More than half of the fathers claimed that they should do these tasks. While the mothers work hard in the city to send their families remittances, the fathers staying behind do not think of their new responsibilities as women's work. They value these tasks and consider them as important as many other kinds of work. Some of them report that they now realize how hard the work is and that they have more sympathy for their wives. For example, Anh, a 52-year-old father, feels that he "should do domestic tasks because my wife has to work for the family!" Men also changed their attitudes because there are increasing numbers of stay-at-home fathers involved in domestic tasks.

Others have placed children's interests above their masculine pride to degender their involvement in domestic tasks. For instance, Khiem, a 50-year-old father, claimed, "I do not think domestic tasks are women's or not. I work for our children's education." Khiem's family has two children studying: a son in college and a daughter in high school. Remittances from the mother primarily cover their children's educational expenses. Khiem considers his assumption of the role of caregiver as his sacrifice for his children's future. This is also another way for him to secure his own livelihood as his children must remember and repay him this sacrifice in his old age.

Yet less than half of the fathers stated that they have to take on these responsibilities because new circumstances compelled them to do so (see also Chesley 2011; Williams 2008). Migration of the mothers is often a family decision made on a cost-benefit analysis. It is economically better for the family if the mother migrates instead of the husband because of gender-segregated labor markets favoring women workers. "All because of economics!" as stated by Hien, a 46-year-old father. Similarly, Hung, a 30-year-old father, agreed to his wife's migration because of his small income. Hung said, "Agreeing to my wife's migration was a last extremity. Income from my carpenter job cannot cover our household expenses. So I have to let my wife migrate." Drawing on a study of Filipino fathers whose wives pursue transnational migration, Asis et al. (2004) also found that the ideal situation, often thwarted by a household's economic circumstances, is a stay-at-home wife and mother. Fifty-one-year-old father Thanh says, "These domestic tasks are for women. I feel quite embarrassed to do them but I have to adapt, no one helps me."

These fathers face difficulties adapting to their new role as carer. They have to perform caring responsibilities in the absence of their wives, but not when their wives are at home. They still consider the domestic tasks to be women's responsibilities and trivial. They accept this reversal as temporary and expect respective roles to revert back to the traditional family model when the wives return permanently to the villages (see also Resurreccion and Ha 2007: 219–20). Interviews with six returned migrant mothers affirm this. However, these women also report that their husbands are more willing to perform domestic tasks than before they migrated to Hanoi.

Migrant Mothers

Although stay-at-home fathers assume domestic tasks, their migrant wives still maintain their caring responsibilities (see also Resurreccion and Ha 2007). The wives make regular home visits at least once a month because their jobs are flexible. During their home visits, they actively reclaim their domestic tasks. As the wives explain, they have sympathy for their husbands, who have to work hard in their absence. Therefore they try and make it up to their families when they are at home by sharing the workload of the household. Before returning to the city, they make sure that their families have enough food and other essentials, like rice, cooking oil, and soap, while they are away in Hanoi. They also calculate when they think their family will run out of rice or money, returning home or sending money to the husbands, rather than waiting to be notified. The wives try to prevent their husbands from feeling economically dependent. They are aware that their earnings weigh on their husbands' senses of self-worth. Says 42-year-old wife Linh: "I am aware of my husband's sense of failure. Sometimes in our quarrels he says, 'So you rely on your money against me.' I therefore try to show that my role at home does not change. I care for my family when I am in Hanoi. I call them very often to know if they are fine, to ask my youngest son about his studying, and to remind my husband to do this and that. I sometimes send gifts to my family. When I am at home, I undertake all domestic tasks."

Fourteen out of thirty-five migrant mothers report that they still fulfill their mothering roles, but the rest concede that they do not fulfill what they see as their caregiving responsibilities. The latter are concerned about maintaining their caregiving roles. In doing so, they interfere with their husband's childcare from afar and during home visits. They are also dissatisfied with their husbands' parenting styles. Sinh, a 55-year-old wife, reports: "I am not satisfied with the way my husband disciplines our children. Sometimes I call him and remind him about it. Once my son called and told me that he had lied to his father. He went out playing but said he had gone to school. His father found out and beat my son. I was mad at my husband. I called and told him that he is not allowed to beat and scold our children."

Migrant mothers pay special attention to their husbands' parenting style when it relates to the children's education. The fact that many mothers migrate because of financial demands for children's education intensifies this conflict between the migrant mothers and their stay-at-home husbands. Mothers blame the latter for not monitoring their children closely enough, which they feel leads to their poor academic attendance and performance. So how do children feel about their stay-at-home fathers as caregivers?

Children

Children have a clear view of the fathers who care for them. Most state that they receive less care when their mothers are away. For example, fathers do not wake them when they oversleep. Children skip breakfast to arrive to class on time. They wear dirty clothing or shirts with missing buttons to class. Their fathers are sometimes absent at school parents' meetings. Two children had to repeat one class. Eighteen-year-old Thien dropped out of school in ninth grade, explaining, "Father did not supervise my studying very closely, so I spent less time studying and more time going out with friends." The children often refer to mothers as good caregivers because these things would not happen in their presence. Eleven-year-old Ngoc said, "When my mother is working in Hanoi, nobody attends parents' meetings at school. My father is absorbed in playing outside: he does not attend the meetings."

The children also learn to care for themselves and help their fathers perform domestic tasks. The older children take care of their younger siblings, washing clothes and helping them with homework (see also Asis 2006: 45–67), tasks their mother would have completed. They explained why some children claim to be at a disadvantage in comparison to friends whose parents are both at home because the latter receive care from both parents, while they only receive care from their fathers. However, receiving care from fathers increases a child's intimacy with his or her father. Ngoc, a 16-year-old son, reported, "My father cares more about me, much more than my mother does." Yet Ngoc's feelings might reflect more resentment for his absent mother than affection for his present father. He claimed that his mother loves his brother more than him and that she often scolds his father for taking his side. He concluded, "To be honest, I like my mother working in Hanoi rather than staying at home."

Villagers

In Binh Ho and Phu Khe, local villagers would gossip about migrant mothers who do not undertake domestic tasks when they are at home as "bad mothers and bad wives." To some extent, the migrant mothers are obliged to resume their responsibilities for domestic tasks to avoid social condemnation. If migrant wives do not undertake domestic tasks while at home, the villagers sneer, saying that they are "lazy" and "don't know what to do" or that they are "coming back home but doing nothing." Some people even say it directly to the women's faces.

At the same time, the villagers have relaxed their views on changing gender roles. They realize that husbands and wives are both responsible for building up the family and that sometimes roles must change for the family's survival. According to one focus group participant, "It doesn't depend on your gender." Moreover, husbands and wives share not only economic, but also domestic responsibilities. A man who undertakes domestic tasks is considered to be a good father and husband.

The Struggle to Hold the Pillar of the Home Front Still

Stay-at-Home Fathers

In Vietnam, a good father is expected to serve as the role model for his children (Huou 1991). Taking on a breadwinning role and serving as the pillar of the home are major parts of realizing this goal. As a 55-year-old father stated, "No change in my position in the family. If my role as a pillar of the home changes, then our children will follow my example. It will be my bad fortune." How does a stay-at-home father with his modest earning from agriculture and seasonal sideline production fulfill this great responsibility? Just two stay-at-home fathers report feeling like they lost power in the family and that their wives are the pillars of the home. The rest claim that they are still the pillars of the home despite their wives' much greater economic contributions. First, they emphasize the contribution of their agricultural income,[7] which is no less important to the family's economy than the wives' remittances. Thus, they equate their economic contribution to their families with that of their wives. Note that agricultural expenses are covered by the wives' remittances and that the total income from agricultural and sideline production comprises just one-quarter of the wives' remittances on an annual basis. Second, the fathers claim that they play an important role in the migration of the mothers. Without them remaining at home and taking on domestic tasks, such migration could never happen.

Nonetheless, the stay-at-home father's position as the pillar of the home is shaking as they struggle to hold it still. A more detailed discussion reveals that stay-at-home fathers' power is being undermined by these changes. Two out of thirty-four fathers report that their wives make the family decisions, although they participate in the negotiation process. Meanwhile, the other fathers report that they have to consult and negotiate with the mothers more than before the migration regarding decisions on expensive purchases and investments; they cannot make these decisions alone. Fathers can either discuss them with the migrant mothers on the telephone or wait until the latter visits the family. Bear in mind that migrant mothers bring remittances into their families and control them during their home visits, giving any money left to the fathers before their departure. The fathers are "free" to spend the money in the absence of the mothers. However, if the fathers misspend the money, the mothers will notice and tighten their control over these remittances. Says Hoang, a 30-year-old stay-at-home husband: "Stay-at-home husbands lose power. If my wife does not agree with me, she would say, 'So you buy whatever you want; you work to buy it.' In our discussion on purchasing things, if I disagree with her, I feel awkward because in fact she earns money, not I. Decisions have to be made by men most of the time, therefore I want to discuss them with her, but it is very hard. It isn't my wish."[8]

Stay-at-home fathers feel uneasy experiencing these changing gender relations. They try to reclaim their power. Even their decisions need money to be executed, while their own earnings, if any, cannot cover these costs. They either borrow money or pay partially. It is common for shop owners to offer villagers deferred payments if their families receive remittances from migrants. When their wives visit the families, debt owners visit them to collect their debt. "So she [his wife] must work harder to pay for it [the debt]," 57-year-old Tien stated when talking about a "beautiful" sideboard that he bought but lacked money to pay for. In doing so, stay-at-home fathers show other family members, especially their wives, that they are still in power. Relates Dinh, a 48-year-old father: "I bought this nice furniture, 5 million VND. I told my wife I like to buy it but she said that she wants to spend money on something else. So I sold rice though it was not enough to pay off but the shop owner let me pay the rest later."

Stay-at-home fathers become depressed because of their inability to fulfill their role as breadwinner. Having robust labor power, they feel that it is unreasonable for men to stay at home and let their wives assume the responsibility for earning a living for their families. The experience of "waiting for the migrant mother to send home money to spend" hurts stay-at-home fathers' sense of masculinity. They feel economically dependent on their migrant wives. Some fathers win back their power by opposing their wives' migration and resuming breadwinning roles. Recounts Quynh, a 45-year-old father: "My position in the family is declining because our children do not obey me. With little and unstable earnings I feel I lost my 'democracy.' When I can earn money I can make decisions. No money, no power. The children feel that a father who can earn money is great.... Since my wife has moved to Hanoi to earn money, I feel I have lost my power. Therefore, for six years I did not let her move."[9] Many stay-at-home fathers experience a threat to their masculine identity because of what they see as an inability to provide financially for their families (see also Chesley 2011). They struggle to maintain their position as the pillar of the home. They use different "micro-political" tactics, and some even prevent their wives' migration and reassume their breadwinning roles. As also found in Africa (Francis 2002) and China (Fan 2003: 42), fathers oppose the migration of mothers because it weakens their own authority in the family.

Migrant Mothers

Migrant mothers acquire more power and improve their position in their families. More than 60 percent of the migrant mothers report participating more and having a stronger voice in negotiating decisions. This is explained by their substantial financial contributions, improved social knowledge, and increased communication skills. Says 55-year-old Huong: "My husband does not earn money. If my husband insists on buying something, but I say 'no money,' then he cannot do anything. Isn't it I who decided? I am the one who makes decisions in my family. I decided to build our house, buy three motorbikes, bring my children to Hanoi, and buy a kiosk at the Long Bien market. I give my husband one million VND a month, just enough for his expenses." On the whole, migrant mothers are independent and have high self-esteem. They are confident in their relations with other family members and villagers. Says 42-year-old Nguyet: "My position in the family has improved. My husband, his siblings, and my children respect me more because if they need to borrow money I can lend it to them. Formerly, my husband could give money to our nephew without telling me. Now he has to ask me before doing so. I am proud because I can earn money to support my husband and children." Although migrant mothers stretch gender boundaries, they do not maximize their challenge to men's dominance. They are careful not to provoke their husbands' senses of failure. In their discourse, in the eyes of the villagers, they show their submission to their husbands. They acknowledge their husbands' role in their migration. They rarely emphasize their breadwinning roles in their families. Some migrant mothers feel sorry for themselves because the financial burdens are placed on their shoulders. They are under pressure to provide for their families. They are also concerned about maintaining and fulfilling their caring roles, which they struggle to balance with their breadwinning roles. These migrant mothers are also careful to minimize what they see as a challenge to traditional family gender norms because they want their children to see the family dynamic as complying with these norms. Hoa, a 44-year-old migrant mother says, "My husband is the master of the family, but I am the decision maker. He is the pillar of the home so that our children will see our model. If I want to make a decision, I make it, then inform my husband before we implement it."

Complying with traditional gender norms allows these parents to maintain their authority over the younger generation. More importantly, their adherence to a traditional family dynamic reinforces the children's responsibilities to care for their parents in their old age (see Pham 1999: 181–228). Mothers and fathers therefore try to build up an image of the traditional family in educating and bringing up their children. They emphasize the father's role as the pillar of the home and the father's authority over the mother.

Children

Children's perceptions on gender roles and relations are influenced by both parents' attempts to educate children according to the traditional gender norms and by their participation in a family dynamic in which fathers take responsibility for caregiving while mothers serve as breadwinners. One-third of the children report that their mother, not the father, is the pillar of the home because she earns the money. Yet one-third claim that fathers and mothers share the same position and hold equal amounts of power in the family as they negotiate when making decisions. Two-thirds of the children claim that their father is the pillar of the home and the decision maker.

Villagers

The local villagers seem relaxed about the new gender division of labor. However, this flexible approach does not extend to their attitude toward gender relations. They underline the importance of the Confucian gender hierarchy in the family, in which women are subservient to men, even when they play breadwinning roles. Without this hierarchy, family order and harmony is lost.

Conclusion

For many families in rural areas of Vietnam, women's migration provides a new way of making a living. Yet it also pushes families into a new way of organizing domestic life: fathers and children stay behind in the village, while their wives and mothers seek paid jobs in the city. This chapter explores the lived experiences of stay-at-home fathers through everyday interactions with their migrant wives around childcare, housework, and gender relations. It examines the ways in which stay-at-home fathers work on their emotions that arise in relation to the migration of their wives. It also examines the implications of women's migration for gender inequalities.

The findings show that fathers view stay-at-home work as a matter of economic necessity. Nonetheless, they greatly involve themselves in domestic tasks and childcare. In the absence of their migrant wives, stay-at-home fathers become carers for their families. The fathers both undo and do gender by taking on these caregiving roles. Most of the fathers value childcare and housework and consider their assumption of these tasks quite ordinary. Others put their children's interests above their masculine pride to degender their caretaking role. Yet some fathers consider this changing role a temporary arrangement and hope to return this role to their wives when the latter eventually return home. In Miller's (2011) words, "They fall back into their gender." At the interactional level, the fact that migrant mothers still maintain their caregiving roles has an ambivalent impact on fathers undoing gender. On the one hand, it supports the mothers and helps reduce gender inequalities. If the mothers neglect their caregiving roles, the fathers may oppose the mothers' migration, returning both to their traditional gender roles. On the other hand, it weakens fathers undoing gender because it permits men to become involved, however minimally, in performing domestic tasks.

Many stay-at-home men feel that their roles as household heads are threatened as their wives take on breadwinning roles. They also fear that their children see them as "soft" and less powerful than the mothers in family matters. Therefore, these stay-at-home fathers struggle to maintain their position as the pillar of the home—doing gender. They attempt to contribute and control some level of financial resources through farming and seasonal sideline production. They emphasize their contribution in their wives' migration. Some even resume their breadwinning roles and prevent their wives from migrating. By doing so, they resist what they see as their wives' challenge to their authority. Nevertheless, the fathers are pushed into undoing gender because they experience a loss of power, though their wives try to make them feel like they have maintained their image of the status quo—the pillar of the home. Through these doing and undoing gender practices, stay-at-home fathers work on their emotions associated with their wives' migration practices.

This chapter documents that structural changes have pushed men into stay-at-home fatherhood as women take responsibility for earning money through migration. In response to women's labor migration, normative gender norms and behaviors are refuted in some ways, but persist in others. Gender inequalities are being reduced, but this transformation is uneven, gradual, and tense.

Acknowledgments

This chapter adapted some of the contents of my 2012 article, "'Doing Family': Female Migrants and Family Transition in Rural Vietnam," co-authored with Jytte Agergaard and published in *Asian Population Studies* 8, no. 1: 103–19.

Notes

1. Author calculated from General Statistics Office (2010).
2. Focus group interviews, 2008.
3. Besides residential rights, permanent household registration is related to many other essential citizens' rights, such as access to housing, education, employment, and healthcare.
4. Forty out of 256 households in Phu Khe, and eighty-one out of 464 households in Binh Ho.
5. On average, the migrant mothers sent home 1 million VND a month (approximately equal to $60 in 2008).
6. One father refused to be interviewed.
7. Agricultural expenses are covered by the mother's remittances and labor contributions in the transplanting and harvesting seasons.
8. When I revisited Hoang's family in 2010, Hoang migrated to Hanoi while his wife was in the village. The wife said they made an agreement that each of them migrate a couple of months out of the year. She was not satisfied with Hoang's care of their children (ages three and seven). For example, Hoang seldom allowed their 3-year-old daughter to play outside.
9. In fact, Quynh's wife had not moved for twelve months up to the time of the interview, and Quynh now migrates to Hanoi.

References

Aboim, Sofia. 2010. *Plural Masculinities: The Remaking of the Self in Private Life.* Surrey: Ashgate.
ActionAid. 2005. *A Summary Research Report on Migrant Workers in Vietnam.* Hanoi: Lucky House Graphic Ltd.

Ashwill, Mark. A., and Thai Ngoc Diep. 2005. *Vietnam Today: A Guide to a Nation at a Crossroads.* Yarmouth, ME; London: Nicholas Brealey Publishing.

Asian Development Bank. 2005. *Vietnam: Gender Situation Analysis.*

Asis, Maruja M. B. 2006. "Living with Migration: Experiences of Left-Behind Children in the Philippines." *Asian Population Studies* 2, no. 1: 45–67.

Asis, Maruja M. B., Shirlena Huang, and Brenda S. A. Yeoh. 2004. "When the Light of the Home is Abroad: Unskilled Female Migration and the Filipino Family." *Singapore Journal of Tropical Geography* 25, no. 2: 198–215.

Chantavich, Supang. 2001. *Female Labour Migration in South-East Asia: Change and Continuity.* Bangkok: Asian Research Centre for Migration.

Chesley, Noelle. 2011. "Stay-at-Home Fathers and Breadwinning Mothers: Gender, Couple Dynamics, and Social Change." *Gender & Society* 25, no. 5: 642–64.

Connell, R. W., and James W. Messerschmidt. 2005. "Hegemonic Masculinity: Rethinking the Concept." *Gender & Society* 19, no. 6: 829–59.

Dermott, Esther. 2008. *Intimate Fatherhood: A Sociological Analysis.* London; New York: Routledge.

Deutsch, Francine M. 2007. "Undoing Gender." *Gender & Society* 21, no. 1: 106–27.

Devasahayam, Theresa. W., Shirlena Huang, and Brenda S. A. Yeoh. 2004. "South East Asian Migrant Women: Navigating Borders, Negotiating Scales." *Singapore Journal of Tropical Geography* 25, no. 2: 135–40.

Doucet, Andrea, and Laura Merla. 2007. "Stay-at-Home Fathering." *Community, Work & Family* 10, no. 4: 455–73.

Elmhirst, Rebecca. 2007. "Tigers and Gangsters: Masculinities and Feminised Migration in Indonesia." *Population, Space and Place* 13, no. 2: 225–38.

Fan, Cindy C. 2003. "Rural-Urban Migration and Gender Division of Labor in Transitional China." *International Journal of Urban and Regional Research* 27, no. 1: 24–47.

Francis, Elizabeth. 2002. "Gender, Migration and Multiple Livelihoods: Cases from Eastern and Southern Africa." *Journal of Development Studies* 38, no. 5: 167–90.

Gatrell, Caroline. 2007. "Whose Child is it Anyway? The Negotiation of Paternal Entitlements within Marriage." *Sociological Review* 55, no. 2: 352–72.

Griswold, Robert E. 1993. *Fatherhood in America: A History.* New York: Basic Books.

General Statistics Office (GSO). 2006. *The 2004 Vietnam Migration Survey: The Quality of Life of Migrants in Vietnam.* Hanoi: Statistical Publishing House.

———. 2010. *The 2009 Vietnam Population and Housing Census: Major Findings.* Hanoi: Statistical Publishing House.

Ha, Thi Phuong T., and Ha Ngoc Quang. 2001. *Lao dong nu di cu tu do: Nong thon- Thanh thi* [Female labor migration: Rural-urban]. Hanoi: Women's Publishing House.

Harris, Jack D. 1998. "Incorporating Men into Vietnamese Gender Studies." *Vietnam Social Science* 5, no. 67: 52–65.

Hoang, Lan A., and Brenda S. A. Yeoh. 2011. "Breadwinning Wives and 'Left-Behind' Husbands: Men and Masculinities in the Vietnamese Transnational Family." *Gender & Society* 25, no. 6: 717–39.

Hochschild, Arlie R. 1979. "Emotion Work, Feeling Rules, and Social Structure." *The American Journal of Sociology* 85, no. 3: 551–75.

Hondagneu-Sotelo, Pierrette, and Ernestine Avila. 1997. "'I'm Here but I'm There': The Meanings of Latina Transnational Motherhood." *Gender & Society* 11, no. 5: 548–71.

Huou, Tran Dinh. 1991. "Traditional Families in Vietnam and the Influences of Confucianism." In *Sociological Studies on the Vietnamese Family*, ed. Rita Liljestrom and Tuong Lai. Hanoi: Social Sciences Publishing House.

Hy, Van Luong. 2003. "Gender Relations: Ideologies, Kinship Practices, and Political Economy." In *Postwar Vietnam: Dynamics of a Transforming Society*, ed. Luong Van Hy. Lanham, MD: Rowman and Littlefield.

Jensen, Rolf, and Donald M. Peppard. 2003. "Hanoi's Informal Sector and the Vietnamese Economy: A Case Study of Roving Street Vendors." *Journal of Asian and African Studies* 38, no. 1: 74–81.

Johansson, Thomas, and Roger Klinth. 2008. "Caring Fathers: The Ideology of Gender Equality and Masculine Positions." *Men and Masculinities* 11, no. 1: 42–62.

Knodel, John, Vu Manh Loi, Rukmalie Jayakody, and Vu Huy Tuan. 2005. "Gender Roles in the Family: Change and Stability in Vietnam." *Asian Population Studies* 1, no. 1: 69–92.

Marsiglio, William, and Mark Cohan. 2000. "Contextualizing Father Involvement and Paternal Influence: Sociological and Qualitative Themes." *Marriage & Family Review* 29, no. 2–3: 75–95.

Miller, Tina. 2010. *Making Sense of Fatherhood: Gender, Caring and Work.* Cambridge: Cambridge University Press.

———. 2011. "Falling Back into Gender? Men's Narratives and Practices around First-time Fatherhood." *Sociology* 45, no. 6: 1094–1109.

Nguyen, Liem, Brenda S. A. Yeoh, and Mika Toyota. 2006. "Migration and the Well-Being of the 'Left-behind' in Asia: Key Themes and Trends." *Asian Population Studies* 2, no. 1: 37–44.

Parreñas, Rhacel Salazar. 2005. *Children of Global Migration: Transnational Families and Gendered Woes.* Stanford, CA: Stanford University Press.

Pham, Van B. 1999. *The Vietnamese Family in Change: The Case of the Red River Delta.* Surrey: Curzon Press.

Pinnawala, Mallika. 2008. "Engaging Trans-Local Management of Households: Aspects of Livelihood and Gender Transformations among Sri Lankan Women Migrant Workers." *Gender, Technology and Development* 12, no. 3: 439–59.

Resurreccion, Bernadette P., and Ha Thi Van Khanh. 2007. "Able to Come and Go: Reproducing Gender in Female Rural-Urban Migration in the Red River Delta." *Population Space and Place* 13, no. 3: 211–24.

Risman, Barbara J. 2009. "From Doing to Undoing: Gender As We Know It." *Gender & Society* 23, no. 1: 81–84.

Silva, Indralal W. 2005. "Family Transition in South Asia: Provision of Social Services and Social Protection." *Asia-Pacific Population Journal* 20, no. 2: 13–46.

Tran, Thi Que. 1996. "Gender Issues in Vietnam's Development." In *Vietnam in a Changing World*, ed. Carolyn Gates, Irene Noerlund, and Vu Cao Dam Vu. Surrey: Curzon Press.

Truong, Si Anh, Patrick Gubry, Vu Thi Hong, and Jerrold Huguet. 1996. "Migration and Employment in Ho Chi Minh City." *Asia Pacific Population Journal* 11, no. 2: 3–22.

United Nations Economic and Social Commission for Asia and the Pacific. 2010. "Key Trends and Challenges on International Migration and Development in Asia and the Pacific." Expert Group Meeting on International Migration and Development in Asia and the Pacific. Population Division, Department of Economic and Social Affairs.

Vuori, Jaana. 2009. "Men's Choices and Masculine Duties: Fathers in Expert Discussions." *Men and Masculinities* 12, no. 1: 45–72.

Wall, Glenda, and Stephanie Arnold. 2007. "How Involved is Involved Fathering? An Exploration of the Contemporary Culture of Fatherhood." *Gender & Society* 21, no. 4: 508–27.

West, Candace, and Don H. Zimmerman. 1987. "Doing Gender." *Gender & Society* 1, no. 2: 125–51.

West, Candace, and Don H. Zimmerman. 2009. "Accounting for Doing Gender." *Gender & Society* 23, no. 1: 112–22.

West, Candace, and Sarah Fenstermaker. 2002. "Power, Inequality and the Accomplishment of Gender: An Ethnomethodological View." In *Doing Gender, Doing Difference: Inequality, Power, and Institutional Change*, ed. Sarah Fenstermaker and Candace West. New York: Routledge.

Williams, Stephen. 2008. "What is Fatherhood? Searching for the Reflexive Father." *Sociology* 42, no. 3: 487–502.

Yamanaka, Keiko, and Nicola Piper. 2005. "Feminized Migration in East and Southeast Asia: Policies, Actions and Empowerment." Occasional Paper 11. United Nations Research Institute for Social Development, Geneva.

Chapter 6

ON FATHERHOOD IN A CONFLICT ZONE

GAZA FATHERS AND THEIR
CHILDREN'S CANCER TREATMENTS

*Daphna Birenbaum-Carmeli, Yana Diamand,
and Maram Abu Yaman*

Introduction

The Israeli-Palestinian conflict has been a focus of international tension for decades. Men living in the region are often caught in dire circumstances that challenge various aspects of their masculinity, including fatherhood. In this chapter we probe the consequences of the international constellation on notions and practices of fatherhood. At the center of our attention are Gaza fathers who attend to their children as the children undergo cancer treatment in Israel. The situation is exceptional: Due to the movement restrictions that Israel imposes on Gaza residents and the uncertainty that accompanies every border crossing to Israel, patients from Gaza remain hospitalized in Israel for the entire duration of the treatment, up to a year and sometimes longer. Moreover, for the same reason, in most cases, just one attendant is allowed to accompany each patient. Often, the child's mother stays home with the other children, while the father travels to Israel with the child. Caught in the midst of this international conflict, these fathers and children are forced to struggle with a life-threatening disease, isolated from their kin, in the country that is greatly responsible for their very need to seek treatment abroad and for the restrictions that prevent them from going back home on treatment breaks. Based on participant observations in two pediatric oncology wards in hospitals in Israel, we describe how Gaza fathers become immersed in childcare, showering their sick children with warmth and affection. The chapter ends by articulating the notion of expressive fatherhood, as it is manifested in regular overt expressions of affection toward one's child under these traumatic political and personal circumstances.

Contemporary Fatherhood and Cancer

Concepts of fatherhood are dynamic and contextual. Throughout the past decades, as part of broader economic and political changes, family formations have undergone profound and diverse transformations. In industrialized countries, fatherhood has come to the fore in a variety of new configurations (Beck and Beck-Gernsheim 1995). Probably related to the proliferation of dual-career and single-parent families, as well as the rise in unemployment, breadwinning-centered fatherhood has given way to a more blurred notion of the new father, who is more involved in childrearing, both logistically and emotionally (Dermott 2008; Lamb 1997; La Rossa 1997; Summers et al. 1999). However, beyond the declared acceptance of these new concepts, the reality of childrearing remains rather traditional even among Western middle classes (Dermott 2008; Fineman 1995; Grzywacz and Marks 2002). In most families, childcare remains primarily the mother's responsibility with the father perceived as her "assistant" (Warin et al. 1999).

In Israel, despite erosion in the traditional family and rising women's participation in the labor market, the gender-role division has remained fairly conservative (Fogiel-Bijaoui 1999). Fathers, both Jewish and Arab, normally spend less time with their children than mothers and have a smaller impact on the child's well-being (Slone 2012).

A child's cancer destabilizes the whole family. Studies conducted in Western countries show that parents assume much of the treatment responsibility, while also attending to the child's education and well-being, as well as those of other family members. Often, one parent quits work in order to be with the sick child while the other attends to the remaining family tasks (Brody and Simmons 2007; Clark 2005).

Commonly, fathers are perceived as secondary carers (Hill et al. 2009). This perception reverberates also in the scarcity of research on fathers of seriously sick children (Ware and Raval 2007). The few existing studies explore middle-class families in industrialized countries and hardly account for the families' contexts. These studies convey a mixed picture. The lives of these fathers were deeply affected by the threat to the child's life (Goble 2004). Some fathers lost their jobs. Some worked longer hours to make up for the mother's lost income. Fathers lamented the loss of normal daily life and the injury to their role as family protectors; some fathers invested great effort in retaining a resilient façade vis-à-vis their wives and children. Men reported bursts of crying, distress, powerlessness, alienation, isolation, lack of social support, and reduced confidence regarding their capabilities as carers and breadwinners (Hovey 2003; Katz and Krulik 1999; Ware and Raval 2007). Some fathers became the primary carers of the family's healthy children (Goble 2004; Jones and Neil-Urban 2003).

Several studies found a fairly traditional role division between sick children's parents, with some fathers sustaining a greater distance from the disease (Clark-Steffen 1997) and medical care, seeking refuge in their work and in financial management (Chesler and Parry 2001). Some fathers expressed a fear of staying by themselves with the sick child (Goble 2004; Jones and Neil-Urban 2003) or of communicating about the disease. Some regretted the growing distance from relatives and friends and the financial difficulties. Fathers also faced greater difficulties in encounters with the healthcare system, which approached mothers as the primary carers and better suited their daily schedules (Chesler and Parry 2001; Clark 2005; Hill et al. 2009; Ware and Raval 2007). Some fathers, however, probably due to the more general change in gender roles (Reaya et al. 1998), described a more expressive, highly emotional involvement in all aspects of the child's life and treatment (Clark 2005). They appreciated the intensifying family support and tried to spend more time with their families (Brody and Simmons 2007; Hill et al. 2009). Many cherished the greater closeness with their wives (Ware and Raval 2007).

Some fathers mentioned the dialogue with parents of children in similar conditions and the help of social workers and support groups as critical to their coping. Other coping strategies included acquiring knowledge about the child's disease, inspiriting the child throughout the treatments, and helping others (Hill et al. 2009; Lavee 2005; Ware and Raval 2007). Wishing to regain control over their lives, some fathers took occasional breaks from the illness setting (Hill et al. 2009).

Little is known about the experiences of Gaza fathers while caring for a child with cancer. In order to elucidate these experiences and contextualize them, we briefly outline key features of the life and health situation in Gaza after describing our methodology below.

Methodology

The chapter is based on participant observation carried out in two major hospitals, both located in large urban settings in Israel. The specific fields of observation were each hospital's pediatric oncology ward, where children from Israel, the Palestinian Authority (PA), as well as medical tourists, primarily from Eastern Europe, were being treated. Fieldwork was conducted for twelve months in one center and for eight months in the other, during the years 2011 and 2012. The material was gathered primarily by means of observation, as well as talks with the Gaza fathers who stayed in the ward as their children's attendants. One researcher speaks Arabic and could communicate fluently with the fathers. The other speaks no Arabic and was therefore more restricted in her ability to converse. However, due to the lengthy stay in the hospital, some channels of verbal—as well as non-verbal—communication evolved, allowing for significant communication. Each researcher took preliminary notes soon after observations, to be later transcribed into Hebrew and Arabic, where applicable. The talks unfolded mostly at quieter hours of the day, during more relaxed phases of the treatment, and were incidental and informal. Here, too, notes were taken shortly after the talks and were later fully transcribed. Owing to the personal and political sensitivity of the subject, various identifying details were omitted. All names have been changed.

Masculinity and Fatherhood in Palestinian Families

Masculinity is performative and contextual. Broadly speaking, in the Palestinian culture, men are perceived as the source of prestige and dignity (Massad 1995). However, decades of international conflict and economic distress affected many Gaza men (as well as many other Middle Eastern men; see Inhorn 2012: 305–7), and brought masculinity to a crisis. One impact of this crisis is the conflation of gender and national boundaries (Kanaaneh 2005; Monterescu 2007). Resistance to the occupation has become an important constituent of Palestinian masculine identity, which manifests, among other features, in the prevalence of overmanning, namely, an overacting of traditional masculine roles (Nashif 2008). In this context, enduring severe physical and mental pain comprises a ritualistic response to the crisis of male productivity, and individual bodies are seen as re-enacting the collective national body (Peteet 1994). Confrontations with Israeli soldiers are constituted as rites of resistance and help transform humiliation into empowerment (Massad 1995; Sa'ar and Yahya-Younis 2008).

A different focus of Palestinian masculinity is that of the family provider. The numerous men who have traveled abroad, often to the Gulf region, to seek livelihood, have not taken part in the phys-ical national struggle. For them, providing for one's family has be-come key to masculine Palestinian agency, so much so that young men compete for masculinity by providing for their family relatives. The national agent is thus also a provider and a nurturer (Herzog and Yahia-Younis 2007; Mar'i and Mar'i 1991; Massad 1995). Even-tually, a man's readiness to sacrifice his life, as well as his money, for the national cause is another aspect of Palestinian masculinity. Nationalism and masculinity are thus inseparable in contemporary Palestinian discourse (Hudson 1994; Massad 1995).

The Field: Masculinity, Fatherhood, and Families in the Gaza Strip

The Gaza Strip is home to more than 1.6 million Palestinians. Since its occupation by Israel in 1967, Gaza and its local population have depended on Israel in all major spheres of life, including economy and health. The area, which is among the densest in the world with 3,881 residents per square kilometer versus 347 in Israel (Central Bureau of Statistics 2012; United Nations Relief and Works Agency 2009), is poverty stricken: 32 percent are unemployed (Central Bu-reau of Statistics 2011). Eighty percent of the local households live in poverty and two-thirds in deep poverty (World Health Organization 2008). As such, malnutrition prevails: 59 percent of Gaza children consume less than 80 percent of the recommended daily intake of calories (United Nations Office for the Coordination of Humanitarian Affairs 2009) and 45 percent are chronically undernourished (Bendel 2005). Over half the toddlers aged six months to thirty-six months suffer from anemia (2005). Four out of five Gaza residents depend on humanitarian aid (Amnesty International 2010). The long eco-nomic crisis has transformed families from productive and reproduc-tive units to almost exclusively reproductive units (Abdo-Zubi 1987).

Gaza residents form families early in life. Men marry between the ages of 22 and 24 and women between the ages of 18 and 20 (Pedersen et al. 2001: 108). They form large families with nearly five children on average. This seemingly high figure represents, however, a steep decline from 7.78 in 1994, (2001: 98) to 5.19 in 2008 and 4.74 in 2011 (CIA World Factbook 2011). The change, which has taken place despite the growing political sensitivity to family planning (Bosmans et al. 2008), may be attributed to the severe and constant economic and political hardship that Gaza women and men face.

Gaza families have undergone profound changes in the last decades. Until the mid 1990s, nearly half of Gaza workers were employed in Israel (Dhillon and Sayre 2009; Farsakh 2002). In the absence of working-age men, older women dominated the extended households, thereby somewhat loosening the patriarchal order. Gently, while maintaining everyday normalcy, Gaza women, especially the younger ones, also negotiated the local patriarchy (Richter-Devroe 2011). Despite some changes, the ideology and image of patriarchy remained, nonetheless, dominant. Indeed, in some parts of the Palestinian society, the control of women became not only a response to masculine insecurity but a symbol of cultural continuity (Herzog and Yahia-Younis 2007; Mar'i and Mar'i 1991; Monterescu 2007).

The closure of Gaza borders in 2001 effectively terminated Gazans' employment in Israel (Miaari and Sauer 2011). This Israeli policy and the subsequent siege (from 2007 on) severed men's ability to earn a living and forced the majority of Gaza families to rely on welfare. Here again, it is women, most of whom are housewives, who obtain the required coupons. Many men, attempting to avoid being seen as useless, prefer to leave home during the day even when they do not work (Muhanna 2010).

This general challenge to masculinity has been found to underlie two interactive effects, pushing some men toward violence while rendering others sympathetic and cooperative. Among the latter, less educated men, especially those living in nuclear households, believe that providing for the family is their gendered obligation. Young women (aged twenty to thirty-nine), again, primarily those in nuclear households, attribute their husbands' growing cooperation and tolerance to the husbands' unemployment, as well as to their own unshaken respect for the husbands' manliness, even while they earn no income (Muhanna 2010). The men also remain the primary disciplinary parent and are seen by youths as the family's main decision makers and providers (Fronk et al. 1999). Probably also in order to restabilize their gendered image, cooperative men, as well as their wives, tend to emphasize the situational, rather than personality, component of their current enactment of masculinity (Muhanna 2010).

The closure, unemployment, and scarcity of interaction with the outside world coincide with the rise of Islamist power to shift youths toward conservatism and patriarchy (Muhanna and Qleibo 2009). Assuming traditionally female childrearing tasks might be highly delicate under these circumstances, as it might further threaten one's masculinity. Our hospital ethnography reveals an opposite trend. We introduce the fatherhood ethnography with a brief contextual outline.

Health and Healthcare in the Gaza Strip

As of the Oslo Accords of 1994, healthcare in the Gaza Strip falls under the responsibility of the PA. However, severe financial and political restrictions resulted in a deficient system unable to offer many common procedures including life-saving ones (Physicians for Human Rights 2010c). Since Hamas's election victory in 2007 and Israel's subsequent blockade of the Gaza Strip, the shortage in medical equipment further intensified. Limitations on fuel imports interrupt the work of clinics and many narrow their services to life-saving procedures (United Nations Office for the Coordination of Humanitarian Affairs 2009). Cancer treatment has long been practically unavailable, if only for the prohibition on the admission of any radioactive materials into the Gaza Strip (Yaron 2008). In 2009, Operation Cast Lead inflicted additional devastation on Gaza's healthcare system, destroying medical centers, clinics, and ambulances. Vital medical equipment and medication became unavailable (World Health Organization 2010a) and foreign experts were not allowed into the region (Human Rights Organizations 2009). Some 1,400 Palestinians, among them 341 children, were killed in the campaign; 1,872 children were injured (United Nations Human Rights Council 2009).

The Israeli siege continued after the attack, impeding the removal of harmful debris and repair of damaged clinics (United Nations Office for the Coordination of Humanitarian Affairs 2009; 2010). Certain relaxation of the restrictions after the 2008–2009 Israeli assault in Gaza has made but small improvement (Physicians for Human Rights 2010a; 2011a; World Health Organization 2010b). Children are among the main sufferers of the healthcare deficiency, the ecological hazards (United Nations Office for the Coordination of Humanitarian Affairs 2009), and the nutritional insecurity (United Nations Office for the Coordination of Humanitarian Affairs 2009; Physicians for Human Rights 2011a; 2011b). Infant mortality in Gaza is nearly six times that of Jewish Israeli babies (17.2 versus 2.9 respectively) (Central Bureau of Statistics 2011; CIA World Factbook 2011). Under these circumstances, Gaza dependency on external medical assistance is acute.

Negotiating Treatment Eligibility

Since the 2007 blockade, patients referred to clinics in Israel—or in East Jerusalem, the West Bank, or Jordan, who must all cross Israel's border checkpoint—have been the only Gaza residents that may apply for an exit permit. The application procedure is riddled with obstacles: a Gaza hospital submits a referral from a local doctor to the Palestinian Ministry of Health in the West Bank. The latter, if it approved the application, would fund the treatment and issue passports for the patient and one accompanying person. This phase takes several weeks owing to the tensions between the PA in the West Bank and the Hamas authorities in Gaza.

Furthermore, the patient and his or her attendant must undergo interrogation by Israel's General Security Service (GSS). The procedure may include harsh inquiries, demands for collaboration, and even arrest (Physicians for Human Rights 2010c). Moreover, the interrogation is often scheduled for a date after the medical appointment, thus imposing additional treatment delay. Between January and August 2009, over one-third of the applicants (1,310 out of 3,758) missed their appointments. From 2008 to 2009, eighty-four Gaza applicants died while awaiting GSS approval (World Health Organization 2010a). Between 2006 and 2008, the rate of rejections rose from 10 to 44 percent (Physicians for Human Rights 2010c). Rejected patients can appeal to an Israeli court via Physicians for Human Rights (PHR) (Yaron 2008). If rejected again, they are offered no alternative.

Gaza Children and Fathers in Israeli Hospitals: An Overview

The treatment of Gaza children is especially expensive. Due to the movement restrictions that Israel imposes on Gaza residents (High

Court of Justice 2007; Human Rights Organizations 2009; Physicians for Human Rights 2010a; 2010b), Israeli doctors keep Gaza children hospitalized for the entire duration of the treatments, thereby pushing up their costs. Funding for the treatment is provided primarily by the PA. As it is deducted by Israel directly from tax transfers, this payment is immune to the PA's financial difficulties and is delivered to the hospitals much sooner than the ordinary payment for Israeli patients. The tariff is also higher than that which is paid by Israeli healthcare providers. Small sums are contributed by the Peres Center for Peace and Israel's PHR chapter, both of which obtain their funds from foreign, mostly European, bodies. The treatment of Gaza children thus does not incur any expense to Israeli taxpayers. Rather, it is a source of income for Israeli hospitals that receive tens of millions of dollars (*Hamakor* 2012). When the treatment includes bone marrow transplantation, a common treatment for childhood cancer, the family needs to contribute approximately $10,000, a task that often contributes to delays in treatment onset. The PA does not cover use of the international donor repository. Another source of postponement of bone marrow transplantation is the approval of entry of all potential donors for tissue typing in the Israeli hospital. In some cases, the donor, too, stays in the hospital for months because of the movement restrictions. It is noteworthy that in the Israeli media, and in various channels that address international audiences, the treatment of Gaza children is praised as an act of benevolence toward the enemy's children on the part of Israel (Birenbaum-Carmeli forthcoming).

Unofficially, Israeli physicians estimate that the chance of a Palestinian child to recover from cancer is some 20 percent lower than that of his or her Israeli counterparts. This gap is attributed to the deficient preliminary workup in Gaza, the delays in treatment onset, the restriction of the donor search to the child's family, and eventually the difficulties in long-term follow-up.

Once in Israel, Gaza children and their attendants are confined by their permit to the hospital premises. This restriction renders life in the ward especially crucial. Commonly, there are two to four Gaza fathers in the ward, depending on the specific agreements with each hospital that affect the number of Gaza patients at a given moment. By and large, the staff try to make the children and their attendants as comfortable as possible. They provide small services and supplies, accommodate various life routines, like praying or playing Arabic music, or playfully mock the situation with the help of (Jewish) clowns. Some staff members, especially nurses and social workers, occasionally develop highly personal relations with particular children and fathers. They would enter these children's rooms more often, initiate long personal talks with the children and their fathers, and provide various "extra" services, such as making inquiries on their behalf or bringing small gifts. The staff members save photographs of the children on their cellular phones and decorate their lockers with the children's drawings. On rare occasions, they take the Gaza children on an organized brief visit outside the hospital, to the zoo or the seaside. An incidental case, when two Jewish patients left the playroom because two Gaza patients refused to lower the music they were listening to, illustrates the confidence that some Gaza children were feeling, at least in one hospital, at least some of the time. One of the studied hospitals, which serves the majority of Israel's Palestinian citizens, has a mosque. It also assigns a mediator to every medical tourist family, including Gaza families. Medically, the children receive the same treatment as that which is provided to Israeli patients.

Structural hardships, however, abound. Gaza children are disconnected from their families, friends, and school settings at a stressful time, isolated in unfamiliar surroundings, toward which they are deeply ambivalent. Most children and their attendants speak only Arabic, a language that few Israeli doctors, especially in the Tel Aviv area, can speak. Among nurses, the percentage of Arabic speakers is higher but the numbers are still small. A few pediatric wards employ an Arabic-speaking social worker, teacher, or therapist. However, they, too, are present for a few hours only and in many cases, their positions are irregular and unstable. The medical staff would therefore have to rely occasionally on a Palestinian attendant or worker to deliver even substantial updates to the family.

If the child's treatment includes bone marrow transplantation, the relatives who arrive for tissue typing are allowed to stay in Israel for one day only, thus exacerbating the anxiety that accompanies the rare reunion. Tensions of national political character also arise. Beyond these daily hardships lies the attendants' great loneliness throughout this tortured period. Normally, it is only when a child is extremely ill that both parents are allowed to exit the Gaza Strip in order to stay with her or him for some time.

The hospitalization is also an encounter with prosperity. Coming from a reality of food insecurity and interrupted electric supply, the sick child and the attendant find themselves in a highly equipped hospital, surrounded by advanced medical and personal technology, opulent playrooms, manicured flowerbeds, artwork in the corridors, and bustling shopping centers. Gaza patients and attendants are by and large outside this circle of prosperity. The wards' rooms have computers and televisions, but the child and the attendant may have to share one pair of earphones meaning they cannot listen simultaneously. Most room keyboards have no Arabic letters. Skype, which is the main channel of communication for many Gaza families, can be downloaded only to specific room computers, while the playroom computers that do have Skype often have no earphones and speakers. Moreover, power cuts in Gaza result in congestion in times of electricity supply, and in competition among families over Skype access. Computers and computer access are therefore a source of recurrent tension among Gaza families.

Between treatments, the child and attendant move to the hospital motel. In some hospitals the motel is a pleasant facility. At least in one, however, it is an old hospital wing, where patients and their attendants—at times, forty people—crowd together, having to share two lavatories, exposing the treated children to infection. When the political situation is relatively calm, some children and their attendants do return to Gaza for a break. While the situations of Gaza fathers and children obviously vary, as do the two hospital wards that are scrutinized here, these structural features apply quite broadly.

Fathers as Carers: Ethnographic Portraits

Some Gaza parents cannot leave home for the long treatment period. Their children are then accompanied by more distant, sometimes older, relatives. Other children are accompanied by their mothers. However, many Gaza parents prefer the mother to stay in the private home sphere. This gender division and the high unemployment among Gaza men underlie the prevalence of fathers among the children's attendants.

Beyond the personal anguish of caring for a severely sick child, these fathers face an especially distressful structural situation. Many Gaza fathers have hitherto met Israelis primarily as oppressors. Trusting the enemy with the life of one's child is probably an extremely difficult and possibly disorienting experience. The prolonged stay and the physical confinement to the hospital, let alone various daily incidents, comprise a continuous reminder of the international conflict and Gaza's situation within it. Second, Gaza fathers endure ongoing material inferiority vis-à-vis their Israeli counterparts. They cannot pamper their sick children with equal material comfort; they cannot bring them personal items from home on a daily basis. In most cases, they do not speak the hospital's language and are therefore less informed and agential. Ultimately, being unable to fully assume the carer role, Gaza fathers are more prone to exhaustion in the course of the treatment. Bearing in mind these difficulties, we turn to the ethnography of Gaza fathers in two Israeli hospitals.

Information Seeking

Many Gaza fathers had very partial command of the Hebrew language. In extreme cases, the linguistic limitation restricted fathers' abilities to help their children. For instance, Rafiq, ten years old, had been accompanied by his grandmother for the first months of his treatment. By the time his father replaced her, Rafiq's Hebrew was much better than his father's. He therefore went to the playroom on his own and played by himself. He would even arrive unaccompanied at the nurses' station, in the evening, to have his blood pressure taken. In fact, owing to his superior linguistic skills, Rafiq often interacted with the professional staff without his father's mediation. Struggling with such linguistic deficiency, many Gaza fathers had to invest much greater effort in order to obtain disease-related information. Professionals' explanations normally required translator's mediation. Internet access was, as mentioned, scarce in the ward and to some fathers alien. Printed material was abundant in Hebrew—describing chemotherapy and other medical treatments and procedures, nutrition, patients' rights, etc.—but much scarcer in Arabic. On the day we looked for material, we found just one leaflet in Arabic, dealing with radiotherapy. Several additional leaflets in Arabic could be obtained from the social worker, but they had to be requested. Despite these limitations, the fathers did try to fill this gap and acquire information. They asked regularly about blood test results, particularly about the crucial and more familiar parameters (hemoglobin, neutrophils, platelets). Though they did not inquire about details of the chemotherapy, they always asked how many IV bags the child would receive. Fathers also sought doctors' explanations about the child's condition and in some cases made their own suggestions for possible causes of changes in his or her condition. A few fathers, especially those who knew some Hebrew from the times they had worked in Israel, were more knowledgeable about the disease. These fathers also negotiated, if delicately, some aspects of the treatment.

Negotiating for one's child was extremely sensitive for Gaza fathers. Beyond the normal dependence on the professionals who treat a severely sick child, Gaza fathers were especially exposed given their political, economic, and linguistic disadvantage. Negotiations were therefore scarce and subtle. Manal's father called the nurse to change his daughter's port sticker. As she was working, he mentioned gently that the other nurse had not disinfected the area properly and pointed at Manal's infected skin. Yaser's father refused to take his son to the crowded motel after bone marrow transplantation, for fear of infection. He approached an (Arabic-speaking) nurse and requested her to tell the doctor that he would not transfer the boy due to the risks that awaited him in the motel. Rima's father requested that his critically ill, 13-year-old daughter be given a platelets transfusion. Though the doctors did not think that such a transfusion was needed, they fulfilled his request. The father also negotiated Rima's psychological well-being. When the grandmother of the other child in the room was telling her son on the phone, loudly, that several children in the ward were dying, Rima's father requested to separate the children to different rooms. This request was also ratified.

While some Gaza fathers were knowledgeable and assertive, as illustrated, such incidents were rare. The scarcity may stem from ethnographic shortcoming. However, even if this was partly the case, the difficulty of spotting such negotiations and their low profile might suggest the fathers' caution in the Israeli system. Indeed, from some fathers' descriptions one learns that they had been more assertive and demanding in Gaza. At least one father said explicitly that he kept quiet in the Israeli hospital as "all I want is that they treat my son well."

More routinely, however, Gaza fathers spent most of their time attending to their children's instrumental needs, feeding and showering them and tidying up the rooms, which had to be immaculate due to the child's immune suppression. This applied also to fathers of very young children. Mussa's father bathed his 7-month-old baby daily, changed his diapers pedantically, and fed him patiently. Manal's father, who stayed with his 2-year-old daughter in the hospital for five months, gently bottle-fed her and then supplemented her meal, showered and dressed her, changed her linen, and cleaned her room. A developmentally disabled daughter was equally well attended: the father of Wafaa, fourteen years old, monitored her eating and reminded her to go to the washroom. When she wet her bed at night, he would change the linen and help her wash, ensuring that she was always neat. Nadia's father changed diapers and washed his 18-year-old daughter, saying he pushed aside the embarrassment and would do anything for fear of losing her. Yasser's father has been confined to the Israeli hospital for over sixteen months of his son's operation and bone marrow transplantation. Throughout this period, he sustained the hospital's routine, dressed and showered Yasser, bought him food as he would not eat the hospital's meals, changed his bedding, and cleaned his room. He also gave Yasser his medications meticulously. Yasser would regularly leave the playroom to check where his father was. At one point, Yasser's father also looked after another boy whose grandmother returned to Gaza after she had suffered a stroke. Occasionally, a father would take part in medical procedures, like Adel's father who learned to handle his son's PICC line in order to operate it in Gaza for intravenous antibiotics.

However, Gaza men expanded their fatherhood beyond functional responsibility and paid much attention to the children's emotional well-being. When Adel, ten years old, had a fever, his father did not leave him for a moment and kept stroking him in bed for hours. The father of 7-month-old Mussa would call him "my sweetie," singing and playing with him as he was treating him. The father regularly took Moussa in his arms for strolls outside the ward. The baby grew extremely attached to his father and seemed unquiet when he lost sight of him.

Manal's father stayed for days in the room of his 2-year-old daughter, who was not allowed to exit, leaving for no more than a few minutes to smoke a cigarette. One day, when he wanted to take a nap, Manal started jumping on him in bed. The father looked happy to see her jumping; he got up right away the moment she said she wanted to paint, and started drawing with her.

Emotiveness took many forms. Rima's father was unemployed; the family was supported, however, by his brothers and wealthy mother-in-law and seemed quite comfortable. Every Friday, the father took Rima to the hospital mall and bought her cooked dishes and sweets from the food bazaar. Yasser's father could not afford such shopping. Even the food he had to buy for Yasser was a heavy burden for him. He also did not play with Yasser or read books to him. He did not even stay in the playroom most of the time. However, for over sixteen months, he watched television with him, stroked him and carefully ensured he was comfortable. Unlike Israeli parents, who take shifts in hospital stays, who interact with their children also by bringing them toys, food, and even friends from home, Yasser's father was his son's sole carer, confined to the hospital for over a year, unable to bring any extra-hospital objects of pleasure.

Continuities and Transformations

Several men described themselves as having been involved fathers already in Gaza. Manal's father described his wife as the family's breadwinner, whereas he, having been unemployed for years, looked after their daughters and practically raised them. Waffa's father had also been unemployed for years, following a work accident. As her mother found it hard to cope with Waffa's slow pace, the father had been her main carer also at home. Waffa's mother never came to the hospital, and all treatment-related discussions were held with the father alone. The father seemed strongly attached to Waffa, and his mood was directly affected by her condition. Rima's father had also been unemployed for years. He, too, was his daughter's main carer in Gaza, taking her to doctors and going out of his way to fulfill her wishes. At the same time, he was an authoritative father who ensured that his children were ready for school and "screened" their friends closely. Occasionally, he would sanction and even spank his children. Nadia's father was also in charge of her medical treatment in Gaza. It was he who suspected that the disease had relapsed, despite the doctor's optimism. It was he who made the critical treatment decisions and who talked with his daughter about the future.

For some fathers, however, the hospital period was transformative. Salwa's father performed all the daily tasks pedantically, but his manner with his 3-year-old daughter was rough. He exerted physical power when he showered her and treated her mouth wounds. When he gave her medication, he would close her nose and inject the drug into her mouth against her will. Feeling uncomfortable with the father's practices, the nurses started to show him—non-verbally, as none of them could speak Arabic—a gentler mode of treatment. The ward's social worker supported him, too, as he quickly endorsed a softer approach and changed his mode of conduct. Beyond his emerging gentleness, the father massaged Salwa's skin with lotion, folded her overlong pajama pants and wrapped her hairless head with a pink kerchief. The stronger Salwa grew, the calmer her father became. He started playing with her, tickled her, sang songs, and took her for strolls outside the ward. When Salwa cooperated with the medical staff, he encouraged her with compliments like "good girl." At this somewhat later stage in the treatment the nurses learned that the father had never participated in childcare at home. They noted that he became much more attached to Salwa during the hospitalization period.

Thirteen-year-old Rima was extremely weak, unable to get out of bed or stand on her feet. She suffered great pain with every movement. Due to her severe condition, both parents were allowed to stay with her. The mother attended to Rima during the day, and the father from the afternoon through the night. Rima preferred to take her shower at night. At first, her father helped her prepare and waited outside. Later, she needed help, and he would wash her up. The father told the nurse:

> When Rima was born, I used to work thirty-six-hour shifts. I returned home exhausted, dead, and she wouldn't stop crying. At first, I found a solution: the swing. Gradually, the swing lost effectiveness. One day, I was extremely tired and she kept screaming. I held her in my arms and threw her off to bed. I have never forgiven myself that day. Now, when she is sick, I have an opportunity to ask for her forgiveness. One day, on her way to the shower, she hugged me and said, "I love you, *ya baba.*" I said that I love her, too, and asked pardon. She said she had forgiven me everything. See, I see her suffering and I can't do anything. When we first found out about the disease, I couldn't part from her. Now, when the disease has relapsed I feel how difficult it is for her to cope again. ... I just pray to God that if he wants to take her, that he please does it without suffering.

Ultimately, some Gaza fathers had to make fatal decisions regarding their children's treatment. Nadia's father decided not to take her home to die but rather stay in the hospital and opt for the faint-chance treatment. Adel's father, at a critical point in his disease, conducted a series of talks with his son's doctors. He also discussed the prognosis over the telephone with his wife. Eventually, in light of these consultations, the father decided to bring Adel back to Gaza to die among his kin rather than in the alien hospital, far away from his mother and six siblings. One can but imagine the loneliness and fear that Adel's father had probably experienced while bearing witness to his son dying, in a hospital abroad, in an enemy country, whose language he could not speak, without a relative or friend to support him. Though he did not discuss these aspects of his final decision with the nurses, his loneliness might have well played a role in its shaping.

Conclusion

The Israeli-Palestinian conflict is the prime factor shaping the lives of Gaza fathers. Political limitations on work, severe restrictions on

movement, and lifelong poverty affect Gaza men—and women—
and their notions of parenthood. These circumstances also underlie the deficiencies of the local healthcare system that can offer no
treatment to seriously ill children, whose parents must seek therapy
abroad and stay away for months. Unemployment renders fathers
functionally more "dispensable" at home, and, as such, able to accompany the children through the long treatments in Israel.

At the social-cultural level, one might expect that fulfilling a traditionally maternal role—childcare—would add to the fathers' gendered distress. Our observations suggest the opposite. The attending
fathers appeared completely immersed in their caring role and fulfilled it wholeheartedly. Indeed, open expressions of affection toward
their children were salient in their behavior. In order to elucidate
this divergence from stereotypical patriarchal images, which are often associated with Gaza men, one needs to contextualize the scene
historically.

The fathers who now accompany their children to treatment
grew up in the 1980s, the years of the First Intifada. Whereas men
led the campaign, women also filled various active roles (Johnson
and Kuttab 2001). Many men, on their part, had worked in Israel
in those years, thus leaving the extended household to the control
of older women (Muhanna 2010). Though gender roles were somewhat destabilized, patriarchy persisted, owing largely to women's
support and the growing significance of gender hierarchy as a symbol of cultural continuity (Mar'i and Mar'i 1991; Monterescu 2006;
Herzog and Yahia-Younis 2007).

The mid 1990s, when most of the participating fathers matured
and married, saw the founding of the Palestinian Authority, followed by relative stability and nucleation of households. Women
were somewhat released from the domination of senior females
though they still depended on their husbands' earning, as they remained essentially confined to housework (Muhanna 2010).

This relative stability came to an end in 2000, with the outbreak
of the Second Intifada. The material and social basis of both masculinity and femininity was undermined: men lost their jobs, and
women were forced out of the home sphere to seek humanitarian
aid (Muhanna 2010). The numerous child casualties have brought
the notion of paternal protection to a crisis (Johnson and Kuttab
2001). The fragility of gender roles, and possibly also some of their
arbitrariness, was unveiled.

Throughout these decades, most Gaza men did not participate actively in the armed struggle (Johnson and Kuttab 2001), but rather

became work migrants. For these men, providing for one's family became their contribution to the national cause (Massad 1995: 477); as such, their service to the nation was never devalued (Muhanna 2010). Again, in contrast to media images of Islamist militancy and passive victimhood that dominate representations of the political subjectivity of Palestinian men (Junka 2006; Birenbaum-Carmeli forthcoming), contemporary Gaza fathers seem to have grown up and to be living today in a fairly mixed gender climate. The fathers' descriptions of their deep involvement in childrearing already in Gaza reinforce this contention.

Similar descriptions of Muslim men's expressiveness abound in Marcia C. Inhorn's (2012) depictions of spousal companionship in the Arab world. Spanning class, education, locality, and life circumstance, these Arab men show great affection toward their wives, also in the face of challenge, such as prolonged infertility. Under those circumstances, too, many men invest much money and time trying to ease and contain the hardship, defying family pressures and bending religious dictates. In both words and practice, men express empathy, tenderness, and long-term commitment toward their wives (Inhorn 2012: 91–121). Some men are equally open in expressing their emotions toward children (295–98).

In our study, we found similar expressiveness among Gaza fathers. Not only were the fathers devoted to their children, but they were absorbed in childcare. They were highly expressive emotionally, revealing their feelings and overtly expressing affection, even in public. Indeed, gestures of affection were integral to their ongoing interactions with their children. Despite their political, economic, and parental challenges, Gaza fathers constantly kept their children's emotional needs high on their priorities and went to great lengths to fulfill them. One could argue that those fathers who stepped forward to attend to their children during illness were more expressive to begin with. Equally plausible is the contention that going through the illness and treatment in itself enhanced those fathers' expressive capacities. Although we are unable to assess these options, our data does suggest the strength of expressive fatherhood among these Gaza men.

Given the exceptional, traumatic circumstances under which this mode of fatherhood has been observed, it is difficult to assess its significance and prevalence. One possibility is that expressive fatherhood has become salient as a result of the extremity of the situation. Another option, however, is that expressive fatherhood is customary in the Muslim world, somewhat contrary to popular images of patriarchal gender-role division in Arab communities.

References

Abdo-Zubi, Nahla. 1987. *Family, Women and Social Change in the Middle East: The Palestinian Case.* Toronto: Canadian Scholars' Press.

Amnesty International. 2010. "Suffocating Gaza—The Israeli Blockade's Effects on Palestinians."

Beck, Ulrich, and Elizabeth Beck-Gernsheim. 1995. *The Normal Chaos of Love.* Cambridge: Polity Press.

Bendel, Maskit. 2005. "The Disengagement from the Gaza Strip: Patients Pay the Price." Physicians for Human Rights. http://www.phr.org.il/uploaded/הזכותpdf.20.20%על%20והשלכותיה%ההתנתקותתכנית20% [in Hebrew]. English summary: http://www.phr.org.il/uploaded/26.9.05Report.pdf.

Birenbaum-Carmeli, Daphna. Forthcoming. "'Wouldn't Stop Praising: The Treatment of Gaza Children in Israeli Hospitals and Its Media Coverage.'"

Bosmans, Marleen, Dina Nasser, Umaiyeh Khammash, Patricia Claeys, and Marleen Temmerman. 2008. "Palestinian Women's Sexual and Reproductive Health Rights in a Longstanding Humanitarian Crisis." *Reproductive Health Matters* 16, no. 31: 103–11.

Brody, Amanda, and Leigh A. Simmons. 2007. "Family Resiliency during Childhood Cancer: The Father Perspective." *Journal of Pediatric Oncology Nursing* 24, no. 3: 152–65.

Central Bureau of Statistics, Israel. 2011. "Israel Statistics Annual." No. 62, Chapter 3, Table 32. http://www.cbs.gov.il/reader/shnaton/templ_shnaton.html?num_tab=st03_32x&CYear=2011.

———. 2012. "Statistical Abstract of Israel." Table 2.14, Population density per sq. km. of land, by district and sub-district. http://www.cbs.gov.il/shnaton63/st02_14.pdf.

Chesler, Mark A., and Carla Parry. 2001. "Gender Roles and/or Styles in Crisis: An Integrative Analysis of the Experiences of Fathers of Children with Cancer." *Qualitative Health Research* 11, no. 3: 363–84.

CIA World Factbook. 2011. https://www.cia.gov/library/publications/the-world-factbook/rankorder/2091rank.html.

Clark-Steffen, Laura. 1997. "Reconstructing Reality: Family Strategies for Managing Childhood Cancer." *Journal of Pediatric Nursing* 12: 278–287.

Clarke, Juanne. 2005. "Fathers Home Health Care Work When a Child Has Cancer: I'm Her Dad, I Have to Do It." *Men and Masculinities* 7, no. 4: 385–404.

Dermott, Esther. 2008. *Intimate Fatherhood: A Sociological Analysis.* London: Routledge.

Dhillon, Navte, and Edward Sayre. 2009. "West Bank and Gaza Economy: Before and After the Crisis." Brookings Institute. http://www.brookings.edu/interviews/2009/0114_west_bank_gaza_dhillon.aspx?p=1.

Farsakh, Leila. 2002. "Palestinian Labor Flows to the Israeli Economy: A Finished Story?" *Journal of Palestine Studies* 32, no. 1: 13–27.

Fineman, Martha A. 1995. *The Neutered Mother, the Sexual Family and Other Twentieth Century Tragedies.* New York: Routledge.

Fogiel-Bijaoui, Sylvie. 1999. "Families in Israel: Between Familism and Postmodernism." In *Sex, Gender, Politics: Women in Israel*, ed. Giora Rozen. Tel Aviv: Hakibbutz Hameuchad.

Fronk, Camille, Ray L. Huntington, and Bruce A. Chadwick. 1999. "Expectations for Traditional Family Roles: Palestinian Adolescents in the West Bank and Gaza." *Sex Roles* 41, no. 9/10: 705–35.

Goble, Ladonna A. 2004. "The Impact of a Child's Chronic Illness on Fathers." *Issues in Comprehensive Pediatric Nursing* 27, no. 3: 153–62.

Grzywacz, Joseph G., and Nadine F. Marks. 2002. "Family, Work, Work-Family Spillover, and Problem Drinking Midlife." *Journal of Marriage and Family* 62, no. 2: 333–48.

Hamakor. 2012. http://news.nana10.co.il/Article/?ArticleID=859243. 17 January.

Herzog, Hana, and Taghreed Yahia-Younis. 2007. "Men's Bargaining with Patriarchy: The Case of Primaries within Hamulas in Palestinian-Arab Communities in Israel." *Gender & Society* 21, no. 4: 579–602.

Hill, Karalyn, Aiveen Higgins, Martin Dempster, and Anthony McCarthy. 2009. "Fathers' Views and Understanding of their Roles in Families with a Child with Acute Lymphoblastic Leukemia: An Interpretative Phenomenological Analysis." *Journal of Health Psychology* 14, no. 8: 1268–80.

Hovey, Judith K. 2003. "The Needs of Fathers Parenting Children with Chronic Conditions." *Journal of Pediatric Oncology Nursing* 20, no. 5: 245–51.

Hudson, Leila. 1994. "Coming of Age in Occupied Palestine: Engendering the Intifada." In *Reconstructing Gender in the Middle East: Tradition, Identity, Power*, ed. Fatma M. Gocek and Shiva Balaghi. New York: Columbia University Press.

Human Rights Organizations (Adalah—The Legal Center for Arab Minority Rights in Israel, Amnesty International Israel Section, Bimkom—Planners for Planning Rights, B'Tselem—The Israeli Information Center for Human Rights in the Occupied Territories, Gisha—Legal Center for Freedom of Movement, Hamoked—Center for Defence of The Individual, Physicians for Human Rights). 2009. "An Israeli Call For Urgent Humanitarian Action In Gaza." Public Committee against Torture in Israel, Yesh Din—Volunteers For Human Rights. http://www.btselem.org/english/press_releases/20090114.asp.

Inhorn, Marcia C. 2012. *The New Arab Man: Emergent Masculinities, Technologies, and Islam in the Middle East.* Princeton: Princeton University Press.

Johnson, Penny, and Eileen Kuttab. 2001. "Where Have All the Women (and Men) Gone? Reflections on Gender and the Second Intifada." *Feminist Review* 69: 21–43.

Jones, Jill B., and Sherry Neil-Urban. 2003. "Focus Groups of Fathers of Children with Cancer." *Social Work in Health Care* 37, no. 1: 41–60.

Junka, Laura. 2006. "Camping in the Third Space: Agency, Representation, and the Politics of Gaza Beach." *Public Culture* 18, no. 2: 348–59.

Kanaaneh, Rhoda. 2005. "Boys or Men? Duped or 'Made'? Palestinian Soldiers in the Israeli Military." *American Ethnologist* 32, no. 2: 260–75.

Katz, Shira, and Tamar Krulik. 1999. "Fathers of Children with Chronic Illness: Do they Differ from Fathers of Healthy Children?" *Journal of Family Nursing* 5, no. 3: 292–315.

Lamb, Michael E. 1997. "Fathers and Child Development: An Introductory Overview and Guide." In *Infant Social Cognition: Empirical and Theoretical Considerations,* ed. Michael E. Lamb. Hillsdale, NJ: Erlbaum.

La Rossa, Ralph. 1997. *The Modernization of Fatherhood: A Social and Political History.* Chicago: University of Chicago Press.

Lavee, Yoav. 2005. "Correlates of Change in Marital Relationships Under Stress: The Case of Childhood Cancer." *Families in Society* 86, no. 1: 112–20.

Mar'i, Miriam M., and Sami K. Mar'i. 1991. "The Role of Women as Change Agents in Arab Society in Israel." In *Calling the Equality Bluff: Women in Israel,* ed. Barbara Swirski and Marilyn Safir. New York: Pergamon Press.

Miaari, Sami H., and Robert M. Sauer. 2011. "The Labor Market Costs of Conflict: Closures, Foreign Workers, and Palestinian Employment and Earnings." *Review of Economics of the Household* 9, no. 1: 129–48.

Massad, Joseph. 1995. "Conceiving the Masculine: Gender and Palestinian Nationalism." *Middle East Journal* 49, no. 3: 467–83.

Monterescu, Daniel. 2007. "Masculinity as a Relational Mode: Palestinian Gender Ideologies and Working Class Boundaries." In *Reapproaching Borders,* ed. Sandra M. Sufian and Mark LeVine. Lanham, MD: Rowman and Littlefield.

Muhanna, Aitemad. 2010. "Changing Family and Gender Dynamics During the Siege against Gaza: Spousal Relations and Domestic Violence." *Review of Women's Studies* 6, no. 3: 40–52. http://home.birzeit.edu/wsi/images/stories/6th_issue/English_article_3_vol_6.pdf.

Muhanna, Aitemad, and Elena Qleibo. 2009. "Negotiating Survival: The Impact of Israeli Mobility Restrictions on Women in Gaza." *Review of Women's Studies* 5: 23–40.

Nashif, Esmail. 2008. *Palestinian Political Prisoners: Identity and Community.* New York: Routledge.

Pedersen, Jon, Sara Randell, and Marwan Khawaja, eds. 2001. *Growing Fast: The Palestinian Population in the West Bank and Gaza Strip.* Tøyen: Fafo Institute for Applied Social Science, http://www.fafo.no/pub/rapp/353/353.pdf.

Peteet, Julie M. 1994. "Male Gender and Rituals of Resistance in the Palestinian Intifada: A Cultural Politics of Violence." *American Ethnologist* 21, no. 1: 31–49.

Physicians for Human Rights. 2010a. "Obstacles to Treatment on the Way of Gaza Patients." http://www.phr.org.il/uploaded/יולי%20-20%עזהhעזה%עדכון/20%202010%עברית%20.pdfסופי.

———. 2010b. "Position Paper: Who Gets to Go? In Violation of Medical Ethics and the Law: Israel's Distinction between Gaza Patients in Need of Medical Care." http://www.phr.org.il/uploaded/Microsoft%20Word%20-%20PP%20-%20English%20_2_.pdf.

————. 2010c. "Israel Promised to Ease the Blockade on Gaza—What Now? Obstacles on the Way of Gaza Patients to Health Care." http://phr.org.il/ uploaded/עדכון%20עזה%20-%20יולי%202010%20עברית%20.pdf.סופי

————. 2011a. "For the First Time in Two Years—Physicians for Human Rights-Israel's Delegation Enters the Gaza Strip." http://www.phr.org.il/ default.asp?PageID=60&ItemID=1040.

————. 2011b. Report: "'Humanitarian Minimum'—Israel's Role in Creating Food and Water Insecurity in the Gaza Strip, December 2010." http:// www.phr.org.il/default.asp?PageID=111&ItemID=799.

Reaya, Diane, Sarah Bignold, Stephan J. Ballcand, and Alan Cribb. 1998. "He Just Had a Different Way of Showing It: Gender Dynamics in Families Coping with Childhood Cancer." *Journal of Gender Studies* 7, no. 1: 39–52.

Richter-Devroe, Sophie. 2011. "Palestinian Women's Everyday Resistance: Between Normality and Normalisation." *Journal of International Women's Studies* 12, no. 2: 32–46.

Sa'ar, Amalia, and Taghreed Yahya-Younis. 2008. "Masculinity in Crisis: The Case of Palestinians in Israel." *British Journal of Middle East Studies* 35, no. 3: 305–23.

Slone, Michelle, Tomer Shechner, and Oula Khoury Farah. 2012. "Parenting Style as a Moderator of Effects of Political Violence: Cross-Cultural Comparison of Israeli Jewish and Arab Children." *International Journal of Behavioral Development* 36, no. 1: 62–70.

Summers, Jean A., Helen Raikes, James Butler, Paul Spicer, Barbara Pan, Sarah Shaw, Mark Langager, Carol McAllister, and Monique K. Johnson. 1999. "Low-Income Fathers and Mothers Perceptions of the Father Role: A Qualitative Study in Four Early Head Start Communities." *Infant Mental Health Journal* 20, no. 3: 291–304.

United Nations Human Rights Council. 2009. "Report of the United Nations Fact-Finding Mission on the Gaza Conflict." http://www2.ohchr.org/ english/bodies/hrcouncil/docs/12session/A-HRC-12-48.pdf.

United Nations Office for the Coordination of Humanitarian Affairs. 2009. "Gaza Blockade—Special Focus: Occupied Palestinian Authority [OCHA]." http://www.ochaopt.org/documents/Ocha_opt_Gaza_impact_ of_two_years_of_blockade_August_2009_english.pdf.

————. 2010. "Gaza Health Fact Sheet." http://www.ochaopt.org/docum ents/ochaopt_who_gaza_health_fact_sheet_20100120_hebrew.pdf.

United Nations Relief and Works Agency. 2009. "New Population Figures." http://unispal.un.org/UNISPAL.NSF/0/B4CC62867AD730A3852576B6 006E251D.

Ware, Jane, and Hitesh Ravel. 2007. "A Qualitative Investigation of Fathers' Experiences of Looking after a Child with a Life-Limiting Illness, in Process and in Retrospect." *Clinical Child Psychology and Psychiatry* 12, no. 4: 549–65.

Warin, Jo, Yvette Solomon, Charlie Lewis, and Wendy Langford. 1999. *Fathers, Work and Family Life*. Oxford: Family Policy Studies Centre for Joseph Rowntree Foundation.

World Health Organization. 2008. "Health Conditions in the Occupied Palestinian Territory, Including East Jerusalem, and in the Occupied Syrian Golan." http://apps.who.int/gb/ebwha/pdf_files/A61/A61_18Rev1-en. pdf.

———. 2010a. "Gaza Health Fact Sheet." http://unispal.un.org/UNISPalestinianAuthorityL.NSF/0/80E8238D765E5FB7852576B1004EC498.

———. 2010b. "Press Statement—Unimpeded Access of Medical Supplies Needed for Gaza." http://www.emro.who.int/palestine/reports/advocacy _HR/advocacy/WHO%20-Press%20statement-June2010.pdf.

Yaron, Ran. 2008. "Holding Health to Ransom: GSS Interrogation and Extortion of Palestinian Patients at Erez Crossing." Physicians for Human Rights. http://www.phr.org.il/uploaded/HoldingHealthToRandsom_4.pdf.

Part IV

CLINICAL FATHERHOOD

Chapter 7

ENHANCING FATHERING THROUGH MEDICAL RESEARCH PARTICIPATION IN MEXICO

Emily Wentzell

Introduction

Arturo,[1] a 50-year-old electronics repairman, told me that physical health was not his only motivation for joining the Cuernavaca, Mexico, arm of the Human Papillomavirus Infection in Men, or HIM, study, a multinational, longitudinal study of human papillomavirus (HPV) occurrence. HPV is the world's most common sexually transmitted infection (STI), and while usually asymptomatic, some strains of the virus can cause genital warts or cervical and other cancers (Clifford et al. 2005). In Mexico, where cervical cancer remains a leading cause of death despite a nearly 40-year-old national screening program (Lazcano-Ponce et al. 1999; Palacio-Mejía et al. 2009), educational and vaccination campaigns framing HPV as a cancer-causing virus are already underway nationwide (Secretaría de Salud 2010). In light of this public health emphasis on HPV, Arturo and his wife Ade, a nurse, said that they were glad that the study provided testing for this disease and that they were especially glad to support scientific research that could enhance treatment. However, Arturo's main reason for participating related to his belief that "the body is a reflection of the soul."

He said that a few years earlier, he had been a "typical Mexican man," who loved his family but spent too much time drinking, working, and engaging in other "unhealthy" pursuits. After surviving a kidnapping, he decided to change his life and become "a good husband and father." He focused especially on increasing his communication and closeness with his two adult daughters, saying that he hoped to model good behavior so that they could expect the same from men in their own lives. He explained that his efforts required a wide range of life changes, from converting to Protestantism (a religion he believed would help him shed his vices), to cultivating bodily health that he said would reflect and enhance his new, healthier inner life. Ade heard about the HPV study at work and told him about it, thinking it would fit well with his new worldview. He decided to join, and described being in the study as an important way for him to live out the new, healthy lifestyle that made him a better parent and husband.

Changing Mexican Masculinities and Multinational Sexual Health Research

Arturo's change is a common one in Mexico today, where men often report midlife shifts away from "traditional" forms of masculinity that they have come to view as problematic, or develop individual ways of being men in consistent and conscious opposition to widely critiqued—but also commonly naturalized—stereotypes of Mexican men as unfeeling, womanizing *machos* (Gutmann 1996; Wentzell 2013a). Amid longstanding calls for "modernization" of gender roles, companionate marriage has become ideal and families are reconfiguring gendered divisions of labor (Domínguez-Ruvalcaba 2007; García and de Oliveira 2004; Hirsch 2003). Critiques of and alternatives to machismo, which often nevertheless reify it as an innate trait to be battled, have arisen from social settings ranging from self-help groups, to increasingly popular forms of Protestantism that call for male temperance and fidelity, to critiques of men's participation in the rising narcoviolence, like poet Javier Sicilia's leading of anti-violence protests following the murder of his son (Amuchástegui 2009; Brandes 2002; Sicilia 2011; also see Smith, this volume, for a comparative case of religious conversion).

Across these cultural sites for debate about masculinities, it is also common to call for men to oppose machismo by engaging in "responsible" sexual health practices and emotionally engaged fathering (Gutmann 2007; Ramirez 2009).

There are thus many ways of "being a man," and many cultural sites that encourage specific performances of masculinity in Mexico today. Masculinities, most straightforwardly defined as "what men say and do *to be men*," are individual practices that vary across men's lives and contexts; the way someone might act "like a man" is likely to vary between environments like work, home, and leisure (Gutmann 1996: 17, italics in the original). Thus, elsewhere I argue that it is productive to understand masculinities not as singular identities or practices but as composites of the multiple ways of being men in which people engage. This approach builds on Annemarie Mol's (2002: 47) argument that objects of medical inquiry perceived as singular items—like a specific disease—are in practice "composite objects," collections of things, events, and experiences called by "the same name" and made to "hang together" through social action. Applying this idea of compositeness to the performance of gender enables analysis of the ways *how* and reasons *why* men incorporate specific and varied actions, experiences, and attitudes into their overall ways of being men. "Composite masculinities" are thus contingent and fluid constellations of acts, attitudes, relationships, and physicalities that men weave into coherent masculine selfhoods through a variety of social and bodily practices (Wentzell 2013b). Developed interactionally and context-dependently, composite masculinities are constructed from the materials available to an individual at a given time. Mexican men today can engage in several of the social movements and actions associated with manliness discussed above—from enacting to protesting violence or machismo, to performing particular parenting or religious practices—and incorporate these context-specific ways of being men into their composite masculinities. This is evident in Arturo's story, which opened this chapter, as he incorporated improved self-care, religious conversion, and expanded fathering practice into his postkidnapping composite masculinity.

Mexican men's participation in sexual health research may thus be an activity that they can incorporate into self-consciously progressive composite masculinities. Medical anthropologists have long argued that people can assert, or be labeled with, specific social identities through their engagement in health practices (Whyte 2009). This is especially apparent in the case of STI testing and treatment, which may be stigmatizing or, conversely, provide an opportunity for asserting responsibility and modernity (Adkins 2001; Biehl et al. 2001; Hammar 2007). Participating in medical research, like clinical trials, can also lead people to become associated with specific labels, including self-generated identities like "professional guinea pig" (Abadie 2010; Epstein 2008). Thus, participating in long-term observational medical research, especially studies like the HIM study that generate STI diagnoses, may present both possibilities and pitfalls for enacting desired forms of masculinity. Positive HPV diagnoses might lead to stigmatizing labeling that challenges participants' desired identities, but the HIM study may also provide a forum for acting out desired identities. HIM study participants are tested biannually for four years with new DNA technology that reveals previously undetectable HPV infection. At their appointments, they are told if they have "high risk" (cancer-causing) and/or "low risk" (wart-causing) viral strains, offered any necessary medical treatment, and instructed to complete computerized surveys regarding their health and sexual practices. As a research site, this study affords the anthropological opportunity to investigate the social consequences for men and their families of participation in long-term sexual health research. This chapter draws on initial data from a research project investigating the consequences of HIM study participation for Mexican couples' practices of gender, self-care, and family life, which will follow thirty couples over the course of their study experience.

In these interviews, participants' narratives about their reasons for joining the HIM study often focused on their desire to "be" specific kinds of men, women, partners, and parents. For male participants, the theme of fathering emerged as a particularly strong motivator for study participation. In their narratives regarding their reasons for joining the study, men and couples often discussed parenting and performing "good" fatherhood as both reasons for participating and ends that could be achieved through participation. Drawing on men's accounts of their reasons for study enrollment voiced during their couple interviews, I argue that participation in a multinational sexual health study enables some men to include self-consciously progressive forms of fathering in their composite masculinities in three key ways: caring for their health in order to model non-macho masculinity, providing a forum for them to enact "better" manhood, and enabling them to feel they are aiding future generations by furthering national modernization and healthcare.

The Study Site and Methods

Cuernavaca, a metropolitan area of almost 800,000 people located eighty-five kilometers south of Mexico City, is a former elite vacation site turned bustling urban center (Instituto Nacional de Estadística y Geografía 2009). In recent history, Cuernavaca has been a key site for population resettlement in central Mexico. Since the 1985 Mexico City earthquake sent refugees to settle in the city, it has been growing quickly and has now sprawled to absorb many local, once rural, municipalities. Wal-Mart supercenters sit at both the north and south edges of town, and busy streets are lined with strip malls and fast-food restaurants, as well as food carts, street vendors, and markets. Residents of Cuernavaca frequently describe it as a modern city that is increasingly similar in attitude to the nearby national capital; this makes it ideal for examining middle-class urban Mexicans' efforts to live out specific gendered identities in the context of cultural debates about "modern" masculinity, femininity, and sexuality.

As a research site, Cuernavaca can also reveal the relationships that the national spread of narcoviolence and insecurity, as well as economic troubles related to that violence, enduring economic inequality, and the recent global financial crisis, have to individual actions and attitudes. Only a few years ago Cuernavaca residents considered their city to be one of the safest in the region, and it appeared to remain so even after the outbreak of extreme narcoviolence in the north in response to the 2006 federal crackdown on drug trafficking. However, this sense of safety ended following incidents of spectacular drug-related violence beginning around 2009, including the hanging of four mutilated bodies off a bridge by a popular, upscale mall in 2010. After repeated, sensational violence, residents now perceive Cuernavaca as fundamentally insecure, and the city has also become the base of anti-violence protests. Further, while economic inequality and instability have long been part of life in Cuernavaca, the economic situation has recently worsened, with investments in construction and tourism decreasing due to both violence and the global economic crisis, eliminating many building and service industry jobs. These new difficulties of life were a constant theme in research interviews, as Arturo's story of focusing on family and health after surviving kidnapping illustrates.

The Mexican arm of the HIM study is associated with a hospital run by the Instituto Mexicano del Seguro Social, or IMSS, a national system that offers healthcare and social services to formally employed private-sector workers, public university students, and their dependents, comprising about 40 percent of the national population (Instituto Nacional de Estadística y Geografía 2005). The Cuernavaca branch of the HIM study has recruited IMSS workers and patients, as well workers from local universities and businesses, primarily through educational lectures on HPV and recruitment posters (Giuliano et al. 2006). While these methods were unlikely to reach the very wealthy or poor, study enrollment includes a wide sample of mostly middle-class men aged eighteen to seventy who did not have an active STI at study enrollment (Giuliano et al. 2008). Participants are literate and mostly formally employed, a status that provides relative economic stability (though not necessarily wealth, especially as even large-scale employers struggle in the current economic climate), in a country where most people work in the informal economy (Instituto Nacional de Estadística y Geografía 2009). HIM participants come to the study offices biannually to donate biological samples and complete sexual and health history questionnaires.

The HIM study staff recruited and scheduled initial interviews for the present anthropological project when they arranged participants' clinical appointments. I interviewed thirty female-male couples in which the male partner had already joined the HIM study and the female partner was planning to enroll in a companion study, as well as ten male and ten participants alone (these women's interviews are not included in the present analysis). For convenience, ethnographic interviews with couples were often scheduled after women's HIM study enrollment visits. I did all interviews in Spanish, in private consulting rooms, and they tended to last from forty-five to ninety minutes. I took written notes and also audio-recorded interviews with participants' permission.

As the first round of semi-structured interviews in a long-term study of the social consequences of HIM study participation for male subjects and their families, these interactions focused on participants' reasons for enrolling in the HIM study, study experiences to date, and health and relationship histories. All participants signed informed consent forms and were told that their decisions regarding participation in the anthropological study would not impact their HIM study eligibility or treatment. The themes of critiquing "machismo" and lauding "modernity" emerged early on, and I sought to avoid guiding subsequent interviewees' narratives toward these themes by avoiding related key words unless the participants themselves used them.

Unlike the resource-poor populations discussed in most anthropological studies of medical research participation, and HIM participants in the study's other two sites in the United States and Brazil, who participate for financial compensation, Mexican HIM participants are uncompensated aside from free STI treatment and medical checkups (Elliott and Abadie 2008; Giuliano et al. 2006). Recruited from the government health service and local businesses, Mexican HIM participants are mostly middle-class, literate, and covered by government health insurance. It is thus likely that participants, like Arturo, decided to enroll for reasons that range far beyond either compensation or the specific health problems under study. Thus, this population may display a "healthy user effect," a sampling bias in which the people who are more interested in healthcare and likely to follow health recommendations are also most likely to enroll in research studies. While this bias poses a problem for medical research sampling, it is a boon for the anthropological aim of investigating how longitudinal study participation may influence gendered identity, since it means that HIM study participants may be especially likely to seek to incorporate aspects of their research participation into existing or desired composite masculinities.

It is a key anthropological insight that interviews are intersubjective encounters, which generate context-specific performances of self rather than unmediated views into someone's "true" experience (Jackson 1998). In this light, couple interviews are especially important for revealing how, in the research setting, spouses negotiate and assert both joint and individual identities. For example, spouses often collaboratively told shared narratives about their lives and health experiences, but also often debated the reasons why the husband joined the HIM study, why "we" were planning to enroll jointly, and what study-related experiences meant for them as a family. Interviews served as a space for participants both to describe their experience and to enact and define who they were trying to be as men, women, parents, and spouses. Thus, I analyze interview data as observation of this social practice, rather than as a journalistic account of participants' experiences. While I focus here on men's accounts of their reasons for study participation in order to discuss the role that ideas of "good" fatherhood played in their decision to enroll, it is important to note that since most men produced these accounts in their wives' company, those narratives represent men's desired self-presentation in the family sphere.

HIM Participation as Modeling Good Manhood

Male study participants frequently characterized study participation as a form of self-care that would ensure their physical fitness to father while providing a good example for their children. A 71-year-

old office worker and father of three children, including two unmarried daughters in their twenties who lived at home, said that
being healthy enabled him to be there for his family. He explained
that he was participating in the study, "More than anything, for my
daughters. If I get sick, what will happen to them? I'm not done
caring for them. That's the obligation you have; to be healthy for
the kids." His wife agreed with this aim, saying that their main goal
in life had been "to raise healthy kids," and that their own mental
and physical health was necessary for doing so. Echoing this theme,
a married 47-year-old hospital warehouse worker with three adult
children described his own health as crucial for his family's well-
being more broadly. He explained that he joined the study, "principally for my health, my well-being. First mine, then my family's. If
I'm healthy, I can work and support them."

While men like the participant described above prioritized their
own health in order to ensure that they could provide for their families, parents more commonly described feeling that their needs
should come second to those of their children. For example, a
48-year-old couple, he a hospital office worker and she a secretary-
turned-housewife, said that they had both been raised to put family first. They framed the HIM study as a resource for ensuring his
health as a way to be sure that he could be there for others. He explained, "Now I don't think of myself, I think of her and the kids.
She thinks the same. When [the kids] grow up, well then, they'll
think the same way. I don't live for myself, but for my children and
wife." She said that this point of view echoed the way she had been
raised to view men's role in marriage and parenting, saying, "My
father said, 'When you marry, your life isn't yours [as a man], it's
your wife's. And when you have children, again, it's not yours, it's
for them. So, you have to take care of yourself.'" He concluded that
they "try to be good models" of this philosophy for their own children, through practices like study participation.

In Mexico, people frequently use the word "healthy" (*sano*) to
describe a broad notion of health that moves beyond the lack of
disease to encompass mental health and positive morality. Parents,
especially fathers like the office worker quoted above, frequently
described the HIM study as a chance to be a good role model of both
the physical and social aspects of health. For example, a 50-year-
old driver living in a common-law relationship with his partner, a
28-year-old stay-at-home mother, treated their study visit as a family outing, bringing their young children to see their father engaged
in health-related activity. He said that because his ex-wife had a

uterine problem that she attributed to HPV, and because she blamed him for transmitting it, he had decided to join the study to try to ensure his and his present partner's health. While neither had symptoms, they saw being healthy for their children as paramount; she said that, "If we're positive, we'll seek treatment, because I want to be healthy for my babies." In describing his reasons for study enrollment, the male partner focused on the need to raise "healthy" children, above and beyond his own physical health. He said, "Being parents is very important. I have them [pointing to his children in the room], my daughter, and children with my ex-partner, who are now grown. We had problems, with the divorce, but luckily my kids came out healthy." This participant reported that he wanted to be a good father by not only staying healthy to ensure that he could care for his children, but also by teaching his children the importance of healthcare by example. Stating that, "We love them [our children] a lot, and try to give them the treatment they deserve," he explained that seeing their father care for his and their mother's health was an important aspect of this treatment.

A 35-year-old couple with two teenage children voiced similar aims. The husband, a worker at a wholesale company, described participating in the study as "killing two birds with one stone. One is our health, the other is demonstrating how to live well." He explained that being a good role model was as important for good fathering as maintaining his physical health, stating, "We have two children, who will also be parents some day or have partners, and we've thought a lot about that. If we don't give them a good example, I can't say anything to them about their behavior if mine is bad." He said that both he and his wife had been taught by their parents to be respectful, and he believed that sexual fidelity was a key part of respecting one's family, as it protected them from sexually transmitted infection. He said that the HIM study provided not only the chance to demonstrate living healthily, but was also an opportunity to model consideration for his sexual health to his children, which would have the added advantage of opening familial lines of communication about sexuality. He said, "We don't want our kids to make mistakes because of lack of information," and that he did not want to replicate the "silence" regarding sex that he had grown up with. His wife agreed, saying, "We try to be very open. We never want it to be like before; my parents never told me anything!" It was important to this couple that the HIM study enabled health maintenance in a way that could foster what they considered healthy family relationships that included openness about potentially taboo topics.

The healthy behavior that fathers said they sought to model often entailed a rejection of the machismo that many characterized as a lingering social problem in Mexico. Many men described study participation as a chance to show that they were not too macho to engage in self-care, and discussed wanting their children to follow their lead. For example, a 50-year-old bartender, married to a 36-year-old nurse with whom he had two teenage boys, said, "It's important to me not to be macho," especially as a father of sons. As his wife nodded emphatically, he described machismo as an attitude that could harm men physically by discouraging them from seeking medical care. Even worse, he said that it would also harm their family relationships and damage their children by modeling and thus transmitting self-destructive behavior. He said, "Here in Mexico, we're *machistas*. But we [gesturing to himself and his wife] are against machismo." He described taking care of his health as one of many ways he tried to demonstrate divergence from machismo. For example, the couple also described doing housework together, a practice that she said was intentional because "gender equity is very important." Overall, he described modeling progressive behavior in life areas traditionally associated with machismo as a key part of being a good father, as he tried to lead his sons to care for their health by example, and to show them that "women have rights" by "model[ing] caring for my wife." He characterized his HIM study visits, which the couple deliberately attended together, as an excellent opportunity for this modeling.

Being a Better Man and Father in the HIM Study

Male HIM participants often said that they were grateful that the study was there to help them be "better" or "different" kinds of men than the stereotypically macho Mexican. Male partners in couples that described themselves as having "modern" divisions of gendered labor and treating each other as equals often said that study participation helped them both to continue trajectories of self-improvement. For example, a 36-year-old male laboratory technician, married to a 39-year-old hospital administration worker, said that the HIM study provided an opportunity to "take care of ourselves, as a couple" in a way that would especially help them to care for their family. Since he had been diagnosed with genital warts before the study began, both viewed the frequent checkups as a way to monitor his sexual health and thus mitigate her health risk, which they saw as especially crucial now that they had a 3-year-old child. Aside from these health-related objectives, he explained that study participation was also "part of our life advancement" as a family. Both had returned to school in order to earn engineering degrees that would increase their pay and status at work. She explained that they had done this because "we have goals," and he finished her thought by stating, "for our children." Thus, by attending to possible HPV-related disease and simultaneously modeling progressive marital relations for their child, they both said that the HIM study was a way to "move forward" in life.

More commonly, male participants described HIM study participation as an activity that both symbolized and furthered a shift away from more macho to more progressive masculinity—exemplified by emotionally engaged fathering—over their life course. For example, the warehouse worker quoted previously describing his study enrollment as supporting his health and thus enabling him to support his family said that his way of being a man had radically changed. He explained, "There's Miguel before and after. I used to drink too much. Thank God, I had the opportunity to leave that behind." He described neglecting his family in favor of drinking and carousing for years, then said that about fourteen years ago, "I opened my eyes and stopped this evil." He said that quitting alcohol was a long and difficult process, and that he had also struggled to treat his family as they deserved. He now saw himself as a good father, provider and spouse, stating, "It was my mistake not to be like that from the beginning, but it's never too late to change." He described the HIM study as something that helped him to live out his new goals of being healthy and non-macho. He said that for Mexican men, "It's common not to get enough healthcare, but the study appointment obliges me to do it. That's why I joined, to be forced to have checkups!" Miguel thus saw study participation as both emblematic of his life change and as providing structure that compelled him to stick with the path he had chosen.

Like Miguel, male participants frequently linked overcoming alcoholism to their study enrollment, saying that these health practices were mutually reinforcing and together made them better fathers and husbands. For example, a 44-year-old taxi driver said that he and his wife, a 44-year-old university instructor, had split up several times over the course of their marriage as a result of his failings in these areas. He said, "I lacked maturity, I lacked personal development. I had an alcoholism problem that's now under control. I worked, and I went drinking with my work friends, and my family relationships suffered. Work and family and alcohol were too much, so at one point I stopped drinking for four years. I was trying to reconstruct my life, to be able to focus on work, family, and myself. I'm in AA now, trying to do what my family needs." He said that curbing his drinking had been important for both his physical and mental health because he had previously been "somaticiz[ing] my problems" and treating them with alcohol. Now, he stated that focusing on his health was helping him to deal with these issues and that being in both AA and the HIM study forced him to become healthy and face his emotional issues directly. He said that these changes, while difficult, had made him a better father and that as a result, "being a father just gives me the most satisfaction in life." He attributed positive changes in his fathering to these health interventions, saying that by participating, "I'm moving us forward, trying to make the damage to [my children] as little as possible." On the whole, many participants sought to revise their composite masculinities by excluding more "traditionally" manly practices like excessive drinking, and including the acts of self-care and enhanced fathering enabled by study participation.

Many participants discursively linked generational change in Mexican society and their individual improvement as husbands and fathers throughout their lives. For instance, a 39-year-old dental technician said that he had found blending families with his second wife, a 36-year-old dental office worker, difficult, since his daughters blamed their new stepmother for the failure of their parents' marriage. He said that he initially responded to this stress by drinking, which increased family fighting and his sense of failure as a parent. However, he strove to change, and said that now, "I drink less; I'm less aggressive and more tolerant. I changed because of being around her [his wife], and our daughters." He explained that he wanted to change rather than replicate his own troubled childhood. "The changes are for my health, but you also have to think of your children...I had a hard childhood, my mom drank a lot. You don't want your kids to suffer what you did. I don't want to teach my daughters to accept bad treatment...We want to have a better life for our kids." He described HIM study participation as one of the ways he was improving his health and his life, which made him feel good about both ensuring a healthier older age that would keep him physically present for his family and being a good role model for his children. The explicit desire to change also itself became a key element of many participants' revised composite masculinities.

Helping Future Generations
through HIM Participation

In addition to discussing the need to model good masculinity and parenting for their own children, study participants frequently voiced a desire to help future generations and their nation as a whole by volunteering for the HIM study. Participants often identified "supporting science" as a key reason why they chose to enroll in the study, and they usually explained the social benefits of this practice in terms of the positive effect it could have on their own children or on future generations in the abstract. For example, a 58-year-old husband and 64-year-old wife, both phone company retirees, described their lives and romantic relationship as having extreme highs and lows, and said that they believed they were at their best as grandparents. His decision to join the study had been prompted by their 11-year-old granddaughter's HPV vaccination, which had brought the dangers of HPV-related cancer to their attention. He said that he hoped that his participation would support the larger cause of HPV research, enabling him "to be one of those grains of sand that, all together, can make a difference." She expanded on the importance of supporting research that would help future generations, explaining, "We've had boys, girls, grandchildren, so we want science to advance, if we can help."

Several participants described "supporting science" and thus improving future generations' health as a way to meet the commonly voiced aim of being better men and fathers. This was the case for a 47-year-old taxi driver in a common-law marriage to a 32-year-old beautician, who lived with two adult children from his previous marriage. He stated that he had joined the HIM study to "support research, support science. I heard about the study while I was waiting on line at the IMSS, and decided to do it to help science, since that's really everyone's job." He related his belief that improving population health was "everyone's job" to the "self-help" education that he had undertaken to improve his parenting after his divorce. He said that he had focused on improving his health habits, taking parent-child enrichment classes, and doing his fair share of housework as a way to be a good father and model for his children, but that he felt frustrated by the suffering of so many other children he could not help. For example, he said that he had recently seen a documentary about impoverished families, in which the "mothers were making dirt cookies to feed to their children; it makes you feel sad, you feel helpless." He told me that participating in the HIM study was his way of trying to help children and society in a broader way.

A 49-year-old physician married to a 46-year-old stay-at-home mother, who had left her job to care for their special needs teenager, also related his study participation to the desire to help less fortunate children. When asked why he decided to join the study, he explained: "Something important is that when you're in the study, you know there will be medical advances. And now there is; a vaccine, that our daughter has gotten. There is a result. Someone has to be the guinea pig, to give a better quality of life to others. To help the next generation avoid aggressive viruses like HPV and HIV, the diseases of the twenty-first century, cancer. You have to be a positive statistic. We hope that we'll be well, and that the study will advance health in Mexico." He went on to relate his desire to advance population health to his own experiences as a father, especially his knowledge that getting help for one's children required means that were not available to everyone. He said, "We're parents of a special needs child, so we've always looked for alternatives, solutions for him. We have a child with mental retardation, nineteen years old, and we are getting there, but we don't want others to suffer. We can afford tests, but others can't."

Just as this participant described his study enrollment as intended to help future generations by combating the "diseases of the twenty-first century," many others said they hoped to help make a better future by modernizing Mexican society. In both their critiques of machismo and their common statements that Mexico lacked a future-oriented health culture, participants frequently cast their nation as insufficiently modern in terms of health and gender. For example, in a typical statement, Arturo's wife explained, "In general, as Mexicans, we treat rather than prevent. We're not into prevention." She identified this as a key problem facing the nation, which she hoped Arturo's study enrollment would help to combat.

Both male and female participants often remarked that Mexico "lacks a culture of prevention" and said that changing this culture by example was a major benefit of HIM study participation. Both implicitly and explicitly, these participants often compared Mexican culture to that of other nations that they saw as more "developed" and "modern," and framed their support for HPV research as a way to emulate the health and gender cultures of those other places. For example, one participant switched to English when describing his progressive attitude toward sexuality and parenting. In an interview conducted otherwise completely in Spanish, he described himself as having an "open mind." He explained that this was what led him to join the study and also use his study experience as a starting point for talking to his kids about sex and encouraging them to take care of their own sexual health. Thus, in addition to hoping to be good role models for their own children, many men saw the ability to live out progressive manhood and fatherhood through HIM study enrollment as a way to "advance" their culture more broadly. Participants sometimes expressed pride in their alliance with a multinational study, for example by wearing complimentary hats and T-shirts bearing the name of the American institution that led the HIM study. It seemed that aligning themselves with an international sexual health study was a way for many participants to include lived "modernity" in their composite masculinities, and to model this attitude for their own children and for the future generations they hoped would benefit from their participation.

Discussion

Most male HIM study participants described HPV testing and periodic checkups as a benefit of enrolling in the study but did not identify healthcare for health's sake as their main reason for participating. Rather than casting healthcare as an end in itself, men often described it as a way to help ensure that they would be able to support and be present for their spouses and children. In keeping with this view of healthcare as a practice done for others, participants often described their ability to model healthy and non-macho self-care behavior for their children as a key benefit of study participation. Overall, male participants described their HIM study experience as a forum that enabled them to be positive role models for their families and enact forms of masculinity that they viewed as "modern" and socially positive. Some men described their study experience as facilitating an ongoing identification with "progressive" fatherhood and manhood, while others incorporated study participation into a shift away from activities they associated with traditional, "macho" masculinity.

It is likely that specific attributes of the HIM study made it attractive as a site for achieving these goals. Firstly, many men reported that the study's focus on sexual health enabled them to not only model self-care, but to actively model care for their wives' health by monitoring their own STI status. This notion reflects framing, on the national level and within the HIM study, of men as "HPV carriers" and women as "victims" of the disease; this discourse replicates the gendered notions of men as sexually active and women as passive that are associated with the "traditional" gender roles that participants often critiqued. Other participants used the HIM study's sexual health focus as a point of departure for talking with their children about sex and STIs, and thus cultivating familial communication that many participants viewed as a hallmark of "good," nontraditional fathering. By engaging in these behaviors, participants were able to act in ways opposite to the poor fathering, thoughtless womanizing, lack of self-care, and emotional closure that they described as hallmarks of machismo. The HIM study's focus on STIs made it an ideal site for Mexican men seeking to "be different" to enact what they viewed as progressive masculinity and fatherhood. Despite the stigma often attached to STI positivity, neither male nor female participants tended to cast positive test results as socially problematic, instead describing study participation as a way to responsibly monitor one's health and thus mitigate any harm that positivity might cause.

Secondly, the HIM study's multinational design enabled participants to understand their study experience as supportive of international values and gender norms that many imagined to be more "modern" than those of Mexican culture. Many men and women critiqued Mexican society in the abstract for fostering gender inequality and deterring men from seeking healthcare; they cast study participation as a way to help their nation "move forward." For example, Arturo explained that he had decided to participate partly because "it's an international study, in Brazil and the U.S., so being part of it is important." In addition to his hopes that participating would help him to model nontraditional masculinity and reflect the inner changes through which he had become a better man, he hoped that participation would help others on a large scale. He described enrolling in the study as "something I can do that can benefit the whole world."

Like Arturo, participants sometimes voiced the desire to have a worldwide impact by participating in an international study, saying that the study enabled them to be a part of global advances in healthcare and attitudes about sexuality. Participants frequently discussed these desires for global change in relationship to children, saying that they hoped that advances in medical knowledge and social change regarding sexuality would improve both their own children's lives, and brighten the future for the next generation. This focus on children—in both the specific and the abstract—makes sense in a pronatalist culture where fatherhood has long been seen as key to male identity, but the ideal of fatherhood has shifted from patriarchal pride in siring offspring to emotional investment in one's children.

While male participants' narratives commonly linked study participation to their desires to be "good" fathers and husbands, it is important to remember that they produced these statements in conversation with their wives and a female interviewer. While Mexican men now commonly voice the desire to move away from the forms of masculinity assumed to be "traditional" to Mexico in order to enact progressive fatherhood and companionate marriage in research studies and life histories (Amuchástegui and Szasz 2007), they do so in the context of ongoing gender inequality (in which, for example, women are assumed to be in charge of domestic duties, and progressive men "help"), and a sexual double standard. In keeping with the fact that many participants who described their fathering and spousal practices as progressive also recounted life phases in which they had enacted more macho masculinity, the discourse of modernization voiced by so many participants is likely one of many potentially conflicting frameworks that they use for acting and making sense of their actions. Thus, men were likely encouraged by the interview context to focus on their desires to be good fathers and husbands in their descriptions of their reasons for study enrollment, rather than presenting other potentially coexisting motives. Indeed, these interviews may have become sites in which men were able to enact progressive masculinities by voicing these narratives. This makes the data presented here a partial view of men's reasons for enrolling in the HIM study, but one that powerfully demonstrates how study-related experiences could fulfill many participants' apparent desires to be seen by wives and researchers as progressive fathers and non-macho men.

Conclusion

In sum, these interviews revealed the ways that many HIM study participants sought to incorporate their experiences of HPV testing and diagnosis into their broader composite masculinities. Some participants recounted consistent attempts to be manly in self-consciously "modern" ways, incorporating histories of engaged fathering, affective partnering, and responsible provision for their families into the composite masculinities presented when we spoke. Other participants sought to remove past "bad" behaviors, like excessive drinking or disengaged fathering, from their composite masculinities, replacing them with "responsible" practices like HIM study participation and foregrounding these narratives of positive change facilitated by medical research involvement in the interviews. For many, HIM study participation appeared to be a single activity that could be incorporated into "good" composite masculinities in multiple ways as it demonstrated an international sensibility, facilitated physical health and self-care, moral uprightness, familial responsibility, and the practice of engaged fathering. The analysis of this phenomenon presented here demonstrates that even activities that on the surface may not seem directly related to fathering, like participation in a medical study, can be linked to altered parenting practices and ideals of family life that men incorporate into self-consciously "progressive" masculinities.

Notes

1. All names are pseudonyms.

References

Abadie, Roberto. 2010. *The Professional Guinea Pig: Big Pharma and the Risky World of Human Subjects.* Durham, NC: Duke University Press.

Adkins, Lisa. 2001. "Risk Culture, Self-Reflexivity and the Making of Sexual Hierarchies." *Body & Society* 7, no. 1: 35–55.

Amuchástegui, Ana. 2009. "Partner Violence, Technologies of the Self, and Masculinity in Mexico." *Culture, Society and Masculinities* 1, no. 2: 155.

Amuchástegui, Ana, and Ivonne Szasz, eds. 2007. *Sucede que me canso de ser hombre* [It happens that I am tired of being a man]. Mexico City: El Colegio de Mexico.

Biehl, João, Denise Coutinho, and Ana Luzia Outeiro. 2001. "Technology and Affect: HIV/AIDS Testing in Brazil." *Culture, Medicine and Psychiatry* 25, no. 1: 87–129.

Brandes, Stanley. 2002. *Staying Sober in Mexico City.* Austin: The University of Texas Press.

Clifford, G. M., S. Gallus, R. Herrero, N. Muñoz, P. J. Snijders, S. Vaccarella, P. T. Anh, C. Ferreccio, N. T. Hieu, E. Matos, M. Molano, R. Rajkumar, G. Ronco, S. de Sanjosé, H. R. Shin, S. Sukvirach, J. O. Thomas, S. Tunsakul, C. J. Meijer, and S. Franceschi. 2005. "Worldwide Distribution of Human Papillomavirus Types in Cytologically Normal Women in the International Agency for Research on Cancer HPV Prevalence Surveys: A Pooled Analysis." *The Lancet* 366, no. 9490: 991–98.

Domínguez-Ruvalcaba, Héctor. 2007. *Modernity and the Nation in Mexican Representations of Masculinity: From Sensuality to Bloodshed.* New York: Palgrave Macmillan.

Elliott, Carl, and Roberto Abadie. 2008. "Exploiting a Research Underclass in Phase 1 Clinical Trials." *New England Journal of Medicine* 358, no. 22: 2316–17.

Epstein, Steven. 2008. "The Rise of 'Recruitmentology': Clinical Research, Racial Knowledge, and the Politics of Inclusion and Difference." *Social Studies of Science* 38, no. 5: 801–32.

García, Brígida, and Orlandina de Oliveira. 2004. "El ejercicio de la paternidad en el México urbano [The practice of paternity in urban Mexico]." In *Imágenes de la Familia en el Cambio de Siglo,* ed. Marina Ariza and Orlandina de Oliveira. México, D.F: Instituto de Investigaciones Sociales, Universidad Nacional Autónoma de México.

Giuliano, Anna R., Eduardo Lazcano, Luisa L. Villa, Jorge Salmeron, Roberto Flores, Martha Abrahamsen, and Mary Papenfuss. 2006. "Natural History of HPV Infection in Men: The HIM Study." AACR Meeting Abstracts 2006, no. 3: B215.

Giuliano, Anna R., Eduardo Lazcano-Ponce, Luisa L. Villa, Roberto Flores, Jorge Salmeron, J. H. Lee, Mary R. Papenfuss, Martha Abrahamsen, E. Jolles, C. M. Nielson, M. L. Baggio, R. Silva R, and M. Quiterio. 2008. "The Human Papillomavirus Infection in Men Study: Human Papillomavirus Prevalence and Type Distribution among Men Residing in Brazil, Mexico, and the United States." *Cancer Epidemiology, Biomarkers & Prevention* 17, no. 8: 2036–43.

Gutmann, Matthew C. 1996. *The Meanings of Macho: Being a Man in Mexico City.* Berkeley: University of California Press.

———. 2007. *Fixing Men: Sex, Birth Control, and AIDS in Mexico.* Berkeley: University of California Press.

Hammar, Lawrence. 2007. "The Many Sexes of Risk: Gender, Disease, and Identity in the Asia-Pacific Region and Elsewhere." *Reviews in Anthropology* 36, no. 4: 335–56.

Hirsch, Jennifer. 2003. *A Courtship After Marriage: Sexuality and Love in Mexican Transnational Families.* Berkeley: University of California Press.

Instituto Nacional de Estadística y Geografía. 2005. Causas seleccionadas de mortalidad por sexo [Selected causes of mortality by sex]. http://www .inegi.org.mx/prod_serv/contenidos/espanol/bvinegi/productos/integra cion/sociodemografico/mujeresyhombres/2007/MyH_2007_2.pdf.

———. 2009. Geográfica [Geography]. http://www.inegi.org.mx/inegi/de fault.aspx?s=geo.

Jackson, Michael. 1998. *Minima Ethnographica: Intersubjectivity and the Anthropological Project.* Chicago: University of Chicago Press.

Lazcano-Ponce, E. C., S. Moss, P. Alonso de Ruíz, Castro J. Salmerón, and M. Hernández-Avila. 1999. "Cervical Cancer Screening in Developing Countries: Why is it Ineffective? The Case of Mexico." *Archives of Medical Research* 30, no. 3: 240–50.

Mol, Annemarie. 2002. *The Body Multiple: Ontology in Medical Practice*. Durham, NC: Duke University Press.

Monahan, Torin. 2011. "Surveillance as Cultural Practice." *The Sociological Quarterly* 52, no. 4: 495–508.

Palacio-Mejía, L. S., E. Lazcano-Ponce, B. Allen-Leigh, and M. Hernández-Avila. 2009. "Regional Differences in Breast and Cervical Cancer Mortality in Mexico between 1979-2006." *Salud Pública de México* 51, no. 2: S208–19.

Ramirez, Josué. 2009. *Against Machismo: Young Adult Voices in Mexico City.* New York; Oxford: Berghahn Books.

Secretaría de Salud. 2010. *Campaña de vacunación contra el virus del Papiloma Humano* [Vaccination campaign against human papillomavirus]. Mexico City.

Sicilia, Javier. 2011. *Javier Sicilia: Carta abierta a políticos y criminales* [Javier Sicilia: Open letter to politicians and criminals]. Vanguardia.

Wentzell, Emily. 2013a. "'I Don't Want to be Like my Father': Masculinity, Modernity and Intergenerational Relationships in Mexico." In *Transitions and Transformations: Cultural Perspectives on the Life Course,* ed. C. Lynch and J. Danely. New York; Oxford: Berghahn Books.

———. 2013b. *Maturing Masculinities: Aging, Chronic Illness, and Viagra in Mexico.* Durham, NC: Duke University Press.

Whyte, Susan Reynolds. 2009. "Health Identities and Subjectivities." *Medical Anthropology Quarterly* 23, no. 1: 6–15.

Chapter 8

THE HIGH-TECH HOMUNCULUS
NEW SCIENCE, OLD CONSTRUCTS

Linda G. Kahn and Wendy Chavkin

Introduction

Any discussion of fatherhood—globalized or otherwise—would be incomplete without considering the basics of human reproduction: biological fathers provide half of the DNA that becomes the template for their offspring. Typically, that genetic material is delivered via sexual intercourse, and there is often a relationship between the provider and recipient that includes a socially determined set of obligations and expectations. The inability to father a biological child interferes with that dynamic and is a source of profound shame in many cultures. Male infertility is a growing problem in certain parts of the world as a result of advancing paternal age, consanguinity, and environmental exposures associated with declining sperm count. Two technological resolutions to the problem have emerged: artificial insemination by third-party semen, also called artificial insemination by donor (although the use of the term "donor" presumes an altruistic motivation that may not be present in today's fertility marketplace); and intracytoplasmic sperm injection (ICSI), which is used for low sperm count and increasingly in cases of unexplained infertility.

The availability of third-party insemination underscores the distinction between social and biological aspects of fatherhood, making it culturally acceptable for men to produce intentionally genetic offspring they have no intention of rearing and for women to bear children in households without a paternal presence. ICSI, while preserving the unity of social and biological paternity, is associated with proven health risks to offspring. Both technologies are cause for substantive ethical, psychological, and medical concern, and in spite of their seeming modernity, they are often interpreted in ways that reinforce old tropes about genetic determinism and the primacy of the male gamete.

An international trade in semen has given new meaning to the term "globalized fatherhood." While a vial of "dream" genes can be sent anywhere on the planet, there is a cost involved, and it is not only monetary. In this chapter we focus on three core issues that highlight the ways in which various countries and cultures around the globe have dealt with third-party insemination: anonymity, regulation, and compensation. Although ostensibly questions of law and ethics, decisions in these three areas have health ramifications—both physical and psychological—that may affect any or all of the parties involved: the provider, the recipient, and the child. Until recently, there has been scant scientific research into the health outcomes of third-party insemination and ICSI. Instead, public space is filled by a marketing blitz by the financially powerful infertility industry, which has a vested interest in downplaying health risks.

As a medical doctor (Chavkin) and epidemiologist (Kahn) working in the field of public health, our primary focus is on the impact of these procedures on both individual and population health. In this chapter we use a combination of published medical, government, and journalistic sources to describe the current state of affairs. Large-scale well-designed studies of the health impacts of third-party insemination and ICSI are rare; we have cited the best available, which compare children born of these interventions to population controls. Research into the psychological and cultural aspects of these technologies is generally conducted among subjects who agree to participate; while informative, these are studies of non-representative, small, self-selected samples. Newspaper and magazine articles rarely provide rigorously obtained empirical findings but are useful sources of anecdotal evidence.

As feminists, we are also fascinated by the issues of gender and power that these brave new technologies highlight. Certainly, it may be liberating both for men and women to be able to reproduce in a wider set of social circumstances and to transcend their biological limitations. Injecting a single sperm into an egg under a high-powered microscope is light years away from old-fashioned sex and—one would think—old-fashioned ideas about procreation. And yet, in the Herculean effort to scavenge a single live sperm from an intended father for ICSI or the aggressive promotion of qualities of semen donors, there remains an unchallenged emphasis on the mystique of the male gamete that stretches back centuries. Spermism, the notion of the all-controlling sperm and the passive egg, dates at least to Pythagoras, an early Preformationist, who believed that miniature human beings resided within male gametes, awaiting the spark of fertilization to begin growing. This theory gained new traction in the seventeenth century with the invention of the microscope. Scientists such as Antonie van Leeuwenhoek and Nicolaas Hartsoeker reported seeing a homunculus—literally, a "little man"—fully formed, curled up inside the head of a sperm, an image that conformed to the prevailing mechanistic view of the natural world (VanSpeybroeck et al. 2002).[1] While we now know that the female contribution to future offspring is equal to the male in terms of genes—and even greater when one includes the impact of the uterine environment—the primitive concept of the primacy of the sperm persists, even in the high-tech field of assisted reproduction.

From Livestock to the Stock Market:
A Brief History of Third-Party Insemination

While it is possible that artificial insemination had been occurring for centuries, the first case of artificial insemination using a third-party donor that is documented in the medical literature took place at Jefferson Medical College in Philadelphia in 1884. Seeking medical advice for their infertility, a wealthy Quaker couple approached the well-known doctor William Pancoast. The wife was found to be healthy, but her husband was found to be azoospermic, producing no sperm in his ejaculate. On the pretense of a follow-up visit, in the presence of a half-dozen medical students, "The woman was chloroformed, and with a hard rubber syringe some fresh semen from the best-looking member of the class was deposited in the uterus" (Hard 1909). The husband was told of the procedure only after his wife was confirmed to be pregnant; at the husband's request, the wife, who delivered a healthy boy, was never made aware of the use of donor semen. The procedure was kept secret until twenty-five years later, when one of the medical students involved, Addison David Hard, reported the procedure in the pages of *The Medical World*. After regaling readers with a lively description of the event in question, Hard went on to extol "artificial impregnation by carefully selected seed" as a solution to the "problem" of "half-witted, evil-inclined, disease-disposed" progeny that result from sentimental marriages between "persons of the worst possible promise of good and healthy offspring" (1909). His communication aired themes that have played in the background over the subsequent century of experimentation with artificial insemination: the shame of male infertility, the female body as a locus of experimentation, and faith in the power of the sperm to transmit desired traits from supplier to offspring.

Over the ensuing decades, third-party insemination to aid infertile couples began to be practiced with increasing frequency, but continued secrecy. Semen was generally supplied by doctors and medical students, who were considered optimal sources because of their presumed intelligence and commitment to an honorable profession. Alan Guttmacher (1962), who utilized the technique in his own practice, preferred "married medical students, or house officers, who themselves have fathered normal children... [as] you can discuss with them their family trees and can rule out those who have likelihood of transmitting cacogenic factors" that might yield offspring with undesirable traits. Furthermore, he trusted that medical doctors would recuse themselves if they carried any venereal diseases.

In spite of Guttmacher's faith in the upstanding nature of medical professionals, the fact remains that throughout the early decades of third-party insemination, donors remained anonymous and underwent at most basic medical screening, leaving women vulnerable to sexually transmitted infections and children at risk of heritable and transmissible conditions. Physicians encouraged women not to reveal their use of donor semen, even to their offspring, in order to protect their husbands from the stigma of infertility and their children from the stigma of illegitimacy (as an added bonus, this protected the doctors from future paternity claims, as they were often the semen suppliers). They often prescribed intercourse the night of the procedure or mixed the husband's semen with the supplier's, leaving open the remote possibility that the husband had sired the child and thereby justifying putting the husband's name on the birth certificate (K. Daniels 1998). Sowing hope—or at least uncertainty— about the husband's genetic relationship to the child was as much a legal matter as a psychological one, as conception via semen donation was considered adulterous, and the progeny thus illegitimate in the eyes of the government. It was not until the Uniform Parentage Act in 1973 that, in the states where it was enacted, the husband of a woman who gave birth via donor insemination was considered to be the child's father, and then only if he had consented to the procedure and it was carried out by a licensed physician (National Conference of Commissioners on Uniform State Laws 2000).

As long as fresh semen was required for third-party insemination, the medical professional donor model continued to be the norm, as samples could be obtained where and when they were needed. The physician in whom the couple had placed their confidence would select the donor, usually so that his phenotypic characteristics approximated those of the infertile husband. Techniques for successfully freezing and thawing human semen had to be developed before the donor pool could be expanded and selection criteria refined. In 1866, the Italian physician Paolo Mantegazza first reported the survival of frozen sperm and speculated on the possibility of storing frozen semen of soldiers for future use should they be killed in battle (Polge et al. 1949). Research into cryogenic preservation continued, driven by efforts to freeze bovine semen for the dairy cattle industry, with the occasional foray into experimentation with human samples (Polge et al. 1949; Sherman 1964). Finally, in 1953, Raymond G. Bunge, a professor of urology, and Jerome K. Sherman, a doctoral student in zoology, both at the University of Iowa, successfully impregnated four women with semen that had been previously frozen and stored in what became the first semen cryobank (Bunge and Sherman 1954).

Once frozen human semen (which could be stored and transported easily) was shown to be effective in achieving pregnancy, the concept of the semen bank of which Mantegazza had only dreamed a century earlier began to take off. For a variety of reasons, including the development of semen-freezing techniques within the agricultural industry, the secrecy in which third-party insemination had been practiced, and the fact that the procedure did not involve drugs or devices that were within the purview of the U.S. Food and Drug Administration (FDA), third-party insemination in the United States flew under the regulatory radar for decades. Semen banks were essentially self-policed until 2005, when rules concerning the safety and handling of human tissue and the eligibility of donors—first proposed only in 1997—finally became effective (U.S. Food and Drug Administration 2009).

Perhaps partly because of this lack of oversight, donor insemination is a huge international industry today. It is estimated that in the United States alone semen banking is a $100 million-per-year business (Newton-Small 2012). Young men are recruited with promises of steady income and often sell their semen to defray university expenses or supplement the income from their first jobs.[2] Semen banks compete for eligible suppliers and aggressively market their frozen wares, with matches made over the Internet between buyers and sellers who may be on opposite sides of the globe. Yet the issues that swirled around that first experiment more than a century ago—anonymity, secrecy, stigma, and emphasis on the primacy of the male contribution—continue to influence how third-party insemination[3] is practiced in various cultural settings today.

Local Regulations versus the Global Marketplace

In Western countries, relatively liberal attitudes toward childbearing outside of marriage, minimal stigma against infertility, and an open marketplace have led to a proliferation of semen banks since the late 1970s. The United States is the world's first and largest supplier of semen—in 2005, the top four U.S. semen banks alone provided 65 percent of third-party semen globally and currently the U.S. exports semen to more than sixty countries (Newton-Small 2012). Therefore, we have chosen to use the United States as the baseline for our discussion of how the semen industry operates, drawing cross-cultural comparisons wherever reliable data could be found.

While semen bank clientele initially comprised married couples exclusively, single women and lesbian couples eventually began to avail themselves of the opportunity to conceive biologically related children. Since the development of ICSI in the early 1990s, many heterosexual couples whose infertility is attributable to male factors have opted to try to conceive using what little reproductive material can be obtained from the male partner, even if it entails a surgical procedure, rather than third-party semen. Consequently, the market for donor semen in certain countries is becoming more and more driven by single and lesbian women. At the 2011 annual meeting of the of the American Society for Reproductive Medicine (ASRM), Michelle Ottey and Suzanne Seitz (2011) reported on the results of an online survey of clients of Fairfax Cryobank and Cryogenics Laboratories, Inc., two of the largest and oldest semen banks in the United States. They sent an Internet survey to all of their clients over a three-year period (total number unspecified) and received more than 7,700 responses (99 percent of which were from women). They found that 35 percent identified themselves as part of heterosexual couples, 30 percent as single mothers by choice, and

35 percent as part of lesbian couples (2011). While the respondents were self-selected, the results are in line with other, much smaller studies, including a survey of 165 women who sought third-party insemination in Perth, Australia, 23.6 percent of whom were partnered heterosexual women, 17.6 percent partnered lesbian women, and 58.8 percent single women (Rodino et al. 2011).

In the United States, semen is predominantly brokered through registered semen banks. Sellers are solicited, often via the Internet, and screened according to procedures outlined by the FDA, which regulates the donation of all human cells, tissues, and cellular- or tissue-based products. Potential semen suppliers are required to undergo physical exams, be tested for communicable diseases, and give complete personal, medical, and sexual histories. There is no requirement that any of the personal or family health information provided during the screening interview be verified. Unless the provider is known to the recipient, the semen sample must be frozen and quarantined for at least six months, and then the supplier must be retested prior to use. Screening and test results of semen providers must be kept for ten years (U.S. Food and Drug Administration 2009). In Europe, similar screening procedures to those of the FDA are mandated by the EU Tissue Directive (The Commission of the European Communities 2006).

Above and beyond the FDA requirements, the ASRM recommends that suppliers undergo psychological counseling, be tested for blood type and Rh, and be rejected if they are considered high risk for sexually transmitted and other blood-borne diseases, or have recently received transplants or been vaccinated against smallpox. In addition to testing all potential suppliers for certain genetic diseases such as Huntington disease and cystic fibrosis, it is recommended that men from ethnic groups at high risk for particular heritable conditions (e.g., Tay-Sachs, sickle cell anemia, thalassemia) also be screened for those. Men should be younger than forty years old and free of major malformations, familial genetic diseases among their first-degree relatives, and known chromosomal abnormalities. Furthermore, the ASRM recommends that semen banks keep permanent records of suppliers' screening and testing results, as well as of the outcomes of each insemination cycle (Practice Committee of the American Society for Reproductive Medicine and Practice Committee of the Society for Assisted Reproductive Technology 2008). Because all but the FDA requirements regarding semen provision in the United States are non-binding, semen banks are essentially left to oversee their own quality control. There is no legal accountability when semen banks fail to maintain high standards and no recourse for families desiring additional medical information from anonymous suppliers, even if they have reason to believe their child has a heritable condition traceable to his or her biological father (Grady 2006; Mroz 2012).

In markets such as that of the United States, where there are no legal limits on the number of children who may be fathered by a single supplier, providers with saleable traits can be major assets to commercial semen banks. Successful suppliers provide samples two to three times a week for six to twelve months. While most semen banks claim to limit the number of offspring produced by a single supplier, recent reports of dozens of children—in one case, more than 150—fathered by one provider suggest that profit may be trumping prudence (Agence France-Presse 2011; Mroz 2011). Large numbers of offspring from a particular supplier can occur because men donate to multiple semen banks. It can also occur because semen banks that sell to private consumers have no way to monitor pregnancy outcomes; they are entirely dependent on recipients voluntarily reporting back. According to the director of Fairfax Cryobank, only 20 to 30 percent do (Pool 2011). In addition, recipients often purchase a number of vials in case repeated insemination is required; if pregnancy is achieved, they may pass on or resell the leftover semen, making it impossible to keep track of the number of offspring produced by a particular supplier.

The private marketplace's lack of comprehensive records of how many children a supplier has fathered and who those children are may have serious consequences. There have been no formal studies of the outcome of discovering that one has scores of siblings or offspring, although an argument has been made that psychological consequences ought to be considered as well as potential consanguinity in terms of setting limits on the number of live offspring permitted from a single supplier (Scheib and Ruby 2009). Furthermore, if it is later discovered that a supplier has a serious heritable medical condition, it is imperative that there be well-kept records in order to inform his progeny.

The most significant cross-country differences regarding semen provision have to do with compensation, restrictions on the number of offspring, and anonymity. While the ASRM guidelines recommend that compensation reflect time and trouble, and not serve as a major incentive, the fact that semen supplies have increased in the United States as the economy has suffered suggests that remuneration is a motivating factor for some (Schiffman 2010). Indeed, when conducting research for this chapter, we were barraged with Internet banner advertisements and paid Google search items offering up to $1,200 a month to semen suppliers. Many other countries prohibit compensation altogether or keep it to a bare minimum in order to insure that the suppliers' motivation is primarily altruistic. In the United States, Russia, Canada, and Israel, there are no limits on the number of children a provider may sire, only loose recommendations—no more than twenty or twenty-five children per 800,000 to 850,000 population. By contrast, Australia, New Zealand, and European countries that permit gamete donation have strict legal limits on third-party insemination, ranging from five full-term pregnancies in Bulgaria to twenty-five offspring in the Netherlands, which are enforceable as long as women are inseminated with semen procured through public sector fertility clinics (Janssens et al. 2011).

While suppliers' rights are privileged in the United States, where anonymous semen donation is the norm, children's rights are privileged in northern Europe and other Anglo countries. In these places, the trend has been toward open-identity donation based on a strict interpretation of the United Nations Convention on the Rights of the Child, which states that a child has the right "to know... his or her parents" and "to preserve his or her identity... including family relations" (Office of the United Nations High Commissioner for Human Rights 1989). Children may learn their biological father's identity by age eighteen, if not earlier. As a consequence of their prohibition of anonymity, countries such as Sweden and the United Kingdom experienced a substantial decline in donations and had to increase their reliance on imported semen to meet domestic demand (Shukla 2013).

An exception to the trend toward open semen donation in Europe is Denmark, home to the world's largest semen bank, Cryos International. Semen donation is big business in Denmark—so much so that in 2006, when the Danish tax authority proposed taxing semen sellers on income earned through their efforts, thereby jeopardizing their anonymity, Cryos threatened to move abroad and the tax authority retreated. Founded in 1987, Cryos became a major player by marketing semen from healthy, blond-haired, blue-eyed sellers who were desired by Cryos's earliest clients, northern European fertility clinics and private U.S. consumers. In 2005, the FDA banned the import of human semen to prevent transmission of Creutzfeldt-Jakob ("mad cow") disease, severely harming the company's bottom line. (The FDA banned donation of blood from those potentially exposed to the disease in 1999.) Cryos now recruits sellers at multiple franchises in Denmark, India, and New York and distributes semen to more than sixty-five countries worldwide, primarily through public sector fertility clinics (Cryos International 2011; Expatica.com 2009).

While concerns about rights dominate public discourse about se-men donation in Western countries, cultural and religious beliefs are the major factors determining use of third-party insemination in Middle Eastern and South Asian countries. Semen donation is pro-hibited by religious *fatwas* among Sunni Muslims, who comprise the majority of Muslims worldwide and have consequently become avid consumers of ICSI (see Inhorn, this volume). There is more diver-sity of opinion among Shiite Muslims, who represent the majority in Iran, Iraq, Bahrain, and Lebanon (Inhorn 2006). In Israel, third-party insemination is widely available and government-subsidized, and among secular Israelis it is freely used by heterosexual couples, lesbians, and single women. Infertile Orthodox Jewish couples may avail themselves of third-party insemination, but only under spe-cific circumstances determined on case-by-case bases by their rabbis (Kahn 2000). In India, where male infertility is highly stigmatized and third-party insemination is often viewed as a radical departure from established beliefs, men frequently request that a brother's or father's semen be used in order to preserve a familial link; how-ever, they will use non-related suppliers if needed, often swearing the physician to secrecy (Bharadwaj 2003). The Indian Council of Medical Research has issued non-binding guidelines about supplier screening and about limiting the number of offspring per supplier, but these are frequently ignored in a lucrative market driven by shame and desperation (Gupta 2008).

Regardless of where on the globe third-party insemination and ICSI are being employed, the discourse primarily focuses on the ful-fillment of desires: the desire of a heterosexual or lesbian couple to produce a child together, the desire of a man to overcome the stigma of infertility, the desire of a single woman to experience the joys of motherhood—as well as the desires of the fertility industry and its suppliers to make money while providing a sought-after service and of the religious authority to maintain control. In the effort to fulfill those desires, health risks to women and children are often down-played or ignored.

From Political to Personal

While human rights, corporate profits, and societal mores affect reg-ulation and legislation regarding the use of third-party semen, other considerations come into play when decisions are made on the personal level. Consumers who purchase semen directly may have the freedom to choose between anonymous and open-identity donation, and if they opt for anonymous, they can further choose whether or not to disclose to their offspring the circumstances of their conception. Buyers may also select suppliers based on particular qualities and sellers can craft profiles that increase their marketability.

Anonymity is appealing to heterosexual couples seeking third-party insemination who desire to maintain the illusion that the social and biological fathers are one and the same. In this case, it is necessary both to obscure the identity of the supplier and to keep the child unaware of this aspect of his or her origin. The growing private market in anonymously supplied semen in countries that mandate open-identity donation—and the legal sanction of anonymous semen provision in large markets such as that in the United States—attest to many recipients' continued desire to maintain secrecy. While the trend is toward greater disclosure, there is still resistance. A longitudinal study of heterosexual married couples in the United Kingdom who used third-party semen to conceive in the early 1990s found that fewer than 9 percent had told their children by age eighteen (Golombok et al. 2002; Owen and Golombok 2009). A second study initiated a decade later found an increased openness among the parents: nearly half expressed an intention to disclose when interviewed during their children's infancy (Golombok et al. 2004), and almost a third had done so by the child's seventh birthday (Casey et al. 2008). Responses to a non-representative online survey of 165 adolescent and adult members of the Donor Sibling Registry, in which respondents were asked their age and emotions when they found out about the circumstances of their conception, show an association between delayed disclosure and feelings of confusion, shock, upset, and anger (Jadva et al. 2009).

For lesbian couples and single mothers by choice, there is no father figure in the household, and thus less reason to try to obscure the existence of the semen supplier. Consequently, lesbian couples and single mothers who use donor semen are more likely to disclose to their children at an early age, often in response to their children's curiosity about their paternity (Jadva et al. 2009). Single women and lesbian couples are also less likely to choose anonymous providers, according to a study by The Sperm Bank of California (TSBC), the first semen bank in the world to offer clients the choice of anonymous or open-identity suppliers. Based on archival data of 515 families who bore at least one child through third-party insemination between 1998 and 2003, this study found that heterosexual couples were equally likely to choose open-identity suppliers as anonymous ones, whereas 76 percent of single women and 79.9 percent of lesbian couples chose open-identity suppliers. Ninety of the families chose to participate in a matching service, which would connect them with other families that had conceived using the same semen donor; participants were nearly all either single women or lesbian couples (34.4 percent and 62.2 percent, respectively), with only 3.3 percent being heterosexual couples (Scheib and Ruby 2008). While these results are in line with other research findings, they derive from the self-selected group that reported live births to TSBC.

When third-party insemination is provided through publicly funded healthcare services, suppliers and recipients are generally matched on phenotypic characteristics by clinic staff. In contrast, when recipients purchase semen through the private marketplace, they can freely browse online catalogs of potential suppliers. Much like personal advertisements, the profiles highlight the men's intelligence, athleticism, good looks, sensitivity, humor—even their popularity among other semen shoppers. Semen bank staff members, who know which attributes will appeal to their clients, may assist suppliers in creating their profiles (Almeling 2011). In keeping with their tendency not to disclose their use of donor insemination and to seek out anonymous suppliers, heterosexual couples most often choose suppliers who physically match the male partner in order to mask the discrepancy between biological and social paternity (C. Daniels 2006). Lesbian couples and single women are not constrained by such considerations. An analysis of the type of information about semen suppliers deemed important by 165 recipients recruited to participate in an online survey through an infertility clinic in Western Australia found that single women differed from partnered heterosexual or lesbian women in the emphasis they placed on the supplier's age, looks, occupation, hobbies and interests, and feelings about contact with his offspring. The authors infer that single women may be looking for characteristics associated with positive long-term mating prospects such as good genes and good character, implying an "as if" relationship with the supplier/father (Rodino et al. 2011).

Of course, there is no guarantee that the qualities on which buyers focus when they purchase semen will be inherited—or are even heritable. Even highly heritable characteristics, such as eye color, are coded for by multiple genes, some of which are inherited from the biological mother and some from the biological father. And often genes interact with the environment, making it impossible to predict how features will develop in a given individual. Yet recipients spend much energy selecting suppliers based on these desired traits, as if their future offspring were latent in the frozen sample, waiting to be born like a high-tech homunculus. Not only does this belie basic biology, but it also presumes that the profiles of suppliers provided by commercial semen banks accurately reflect the qualities of the men who provided the samples, the truth of which is undetermined.

Equally unknown are providers' motivations. While semen banks emphasize provider altruism, pointing to the laborious screening process and the periods of abstinence required prior to each donation, it is clear that in most cases money is a significant factor. In interviews with twenty U.S. semen donors, sociologist Rene Almeling (2011) found the majority worked in low-paying jobs, were unemployed, and/or were part-time students. When Canada outlawed payment for semen samples in 2004, the supply plummeted and imports had to be brought in from the United States (Yee 2009). A systematic review of 29 studies of semen suppliers, including potential, actual, and non-providers, found that younger men tend to be more strongly motivated by financial remuneration, while older men tend to be motivated by more altruistic feelings. Secondary motivations include men's curiosity about their fertility and the desire to procreate and/or to disseminate their genes (Van den Broeck et al. 2013). In a *Newsweek* article in which he investigated the world of do-it-yourself free semen donation, Tony Dokoupil (2011) writes, "Many donors say they are motivated not by sex so much as a desire to spawn as many children as possible."

The Grey Market for Semen

In addition to regulated registered semen banks, there is a vast unregulated market for semen. While some U.S. semen banks run "directed donor" programs, in which a supplier known to the recipient provides semen for artificial insemination that is then screened according to FDA rules, many women and couples make private arrangements with a friend or relative and use fresh semen. In these cases, the donor does not undergo a physical exam or medical history assessment, nor is he tested for sexually transmitted infections (STIs) or genetic diseases, putting both mother and child at risk of adverse health consequences.

Those who prefer fresh semen but do not have a willing friend or relative can avail themselves of numerous web sites and Internet groups where donors and recipients directly arrange for the exchange of free fresh semen. These sites have become particularly popular in the United Kingdom, Canada, and Australia, where the amount of semen available through semen banks has dwindled since laws prohibiting anonymous donation have gone into effect. Interestingly, they are becoming popular in the United States for the opposite reason—in a reaction against the cost and enforced anonymity of semen banks (even open-identity suppliers remain anonymous until the child requests information after age eighteen), recipients are seeking donors who wish to be part of their children's lives. Men usually provide semen samples in a cup, although some will oblige women who prefer natural insemination (Dokoupil 2011). In addition to the legal and health risks associated with other forms of fresh semen donation, there is a heightened risk of STI transmission with practitioners of natural insemination who may have a widespread clientele.

The Health Consequences of Using Frozen Semen

The ability to freeze semen has had far greater ramifications than Mantegazza could have ever imagined. It has exponentially increased the ability of medical professionals to treat male-factor infertility and has allowed single women and lesbian couples to produce biologically related children. Furthermore, men who risk infertility because they need to undergo chemotherapy or radiation, who have occupational exposure to toxic substances, or who may be exposed to chemical warfare agents can bank frozen semen before the noxious exposure. The ability to freeze and quarantine semen has improved the safety of artificial insemination by preventing the transmission of HIV and other communicable diseases. But the process is not risk free.

When a frozen semen sample is thawed, there is a significant decline in normal sperm morphology, motility, and mitochondrial function, contributing to a reduction of approximately one-third in the number of functional sperm (O'Connell et al. 2002). A study of semen samples from ninety-two men, both fertile and subfertile, found that freeze-thawing especially damaged sperm in the tail and head regions, impairing the ability to swim toward the egg and pen-

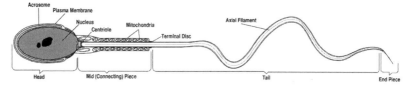

FIGURE 8.1 The Anatomy of a Sperm. Sperm are single cells comprising three parts: head, midsection, and tail. The head contains the nucleus, in which the paternal DNA is tightly coiled. Enveloping the top of the head is the acrosome, which contains enzymes that digest the outer membrane of the ovum, allowing the sperm to penetrate the egg's shield, the zona pellucida. The midsection is filled with mitochondria, which produce the energy that the sperm needs to swim up the female reproductive tract. The tail provides the spiraling and lashing movements needed to propel the sperm forward. When the sperm enters the ovum, the tail detaches. *Source:* Mariana Ruiz Villarreal [public domain], via Wikimedia Commons.

etrate its zona pellucida. In addition, the proportion of condensed chromatin (DNA in its most stable form), morphologically normal sperm, and sperm with normal membrane structure were all significantly reduced after the samples had been frozen and thawed (Hammadeh et al. 1999). In a much smaller study, semen samples were collected from five fertile men. One half of each man's sample was analyzed immediately, while the other half was frozen and thawed prior to analysis. The researchers found increased fragmentation of nuclear DNA in sperm that had undergone the freeze-thaw process compared to fresh, suggesting a possible mechanism for the reduced fertility rate associated with using frozen semen (Gosalvez et al. 2011).

Whether the damage to sperm incurred during the freeze-thaw process negatively affects the health of the offspring is unclear. In the 1990s, two large cohort studies were undertaken to compare pregnancies resulting from use of frozen semen to population-based controls: one included 11,535 pregnancies attained through a consortium of twenty-two French sperm banks, the other included 1,552 pregnancies achieved at two large fertility clinics in Victoria, Australia. Neither showed any statistically significant increase in adverse birth outcomes attributable to the use of frozen semen (Hoy et al. 1999; Lansac et al. 1997; Thepot et al. 1996). We could find no follow-up studies of these or other individuals conceived via cryogenically preserved semen, however. The long-term health consequences to offspring are therefore still unknown.

Intracytoplasmic Sperm Injection

Freezing sperm presumes, of course, that there are sperm to freeze. In 1992, Gianpiero Palermo and colleagues working at the Centre for Reproductive Medicine in Brussels published a short report in *The Lancet* announcing the first human births following direct injection of a single sperm into a human egg (Palermo et al. 1992). ICSI was the most important technological advance in assisted reproduction since the birth of the first "test-tube baby" in 1978 and was quickly adopted, as it permitted men with few normal or viable sperm to father genetically related offspring and avoid the stigma, secrecy, religious prohibitions, and psychological difficulties often associated with using third-party semen.

ICSI now features in a substantial portion of all ART cycles worldwide. A 2007 study of ICSI use internationally found rates were

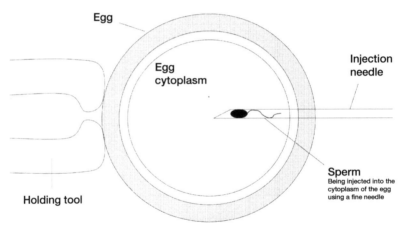

FIGURE 8.2. How ICSI Works. In ICSI, a single sperm, sperm head, or nucleus is inserted directly into the cytoplasm of a mature oocyte to create a fertilized embryo that is then transferred into the uterus of a woman. The sperm is generally retrieved from ejaculate. If ejaculation is not possible because of nerve damage, or if there are no sperm in the ejaculate because of vasectomy or blocked sperm ducts, sperm may be retrieved from the testes or epididymis. In order to allow penetration of the zona pellucida, the protective cumulus cells on the outermost surface of the egg must be chemically stripped away. In natural or in vitro fertilization (IVF), the acrosome of the sperm must bind with the zona pellucida prior to the sperm being granted entry into the egg—one of nature's quality-control measures. Cumulus cells are believed to play a role in oocyte maturation, and it has been suggested that removing them may affect the successful development of the fertilized egg into a viable embryo (Ebner et al. 2006). *Source:* Sims IVF, Dublin, Ireland.

highest in the Middle East (89.2 percent of ART cycles), reflecting both the prohibition against using third-party semen among Sunni Muslims and varying restrictions on the practice among Shiites, as well as the high rate of male infertility in the region resulting from the practice of consanguineous marriage (see Inhorn, this volume). ICSI was popular in Poland (84.3 percent) and the predominantly Catholic countries of Southern Europe and Latin America (73.9 and 70 percent, respectively), and less so in Nordic and Eastern European countries (44.3 and 46.2 percent, respectively). Interestingly, although the Catholic Church has banned all ART, including ICSI and third-party insemination, practicing Catholics appear to perceive the former to be more acceptable than the latter. While ICSI was designed for use in cases where the man has few viable sperm, it is now also being used in cases of mixed and unexplained infertility (Nyboe Andersen et al. 2008). Although there is conjecture that some physicians believe that it yields a higher conception rate than traditional IVF, the latest data from the European Society of Human Reproduction and Embryology (ESHRE), reporting on 84.5 percent of clinics in thirty-six countries, show that pregnancy rates for IVF and ICSI are virtually identical (Ferraretti et al. 2012).

The primary indication for ICSI is few or abnormal sperm, which may be caused by an underlying genetic abnormality and theoretically lead to the transmission of heritable conditions to the ensuing children. A large and rigorous Australian study found that after controlling for potential confounders, children conceived via ICSI had between 1.10 and 1.73 times the likelihood of a birth defect or chromosomal abnormality (depending on whether frozen or fresh embryos were implanted) compared to non-ART-conceived children (Davies et al. 2012). This may reflect chromosomal damage to paternal DNA that is already present in subfertile men (Dohle et al. 2002). Infertile men often have a mix of normal and abnormal looking sperm from which morphologically normal and motile sperm are generally chosen to be used for ICSI. However, compared to men with completely normal looking sperm, a study of forty-nine infertile men found that even their normal looking sperm were more likely to harbor DNA damage (Avendano and Oehninger 2011). Some of these defects may be incompatible with life and lead to early miscarriage; others may put offspring at risk of congenital malformations, mental retardation, childhood cancer, male-factor subfertility or infertility, bilateral absence of the vas deferens, or cystic fibrosis (Aittomaki et al. 2004).

In addition to the possibility of passing on genetic abnormalities, there is concern about epigenetic changes that may be transmitted through ICSI. At different stages of development, genes are turned "on" or "off" in a carefully choreographed pattern by the addition of certain chemical groups to the DNA itself or to the proteins surrounding it (the epigenome). Genes are said to be imprinted when their expression is dependent on the parent of origin; epigenetic changes silence, or imprint, the version of the gene (allele) inherited from one of the parents, often by the addition of a methyl group to the DNA. When that silencing fails to occur, or when the wrong parent's allele is turned off, an embryo may not survive, or the ensuing child may have one of a number of diseases known as imprinting disorders, such as Angelman and Prader-Willi syndromes, the risk of which is increased in children conceived via IVF (Manipalviratn et al. 2009). One Japanese study found that the sperm of twenty-four out of ninety-seven men with moderate to severe oligospermia had abnormal methylation of imprinted genes (Kobayashi et al. 2007), while another smaller Portuguese study found that seven out of fifteen patients with a sperm concentration of less than 10×10^6/ mL had abnormal methylation of imprinted genes (Marques et al. 2008), suggesting that the sperm may be the source of the imprinting disorder.

When either genetic or epigenetic problems are present but either undetected or undetectable in the sperm of infertile men, ICSI raises the likelihood of passing on compromised genetic material—the opposite of Darwinian natural selection. In addition to the health consequences, it is also worth considering the ethical implications of deliberately bringing into the world children with an increased risk of disease. Because these diseases are coded for in the genome and epigenome, they may be passed on from children to grandchildren and beyond. It will take another generation to discern the long-term effects of ICSI, including whether it transmits to male offspring the infertility that made the procedure necessary in the first place. Given the increased incidence of birth defects and unknown long-term effects among ICSI children, the widespread and ever-expanding use of this procedure is worrisome.

Conclusion

Gratifying the desire to become a parent in a world where biological constraints have been loosed leads to a host of social questions about the meaning of paternity, sibships, genetics, and identity. It also leads to serious questions about the health impact of technologies such as third-party insemination and ICSI, especially when practiced in the context of slick marketing, lax regulation, and religious demands. In this chapter, we report the known data and outline the many questions for which we lack empirical findings.

Some view third-party insemination and ICSI as liberating and progressive, as they offer a means to sidestep the stigma of male infertility, avoid overt conflict with religious dicta, and broaden the sanctioned options for achieving parenthood. Yet employing a medical intervention to circumvent these social obstacles does nothing to resolve them; indeed, these procedures are often marketed and consumed in ways that reinforce age-old ideas and conservative gender relationships. Third-party insemination recipients who select suppliers based on qualities they would like to see replicated in their future child impute the sperm with attributes that are not biologically plausible. Couples who undergo ICSI place so much emphasis on preserving genetic connection to the social father that they hazard passing on genetic risk to their offspring. In both cases, their engagement with these technologies is mediated by a decidedly unscientific belief in the primacy of the sperm, harking back to the homunculus. And it is this fetishization of the male gamete that allows them to avoid confronting the very real potential health consequences of these high-tech procedures.

Notes

1. While we understand that there is an established anthropological literature about the homunculus, we refer here to its medical and historical meaning.
2. Because men who provide semen for artificial insemination often receive compensation, we feel it is inaccurate to refer to them universally as semen donors, which implies the giving of a gift for purely altruistic reasons. Although altruism may certainly play a part, some men are incentivized to provide semen by the promise of financial reward. Wherever possible, we substitute the term "supplier" for "donor," and in cases where a financial transaction has clearly taken place, we use the most appropriate term, which is "seller."
3. Similarly, we choose not to use the standard term "donor insemination" because it whitewashes the fact that for many men, the motivation to supply semen is at least partially monetary. We realize that the term "third-party insemination" is not wholly accurate, as a growing proportion of consumers are single women. Even if there is no second party involved, however, we feel the term may still be considered appropriate as

it emphasizes that the semen provider is outside the constructed family unit.

References

Agence France-Presse. 2011. "Sperm Donors Father Huge 'Families' in U.S., Canada." http://www.rawstory.com/rs/2011/10/08/sperm-donors-father-huge-families-in-us-canada/.

Aittomaki, K., U. B. Wennerholm, C. Bergh, A. Selbing, J. Hazekamp, and K. G. Nygren. 2004. "Safety Issues in Assisted Reproduction Technology: Should ICSI Patients Have Genetic Testing before Treatment? A Practical Proposition to Help Patient Information." *Human Reproduction* 13, no. 3: 472–76.

Almeling, Rene. 2011. *Sex Cells: The Medical Market for Eggs and Sperm*. Berkeley: University of California Press.

Avendano, C., and S. Oehninger. 2011. "DNA Fragmentation in Morphologically Normal Spermatozoa: How Much Should We Be Concerned in the ICSI Era?" *Journal of Andrology* 32, no. 4: 356–63.

Bharadwaj, A. 2003. "Why Adoption is Not an Option in India: The Visibility of Infertility, the Secrecy of Donor Insemination, and Other Cultural Complexities." *Social Science and Medicine* 56, no. 9: 1867–80.

Bunge, Raymond G., and Jerome K. Sherman. 1954. "Clinical Use of Frozen Semen: Report of Four Cases." *Fertility and Sterility* 5, no. 6: 520–29.

Casey, P., J. Readings, L. Blake, V. Jadva, and S. Golombok. 2008. "Child Development and Parent-Child Relationships in Surrogacy, Egg-Donation and Donor Insemination Families at Age 7." Presentation at 24th Annual Meeting of the European Society of Human Reproduction and Embryology (ESHRE). Barcelona.

Cryos International. 2011. "Worldwide Network of Sperm Banks." http://www.cryosinternational.com/home.aspx.

Daniels, C. R. 2006. *Exposing Men: The Science and Politics of Male Reproduction*. Oxford: Oxford University Press.

Daniels, K. 1998. "The Semen Providers." In *Donor Insemination*, ed. K. Daniels and E. Haimes. *International Social Sciences Perspectives*. Cambridge: Cambridge University Press.

Davies, M. J., V. M. Moore, K. J. Wilson, P. VanEssen, K. Priest, H. Scott, E. A. Haan, and A. Chan. 2012. "Reproductive Technologies and the Risk of Birth Defects." *The New England Journal of Medicine* 366: 1803–13.

Dohle, G. R., D. J. Halley, J. O. Van Hemel, A. M. W. van den Ouwel, M. H. Pieters, R. F. Weber, and L. C. Govaerts. 2002. "Genetic Risk Factors in Infertile Men with Severe Oligozoospermia and Azoospermia." *Human Reproduction* 17: 13–16.

Dokoupil, T. 2011. "You Got your Sperm Where?" http://www.thedaily beast.com/newsweek/2011/10/02/free-sperm-donors-and-the-women-who-want-them.html?cid=yourtangodailybeastbutton.

Dr. Rama's Institute for Fertility. 2005. "The Insemination Procedure." http://www.fertilityindia.com/husband_insemination.php.

Ebner, T., M. Moser, M. Sommergruber, O. Shebl, and G. Tews. 2006. "Incomplete Denudation of Oocytes Prior to ICSI Enhances Embryo Quality and Blastocyst Development." *Human Reproduction* 21, no. 11: 2972–77.

Expatica.com. 2009. "Business Booms at World's Biggest Sperm Bank." http://www.expatica.com/de/family/Partners/Business-booms-at-world_s-biggest-sperm-bank_14082.html.

Ferraretti, A. P., V. Goossens, J. deMouzon, S. Bhattacharya, J. A. Castilla, V. Korsak, M. Kupka, K. G. Nygren, A. Nyboe Andersen, and ESHRE. 2012. "Assisted Reproductive Technology in Europe, 2008: Results Generated from European Registers by ESHRE." *Human Reproduction* 27, no. 9: 2571–84.

Golombok, S., E. Lycett, F. MacCallum, V. Jadva, C. Murray, J. Rust, H. Abdalla, J. Jenkins, and R. Margara. 2004. "Parenting Infants Conceived by Gamete Donation." *Journal of Family Psychology* 18: 443–52.

Golombok, S., F. MacCallum, E. Goodman, and M. Rutter. 2002. "Families with Children Conceived by Donor Insemination: A Follow-Up at Age Twelve." *Child Development* 73, no. 3: 952–68.

Gosalvez, J., R. Nunez, J. L. Fernandez, C. Lopez-Fernandez, and P. Caballero. 2011. "Dynamics of Sperm DNA Damage in Fresh versus Frozen-Thawed and Gradient Processed Ejaculates in Human Donors." *Andrologia* 43, no. 6: 373–77.

Grady, Denise. 2006. "Sperm Donor Seen as Source of Disease in 5 Children." *The New York Times.* 19 May. http://www.nytimes.com/2006/05/19/health/19donor.html.

Gupta, J. A. 2008. "Trade Secrets from a Sperm Bank in India." *Indian Journal of Medical Ethics* 5, no. 1: 9–12.

Guttmacher, Alan F. 1962. "Artificial Insemination." *The Cervix* 97: 623–31.

Hammadeh, M. E., A. S. Askari, T. Georg, P. Rosenbaum, and W. Schmidt. 1999. "Effect of Freeze-Thawing Procedure on Chromatin Stability, Morphological Alteration and Membrane Integrity of Human Spermatoza in Fertile and Subfertile Men. *International Journal of Andrology* 22, no. 3: 155–62.

Hard, Addison David. 1909. "Artificial Impregnation." *The Medical World* 27: 163–64.

Hoy, J., A. Venn, J. Halliday, G. Kovacs, and K. Waalwyk. 1999. "Perinatal and Obstetric Outcomes of Donor Insemination using Cryopreserved Semen in Victoria, Australia." *Human Reproduction* 14, no. 7: 1760–64.

Inhorn, Marcia C. 2006. "Making Muslim Babies: IVF and Gamete Donation in Sunni versus Shi'a Islam." *Culture, Medicine and Psychiatry* 30, no. 4: 427–50.

InVia Fertility. 2012. "Does the Shape of the Sperm (Morphology) Matter?" http://www.inviafertility.com/blog/wp-content/uploads/2012/01/04b_sperm_cell.jpg.

Jadva, V., T. Freeman, W. Kramer, and S. Golombok. 2009. "The Experiences of Adolescents and Adults Conceived by Sperm Donation: Comparisons by Age of Disclosure and Family Type." *Human Reproduction* 24, no. 8: 1909–19.

Janssens, P. M. W., A. W. Nap, and L. F. Bancsi. 2011. "Reconsidering the Number of Offspring per Gamete Donor in the Dutch Open-Identity System." *Human Fertility* 14, no. 2: 106–14.

Kahn, Susan Martha. 2000. *Reproducing Jews: A Cultural Account of Assisted Conception in Israel.* Durham, NC: Duke University Press.

Kobayashi, H., A. Sato, E. Otsu, H. Hiura, C. Tomatsu, T. Utsunomiya, H. Sasaki, N. Yaegashi, and T. Arima. 2007. "Aberrant DNA Methylation of Imprinted Loci in Sperm from Oligospermic Patients." *Human Molecular Genetics* 16: 2542–51.

Lansac, J., F. Thepot, M. J. Mayaux, F. Czyglick, T. Wack, J. Selva, and P. Jalbert. 1997. "Pregnancy Outcome after Artificial Insemination or IVF with Frozen Semen Donor: A Collaborative Study of the French CECOS Federation on 21,597 Pregnancies." *European Journal of Obstetrics, Gynecology, and Reproductive Biology* 74, no. 2: 223–28.

Manipalviratn, S., A. DeCherney, and J. Segars. 2009. "Imprinting Disorders and Assisted Reproductive Technology." *Fertility and Sterility* 91: 305–15.

Marques, C. J., P. Costa, B. Vaz, F. Carvalho, S. Fernandes, A. Barros, and M. Sousa. 2008. "Abnormal Methylation of Imprinted Genes in Human Sperm Is Associated with Oligozoospermia." *Molecular Human Reproduction* 14: 67–74.

Mroz, Jacqueline. 2011. "One Sperm Donor, 150 Offspring." *The New York Times.* http://www.nytimes.com/2011/09/06/health/06donor.html?_r=1&pagewanted=all.

———. 2012. "In Choosing a Sperm Donor, a Roll of the Genetic Dice." *The New York Times.* http://www.nytimes.com/2012/05/15/health/in-sperm-banks-a-matrix-of-untested-genetic-diseases.html?_r=1&pagewanted=all.

National Conference of Commissioners on Uniform State Laws. 2000. "Uniform Parentage Act." http://www.law.upenn.edu/bll/archives/ulc/upa/final2002.htm.

Newton-Small, J. 2012. "Frozen Assets." *Time Magazine.* http://www.time.com/time/magazine/article/0,9171,2111234,00.html.

Nyboe Andersen, A., E. Carlsen, and A. Loft. 2008. "Trends in the Use of Intracytoplasmic Sperm Injection Marked Variability between Countries." *Human Reproduction Update* 14, no. 6: 593–604.

O'Connell, M., N. McClure, and S. E. M. Lewis. 2002. "The Effects of Cryopreservation on Sperm Morphology, Motility and Mitochondrial Function." *Human Reproduction* 17, no. 3: 704–9.

Office of the United Nations High Commissioner for Human Rights. 1989. Convention on the Rights of the Child. http://www2.ohchr.org/english/law/crc.htm.

Ottey, Michelle, and Suzanne Seitz. 2011. "Trends in Donor Sperm Purchasing, Disclosure of Donor Origins to Offspring, and the Effects of Sexual

Orientation and Relationship Status on Choice of Donor Category: A Three-Year Study." Presentation at Annual Meeting. American Society of Reproductive Medicine, Orlando, FL.

Owen, L., and S. Golombok. 2009. "Families Created by Assisted Reproduction: Parent-Child Relationships in Late Adolescence." *Journal of Adolescence* 32, no. 4: 835–48.

Palermo, G., H. Joris, P. Devroey, and A. C. VanSteirteghem. 1992. "Pregnancies after Intracytoplasmic Injection of a Single Spermatozoon into an Oocyte." *The Lancet* 340: 17–19.

Polge, C., A. U. Smith, and A. S. Parkes. 1949. "Revival of Spermatozoa after Vitrification and Dehydration at Low Temperatures." *Nature* 164: 666–69.

Pool, Stephan H. 2011. "Importance of Pregnancy/Live Birth Reporting." http://www.fairfaxcryobank.com/blog/?p=125.

Practice Committee of the American Society for Reproductive Medicine and Practice Committee of the Society for Assisted Reproductive Technology. 2008. "2008 Guidelines for Gamete and Embryo Donation: A Practice Committee Report." *Fertility and Sterility* 90, Suppl. 3: SS30–44.

Rodino, I. S., P. J. Burton, and K. A. Sanders. 2011. "Mating by Proxy: A Novel Perspective to Donor Conception." *Fertility and Sterility* 96, no. 4: 998–1001.

Scheib, J. E., and A. Ruby. 2008. "Contact among Families Who Share the Same Sperm Donor." *Fertility and Sterility* 90, no. 1: 33–43.

———. 2009. "Beyond Consanguinity Risk: Developing Donor Birth Limits that Consider Psychological Risk Factors." *Fertility and Sterility* 91, no. 5: e12.

Schiffman, Betsy. 2010. "U.S. Sperm Bank Donations Rise in Recession." http://www.dailyfinance.com/2010/05/06/sperm-bank-donations-rise-in-recession/.

Sherman, J. K. 1964. "Low Temperature Research on Spermatozoa and Eggs." *Cryobiology* 1, no. 2: 103–29.

Shukla, U., B. Deval, M. Jansa Perez, H. Hamoda, M. Savvas, and N. Narvekar. 2013. "Sperm Donor Recruitment, Attitudes and Provider Practices—5 Years after the Removal of Donor Anonymity." *Human Reproduction* 28, no. 3: 676–82.

SIMS IVF. 2012. "Intracytoplasmic Sperm Injection (ICSI)." http://www.sims.ie/Home/Intracytoplasmic_Sperm_Injection_ICSI.1040.html.

The Commission of the European Communities. 2006. Commission Directive 2006/17/EC. http://eur-lex.europa.eu/LexUriServ/LexUriServ.do?uri=OJ:L:2006:038:0040:0052:EN:PDF.

Thepot, F., M. J. Mayaux, F. Czyglick, T. Wack, J. Selva, and P. Jalbert. 1996. "Incidence of Birth Defects after Artificial Insemination with Frozen Donor Spermatozoa: A Collaborative Study of the French CECOS Federation on 11,535 Pregnancies." *Human Reproduction* 11, no. 10: 2319–23.

U.S. Food and Drug Administration. 2009. "Donor Eligibility Final Rule and Guidance Questions and Answers." http://www.fda.gov/BiologicsBloodVaccines/TissueTissueProducts/QuestionsaboutTissues/ucm102842.htm.

Van den Broeck, U., M. Vandermeeren, D. Vanderschueren, P. Enzlin, K. Demyttenaere, and T. D'Hooghe. 2103. "A Systematic Review of Sperm Donors: Demographic Characteristics, Attitudes, Motives and Experiences of the Process of Sperm Donation." *Human Reproduction Update* 19, no. 1: 37–51.

VanSpeybroeck, L., D. DeWaele, and G. VandeVijver. 2002. "Theories in Early Embryology: Close Connections between Epigenesis, Preformationism, and Self-Organization." *Annals of the New York Academy of Sciences* 981, no. 1: 7–49.

Yee, S. 2009. "'Gift without a Price Tag': Altruism in Anonymous Semen Donation." *Human Reproduction* 24, no. 1: 3–13.

Part V

INFERTILE FATHERHOOD

Chapter 9

ASSUMED, PROMISED, FORBIDDEN
INFERTILITY, IVF, AND FATHERHOOD IN TURKEY

Zeynep B. Gürtin

Introduction

This chapter discusses the role and meanings of fatherhood in the lives of involuntarily childless Turkish men going through in vitro fertilization (IVF) treatment. Although the IVF clinic may not seem like the most obvious place to search for fatherhood, it nevertheless provides a space in which fatherhood is a constant "absent presence"—whether in consultations with doctors, in the exacting work of embryologists, or in the co-constructed narratives of couples striving to conceive their longed-for children. Although cultural taboos and the materiality of the fertility treatment process marginalizes notions of male infertility and the affective responses of men to childlessness, relegating men as "the second sex" (Inhorn et al. 2009), assumptions and anxieties around achieving fatherhood, as well as the excitement and hope at its anticipation, bubble palpably just underneath the surface.

It is these notions of fatherhood, gathered through ethnographic fieldwork in a Turkish IVF clinic, that this chapter articulates. I begin by sketching the social context, before moving on to three thematic explorations of fatherhood. In the first, I reflect on fatherhood as an assumed part of the life trajectory and the ways in which involuntarily childless men, and women, retrospectively engage with the disruption they experience to this expected norm. In the second, I move on to discuss how the rhetorical and practical choreographies surrounding infertility and assisted reproduction treatments promise fatherhood, even to men with severe fertility problems. In the third, I analyze how legitimate or acceptable fatherhood is framed, and in turn how certain forms of fatherhood are forbidden. It is worth noting that the involuntarily childless men who are the protagonists of this chapter provide only marginal perspectives on fatherhood, yet paying close attention to their articulations, desires, and morals reveals broader patterns regarding how contemporary Turkish fatherhood is constructed.

Methodology

The data discussed in this chapter are drawn from my doctoral research into the cultural constructions of IVF treatment in Turkey. This research includes various periods of ethnographic observation between 2006 and 2009, combining interviews with male and female IVF patients and IVF experts with documentary analysis of media items and regulatory materials. In particular, I draw heavily on fifty semi-structured in-depth interviews with IVF patients, which were conducted during my second period of field research in an IVF clinic in Ankara in 2006. As per the stated preferences of the participants, in twenty-nine of fifty cases, husbands of female IVF patients were included in the interview (of these, in sixteen cases the couple was interviewed together; in eleven the husband joined following the individual interview of the wife; in two the husband was interviewed separately). The interviews were all conducted directly after the embryo transfer procedure, and lasted between forty-five minutes and two and a half hours. In addition, I conducted interviews with thirty-three IVF experts, including practitioners, embryologists, nurses, and regulators, and engaged in countless informal conversations with men and women during the course of my ethnography. All the interviews were conducted in Turkish, digitally recorded (unless interviewees expressed a preference against recording) and transcribed in the original; conversations were noted as part of field notes. All the quotes provided here have been translated by me and where names appear they are pseudonyms in order to protect the anonymity of participants.

The Social Context

Family remains one of the most important social institutions in Turkish society. Entering a heterosexual marriage and bearing children within that relationship are central to the normative life narrative, presumed and desired by both men and women (Kâğıtçıbaşı and Ataca 2005). Establishing a family is seen as the "most natural" (*en doğal*) and "normal" (*normal*) progression in the life cycle—the culmination and proof of both biological and social maturation. Thus, Turkish couples marry young and produce children early within their marriages (Boyacioğlu and Türkmen 2008). According to the Turkish Statistical Institute (2006), the mean age of first marriage is 26.1 for men and 22.8 for women, and although a woman's level of education greatly impacts her age at first marriage and the age at which she first becomes a mother, the average woman in Turkey already has one child by the age of 25 and two by the age of 30 (Institute of Population Studies 2004). Parenting, however, though pivotal to the life-course expectations of men and women, is morally contained firmly within a traditional family structure, with a strong unification of marriage and procreation as mutually constitutive ideals. Indeed the two often appear as ideologically and statistically, inseparable (2004), with children born out of wedlock and childless marriages both regarded as social anomalies.

Desire for and love of children (*çocuk sevgisi*) are regarded as cultural characteristics in Turkey, a reflexive attribution that cuts across profound socioeconomic and educational differences in a widely diverse country. Social psychologist Çiğdem Kâğıtçıbaşı (1981; 1982; 1986) has written extensively about the reasons parents desire children and the value of children in Turkish society (see also Kâğıtçıbaşı and Ataca 2005). She defines three categories of values that can be ascribed to children: psychological (which includes the pleasure of having them around and watching them grow); social/traditional; and economic/material/utilitarian. Other studies divide motives for childbearing between the individual and the social; although the former, related to the joy of childrearing (and correlating with Kâğıtçıbaşı's psychological motives) seems to be held universally across all cultures, cross-cultural differences exist in relation to the articulation of social motivations (Inhorn and van Balen 2002). It may thus be surprising for those from Northern European or North American cultures, which emphasize the non-instrumental values of children, that "The Family Structure Survey," conducted by the

Turkish Statistical Institute (2006), found that the two most important child-related values held by men and women are that "children
should look after their parents in old age" and that "a child brings
the spouses closer together."

While individual autonomy in matters concerning reproduction
may be a central value in both Northern Europe and the United
States (Day Sclater et al. 2009), in Turkey reproduction more commonly occurs within the context of broader intergenerational kinship relations, often viewed as a responsibility toward other family
members and even a civic contribution to the nation (Dole 2004).
Having children then, is not simply a matter of individual or couple
"choice" or "reproductive autonomy," but rather a social and familial
expectation, and even sometimes an obligation. This perception is
strongly endorsed both by Islam (Inhorn 2003a; Schenker 2000) and
by perpetuating cultural patterns that place the family practically and
ideologically at the center of social organization. Although throughout my research all informants articulated a variety of reasons, often
combining individual and social motives regarding why they wanted
to bear and raise children, certain group-based patterns existed in
these articulations. First, in line with Kâğıtçıbaşı's work, in general
socioeconomic development and increased education are linked with
a decrease in the economic/material/utilitarian value of children and
an increase in the psychological value. Similarly, although almost
all individuals referenced some social reasons for wanting children,
these were less often cited by men and women who regarded childbearing as a private or couple decision, and more prominently by
those who saw it as a familial and community expectation.

As has been found throughout the Middle East more generally
(see Inhorn 2003a), in Turkey too, the instantiation of hegemonic
masculinities and femininities through procreation means that childlessness and infertility have a profound impact on the gendered
identities of both men and women. However, the practical roles and
statuses assigned to motherhood and fatherhood are considerably
different. Although ideals about fatherhood may be undergoing
changes, with many new and expectant fathers expressing a desire
to be both physically and emotionally closer to their children than
their own "distant" fathers (Turan et al. 2001), it remains true that
childcare and the rearing of children are situated predominantly
within the female sphere. Fathers, to whose lineage offspring belong, are expected to support and partake in their families, but their
practical presence in the lives of their children is very much sup-
plementary to that of a central mother. This phenomenon has been

described by Emelie A. Olson (1982) as a "duofocal" social structure, which designates separate spheres of influence for men and women, and by Yildiz Ecevit (2003) as the persistence of strict gender roles, according to which women are designated caregivers and men are "straight-jacketed" as breadwinners. These gender roles, in many ways constraining for both sexes and undoubtedly mediated by socioeconomic circumstances, impact the motivations men and women articulate for wanting to parent, their concomitant expectations of fatherhood and motherhood, and the repercussions they face when they fail to become the parents they imagined. Involuntary childlessness and infertility (which may be caused by a variety of female, male, combined, or unexplained factors), though associated with a range of emotional, familial, and social difficulties for both groups, impacts the lives of men and women differently.

The global technology of in vitro fertilization (IVF) has been embraced in Turkey, as in many other locations (see Inhorn and Birenbaum-Carmeli 2008) as a means to combat infertility. Referred to locally as *tüp bebek* (literally "tube baby"), IVF is regarded on the one hand as a cutting-edge medical technology and on the other as a desirable commodity, becoming a central weapon in Turkish couples' battles against childlessness. Although Turkey's first IVF baby was born in 1989, it was not until the new millennium that assisted reproductive technologies (ARTs) expanded rapidly throughout the country. Funding for two cycles of IVF treatment, redeemable through state and social insurance institutions as of 2005, expanded the accessibility of IVF, accelerating demand and encouraging the growth of the industry. The number of IVF centers increased by 50 percent between 2005 and 2007, from 66 to 91, and the number of annual treatment cycles doubled. The total IVF expenditure in 2007 was reported to be in excess of 300 million dollars, which according to national newspapers (e.g., *Hürriyet* 2008) ranked Turkey as "The World's 7th Biggest IVF Market" (behind Israel, France, Spain, England, the United States, and Germany). Currently, there are over 110 clinics throughout Turkey, and while many are concentrated in urban areas, clinics are increasingly opening across the nation, signaling both an increase in access and a decrease in social taboos toward infertility and its treatment (Gürtin 2012a; 2012b). The growth of the IVF sector has generated greater public education around infertility and has, in some ways, transformed public perceptions. The social malady of childlessness is being recast as a medical condition with a technological "cure," though IVF does not always deliver on the promises of parenthood that it makes to the childless.

Assumed Fatherhood

Anthropologist Gay Becker (1994; 1997), in her large body of work examining life disruptions, demonstrates the central claim that cultures harbor the expectation of an orderly progression of the life course, with cultural discourses of "normalcy" defining its contents and timing. Within Turkish culture, and for most Turkish men and women, an assumption of parenthood forms a central life-course expectation. The men and women who I encountered in my research, who ended up facing involuntary childlessness, were no different than their "fertile" counterparts in harboring these expectations. For them too, hegemonic gender identities and the culturally prevalent normative procreation mandate had been internalized to form a tacit assumption of parenthood. It was these assumptions that formed a steady backdrop against which narratives of childlessness were thrown into relief as deviant from both social norms and personal desires.

Many of my interviewees reflected on a time when they—in line with peers, families, and members of wider society—had assumed a seamless, sequential progression from getting married to having children. Some detailed how important life decisions, including where to live or which job to do, had been indexed on the idea of becoming a parent. While women often referred to a "natural desire" to mother, men referenced the various ways in which they planned and prepared for the time they would head their own families. In many cases, responsibility (especially economic) for the care of a child began long before the child was conceived. Taking this responsibility seriously was a sign of a man's maturity and the strength of his character, as well as an indication of his aptitude and desire to be a father. Says Zülfü Alifer, "I earn 10 *kuruş*, I spend 2, I save 8—why? For the good of our child. I limit myself, my clothes, so that when we have a child we can give the best to that child."

Because parenthood had been taken so much for granted, for most couples and their families, the occurrence of a reproductive disruption (Inhorn 2007) was an "ontological assault" (Sandelowski et al., 1990)—a startling contradiction to their implicit expectations for which they lacked context or preparation. However, the retrospectively remembered certainty of parenthood in many accounts was part of a broader pattern of "reproductive innocence," whereby men and women were both unaware of potential concerns regarding reproduction and also held unrealistic expectations (e.g., of immediate conception). One consequence of this was that couples who had generally been free of "anticipated infertility" prior to attempts at conception (cf. Roberts 2008) were liable to develop premature anxieties in a very short period. During my ethnography in fertility clinics, I encountered seriously concerned couples, sometimes with extended family members, demanding invasive high-tech fertility treatments after as little as three months of marriage because, according to their expectations, their actions should already have resulted in conception. Yet, in addition to these newlyweds eager for immediate solutions, it was also possible to meet within the fertility clinic men and women who had—for lack of alternatives—shouldered the burdens of involuntary childlessness for many years and were only now—as IVF became more accessible—pursuing the glimmers of hope they had continued to harbor. Such couples were not resigned to childlessness, but more often regarded themselves simply as "not yet pregnant" (Greil 1991).

Culturally, parenthood was often cited as both the *raison d'être* and blossoming of marital unions. This means not only that children's power to strengthen and secure conjugal ties by "binding a couple together" (*eşleri birbirine bağlar*) was emphasized, but also on the flipside, that childless marriages were stereotyped as "fruitless," irresolute, or fractious, and ultimately doomed for misery or failure. However, in place of these gloomy stereotypes, I encountered involuntarily childless couples who emphasized their commitment and deep emotional attachment to each other. Although I was routinely presented with anecdotes in which men divorced "barren" wives in order to attempt conception with new partners (something I encountered only three times during the full course of my investigations), the real-life examples I saw were of men and women who resisted and challenged such stereotypes. With phrases such as "life is for sharing" (*hayat müşterektir*) and "a home can't be broken for the sake of a child" (*yuva çocuk uğruna yıkılmaz*), they articulated that they considered their marriages to be more important than the pursuit of children. Again and again, despite medical diagnoses that usually deemed only one partner or the other as "infertile," or perceived social pressures for their separation, many couples reiterated their view of involuntary childlessness as an *"ortak"* (shared) problem. Most spontaneously engaged with the prejudice of marriage dissolution as a response to childlessness and—even when they did not challenge the general applicability of this wisdom—insisted on their cases as exceptions, where the husband and wife were devoted to each other. Even in what may be considered "arranged" marriages, husbands and wives articulated how their tacit assumptions and generalized desires to become parents had, after marriage, transformed into more concrete and specific desires to become parents together and to raise each other's children.

However, even among the most dedicated couples, the disruption caused by involuntary childlessness and the inability to proceed to parenthood as assumed and imagined generated some tensions and difficulties. Lerzan and her husband Tarık, a visibly loving and intimate couple, told me how their "common wound" could sometimes make them abrasive and irritating toward each other, as their different personalities gave them different ways of "tending to that wound." Lerzan referred to the omnipresent topic of childlessness as "a bomb that is constantly about to explode" between her and her husband, conveying the extent to which it permeated their thoughts and discussions. Emel Yalın worried that her "hypersensitivity" and her husband's "cooling" caused by a prolonged failure to conceive led unnecessarily to "many little upsets during the day" between them. Kâmil was saddened that the experience of involuntary childlessness had created distance and tensions between him and his wife, which he explained as a consequence of their frustration: "We used to discuss everything openly, but it is hard to discuss this. It is because we do not want to break each other's heart. Even though this is a God-given situation (*Allah vergisi*), sometimes you get so frustrated and accuse (*suçla*) and hurt (*kır*) each other." Dilber, thirty-four, who emphasized how lucky she felt to have "a wonderful husband," nevertheless captured the emotions experienced by many couples, when she poignantly assessed the impact of involuntary childlessness on her marriage in the following way: "I cannot lie; I cannot say that it didn't have an effect on our marriage. We love each other very much, of course we do. But there is always a missing child between us, a child that couldn't be despite all our desires."

Although involuntary childlessness was experienced as a shared condition, husbands and wives were aware of, and keen to comment on, what they saw as the gendered differences of their experiences. As Kâmil noted, "[Childlessness] is more difficult for a woman, she [a childless woman] is stuck within four walls all day, with no occupation, no distraction and no friends."

In addition to the difficulties encountered by childless couples, many women reported facing increased challenges regarding how to occupy oneself, how to negotiate predominantly child-centered social life, and how to deal with a wide range of imperfections imputed to accompany involuntary childlessness. Most women I encountered, regardless of their socioeconomic status, articulated some feelings of discomfort during predominantly female social activities, which they characterized as "child-centered," and envied their husbands who did not have to endure such constant reminders of involuntary child-lessness and explicit encounters regarding children. Said 29-year-old Yeliz Alifer: "The men are lucky, because they are not reminded of their childlessness as much as the women. They can go to the *kahve* (coffee house) and play cards, and no one talks about babies with them. It is not a man's world. But with us, it is always, "There was this baby, there was that baby, there was the other baby!" It is almost every second someone is saying something about babies."

However, there was also a general agreement among women that their world enabled more intimate relations, more open communication, and more affective support regarding childlessness. Men, although buffered from many of the everyday encounters, were also required to contain their emotions. Against the general trend, a few interviewees assessed this as making involuntary childlessness harder for men. Said Feyza Anahtar, thirty-three: "I think it is more difficult for men. A woman can share with other women, she can unburden herself somewhat, she can share her troubles. But a man is closed-up. So he is more troubled, he cannot talk, he is all alone in his thoughts."

Promised Fatherhood

Many of the men and women I encountered in the fertility clinic spoke of their childlessness as a state of social suspension marked by a disparity between the passage of chronological time and the arresting of life-course progression. Their hopes and assumptions for parenthood had been central to their imagined lives, so this reproductive disruption was felt keenly to affect their past, present, and future. IVF treatment, which many were in the middle of at the time I interviewed them, seemed to promise a resolution to their "in limbo" existence. Indeed, those for whom treatment was successful found themselves "back on track" and able to, finally, enjoy the anticipated pleasures of parenthood. One couple who came back to visit the clinic and to introduce their 4-month-old twins to the doctors and nurses articulated their experience as "being born again." "I am profoundly grateful," said the man as he presented an enormous box of chocolates to the clinic staff; "you have sweetened our lives, and I hope this will sweeten your taste buds." I asked him how his life had changed with the birth of his children, to which he responded, "My life has been completed! We had everything except our children, and now these two boys have come as the answer to all our prayers." He went on to detail how he enjoyed every aspect of becoming a father and expressed pride in his involvement of caring for the twins. "He is very good, very gentle," his wife confirmed. "It is lovely for me because I am also getting to know him again, this time as a father. We are seeing a new side to one another." Having given birth to twins as a result of their first round of IVF, following eight years of involuntary childlessness, this couple provided the perfect illustration of an IVF success story, so much so that encouraged by their example six other couples from the same town had subsequently sought treatment in this clinic; one of the nurses joked that they should be receiving commissions.

However, not all IVF stories are as victorious. For some couples the results are failure, complications, pregnancy loss, or repeated cycles of disappointment. As Sarah Franklin (1997) writes about in depth, in these situations the promised resolution—whether through conception or the "peace of mind" of having tried everything—is elusive, as fertility treatment takes on its own momentum. For example, for Sibel Cumalı and her husband, who were undergoing their fifth cycle of IVF when I met them, fertility treatment had become an increasingly ambivalent prospect. "On our third time, we said 'This is the last!' Then we thought maybe one more, and then... one more," she told me. Their case was designated as "unexplained" infertility; no explanation could be provided for their inability to conceive naturally or for the repeated failure of treatment. Sibel referenced this as a factor that made their decisions more difficult: "Technically, there is no reason for it not to work, and so we need to exhaust all of our options." But this idea of exhausting all options was also liable to prove ambiguous and continuously shifting, as the promise of fatherhood and motherhood incited such couples to continue on yet another cycle. Thus, for some couples, the uncertainty of the fertility treatment process echoed the "limbo" of involuntary childlessness.

Moreover, in some cases the recent availability of fertility treatments created an additional disruption. Some couples, for whom childlessness had been a reality they had reluctantly accepted, subsequently rethought their prior resignation. Rıza Yerli, in his second marriage and involuntarily childless for "a very, very long time," remarked that IVF offered him new optimism: "Life has not been so enjoyable thus far, but perhaps a child will come and brighten the rest of it." He was clear that a child would be welcomed with open arms, whenever he or she might make an appearance. He spoke poignantly about how the arrival of a child would make him feel that his life and all his hard work to date had been "worthwhile," how he would appreciate the chance to pass on his knowledge, and how he would feel that a part of him would continue on to the next generation. For Rıza, his ability to be a good father was not compromised by his age; in fact he could see some advantages to older fatherhood, such as being calmer and wiser. The conception of fatherhood in this account was very different to the concept voiced by some of the younger men I interviewed. Sezgin Şükür, for example, described how his image of fatherhood involved playing games with his children, being "young, active, and strong" and "as much a friend as a parent to my children." The difference between their conceptions was attributable not only to generational and socioeconomic differences, but also to their different histories of involuntary childlessness. Still in their twenties and embarking on their first cycle of IVF, Sezgin and Aleyna Şükür were confident in talking about an appropriate and normative "timeliness" (*zamanlama*) to procreation. Though they spoke of mounting apprehensions as their childlessness continued despite efforts to remedy it, they also felt that deviations from this timeliness were associated with undesirable psychological and physical consequences for childrearing. "I want it to happen soon. I am getting older, and I want to grow older with my child. I want to be able to relate to my child, to run around with my child," Sezgin explained. "I do not want to be an old man still dreaming of becoming a father!"

Although high-tech fertility treatments in general are prone to hype, the promises made on behalf of technological advances in the Turkish press were particularly striking with regard to male infertility. The rhetoric and practice of assisted reproductive technologies cooperated to construct male infertility in particular ways that made it least threatening and most amenable to treatment. On the one hand, fertility practitioners and the industry more broadly were keen to raise awareness of male infertility: this was seen as an integral part of doctors', nurses', and the media's duty of public education, particularly since cultural prejudices often blamed women for a couple's childlessness. On the other hand, the very same education campaigns stressed the "curability" of male infertility, dismissed it as a problem of the past, and triumphantly announced the efficacy of available treatments. Thus, for example, one newspaper headline exclaimed: "First they have sperm, then they have babies!" (*Sabah* 2006). The article explains that male infertility can account for up to one half of all fertility problems and that men are finally beginning to accept that they may have a "curable medical condition"; it proceeds to detail various hormone treatments, sperm extraction using testicular biopsies, and intracytoplasmic sperm injection, and concludes that, "Thanks to recent advances in medicine even men with no sperm can now become fathers the natural way." In the least, this message is confusing, but it was not an isolated example. Indeed, during the course of my research I found many similar examples where technological and medical advances were heralded as promising fatherhood to men with even the most intractable infertility problems.

In the clinic too, male infertility was often minimized, or presented as easy to overcome through technological intervention. Some reflected on this as part of the necessary "sensitivity" required to deal with this issue, particularly since infertility was culturally more problematic and stigmatizing for men. There was general recognition, by practitioners and patients alike, that male infertility was harder not only for men but also for their wives to accept and deal with. Indeed, women's willingness to shoulder the burden and stigma of their husband's infertility has been noted in various cultural contexts (e.g., Inhorn 2003a; 2003b; 2004), and theorized as a form of "patriarchal bargain" (Lorber 1989) or "marital bargaining" (Lorber and Bandlamudi 1993). But here clinicians too conspired to soften the perceived emotional blow and social consequences of infertility for men. One IVF practitioner explained: "It is difficult to know exactly why a man might have fertility problems. One possible cause is childhood disease. So we ask, 'Did you ever have a bad childhood illness, with high fever?'—and let's be honest, who has not? It is easier for them to accept that it might be because of a disease. That way, they can say, 'Oh, I was not born this way. This happened because of an unfortunate illness; it does not make me less of a man.'"

The attribution of male infertility to childhood disease, rather than to genetic or familial causes on the one hand or lifestyle factors on the other, served two important functions. First, by distancing the cause from the man himself and absolving him of responsibility, the infertility was made both less stigmatizing and "easier for them to accept." Second, through association with more familiar and mundane illnesses, male infertility was placed in the medical realm and cast as a treatable condition. In combination with the triumphant discourses surrounding assisted reproduction, these rhetorical and practical choreographies promised that fatherhood was attainable to all men. However, the reality did not always match the promise: Assisted reproduction treatments in Turkey (as elsewhere) sometimes succeeded, but equally often failed to deliver longed-for babies. Though the idea of intractable male infertility has been erased from discourses surrounding fertility treatment, actual cases persist, presenting a serious paradox for patients and practitioners.

Forbidden Fatherhood

During my research, it became clear that the education and aware-ness campaigns about infertility and its construction as a treatable condition were part of a broader social context that both mandated reproduction and promoted medical treatment—even high-tech re-productive assistance—in its pursuit. There were, however, strict le-gal and moral boundaries that defined the acceptable and legitimate parameters within which parenthood, and fatherhood in particular, could be pursued. These referred, most importantly, back to cul-tural ideals of marriage and parenting as co-constitutive and mu-tually reinforcing, and thus excluded all forms of procreation that fell outside of this union. The most unambiguous example of this is Turkey's regulatory framework for assisted reproduction, which curtails its use to the treatment of heterosexual couples using their own gametes.

The ÜYTEM statute regulating the price of assisted reproduction in Turkey immediately defines ARTs as: "Procedures, accepted as treat-ment methods by modern medicine, which involve assisting the fertil-ization of *the prospective mother's egg* with *her husband's sperm* in various ways, enabling them to fertilize outside of the body when necessary, and transferring the gametes or the embryo back to the *prospective mother's* genital organs" (ÜYTEM 2005: Item 4f, my emphasis).[1] This definition is extremely important, not just semantically or symbol-ically, but for its actual regulatory implication. By referring to the "prospective mother" and her "husband" (rather than to the socially or relationally indeterminate male and female, or man and woman), the statute places the marital unit as legally central and clinically in-dispensable for ART practice. Moreover, by providing this as a defi-nition of ART (rather than more explicitly as a definition of its legal application), it collapses the distinction between what is scientifi-cally possible and what is socially acceptable. The exclusivity of treat-ment provision to married couples, using their own gametes, is re-iterated at the start of Section Five entitled "Prohibitions": "The use of the egg and sperm or the embryo of applicants undergoing ART for any other purpose, or in the treatment of other applicants, or the use of those [sperm, egg, or embryos] obtained from anyone other than the applicants in the treatment of the applicants, or the storage, use, transfer, and sale [of sperm, eggs, or embryos] for any sort of purpose, falling outside the definitions of this legislation, are prohibited" (ÜYTEM 2005: Item 17).

These regulations not only preclude the treatment of unmarried couples, or of single women, but also create a legal and moral obstruction for married couples who are unable to conceive without the use of donor gametes (cases where intractable male or female infertility makes conception using own gametes impossible). Thus, while assisted reproduction globally has been associated with the "creation of family *types* that would not otherwise have existed" (Fasouliotis and Schenker 1999: 26, my emphasis), including gay and lesbian families, single mothers by choice, and myriad family types formed through the use of donor eggs, donor sperm, and surrogacy, within Turkey, the use of these technologies has been framed within the strict confines of a traditional, heteronormative family structure. These civic regulations, although constructed as secular (Arda 2007), echo exactly the parameters defined by Sunni Islam for the acceptable use of reproductive technologies (Gürtin 2012a; Inhorn 2003a; 2006a; 2006b; 2006c) and were often represented to me, by practitioners, regulators, and patients, as directly representative of general Turkish opinions.

Unfortunately, sound empirical data regarding public opinions on third-party assisted reproduction in Turkey are not available. However, Baykal et al.'s (2008) study of the attitudes of 368 women who had applied for infertility treatment showed acceptance rates of 23.3 percent for egg donation, 15.1 percent for surrogacy, and only 3.4 percent for sperm donation. Although it is difficult to know how to interpret what is meant by "acceptance" in this study—since they also report that when asked what they would do if their IVF treatment failed, 59.7 percent of respondents answered that they would "do nothing," 38.3 percent would pursue adoption, and only 2 percent would consider gamete donation—the data is nevertheless reflective both of the existence of some acceptance and of the differing attitudes toward donor eggs and donor sperm. Indeed, this asymmetry was evident in my study, as participants repeatedly voiced fears about the potential "mixing" of sperm in clinics and referenced taboos around sperm donation. The use of donor eggs, on the other hand, was rarely discussed as a fear and was generally considered as far less problematic from both a religious and a social perspective.

The majority of the men and women I interviewed were emphatic about never considering using donor sperm. While for some it was out of the question because it was forbidden by their religion (Islam), others explained and engaged with the rationality behind their objections, outlining myriad personal, marital, and social catastrophes that might result from the use of donor sperm. Imagined scenarios included a father or mother's inability to love or bond with a child conceived "by the sperm of a stranger"; marital frictions created by the secrecy and stress of donor conception; accidental incest among donor siblings; and the transmission of genetic illnesses or psychotic conditions from sperm donors. However, although the use of donor sperm was represented broadly as "against our culture" and dismissed as something unethical and dangerous that only happens in "other"—Western—nations (Gürtin 2012b), these claims do not paint an accurate picture. Many practitioners confided in me during private conversations that they had encountered patients who had requested such "secret" solutions. Although all of the practitioners I interviewed reiterated that they would never consider partaking in illegal practices, in one case, widely dubbed the Çukurova Sperm Scandal, Dr. Ismet Köker was found guilty of "impregnating women who came to his clinic with sperm from strangers" (NTV-MSNBC 2006) and in 2006, sentenced to the maximum three years imprisonment for the general offence of "abusing professional power" (*görevi kötüye kullanmak*). The couples had been complicit in their covert donor treatments, although the medical students and junior doctors from whom the semen was procured claimed to be entirely ignorant regarding the use of their donations.

Practitioners who reflected on this demand for covert treatments generally seemed to find their common occurrence surprising particularly when voiced by what they considered to be conservative sectors of the population that they thought ought to display religious aversions. They attributed this apparent contradiction to the social pressure to have children. According to one IVF practitioner:

> It is interesting that so many patients do consider it. People you wouldn't imagine. For example, a policeman. I mean this is a policeman; the man's profession is to uphold the laws! But he's wanted a child for years, so he asks if there is any way at all.... Of course, they imagine that at the end of the day no one will know about it—his wife will be pregnant. There is a lot of social pressure, pressure from the family, from the wider kin group. Imagine you've been married for ten years or twenty years and there is still no child! ... What is more interesting is that [demand for donor gametes] is more common

among the covered population, how should we call them, the "conservative" population, because they are also subjected to more social pressure [to have children].

The social pressure and normative mandate to become a father was understood to compel some men to pursue fatherhood beyond its acceptable parameters, forcing them into the forbidden frontiers of donor sperm use. These men and their wives acted as "moral pioneers" (Rapp 2000), negotiating novel choices and navigating unchartered waters. Although there are no official statistics, and secrecy surrounded its practice, the existence of a demand from such men and their wives led to the development of a cross-border solution, whereby couples requiring donor sperm could, with the covert aid of Turkish IVF clinics and practitioners, visit ART clinics in neighboring Greece or Cyprus. When I interviewed experts and clinic directors in December 2008, there were divided opinions about these cross-border clinical collaborations and the growth of "reproductive tourism." Some argued that the Turkish government and the Turkish public were "not yet ready" to legalize the use of donor gametes, especially donor sperm, as part of assisted reproduction, but since they saw it as a private matter, were glad to be able to offer their desperate patients an alternative solution, by directing them to clinics in other jurisdictions. Others criticized the practice as commercialized, deceitful, and unethical. Ultimately, it seems the latter opinion prevailed in the regulatory context, as in 2010 Turkey became the first country to legislate against reproductive travel (Gürtin 2011).

Amendments made to Turkey's ART regulation in March 2010 addressed, among other matters, the growth of reproductive tourism. According to Articles 18.6 and 18.7 referring patients abroad for donor treatments became forbidden, and it was specified that in the event of a discovery, at any point, of such prohibited activities: "The person who has conducted this procedure, the persons who have referred patients or acted as an intermediary, the impregnated person, and the donor" would be reported to the state prosecutor. Turkish clinics engaged in providing or facilitating cross-border reproductive care (CBRC) with donor gametes would face closure for three months in the first instance, and indefinitely on subsequent instances, and all professionals involved would have their practice certificates nullified. These strict prohibitions against CBRC involving donor gametes were justified with reference to (the existing) item 231 of the Turkish Penal Code, according to which it is illegal to "change or obscure a child's ancestry," with a punishment of one to three years imprisonment. According to Irfan Şencan, the director of the Ministry of Health's Treatment Services department, the new ban on reproductive travel was added in response to the growth of this phenomenon in recent years, which he argued constituted "a way of breaking Turkish law abroad" (*Hürriyet Daily News* 2010).

It is clear that, quite aside from any moral implications, such regulation creates myriad regulatory conundrums. Several commentators have pointed out the impossibility of controlling and detecting such extraterritorial activities, particularly since, as Sibel Tuzcu, president of ÇIDER (Turkey's prolific infertility support organization) states, Turkish couples who use donor gametes as a last resort are already extremely secretive about this information. Realistically, it can only be the activities of Turkish clinics, rather than the activity of individuals, that can be policed by these amendments. But even this will significantly impact the choices of men and women who are already in an extremely difficult situation, and by effectively tying the hands of professionals, will curtail their access to information, guidance, and preparatory treatment at home. Moreover, it is also very clear that the regulation sends a message about moral parameters, designating the use of donor sperm, whether in Turkey or abroad, as forbidden fatherhood.

Conclusion

This chapter reflects on notions of assumed, promised, and forbidden fatherhood as articulated in a fertility clinic and in the contexts surrounding it. These perspectives from the margins, where fatherhood is an absent presence, not only display how fatherhood is constructed but also how individuals faced with difficulties or paradoxes negotiate the novel choices that may be available to them. In the first thematic section, I outlined how fatherhood is an assumed part of the life trajectory for men, with fundamental consequences for gender identity, marital relations, and important life decisions. In the second, I examined how discourses and practices of assisted reproduction conspire to promise fatherhood to all men, by minimizing male infertility and by exaggerating technomedical capabilities. In the third, I turned to the case of men who fall outside of this rhetorical construct, whose infertility is indeed intractable and for whom the only "solution" involves resorting to the forbidden frontiers of the use of donor sperm. These reflections portray the paradoxes that arise when men are faced, on the one hand, with a normative mandate for fatherhood and, on the other, with strict parameters within which to accomplish this personal, familial, and community mission. While some feel bound with the parameters dictated by religious, moral, or social codes, a minority of others are willing to become "moral pioneers," albeit in secret, in the pursuit of forbidden fatherhood.

Notes

1. A structure for the regulation of assisted reproduction in Turkey was first introduced in 1987, under the title "Statute on Centres for In Vitro Fertilization and Embryo Transfer" (ÜYTEM 1987). This was superseded by "The Statute on Assisted Reproduction Treatment Centres" (ÜYTEM 1996), which has subsequently been amended five times, with the latest two changes made in 2005 (ÜYTEM 2005) and 2010 (ÜYTEM 2010). All issues of the *Official Gazette* may be accessed through the online *Official Gazette* archives at: http://rega.basbakanlik.gov.tr/.

References

Arda, Berna. 2007. "The Importance of Secularism in Medical Ethics: The Turkish Example." *Reproductive BioMedicine Online* 14, no. 1: 24–28.

Baykal, Baris, Cem Korkmaz, Seyit T. Ceyhan, Umit Goktolga, and Iskender Baser. 2008. "Opinions of Infertile Turkish Women on Gamete Donation and Gestational Surrogacy." *Fertility and Sterility* 89: 817–22.

Becker, Gay. 1994. "Metaphors in Disrupted Lives: Infertility and Cultural Constructions of Continuity." *Medical Anthropology Quarterly* 8, no. 4: 383–410.

———. 1997. *Disrupted Lives: How People Create Meaning in a Chaotic World.* Berkeley: University of California Press.

Boyacioğlu, Aslihan Öğün, and Ayfer Türkmen. 2008. "Social and Cultural Dimensions of Pregnancy and Childbirth in Eastern Turkey." *Culture, Health & Sexuality* 10: 277–85.

Day-Sclater, Shelley, Fatemeh Ebtehaj, Emily Jackson, and Martin Richards, eds. 2009. *Regulating Autonomy: Sex, Reproduction and Family.* Oxford: Hart Publishing.

Dole, Christopher. 2004. "In the Shadows of Medicine and Modernity: Medical Integration and Secular Histories of Religious Healing in Turkey." *Culture, Medicine and Psychiatry* 28: 255–80.

Ecevit,Yildiz. 2003. "Women's Labor and Social Security." Poverty Reduction and Economic Management Unit, Europe and Central Asia Region. World Bank. 16 September. http://siteresources.worldbank.org/INTEC AREGTOPGENDER/Resources/TurkeyCGA.pdf.

Fasouliotis, Sozos J., and Joseph G. Schenker. 1999. "Social Aspects in Assisted Reproduction." *Human Reproduction Update* 5: 26–39.

Franklin, Sarah. 1997. *Embodied Progress: A Cultural Account of Assisted Conception*. London: Routledge.

Greil, Arthur L. 1991. *Not Yet Pregnant: Infertile Couples in Contemporary America*. New Brunswick, NJ: Rutgers University Press.

Gürtin, Zeynep B. 2011. "Banning Reproductive Travel? Turkey's ART Legislation and Third-Party Assisted Reproduction." *Reproductive BioMedicine Online* 23: 555–65.

———. 2012a. "Assisted Reproduction in Secular Turkey: Regulation, Rhetoric, and the Role of Religion." In *Islam and Assisted Reproductive Technologies: Sunni and Shia Perspectives*, ed. Marcia C. Inhorn and Soraya Tremayne. New York; Oxford: Berghahn Books.

———. 2012b. "IVF Practitioners as Interface Agents between the Local and the Global: The Localization of IVF in Turkey." In *Reproductive Technologies as Global Form*, ed. M. Knecht, M. Klotz, and S. Beck. Frankfurt: Campus Verlag.

Hürriyet. 2008. 31 January.

Hürriyet Daily News. 2010. 15 March.

Inhorn, Marcia C. 2003a. *Local Babies, Global Science: Gender, Religion, and In Vitro Fertilization in Egypt*. New York: Routledge.

———. 2003b. "'The Worms are Weak': Male Infertility and Patriarchal Paradoxes in Egypt." *Men and Masculinities* 5, no. 3: 236–56.

———. 2004. "Middle Eastern Masculinities in the Age of New Reproductive Technologies: Male Infertility and Stigma in Egypt and Lebanon." *Medical Anthropology Quarterly* 18, no. 2: 162–82.

———. 2006a. "*Fatwas* and ARTs: IVF and Gamete Donation in Sunni vs. Shi'a Islam." *The Journal of Gender, Race and Justice* 9: 291–317.

———. 2006b. "Making Muslim Babies: IVF and Gamete Donation in Sunni versus Shi'a Islam." *Culture, Medicine and Psychiatry* 30, no. 4: 427–50.

———. 2006c. "Islam, IVF and Everyday Life in the Middle East: The Making of Sunni versus Shi'ite Test-Tube Babies." *Anthropology of the Middle East* 1, no. 1: 42–50.

———, ed. 2007. *Reproductive Disruptions: Gender, Technology, and Biopolitics in the New Millennium*. New York; Oxford: Berghahn Books.

Inhorn, Marcia C., and Daphna Birenbaum-Carmeli. 2008. "Assisted Reproductive Technologies and Culture Change." *Annual Review of Anthropology* 37: 177–96.

Inhorn, Marcia C., Tine Tjørnhøj-Thomsen, Helene Goldberg, and Maruska la Cour Mosegaard, eds. 2009. *Reconceiving the Second Sex: Men, Masculinity and Reproduction*. New York; Oxford: Berghahn Books.

Inhorn, Marcia C., and Frank van Balen, eds. 2002. *Infertility around the Globe: New Thinking on Childlessness, Gender, and Reproductive Technologies*. Berkeley: University of California Press.

Institute of Population Studies. 2004. "Turkey Demographic And Health Survey." Hacettepe University, Ankara, Turkey.

Kâğıtçıbaşı, Çiğdem. 1981. "Value of Children, Women's Role and Fertility in Turkey." In *Women in Turkish Society,* ed. Nermin Abandan-Unat. Leiden: E. J. Brill.

———. 1982. *The Changing Value of Children in Turkey.* Honolulu: East-West Population Institute.

———. 1986. "Status of Women in Turkey: Cross-Cultural Perspectives." *International Journal of Middle East Studies* 18: 485–99.

Kâğıtçıbaşı, Çiğdem, and Bilge Ataca. 2005. "Value of Children and Family Change: A Three-Decade Portrait From Turkey." *Applied Psychology* 54: 317–37.

Lorber, Judith. 1989. "Choice, Gift or Patriarchal Bargain? Women's Consent to In Vitro Fertilization in Male Infertility." *Hypatia* 4: 23–36.

Lorber, Judith, and L. Bandlamudi. 1993. "The Dynamics of Marital Bargaining in Male Infertility." *Gender & Society* 7: 32–49.

NTV-MSNBC. 2006. 24 November.

Olson, Emelie A. 1982. "Duofocal Family Structure and an Alternative Model Husband-Wife Relationship." In *Sex Roles, Family and Community in Turkey,* ed. Nermin Abandan-Unat. Bloomington: Indiana University Press.

Rapp, Rayna. 2000. *Testing Women, Testing the Fetus: The Social Impact of Amniocentesis in America.* New York: Routledge.

Roberts, Elizabeth F. S. 2008. "Biology, Sociality and Reproductive Modernity in Ecuadorian *In-Vitro* Fertilization: The Particulars of Place." In *Biosocialities, Genetics and the Social Sciences: Making Biologies and Identities,* ed. Sahra Gibbon and Caros Novas. London: Routledge.

Sabah. 2006. "First They Have Sperm, Then They Have Babies!" April 27.

Sandelowski, Margarete, Diane Holditch-Davis, and Betty G. Harris. 1990. "Living the Life: Explanations of Infertility." *Sociology of Health and Illness* 12, no. 2: 195–215.

Schenker, Joseph G. 2000. "Women's Reproductive Health: Monotheistic Religious Perspectives." *International Journal of Gynaecology & Obstetrics* 70: 77–89.

Turan, J. M., H. Nalbant, A. Bulut, and Y. Sahip. 2001. "Including Expectant Fathers in Antenatal Education Programmes in Istanbul, Turkey." *Reproductive Health Matters* 9, no. 18: 114–25.

Turkish Statistical Institute. 2006. "Family Structure Survey." Prime Ministry of Turkey.

ÜYTEM. 1987. "Statutes on Centres for in Vitro Fertilization and Embryo Transfer." *Official Gazette 19551.* 21 August.

———. 1996. "The Statute on Assisted Reproduction Treatment Centres." *Official Gazette 22822.* 19 November.

———. 2005. *Official Gazette 25869.* 8 July.

———. 2010. *Official Gazette 27613.* 6 March.

Chapter 10

NEW ARAB FATHERHOOD
MALE INFERTILITY, ASSISTED REPRODUCTION, AND EMERGENT MASCULINITIES

Marcia C. Inhorn

Introduction

Male infertility is one of the world's best-kept secrets. Few people realize that male infertility contributes to more than half of all cases of childlessness worldwide (Greil et al. 2010; Vayena et al. 2002). In the Middle Eastern region, the rates of male infertility are even higher—generally contributing to 60 to 70 percent of all cases—with very severe forms that may be genetic in origin (Inhorn 2012; Inhorn et al. 2009).

Since 2003, I have been studying male infertility in the Middle East, interviewing more than 330 men from a variety of Arab countries (including Lebanon, Syria, Palestine, Egypt, Iraq, Yemen, and the United Arab Emirates).[1] In all of these cases, men were undergoing assisted reproduction, particularly intracytoplasmic sperm injection (ICSI), a variant of in vitro fertilization (IVF) designed to overcome male infertility (see Kahn and Chavkin, this volume). Since 1994, when ICSI first arrived in Egypt, demand for this assisted reproductive technology (ART) has skyrocketed across the Arab world (Inhorn 2003; 2012).

This chapter seeks to shed light on Arab men's twenty-first-century engagements with this rapidly globalizing reproductive technology. On the one hand, Middle Eastern men today are active seekers of ARTs and are generally invested in many aspects of the reproductive process, from high-tech conception to hands-on parenting. Such commitments are a manifestation of changing notions of manhood and fatherhood across the region—what I call "emergent masculinities" in my recent book, *The New Arab Man: Emergent Masculinities, Technologies, and Islam in the Middle East* (Inhorn 2012).[2] Inspired by the work of Raymond Williams (1978) on "emergence" and R. W. Connell (1995) on "hegemonic masculinity," I offer the new trope of "emergent masculinities" to capture changing practices of masculinity in the Middle East, as elsewhere (Inhorn and Wentzell 2011). Emergent masculinities encapsulate change over the male life course as men age, change over the generations as male youth grow to adulthood, and changes in social history that involve men in transformative social processes such as the Arab Spring. In the Middle East today, many men are engaged in a self-conscious critique of local gender norms, unseating patriarchy in the process. Part of this critique involves the desire to share the responsibility for reproduction and parenting with wives and to utilize the full panoply of reproductive technologies, from contraception to assisted conception. Indeed, Middle Eastern IVF clinics are full of men seeking ICSI to overcome their male infertility, as well as men supporting the IVF-seeking of their infertile wives.

As this chapter outlines, however, Arab men's attempts to become fathers via assisted conception may enact significant tolls on their bodies, their wallets, and their emotions. The "male quest for conception" (Inhorn 1994) may entail endless rounds of ICSI repetition and failure, costly transnational travel, moral anxieties and dilemmas, and questions concerning both wives' and children's future well-being. In other words, ICSI may be considered a breakthrough technology to overcome male infertility, but it is never a panacea, particularly in a region of the world where male infertility is a highly prevalent and often intractable condition.

Male Infertility in the Middle East

It is important to outline, at least briefly, the scope of the male infertility problem in the Middle East and the history of ICSI there. On a global level, infertility affects more than 10 percent of all reproductive-aged couples, and male infertility contributes to more than half of all of these cases (Vayena et al. 2002). Male infertility involves four major categories of sperm defects, any one of which leads to a diagnosis of male infertility. These include low sperm count (*oligozoospermia*), poor sperm motility (*asthenozoospermia*), defects of sperm morphology (*teratozoospermia*), and total absence of sperm in the ejaculate (*azoospermia*). Azoospermia may be due to lack of sperm production (*non-obstructive azoospermia*) or blockages in sperm transport (*obstructive azoospermia*). These four types of male infertility account for about 40 percent of all cases of infertility in the Western countries (Vayena et al. 2002). However, as noted earlier, 60 to 70 percent of all cases presenting to Middle Eastern IVF centers may involve a diagnosis of male infertility, according to most physicians' estimates. Moreover, non-obstructive azoospermia is highly prevalent in the Middle East, as are cases of severe oligoasthenozoospermia (i.e., very low sperm count and poor motility).

Because of advances in the field of genetics, it is now realized that a significant percentage of these kinds of severe cases are due to genetic abnormalities affecting sperm production (Maduro and Lamb 2002). Probably the most frequent genetic cause of infertility in men involves microdeletions of the long arm of the Y chromosome, which are associated with spermatogenic failure. In men with such Y microdeletions, the spermatozoa will always be infertile, because these genetic alterations are incurable and will be present throughout a man's lifetime. Thus, genetic forms of male infertility are recalcitrant to prevention and represent a chronic reproductive health problem for thousands upon thousands of Middle Eastern men (Inhorn and Birenbaum-Carmeli 2010).

Furthermore, in the Middle East, male infertility tends to run in families, and is probably related to intergenerational patterns of consanguineous, or cousin marriage. Cousin marriage is found in societies around the world, with more than 1.1 billion people estimated to be in consanguineous unions worldwide (Bittles 2012). Consanguineous marriage may be preferred for a variety of social, economic, religious, and practical reasons. In the Middle East, for example, cousin marriage receives support within the Islamic scriptures, given that the Prophet Muhammad married his daughter, Fatima, to his first cousin, Ali (Inhorn et al. 2009). According to a variety of recent studies, cousin marriage continues to be practiced widely across the Middle Eastern region, with the lowest levels found in Lebanon (16 percent) and the highest found in parts of Iran (78 percent); between 8 and 30 percent of these marriages are first-cousin marriages, or the closest form (Inhorn et al. 2009; Shavazi et al. 2006).

A growing literature suggests that genetically based sperm defects cluster in families and may be linked to consanguineous unions. For example, recent studies conducted in Italy show that consanguineous unions highly correlate with rare genetic sperm defects (Baccetti et al. 2001; Latini et al. 2004). These include a range of syndromes that impact sperm morphology (shape) and motility (movement) and may be transmissible to male offspring. Studies strongly suggest that male infertility may be heritable and may cluster in families and communities, depending upon the level of consanguineous marriage in the general population.

In my own study of both fertile and infertile men attending IVF clinics in Lebanon, significantly more of the infertile men than the fertile ones were the offspring of prior consanguineous unions, suggesting that cousin marriage may produce infertile male offspring (Inhorn et al. 2009). Many infertile men in my study also had infertile brothers, and some had other infertile male relatives as well. Indeed, more than 40 percent of infertile men in my study could identify other known cases of male infertility in the immediate family, particularly among brothers, first cousins, uncles, and, in some cases, fathers. In addition, infertile men with the most severe cases of oligozoospermia and azoospermia were significantly more likely to be the offspring of first- (parents') and second-generation (grandparents') consanguineous unions. Among this "most infertile" subset, nearly half of all men were born from consanguineous marriages among parents, grandparents, or both. Clearly, these findings suggest that consanguineous marriage over generations may lead to familial patterns of male infertility. Given the high prevalence of cousin marriage in the Middle East, male infertility represents a significant reproductive health problem there.

Until the early 1990s, the only known solution to male infertility was sperm donation, which, although practiced in the West (Becker 2002), is widely prohibited in most Muslim-majority countries (Inhorn and Tremayne 2012). Most Arab men refuse to consider sperm donation, equating it with mistaken paternity, genealogical confusion, and illicit sexuality (Inhorn 2012). Similarly, legal adoption as it is practiced in the West—where a child takes the adoptive parents' surname, can legally inherit from them, and is treated "as if" he or she is a biological child—is prohibited in Islam for reasons of patrilineal purity.[3] In the absence of sperm donation and child adoption, infertile men are left with few avenues to fatherhood.

Given these prohibitions, the introduction of ICSI, which overcomes male infertility using a man's own sperm, was a watershed event within the Arab world. As a variant of IVF, ICSI solves the problem of male infertility in a way that IVF cannot. With standard IVF, spermatozoa are removed from a man's body through masturbation, and oocytes (eggs) are surgically removed from a woman's ovaries following hormonal stimulation. Once these male and female gametes are retrieved, they are introduced to each other in a petri dish in an IVF laboratory, in the hopes of fertilization. However, "weak" sperm (i.e., low numbers, poor movement, misshapen) are poor fertilizers. Through "micromanipulation" of otherwise infertile sperm under a high-powered microscope, they can be injected directly into human oocytes, effectively aiding fertilization. As long as one viable spermatozoon can be extracted from an infertile man's body, it can be "ICSI-injected" into an oocyte, leading to the potential creation of a human embryo. With ICSI, then, otherwise sterile men can father biogenetic offspring. This includes azoospermic men, who produce no sperm in their ejaculate and must therefore have their testicles painfully aspirated or biopsied in the search for sperm. In short, ICSI gives even the most infertile men a chance of producing a "test-tube baby."

First invented in Belgium in 1991–92, and then introduced in Egypt in 1994, ICSI has led to a virtual "coming out" of male infertility across the Middle East, as men acknowledge their infertility and seek the ICSI solution (Inhorn 2003; 2012). The coming of this new "hope technology" (Franklin 1997) has repaired diminished masculinity in men who were once silently suffering from their infertility. Furthermore, ICSI is being used in the Middle East and elsewhere as the preferred assisted reproductive technology, effectively replacing its predecessor, IVF. Basically, IVF leaves fertilization up to chance, whereas ICSI does not. Thus, ICSI provides a more guaranteed way of creating "the elusive embryo" (Becker 2000). With ICSI, human fertilization is increasingly aided and abetted by human embryologists working in IVF laboratories around the world.

ICSI may be a revolutionary technology, but it also entails many challenges for infertile men and their wives. For one, the precisely timed collection of semen can produce deep anxiety and even impotence, but is imperative for all ICSI procedures (Inhorn 2012). Some men may produce no spermatozoa whatsoever, even within their testicles, eliminating ICSI as an option. Furthermore, ICSI may not succeed, leading to endless rounds of fruitless repetition among some couples. For women, ICSI involves a grueling surgical procedure, which is highly dependent upon the complicated hormonal stimulation and extraction of healthy oocytes from women's bodies. Whereas the fecundity of older men can often be enhanced through ICSI, women's fertility is highly age sensitive, with oocyte quality declining at later stages of the reproductive life cycle. In short, older women may "age out" of ICSI, causing highly gendered, life-course disruptions surrounding women's "biological clocks" (Inhorn 2003; 2012). In addition, men may arrive at ICSI after years of other failed treatment options. ICSI is expensive, usually costing U.S. $2,000 to $6,000 per cycle in the Middle East. Thus, it is often deemed a "last resort," especially for men without adequate financial resources. Finally, when it does succeed, ICSI may perpetuate genetic defects into future generations, through the sperm defects and other inherited disorders that may be passed by infertile men via ICSI to their male offspring. The ethics of passing genetic mutations to children has been an increasing cause for concern (Bittles and Matson 2000).

Despite these challenges, nearly 5 million "test-tube babies" have now been born around the world (Franklin 2012), nearly half a million of whom are the result of ICSI. As suggested earlier, ICSI is a "hope technology" (Franklin 1997), creating the "only hope" for most infertile men, especially those with serious infertility problems. The emergence of ICSI in the Middle Eastern region has led to a boom in demand for this technology—a demand that has never waned. ICSI is by far the most common ART now undertaken in the Middle East, and IVF clinics today are filled with ICSI-seeking men and their wives. For many of these men, the search for ICSI success is relentless. As one infertile Lebanese man put it, "I will try again and again and again. I will never lose hope." Or, as another concluded, "I will try until I die."

In order to exemplify the emergence of ICSI and all that it entails in the Middle East, I turn here to the story of a man who I shall call Ibrahim,[4] whose ardent desire for fatherhood propels him on a valiant and transnational ICSI quest. Ibrahim's story exemplifies many aspects of new Arab manhood as it is emerging in the twenty-first century. In Ibrahim's case, he engages creatively and persistently with a variety of new medical possibilities in his hope of becoming a new Arab father. Ibrahim was one of several Middle Eastern men who volunteered for my ethnographic study, eager to tell his story and to relay his treatment quest to me. I met Ibrahim and his wife

Nura in January 2007 outside an ultrasound scanning suite in an IVF clinic on the outskirts of Dubai, United Arab Emirates (UAE). I was packing my bag to leave for the day when Ibrahim approached me, having read my study advertisement placed on the waiting room tables. We made a tentative appointment to meet later in the month. But as soon as I stepped into a waiting taxi, I received a call from Ibrahim on my cell phone, asking if we could meet sooner, ideally at his home. I agreed, and two days later, on Ibrahim's way home from work, he picked me up at the clinic for the short ride to his and Nura's spacious, high-rise apartment, overlooking an inland lake. I commented on the beauty of the couple's home and its view, and Ibrahim proceeded to give me a tour, showing me the second bedroom where he hoped there would soon be a child. We then sat down on the ornate, Louis XIV–style furniture in the living room to talk about Ibrahim's infertility problem and the couple's ICSI quest.

Ibrahim and His ICSI Quest

Married for thirteen years, Ibrahim and Nura were first cousins, the children of two Palestinian sisters. Ibrahim had grown up in a Palestinian family in Kuwait, but when he visited his mother's family in Jenin (on the West Bank), he met his beautiful cousin Nura, falling madly in love with her. They married "for love" in 1993, and by 1994, the questioning began about why Nura was not yet pregnant. "You know our traditions in the Middle East," Ibrahim said to me. "We get married, and after one year, everybody starts asking what's going on. If you go for more than one year [without a pregnancy], this comes to be seen as a problem."

Nura began the treatment quest by visiting a doctor in 1995. When the doctor told her that she was able to become pregnant, Ibrahim did his first "checkup," a semen analysis that proved to be "very bad." The physician advised Ibrahim to go to a "specialist." Ibrahim consulted a urologist and, per Middle Eastern medical tradition, ended up undergoing a varicocelectomy (to remove varicose veins on the scrotum) in 1995. As is generally the case, the varicocelectomy did nothing to improve Ibrahim's sperm count. "After that, I did many tests," Ibrahim explained. "And still, the results turned out to be very bad." He then volunteered, "I have a copy of all my medical reports. I could show them to you on Sunday. Always, the semen count was 400,000 to 500,000, very, very weak. And after one-half hour, everything died. There was fragmentation, also."

"Our journey starts here," Ibrahim told me, immediately launch-
ing into a story of thirteen failed ICSI attempts between 1995 and
2007, the last one conducted during the sacred month of Ramadan
the year before. In the early days of their ICSI quest, Ibrahim and
Nura focused on Jordan, a country with a Palestinian majority, Pal-
estinian-run IVF clinics, and a "famous" IVF hospital in Amman,
one of the first to perform IVF in the Middle East. Traveling from
their home in Kuwait to Jordan was both taxing and expensive.
Nonetheless, Ibrahim and Nura attempted ICSI seven times in Jordan at three different IVF centers. At that time, the cost of one ICSI
cycle was 1,500 to 2,000 Jordanian dinars (approximately $2,100
to $2,800), but Ibrahim's monthly salary was only 200 Jordanian
dinars, or one-tenth the amount of one ICSI procedure. In desperation, Nura contemplated selling her bridal gold. Fortunately, however, Ibrahim secured a good job in Dubai as an accountant, and
the couple moved there in 1999. Within their first year in Dubai,
Ibrahim and Nura underwent two ICSI procedures in Emirati government hospitals, where ARTs were partially state-subsidized. However, both cycles failed, and the couple became concerned about
standards of cleanliness, having seen cockroaches on the hospital
walls.

As the new millennium was fast approaching and their nine ICSI
cycles had all failed, Ibrahim became convinced to "stop searching in Arab countries." A Palestinian friend in France made an appointment for Ibrahim and Nura at an IVF clinic in Rouen. There,
a chromosome test of Ibrahim's sperm showed "fragmentation," an
indication of a chromosomal defect. Reviewing Ibrahim's case, the
French doctors told him bluntly, "We can't do anything for you.
And since you did ICSI more than nine to ten times, we cannot do
it again, because the French rules say that we cannot do ICSI after
four times." They then suggested adoption, which shocked Ibrahim.
"That's fine for you," Ibrahim told the French doctors. "But for us,
as Muslims, we have a different tradition."

Demoralized but not destroyed, Ibrahim began his "research,"
drawing upon his global network of relatives and acquaintances in
the Palestinian diaspora. Fortunately, one of Ibrahim's Palestinian
friends in Los Angeles told him that he would be willing to help with
the ICSI quest. Despite the difficulty of obtaining visas for travel
to the post-9/11 United States, Ibrahim and Nura's patience paid
off. They were eventually allowed to seek medical care in America.
There, they visited IVF centers in both Las Vegas and Los Angeles,
agreeing that their best chances for ICSI success were at the Uni-

versity of California, Los Angeles, where, in the words of Ibrahim, a "master doctor" was in charge of the IVF clinic.

For the first time in a decade of ICSI-seeking, Ibrahim and Nura were offered preimplantation genetic diagnosis (PGD). In Ibrahim and Nura's case, the UCLA physician wanted to determine whether the couple's ICSI embryos were carrying genetic defects, causing repeated ICSI failures. After verifying that PGD was religiously acceptable, Ibrahim and Nura agreed to PGD, and learned that eight of their twenty embryos were free from obvious genetic disease. As Ibrahim recalled, "He [the IVF doctor] told me something funny then. He said, 'You have seven girls and one boy.' I said, 'I don't give a damn shit for girls or boys, Doctor! All I want is a child!' So he returned back [to Nura's uterus] three girls and one boy."

Ibrahim and Nura were scheduled to return to Dubai a week after the embryo transfer, and Ibrahim carefully changed their tickets from economy to business class, so that Nura and the four ICSI embryos could "recline" in transit. After their return to Dubai, Nura underwent a pregnancy test—again negative. "My God, you cannot imagine how disappointed we were," Ibrahim exclaimed. Calling me by my first name, he continued:

> In the U.S., Marcia, the trip cost me, with the travel, with everything, around $35,000. Maybe I've spent more than $100,000 in total for all of the [ICSI] trials. If somebody else had done this to Nura, I'm sure she couldn't stand it. Sometimes, I come back home, and I find her crying. The environment here in the Arab countries, I mean, her sister is getting pregnant, my brother's wife is getting pregnant, and sometimes they cannot stop it [their fertility]! Our family is not interfering, and it's a love marriage. But sometimes, you know, I told her, "All of the problem is because of me, not you. It's from my side. If you want, we can divorce." But she refused. She told me, "If there is going to be a baby, it has to come from you."[5]

He then asked me, "It's *so* frustrating; I have to do ICSI. But how and where?" At this point, I broached the delicate topic of sperm donation. Ibrahim responded:

> Somebody suggested sperm donation, but we totally refused. For both of us, it's not in consideration. [*Inhorn*: Why?] Because I refuse it. If the sperm comes from somebody else, you know, inside your heart, you will know it is not yours. Not our color, not our eyes, different things will come out. That's why we refuse. He will not be my son. But maybe I will go for the other one, cloning, or how they did Dolly the sheep. This cloning I have no problem with. [*Inhorn*: Even if Islam

doesn't allow it?] I'm sure they *will* allow it eventually. IVF started in the 1980s, and at first, the Islamic authorities didn't accept, but now they accept. Maybe after five years, they will accept cloning.[6] But using a donor, no. It's not from your back [where sperm are thought to be made]. It's not from you."

Nura, who had been quietly following the conversation added, "It's like adoption. I wouldn't do it because I don't like the idea."

Given their opposition to adoption and gamete donation, both of which are prohibited in Sunni Islam, Ibrahim and Nura explained that they must use their own gametes. According to Ibrahim, their reproductive fate is ultimately in God's hands:

> I believe in science, but also God. I believe in science, but if God wants to give, He will. We have the same belief, that if God wants to get us something [a baby], he will give. One of my friends, he was having the same problem as me. Every year, he was going on a vacation with his wife to Jordan and doing ICSI, and it was not happening. Then two years ago, I got back in touch with him. He said, "You'll never believe what happened! I got fed up going to clinics here and there and just spending money. So my wife and I went to Saudi Arabia on the *umra* [a form of pilgrimage], and we were staying there and praying to God. And, yes, it happened."

"So you see," Ibrahim said, "This is from God. You have to believe." According to Ibrahim, he would be satisfied if God granted him one child. "One baby and that's it! Not more. I told Nura, 'If I get one baby, your ovary, I will remove it!' I don't want to think about it anymore! This is the only, and lonely problem in my life. I don't have any other problem."

Ibrahim told me that he had contemplated going to Belgium, where ICSI was invented, but he had decided against it. "One doctor, he advised us to go to Belgium. But after we tried ICSI in America, I feel that what we do here [in the Middle East] is the same." At the time of our meeting, Ibrahim had placed his hopes in the private IVF clinic on the edge of Dubai where I first met him. Although the IVF physician was a Hindu from India, Ibrahim found him "down to earth," a physician who had still "found hope" in Ibrahim's poor sperm profile. Ibrahim continued,

> When I'm alone, I start thinking, "What's wrong with me?" I don't know how to explain it. Sometimes, I think my problem was caused by the fear I faced in Kuwait in 1991. The Kuwaiti people came back to Kuwait [from Iraq], and I was there after the [First Gulf] war finished. They came back and caught all of the Palestinians they could

find [whose leader, Yasir Arafat, had supported Saddam Hussein]. They caught me for one night and tortured me, blindfolding my eyes and beating and slapping me. They took me from my house and I didn't know where I was going because they put a blindfold over my eyes. I was blindfolded, but I felt that there were about eight people there, in a building or a basement, and they tortured me. Then after that, they threw me out, and when the blindfold was removed from my eyes, my eyes opened, but I couldn't see anything for about one-half hour. This happened two years before marriage, and the shock of that, of this happening in the place where I was born and lived for twenty-five years, I don't know, but I think this experience may have caused my problem.

After this sobering conclusion to our interview, Ibrahim and Nura drove me home, chatting amiably about how much they enjoyed the United States and the "friendliness" of Americans. I was able to show them around the pretty, American-affiliated desert campus where I lived with my family. I promised to keep in touch and to make a few inquiries on their behalf. I was heartened by the fact that Ibrahim and Nura still had three female embryos in frozen storage at UCLA. Ibrahim had told me that returning to America to try a so-called "frozen cycle" with these embryos was too difficult, financially and emotionally. "If it is guaranteed that I will 'catch' these three girls [as my children], I will go and put!" he had exclaimed during the interview. But, rightly so, Ibrahim realized that there were no such guarantees.

Several weeks after our interview, I inquired with the clinic's "embryo courier" service about whether it was possible to transport three viable embryos all the way from Los Angeles to Dubai. When the courier replied "yes," I decided to introduce him to Ibrahim, a meeting that took place after Ibrahim and Nura experienced their fourteenth failed ICSI cycle at the Dubai IVF clinic. Ibrahim was very excited about the prospect of transporting their three embryos from the United States to the UAE, but was told by the courier that this would cost approximately $2,500. Ibrahim laughed, "What the hell! After all I've paid, this is nothing!"

I left the UAE in July 2007, after six months of fieldwork at the clinic. I learned from the clinic's embryologist—a fellow Palestinian who had taken a special interest in Ibrahim and Nura's case—that the three embryos were flown from Los Angeles in a cryopreservation tank that was hand-carried all the way from LAX through customs at Dubai International Airport. With the help of the Indian doctor, Ibrahim's and Nura's "three girl embryos," made in America and thawed in the UAE, were transferred into Nura's uterus on the Emirati IVF clinic's operating table.

Unfortunately, God decided that the time was still not right for Ibrahim and Nura to become parents. On the fifteenth attempt at ICSI, the three female embryos did not implant in Nura's womb, and Ibrahim's dreams of fathering three little "American-made" Palestinian daughters vanished.

An ICSI Revolution?

Ibrahim's story is emblematic of emergent masculinities in the Middle East today, including men's engagements with the latest forms of reproductive technology as they become available around the globe. Ibrahim is a happily married man, who wants to father a child with his beloved wife, Nura. When he learns early in marriage that he is infertile, he begins a relentless quest to overcome his infertility, involving, among other things, repeated sperm tests, an unproductive genital surgery, and eventual resort to assisted reproduction. Ibrahim's ICSI quest involves, among other things, thousands of dollars, intraregional "doctor shopping," transnational reproductive tourism to both Europe and America, sophisticated genetic embryo testing, transnational embryo couriership, and fifteen repeated ICSI failures. The toll this takes on Ibrahim and Nura is profound. Nura, for her part, must suffer through the hormonal stimulation and invasive oocyte retrievals and embryo transfers of each failed ICSI cycle. Because Nura herself is healthy and fertile, Ibrahim feels great guilt and empathy for Nura's embodied sacrifice. In an attempt to prevent Nura's suffering, he proposes the option of divorce, which Nura refuses. Nura also refuses the option of legal adoption, which is prohibited by Islam. Ibrahim, for his part, cannot accept sperm donation, which is also religiously illicit and which is rarely accepted by Sunni Muslim men, according to my studies (Inhorn 2006; 2012). Instead, Ibrahim hopes for the day when human reproductive cloning will become available and accepted by the Islamic religious authorities. Until then, he has no option but to wait, or to try ICSI again.

In Ibrahim's case, he is extremely unlikely to impregnate Nura without technological assistance. Like so many Middle Eastern men, Ibrahim has a severe case of male infertility, of likely genetic origin. Although he believes in "science" and understands that his sperm manifest chromosomal "fragmentation," he also believes in God's omnipotence in matters of human reproduction. So far, God has not blessed him with a child, for reasons he cannot dare to question.

Instead, Ibrahim attributes his infertility to the stresses of war-related physical violence, of which he was the victim. In fact, Ibrahim is quite astute in his analysis. In the war-torn Middle Eastern region, war and other forms of political violence have, indeed, increased both male and female infertility on a population level (Abu-Musa et al. 2008; Kobeissi et al. 2008). However, war is probably not the major reason why so many Middle Eastern men are infertile, manifesting severe cases with extremely low sperm counts, poor motility, or absence of sperm altogether. These severe cases tend to run in families and, as noted earlier, are probably genetically based. Men in my studies were often able to note familial patterns of male infertility, calling them *wirathi* (hereditary).

If most male infertility is, indeed, genetically based, then the use of ICSI as the major technological solution to overcome male infertility problems is also ethically questionable. Through ICSI, the genetic mutations causing male infertility may be transmitted to male offspring, requiring the intervention of ICSI generation after generation. To prevent this from happening, some Middle Eastern IVF practitioners are beginning to recommend the PGD-assisted culling of all male embryos in severe male infertility cases, before they are ever implanted. In this way, only female offspring, who do not carry the Y chromosome, are born to such infertile men.

Unfortunately, many infertile Middle Eastern men will never produce an ICSI child, because ICSI cannot guarantee conception. As with IVF, overall ICSI success rates are usually less than 40 percent per cycle, even in the world's best centers (Osmanagaoglu et al. 1999). Depending upon other factors, such as age-related egg quality and the severity of the male infertility, ICSI success rates can be significantly lower. For example, of 220 men participating in my study of male infertility in Lebanon (Inhorn 2012), 177 of them had already undertaken ICSI. Among these 177 men, there was a grand total of 434 ICSI attempts—274 among the infertile men, and 160 among the fertile men with infertile wives. Yet, only eighteen ICSI children were born to these men, including thirteen ICSI sons and five ICSI daughters (including one set of female twins). Thus, the so-called "take-home baby rate" was astonishingly low—only 4 percent. This low rate of ICSI success increased considerably if all conceptions were considered, including current pregnancies (seven), ectopic pregnancies (nine), miscarriages and stillbirths (twenty-nine), and neonatal deaths (four). In this case, sixty-six conceptions took place after 434 ICSI attempts, for a pregnancy rate (as opposed to a "take-home" baby rate) of 29 percent. This makes the overall success of ICSI in this Middle Eastern population seem closer to global standards. Nonetheless, most of these ICSI conceptions ended in heartbreak and suffering, including life-threatening ectopic pregnancies among men's wives, the stillbirth of seven sets of twins, and the deaths of three ICSI sons (including one with Down syndrome) and one ICSI daughter (due to a congenital heart defect). Recounting their losses, men often wiped tears from their eyes.

Furthermore, some men—especially ICSI repeaters like Ibrahim—spent small fortunes on their attempts. The average number of ICSIs was 2.5, but a few men in my study had undertaken ICSI more than ten times. When I asked men to estimate how much they had spent on their ICSI quests, those who were able to calculate averaged $17,000, with total costs ranging from $1,500 to $100,000. These costs are exceedingly high for the Middle East, if it is considered that most men in my study made well under $12,000 per year. In the United States, by comparison, the average cost of one ICSI cycle is more than $12,000, and the cost of making one "take-home" baby reaches nearly $70,000 (Spar 2006).

Because of the costs of repetition, ICSI is an incredibly expensive technology, which many of the men in my study could ill afford. Some of them used up their life savings; some borrowed against their future retirement benefits; others took out bank loans; some sold land; some of their wives sold bridal gold; and in many cases, men relied on family financial aid, particularly from wealthier relatives in the diaspora. Some men literally impoverished themselves in their ICSI quests. Others waited years to save the requisite money for a single ICSI cycle. In a few cases, men told me matter-of-factly that they could only afford one ICSI. Thus, they were praying to God that their single attempt would succeed.

This brings us to an important question: Is ICSI a revolutionary technology? A miracle solution for male infertility? A form of technological assistance? A way to give nature a helping hand? Or is it something less promising? A form of false hope? A deleterious eugenic technology? A means of stratified reproduction?

Neither philosopher nor bioethicist, I find it difficult to answer these questions definitively. Many feminist scholars before me have attempted to "theorize infertility," by condemning the ARTs for their negative gender effects. Yet, in the most comprehensive feminist assessment of assisted reproduction, Charis Thompson (2002; 2005) urges caution in this regard. As she points out, the ethnography of infertility clearly demonstrates the power of ARTs such as ICSI to generate hope, fulfill desire, and make parents of infertile couples. IVF clinics in the Middle East today are filled with ICSI-seeking couples such as Ibrahim and Nura. Baby photos prominently displayed on clinic walls, including in the operating theaters where ICSI is performed, keep hope alive for these couples. ICSI is by far the most common form of assisted reproduction now undertaken in the Middle East, because in the absence of sperm donation and adoption as legal options, ICSI is infertile men's only hope for fatherhood.

ICSI, Emergent Masculinities, and New Arab Fatherhood

Despite the ambiguous effects of ICSI and other forms of assisted reproduction, ICSI brings with it hopes and dreams for the high numbers of infertile men in the Middle East, a region that can now boast one of the strongest and largest assisted reproduction industries in the world (Abbasi-Shavazi et al. 2008; Inhorn and Tremayne 2012). If male infertility threatens fatherhood, it is now typically viewed as a medical condition to be overcome through high-tech assisted reproduction, rather than as a sign of diminished manhood. In a region with high rates of male infertility, men often have friends and male relatives who struggle with infertility. The modern-day treatment quest—which often includes repeated semen analysis, clinic-based masturbation, testicular needlework, genital surgeries, and other forms of embodied agony—is men's badge of honor, signifying the ways in which men suffer for reproduction and love. Their feelings of sympathy and sacrifice—of doing all of this "for her"—are prominent motivating factors in emergent marital subjectivities in the Middle East today.

Gender scripts surrounding conjugality are also being reworked in complex ways as ICSI and other ARTs reach wider audiences in the Middle East. I would argue that assisted reproduction itself is changing the Middle East in unprecedented ways, creating many new possibilities for marital, gender, and family relations. The very growth of a booming Middle Eastern IVF industry—for example, with nearly 250 IVF clinics between the three Middle Eastern countries of Turkey, Iran, and Egypt—bespeaks not only regional pronatalism, but also the physical, financial, and emotional commitments of thousands upon thousands of married couples.

It is important to point out that Middle Eastern men embark on IVF and ICSI within marriage, which is highly valorized. Most Arab men desire romantic love, companionship, sexual passion, and monogamy, surrounded by a sphere of conjugal privacy within a nuclear household setting (Inhorn 1996; 2012). Increasingly, Middle Eastern couples are remaining together in long-term childless marriages, while trying repeated rounds of IVF and ICSI in the hopes of achieving parenthood. Furthermore, Middle Eastern men work hard, often emigrating for periods of their lives, in order to save the money necessary for these IVF and ICSI cycles. Fatherhood of two to three "test-tube babies"—a mixture of sons and desired daughters—is wanted as much for sheer joy and marital fulfillment as it is for patrilineal continuity, patriarchal power, or old-age security.

These changes in men's attitudes, expectations, and practices of reproduction and family life are indicative of what is being called "ideational change" across the Middle East (Yount and Rashad 2008). To wit, total fertility rates have fallen across the region; nuclear families are becoming the socially accepted norm; levels of education for both men and women, but especially women, are rising; and assumptions about son preference and men's patriarchal rights are being questioned. This "new Arab family"—to use the term coined by anthropologist Nicholas Hopkins (2004)—no longer resembles the Middle Eastern family of a generation ago. These emergent changes in family life are being followed by several Middle Eastern anthropologists, who have formed the Arab Families Working Group (AFWG) led by pioneering Lebanese-American scholar Suad Joseph (1999).

Just as these anthropologists are speaking of the new Arab family, I would like to coin the terms "the new Arab man" and "the new Arab father." New Arab men are rejecting the assumptions of their Arab forefathers, including what I have called in my work the "four notorious P's" (Inhorn 2012)—namely, patriarchy (i.e., male dominance), patrilineality (i.e., kinship traced only through the male line), patrilocality (i.e., residence with husband's family after marriage), and polygyny (i.e., marriage of one man to more than one wife). According to the men in my studies, these four P's are becoming a thing of the past. Instead, emergent masculinities in the Middle East are characterized by resistance to patriarchy, patrilineality, and patrilocality, which are being undermined. Polygyny is truly rare, comprising less than 1 percent of marriages in most Middle Eastern societies, just as it has been throughout history (Charrad 2001; Musallam 2009). Certainly, polygyny is not a common strategy today to overcome childlessness, nor a social norm for which contemporary Middle Eastern men strive. Although most Middle Eastern men want to father their own children, taking a second wife is not viewed as a solution to infertility. Instead, men seek to help their infertile wives find appropriate treatment. Middle Eastern men today also realize that they themselves may be infertile. Indeed, determining whether a man is infertile is now one of the first steps taken in the medical examination of childless couples across the Middle Eastern region. Men's acceptance of ICSI as the preferred solution for male infertility is also, in my view, highly indicative of ideational change and emergent masculinities in the Arab world today.

Conclusion

All in all, the Middle East is in the midst of double forms of emergence—both technological and masculine. On the one hand, new forms of reproductive technology are continuously emerging, and once they reach the reproductive marketplace, they are being rapidly discussed, debated, and, in most cases, deployed in Middle Eastern IVF settings. ICSI is a case in point: after its introduction in Belgium in 1992, it spread within two years to Egypt, where Sunni Muslim couples were the first to access this reproductive technology. By 2007, when Ibrahim and Nura were about to embark on their fourteenth ICSI cycle in Dubai, ICSI was widely available across the entire Middle Eastern region from Morocco to Iran, with couples from all religions, Sunni, Shia, Druze, and Christian, employing this technology in hopes of overcoming male infertility.

The willingness of Middle Eastern men such as Ibrahim to engage with ICSI as a form of assisted reproduction is a powerful marker of their emergent masculinities. For example, in Ibrahim's case, he has undergone repeated forms of embodied agony to assess and improve his sperm profile. He has worked hard as a male labor migrant to fund his treatment quest. He has become a twenty-first-century male "reproductive tourist," even venturing to the West, where Palestinians are generally unwelcome. He has authorized the use of the latest forms of reprogenetic technology to advance his chances of ICSI success, and he has engaged in a sophisticated transnational process of embryo couriership in order to retrieve what he hoped would become his future daughters. Furthermore, although Ibrahim has demonstrated his marital love and commitment to Nura, he is sensitive to her own motherhood desires and embodied suffering, believing that she has made a major sacrifice in order to be with him—an infertile husband. Ibrahim extols the virtues of his conjugal love. Indeed, his greatest hope is to become *both* a loving husband *and* a loving father—to a son *or* a daughter, the sex of the child being unimportant in his quest for fatherhood.

In conclusion, in the Middle East today, emergent masculinities entail love, tenderness, and affection, as well as untold sacrifice and suffering, all elements of contemporary Arab manhood that go unnoticed and unappreciated. It is my hope that this chapter provides a fundamentally humanizing account, moving us one step closer to understanding how Arab men encounter their reproductive setbacks. Through these encounters, Arab men such as Ibrahim are living proof that manhood is being transformed in the Middle East today, with men themselves reconceiving their masculinity.

Notes

1. Since 1988, I have been undertaking ethnographic fieldwork on infertility and assisted reproduction in the Middle East, beginning in Egypt. Following the publication of my "Egyptian trilogy" (Inhorn 1994; 1996; 2003), I embarked on a major study of male infertility in Lebanon in 2003, undertaking semi-structured reproductive history and unstructured ethnographic interviews with 220 Lebanese, Syrian, and Palestinian men coming for infertility services in two major IVF clinics in Beirut, Lebanon. In 2007, I returned to the Middle East to undertake an ethnographic study of "reproductive tourism" in the United Arab Emirates, interviewing more than 200 reproductive travelers from fifty countries (Inhorn and Shrivistav 2010). In the intervening years, I conducted a study of infertile Arab immigrant and refugee men in southeastern Michigan, the so-called "capital of Arab America" (Inhorn and Fakih 2005). Most of these men were Lebanese, Iraqi, and Yemeni. In total, I have interviewed more than 330 Arab men in infertile marriages, the majority of these men being infertile. The interviews were conducted in either Arabic or English, depending on the preference of the informant. In Ibrahim's case, we spoke in English, a language in which he was fully fluent.

2. This chapter is excerpted from a variety of sections of my recent book, *The New Arab Man: Emergent Masculinities, Technologies, and Islam in the Middle East* (Inhorn 2012).

3. Legal adoption, as it is understood in the West, is not allowed in Islam. According to Islam, orphaned children can be permanently fostered, but they cannot be given the adoptive parents' family name, nor can they inherit from them (Sonbol 1995). Three Muslim Middle Eastern countries—Iran, Tunisia, and Turkey—have nonetheless circumvented these adoption rules, allowing formal legal adoption to take place. Informal

"adoption" (i.e., fostering) of relatives' children sometimes takes place, but, according to my studies, is relatively uncommon among infertile couples.

4. All names are pseudonyms.

5. At some point during long-term childless marriages, infertile men and women in the Middle East often offer to "free" their fertile spouses through divorce. These offers are generally refused, on the parts of both men and women.

6. Currently, there is an Islamic bioethical ban in place on human reproductive cloning, which follows worldwide trends in this regard (Eich 2002; Moosa 2003). Nonetheless, at least one Lebanese Shia cleric has condoned human reproductive cloning as a solution for childlessness (Clarke and Inhorn 2011; Inhorn 2012).

References

Abbasi-Shavazi, Mohammad Jalal, Marcia C. Inhorn, Hajiieh Bibi Razeghi-Nasrabad, and Ghasem Toloo. 2008. "The 'Iranian ART Revolution': Infertility, Assisted Reproductive Technology, and Third-Party Donation in the Islamic Republic of Iran." *Journal of Middle East Women's Studies* 4, no. 2: 1–28.

Abu-Musa, Antoine A., Loulou Kobeissi, Antoine B. Hannoun, and Marcia C. Inhorn. 2008. "Effect of War on Fertility: A Review of the Literature." *Reproductive BioMedicine Online* 17 (Suppl. 1): 43–53.

Baccetti, B., S. Capitani, G. Collodel, G. Cairano, L. Gambera, and E. Moretti. 2001. "Genetic Sperm Defects and Consanguinity." *Human Reproduction* 16: 1365–71.

Becker, Gay. 2000. *The Elusive Embryo: How Women and Men Approach New Reproductive Technologies.* Berkeley: University of California Press.

———. 2002. "Deciding Whether to Tell Children about Donor Insemination: An Unresolved Question in the United States." In *Infertility around the Globe: New Thinking on Childlessness, Gender, and Reproductive Technologies,* ed. Marcia C. Inhorn and Frank van Balen. Berkeley: University of California Press.

Bittles, Alan H. 2012. *Consanguinity in Context.* Cambridge: Cambridge University Press.

Bittles, Alan H., and P. L. Matson. 2000. "Genetic Influences on Human Infertility." In *Infertility in the Modern World: Present and Future Prospects,* ed. R. Bentley and C. G. Nicholas Mascie-Taylor. Cambridge: Cambridge University Press.

Charrad, Mounira. 2001. *States and Women's Rights: The Making of Postcolonial Tunisia, Algeria, and Morocco.* Berkeley: University of California Press.

Clarke, Morgan, and Marcia C. Inhorn. 2011. "Mutuality and Immediacy between *Marja'* and *Muqallid:* Evidence from Male IVF Patients in Shi'i Lebanon." *International Journal of Middle East Studies* 43, no. 3: 409–27.

Connell, R. W. 1995. *Masculinities.* Berkeley: University of California Press.

Eich, Thomas. 2002. "Muslim Voices on Cloning." *ISIM Newsletter* 12: 38–39.

Franklin, Sarah. 1997. *Embodied Progress: A Cultural Account of Assisted Conception.* London: Routledge.

———. 2012. "Five Million Miracle Babies Later: The Biocultural Legacies of IVF." In *IVF as Global Form: Ethnographic Knowledge and the Transnationalization of Reproductive Technologies,* ed. Michi Knecht, Maren Klotz, and Stefan Beck. Chicago: University of Chicago Press.

Greil, Arthur L., Kathleen Slauson-Blevins, and Julia McQuillan. 2010. "The Experience of Infertility: A Review of Recent Literature." *Sociology of Health and Illness* 32, no. 1: 140–62.

Hopkins, Nicholas S., ed. 2004. *The New Arab Family.* Cairo: American University of Cairo Press.

Inhorn, Marcia C. 1994. *Quest for Conception: Gender, Infertility, and Egyptian Medical Traditions.* Philadelphia: University of Pennsylvania Press.

———. 1996. *Infertility and Patriarchy: The Cultural Politics of Gender and Family Life in Egypt.* Philadelphia: University of Pennsylvania Press.

———. 2003. *Local Babies, Global Science: Gender, Religion, and in Vitro Fertilization in Egypt.* New York: Routledge.

———. 2006. "'He Won't Be My Son': Middle Eastern Muslim Men's Discourses of Adoption and Gamete Donation." *Medical Anthropology Quarterly* 20, no. 1: 94–120.

———. 2012. *The New Arab Man: Emergent Masculinities, Technologies, and Islam in the Middle East.* Princeton: Princeton University Press.

Inhorn, Marcia C., and Daphna Birenbaum-Carmeli. 2010. "Male Infertility, Chronicity, and the Plight of Palestinian Men in Israel and Lebanon." In *Chronic Conditions, Fluid States: Chronicity and the Anthropology of Illness,* ed. Lenore Manderson and Carolyn Smith-Morris. New Brunswick, NJ: Rutgers University Press.

Inhorn, Marcia C., and Emily A. Wentzell. 2011. "Embodying Emergent Masculinities: Reproductive and Sexual Health Technologies in the Middle East and Mexico." *American Ethnologist* 38, no. 4: 801–15.

Inhorn, Marcia C., Loulou Kobeissi, Zaher Nassar, Da'ad Lakkis, and Michael Hassan Fakih. 2009. "Consanguinity and Family Clustering of Male Infertility in Lebanon." *Fertility and Sterility* 91: 1104–9.

Inhorn, Marcia C., and Michael H. Fakih. 2005. "Arab Americans, African Americans, and Infertility: Barriers to Reproduction and Medical Care." *Fertility and Sterility* 85: 844–52.

Inhorn, Marcia C., and Pankaj Shrivistav. 2010. "Globalization and Reproductive Tourism in the United Arab Emirates." *Asia-Pacific Journal of Public Health* 22, Suppl: 68–74.

Inhorn, Marcia C., and Soraya Tremayne, eds. 2012. *Islam and Assisted Reproductive Technologies: Sunni and Shia Perspectives.* New York; Oxford: Berghahn Books.

Joseph, Suad, ed. 1999. *Intimate Selving in Arab Families: Gender, Self, and Identity.* Syracuse, NY: Syracuse University Press.

Kobeissi, Loulou, Marcia C. Inhorn, Antoine B. Hannoun, Najwa Hammoud, Johnny Awwad, and Antoine A. Abu-Musa. 2008. "Civil War and Male Infertility in Lebanon." *Fertility and Sterility* 90, no. 2: 340–45.

Latini, Maurizio, Loredana Gandini, Andrea Lenzi, and Francesco Romanelli. 2004. "Sperm Tail Agenesis in a Case of Consanguinity." *Fertility and Sterility* 81, no. 6: 1688–91.

Maduro, M. R., and D. J. Lamb. 2002. "Understanding the New Genetics of Male Infertility." *Journal of Urology* 168: 2197–2205.

Moosa, Ebrahim. 2003. "Human Cloning in Muslim Ethics." *Voices Across Boundaries* (Fall): 23–26.

Musallam, Basim F. 2009. "The Ordering of Muslim Societies." In *Cambridge Illustrated History: Islamic World,* ed. Francis Robinson. Cambridge: Cambridge University Press.

Osmanagaoglu, Kaan, Herman Tournaye, Michel Camus, Mark Vandervorst, Andre Van Steirteghem, and Paul Devroey. 1999. "Cumulative Delivery Rates after ICSI: A Five-Years Follow-up of 498 Patients." *Human Reproduction* 14, no. 10: 2651–55.

Shavazi, M. J. A., P. McDonald, and M. Hosseini-Chavoshi. 2006. "Modernization and the Cultural Practice of Consanguineous Marriage: A Study of Four Provinces of Iran." Paper Presented at the European Population Conference, Liverpool, England. 21–24 June.

Sonbol, Amira el Azhary. 1995. "Adoption in Islamic Society: A Historical Survey." In *Children in the Muslim Middle East,* ed. Elizabeth Warnock Fernea. Austin: University of Texas Press.

Spar, Deborah L. 2006. *The Baby Business: How Money, Science, and Politics Drive the Commerce of Conception.* Boston: Harvard Business School Press.

Thompson, Charis. 2002. "Fertile Ground: Feminists Theorize Infertility." In *Infertility around the Globe: New Thinking on Childlessness, Gender, and Reproductive Technologies,* ed. Marcia C. Inhorn and Frank van Balen. Berkeley: University of California Press.

———. 2005. *Making Parents: The Ontological Choreography of Reproductive Technologies.* Cambridge: MIT Press.

Vayena, Effy, Patrick J. Rowe, and P. David Griffin, eds. 2002. *Current Practices and Controversies in Assisted Reproduction.* Geneva: World Health Organization.

Williams, Raymond. 1978. *Marxism and Literature.* Oxford: Oxford University Press.

Yount, Katherine, and Hoda Rashad, eds. 2008. *Family in the Middle East: Ideational Change in Egypt, Iran and Tunisia.* New York: Routledge.

Part VI

GAY/SURROGATE FATHERHOOD

Chapter 11

RELATING ACROSS INTERNATIONAL BORDERS

GAY MEN FORMING FAMILIES THROUGH OVERSEAS SURROGACY

Deborah Dempsey

Introduction

Since the early 2000s, it has been popular for Australian gay men to form families through commercial surrogacy arrangements in the United States, although commercial surrogacy is illegal throughout Australia (see Dempsey 2006; Millbank 2011; Murphy 2013; Tuazon-McCheyne 2010).[1] In the mid 2000s, India became a particularly attractive surrogacy destination due to the favorable legal climate for intended parents and the lower cost of clinical services (see Millbank 2011; Whittaker 2010). A survey commissioned by lobby group Surrogacy Australia in 2012 indicated that India had outstripped the United States in popularity as a surrogacy destination for gay men and heterosexual couples alike (Stethoscope Research 2012).

Commercial surrogacy remains a controversial practice. The burgeoning surrogacy industry in developing countries such as India and Thailand invites a renewed focus on the global ethics and politics of cross-border reproductive care (Inhorn and Gürtin 2011) in which the socioeconomic divide between the genetic and gestational

mothers and the mostly Western couples who contract their services is vast (see Chavkin and Maher 2010; DasGupta and DaGgupta
2010; Hochschild 2009; Pande 2011; Whittaker 2010). Indeed, the
politics of Australian gay men's potentially uncritical participation
in that industry is beginning to be subject to research scrutiny (see
Riggs and Due 2010).

Despite the above, in this chapter I assume a perspective on commercial surrogacy that is consistent with what Dumit and Davis-
Floyd (1998) refer to as an "agnostic" view. This leaves open the possibility that the commercialization of human reproduction can potentially give rise to a range of creative, innovative, and personally
rewarding experiences for the men, women, and children involved.
For instance, Elly Teman (2010) observes that researchers generally find surrogacy in Western countries to be a fulfilling process for
the surrogates, including benefits for their sense of self-worth and
self-confidence (see also van den Akker 2003; Blyth 1994; Jadva et
al. 2003; Teman 2006). With regard to circumstances in developing
countries, Sharmila Rudrappa (2012; this volume) contends that Indian commercial surrogates in Bangalore view their reproductive
labor as less dehumanizing and arduous than other employment
alternatives open to them, such as those in the poorly paid garment
industry.

In the discussion that follows, I document the "relational fatherhood work" that gay men utilizing surrogacy perform in creating
and maintaining their families. Jude Browne (this volume) uses the
concept "relational fatherhood" to convey men's time spent personally interacting with their children, in the sense of "hands-on"
care, play, and associated responsibilities. Following this, and Viviana Zelizer's (2005) notion of "relational work," I argue that relational fatherhood work includes time spent thinking through and
enacting relationships relevant to children's senses of identity and
belonging within a constellation of extended family relationships.
For instance, gay men's decision-making processes regarding the
selection of oocyte donors and surrogates reveal a range of often
deeply reflective relational considerations that are strategic for intended family relationships. These may be based on clinical guidance or on men's personal beliefs about the significance of maternal
genetic and gestational connections for future family relationships.
In the latter part of the chapter, I also briefly discuss the implications
of the relational priorities of men forming families through commercial surrogacy in the United States for families formed through
commercial surrogacy in India.

Surrogacy, Kinship, and Commerce

The field of postmodern kinship studies in anthropology has illuminated the creative and dynamic nature of relatedness made possible by developments in assisted reproductive technologies (ARTs). The use of insemination, in vitro fertilization (IVF), and surrogacy, particularly when donated gametes are used, may expose hitherto taken-for-granted Western assumptions about the relational bases on which family and parental relationships rest, while at the same time adapting, undermining, and transforming them (e.g., Carsten 2000; 2004; Edwards 2000; Franklin 1997; Ragoné 1994; Strathern 1992a; 1992b; Thompson 2005).

A growing body of scholarship on lesbian and gay parenthood in the ART era emphasizes a greater degree of choice and flexibility regarding the meaning of biological or family of origin relationships (e.g., Weeks et al. 2001; Weston 1991). Yet it also accentuates the continuing symbolic and social power of biogenetic connections in lesbian mothers' and gay sperm providers' decision making about forming families with children (Dempsey 2005; 2010; Gabb 2004; Nordqvist 2010; Riggs 2008a; 2008b). For instance, lesbian prospective parents will often attempt to match characteristics of the sperm donor to the non-birth mother in an attempt to create a stronger sense of family unity through resemblances, and to make it difficult for onlookers to pick who the "real" mother is (Hayden 1995; Nordqvist 2010).

The tension between notions of choice in forming families through ART and the perceived inalienability of biogenetic ties is also a strong theme in literature on the potential significance of these ties to the children born. Marilyn Strathern (1992a) reminds us that although personal choice may to some extent adjudicate how biological relationships remain relevant when ART is used, the passing on of biogenetic substance from one generation to the next remains important in understandings of relatedness in the developed West. Arguably, the phenomenon known in Australia as the Stolen Generation, whereby thousands of indigenous children were removed by government authorities from their families in the post–World War II era and placed with white families, has done much to sensitize the Australian public and law and policy makers to the ongoing significance of connectedness to families of origin. Adoption policy and practice in Australia has for many years focused on encouraging single birth mothers, where possible, to raise their children, and favored open adoptions, in which social ties with family of origin are retained (Marshall and McDonald 2001).

In keeping with the above, donor conception policy in Australia now strongly supports the importance of having identity-release donor gamete programs that enable children born from donor egg and sperm procedures to access identifying information about their donor, in addition to other information such as health history and family background (see Rodino et al. 2011). Australian law and social policy on ART favors identity registration for oocyte and sperm donors in at least three Australian states (Victoria, New South Wales, and Western Australia) and supports children's entitlements to have knowledge of their biogenetic heritage through policy initiatives, such as parental resources on how to tell children they are donor-conceived. Support for identifiable donors is also known to exist in Australian lesbian parenting communities. Australian research conducted with lesbian mothers has found women often prefer the opportunity to utilize identity-release sperm providers through clinics or their own social networks rather than anonymous clinical supplies of donor sperm in the interests of providing children with knowledge of their biological origins or the possibility of social contact with the biological father (see Dempsey 2005; 2012; McNair et al. 2002).

The relational considerations of gay men in international commercial surrogacy arrangements take place against a backdrop of a dearth of options for them to become full-time parents and the prohibition on commercial surrogacy in Australia. Few Australian children are available for permanent adoption outside of their families of origin, and people in same-sex relationships are ineligible to adopt locally or internationally born children throughout the country. Commercial surrogacy is illegal in keeping with legislation and clinical guidelines that forbid the explicit application of a market economy to assisted reproduction.[2] The principles on which the Australian prohibition of commercial surrogacy rest are coextensive with what Nikolas Rose (2001: 15) calls the classical distinction in Western moral philosophy between "that which is not human— ownable, tradeable, commodifiable—and that which is human— not legitimate material for such commodification." Here, Australia follows the United Kingdom's legislative model rather than that of the United States. While some payment for out-of-pocket expenses is allowed to gamete donors in Australian clinics, paying a man for his sperm or a woman for her oocytes or to gestate a child is illegal.

The Australian ART legislation assumes a familiar dualism between commerce and altruism, and implicit in this is the assumption that exploitation is inherent to paid or commercialized ART whereas there is superior moral or relational value in unpaid or altruistic exchange of donor gametes or reproductive services. On the contrary, Strathern (1992b) contends that ARTs in the presence or absence of explicit commerce have developed as part of an enterprise culture, in which the commoditization of human reproductive capacities is taken for granted. For Strathern, prospective participants in assisted reproduction are construed as customers seeking services. This is evident in the language of voluntarism or desire characteristic of some government reports on ART policy and practice, and indeed many biographical accounts written by those using the technologies. This imbrication of assisted reproduction with the language and practice of choice common to a market economy may be veiled because other culturally dominant beliefs deem such commoditization of human reproduction undesirable. In Australia, for instance, the actual practices of ART clinics may reveal the blurriness between altruism and commerce. Although payment for semen is prohibited, in keeping with reticence about commerce in body organs or substances, considerable expenses may be paid that are an attractive incentive to students and other low-income men. Conversely, in countries such as the United States, in which commerce in gametes and reproductive services is legal in a number of states, a market in altruism is customary. Although the donors are paid for their gametes, those considered most suitable are those whose motives are primarily to help those who cannot have children unassisted over and above financial gain (see Almeling 2011; Haylett 2012).

Relational Fatherhood Work

In exposing as overstated the conventional binary opposition between altruistic and commercial ART processes, it is also possible to concede that a broad spectrum of relational logic can inform the commercial transactions gay men enter into when they embark on surrogacy overseas. As Viviana Zelizer (2005) notes, commercial transactions can and often do involve closeness, emotional connection, and intimacy rather than alienated social relations or ties. They invariably necessitate complex social exchanges that require what Zelizer calls "relational work" to make explicit the ambiguous meaning of the transactions. If we apply this logic to families created through surrogacy, it can be seen in the bonding and matching processes that surrogacy agencies encourage (see Ragoné 1994) and in the encouragement of altruistic rather than motherly feelings in egg donors (see Haylett 2012) in order that surrogates, egg donors and intended parents will feel committed to each other and the contract into which they have entered. In the case of gay men forming families through surrogacy, it can be argued that relational fatherhood work is also done by the men in order to conceptualize how the genetic and gestational mother are present in or related to the children. At one extreme of the relational spectrum, donor eggs or gestational services may be construed by intended parents as instrumental to achieving a pregnancy and becoming a parent rather than embodying future relations or connections. At the other, the genetic material or gestational process is conceived as creating ties of relatedness that are to some degree inalienable. In this view, the oocyte donor or surrogate is perceived to remain present in or connected to the child or the adults involved in these transactions.

Elsewhere, I consider how gay male couples forming families through surrogacy are challenged by their circumstances to reflect on the conventional wisdom that social and biological fatherhood overlap in the decisions they make about whose sperm will contribute to embryo formation (Dempsey 2013). The men's decision-making processes regarding egg donors and surrogates explored in this chapter shed additional light on the establishment and enactment of relational fatherhood work. This engages men's emotional labor and communicative effort in an endeavor to create the conditions under which children born of transnational surrogacy arrangements will feel secure in their identities and the families into which they are born. As I will demonstrate in the analysis of the men's stories, it requires considerable reflection by the men on how their transnational family formation decisions will influence their child's sense of belonging in the future, to the couple's immediate family, and within the context of extended family relationships.

About the Study

The interview material presented in this chapter is based on five male couples' stories. Four of these couples participated in my 2008 Australian study of thirty-two gay and heterosexual fathers who utilized ART, and a fifth couple was interviewed as part of an earlier study of concepts of family and kinship among Australian lesbian and gay parents (see Dempsey 2006). The aims of the 2008 study were to examine the relative significance of biological and social relatedness among men who become fathers through unconventional means and to explore the effects of the normative cultural distinction between biological and social relatedness on family formation decisions. I conducted face-to-face, semi-structured, in-depth interviews to elicit what Ken Plummer (2001) calls short, topical life stories. I sought subjective meanings and experiences of family and kinship, given my interest in how men conceptualized, understood, and negotiated the terms of their participation in procreative and parenting relationships.

Given the relatively small number of interviews with gay fathers by surrogacy, these were checked against and supplemented with other source material such as two widely disseminated Australian documentaries on gay men and surrogacy, *Two Men and A Baby* and *Two Men and Two Babies*; information obtained from a public gay community forum about surrogacy held in Melbourne, Australia, in November 2011; and "Baby Business," a surrogacy debate that screened on Australian television in 2010 (Special Broadcasting Service 2011). The analysis is also informed by presentations at a national Australian surrogacy conference for intended parents and clinicians, held in Melbourne in May 2012.

The ten Australian men whose experiences are discussed herein are inner urban resident, well-educated professionals. This high socioeconomic status is consistent with the costs and with the legal and logistic complexity associated with achieving parenthood through surrogacy in the United States and with recent studies of gay male parents conducted in Australia and overseas (see Bergman et al. 2010; Berkowitz and Marsiglio 2007; Murphy 2013). The couples lived in Melbourne or Sydney. All cohabited, and one had married in the United States. Their relationship duration ranged from five to sixteen years, and they were aged between thirty-one and fifty. Three of the couples had children under the age of five, and two were prospective parents awaiting the births of children. Seven men identified as Anglo-Australian, one as Anglo-American, one as Anglo-Canadian, and one as of Chinese-Malaysian background. All five couples became parents through commercial surrogacy in the United States.

Relational Considerations in Selecting Oocyte Donors

Finding a suitable oocyte donor through a California clinic was one of the first challenges the men encountered. Oocyte donors sourced through these agencies are typically young attractive women under the age of thirty and are often college students. This is because pregnancy success rates tend to be higher with younger donors, and because intelligence and physical attractiveness are highly marketable traits that are known to be popular among agency clientele (Almeling 2011; Haylett 2012). In the United States clinical context, women are given a choice about whether they are willing to be identified to the intended parents or children born of their gametes. However, anecdotal evidence circulating within the Australian gay male communities indicates that most of the available egg donors choose to remain anonymous.

Victor and Terry described the process of selecting their anonymous egg donor as involving a spreadsheet and a list of key criteria, comparing it to the process they used to buy their house. Armed with the knowledge from their specialist that they were unlikely to get their first choice, they saw it as a question of creating a "wish list" of possibilities, then making a selection of their top five choices. Their emphasis was thus on ensuring that the women on their short list met certain standards of youth—for the viability of her eggs— and health, education, and appearance, traits that they believed could be passed on to offspring.

This couple reported that their clinicians had strongly guided them in egg donor selection, with the emphasis on selecting a woman as young as possible. Victor described himself as quite taken aback by how opinionated the fertility specialist had been with regard to the importance of choosing a donor of twenty-five years of age or under: "It's all age, age, age. We were really steered towards going with someone who was twenty-five or under. We were advised that we were unlikely to get our first choice, and told to not even look at the ones over twenty-five."

Although the men decided to follow their specialist's advice, in hindsight, Terry expressed some reservations about their choice of an anonymous and very youthful egg donor. He was concerned that women that young are perhaps too young to "understand the consequences of their decision down the track" and would have preferred more opportunity to select a donor who "was prepared to be known to our child."

It was also clear that Victor and Terry viewed selection of the oocyte donor as potentially a critical relatedness decision, with regard to how their child's appearance would fit with their own. Along with three of the other five couples, they were of Anglo-Australian or Anglo-American origins, and they believed it important to have a child whose racial and ethnic background matched their own. This was primarily due to concerns about potential discrimination their child could face in the future. Having a child who looked ethnically or racially similar to the gay parents emerged as an important consideration because it was perceived to better enable that child's sense of belonging in the face of already having to contend with the social stigma of having gay parents. As Victor explained, "We figured a child of gay parents may face some challenges growing up because of our sexuality. So we didn't want to create even more challenges for our child because ethnically or racially they didn't seem to fit with us."

Similarly, for Ian and Sami, a biracial couple, their main consideration in selecting an oocyte donor had been matching phenotypic characteristics so that their children would look Eurasian. Unlike Victor and Terry, who were concerned about discrimination in general, this couple was concerned about potential discrimination by extended family members toward a "non-biological" child. They did not want their extended families or friends to be able to conclusively discern the identity of their children's biogenetic father by virtue of the child's distinctively Asian or Anglo-Australian appearance. They believed this could mean the biologically related extended family would try to exact special relational privileges, or that the non-biological extended family could reject a child they didn't believe was "theirs."

The California fertility clinics patronized by these men supplied extensive written profiles about the egg donor's health and family background, and sometimes videotaped recordings that enabled them to see what she looked like and get a sense of her personality (see Almeling 2011; Haylett 2012). Beyond obtaining these sources of knowledge about the egg donor, it was apparent that men could go to considerable lengths and cost in order to find a woman who was prepared to meet them and be identified to their child in the future.

Stephen and Michael's story of meeting their oocyte donor, Sophie, whose photograph was prominently positioned along with that of surrogate, Katerina, and her family in their children's bedroom, indicated several reasons for wanting to meet her in person. After spending several months selecting her from their agency's online profiles and videos, the men subsequently made a special trip to the United States to meet her:

> Stephen: For us, it was important for the egg donor to say that she was happy to meet the kids in the future in the event that our kids

ever wanted to track her down and meet her... And we wanted to meet her too. So we flew to New York....

Michael: And fell in love with her.

Stephen: Yeah, Sophie was great. She was just gorgeous... She said, "Oh, it's been great you were able to catch up with me on your trip to New York."

Michael: We said... "We flew here to meet you, we don't just happen to be in New York, you know, and while we're here we'll catch up with Sophie." But it's funny because you're sitting there, you know, looking at her and interacting with her, but in the meantime you're checking her out.... You think, "Well, potentially my daughter, you know, could look just like you" [laughs].

It is apparent in the men's story that Sophie's physical attributes were important to them as traits potentially expressed in their children in the future. However, beyond this there was a desire to feel a sense of rapport and connection to her, as a person who their children might be interested in meeting in the future, which could, in turn, lead to an ongoing interpersonal relationship. The lengths the men went to in order to meet her and obtain her contact details indicated the value they placed on choosing exactly the right person as opposed to other men's greater emphasis on short-listing oocyte donors who met certain criteria.

Relational Considerations in Selecting Surrogates

It has been stated that a radical redeployment of mother/infant bonding occurs in the setting of U.S.-based commercial surrogacy agencies where bonding is instead fostered between the surrogate and the commissioning parents, usually successfully, in order that she fulfill her promise to the intended parents (Ragoné 1994; Teman 2010). This process, in tandem with gestational surrogacy using a donated rather than the surrogate's own oocyte, works well to ensure that surrogacy contracts are successfully fulfilled due to the genetic essentialism often taken for granted in Western cultures (see Thompson 2005). It is now well established in the literature that most gestational surrogates contracted through U.S. agencies do not consider themselves the mother of the baby, that they report high satisfaction with the surrogacy arrangements, and that their attitudes remain stable over time after the children are born (see Teman 2010 for a comprehensive review).

The five couples discussed in this chapter had been encouraged by the agency they dealt with to meet their intended surrogate and her family prior to conception. All had flown to the United States from Australia in order for this meeting to occur. While all of the men commented on a considerable socioeconomic divide between themselves, the surrogate, and her family, all identified some basis for rapport and connection with her, that had been ongoing since the births or it was believed would be ongoing after the child was born. Two of the couples interviewed reported their surrogate had told them she preferred to work with a gay couple because she wanted to avoid potential emotional anxiety or jealousy from an infertile woman.

Josh and Marty explained how being matched with their surrogate involved initial form-filling and then arranged meetings between available women and themselves to find out if there was suitable rapport and shared values about how the pregnancy and birth would proceed. In the quotation below, it was apparent Marty had experienced this as a two-way process between relative equals who each had some say in the matter:

> We filled out a form with our preferences, that is, telling the surrogate about us, you know, a story about ourselves and why we wanted to be parents. Because, essentially, they are choosing us, it's not necessarily us choosing them. They have to like us.... Surrogates are also invited to have some involvement and knowledge of the child's development. So that's important as well that you agree about those things. Then once we selected a surrogate and she selected us back, we had to meet her.... That was to see if we could get along appropriately and you take it from there if it all works out.

There was remarkable uniformity in the men's descriptions of the personal and interpersonal attributes they valued in their chosen surrogate. Victor's explanation of how he and Terry had come to select Rita emphasized qualities typical of those given by the participant group as a whole. There was a sense of interpersonal connection based on personality traits such as a good sense of humor. Character traits such as perceived self-reliance and honesty were also valued by this group of men as these indicated to them that the surrogate would be capable of fulfilling the requirements of the contract. Despite the rhetoric of gifting and help in agencies' promotional materials about surrogates' motives (see Ragoné 1994; Teman 2008) the men appeared undeterred by women who expressed an overt financial motive for becoming a surrogate, particularly if the payment were being used to further her existing children's interests, such as for an education or college fund. Indeed, they took this as evidence of a certain strength of character, or indicative that the surrogate was interested in her own life plans and goals as opposed to over-concerned in welfare or parenting of the child she would gestate on the men's behalf:

> Victor: We had a meeting in their offices for a couple of hours and then we got to spend a few hours with her, just ourselves, having a coffee and a chat. Yeah, so that was the initial meeting. And we both liked her sense of humor and felt comfortable, and it just sort of went from there, so—
>
> [*Dempsey*: And were there other things about her that made you feel comfortable?]
>
> Terry: She was doing it for the money. To put her kids through college.
>
> Victor: That was good.
>
> Terry: She did mention that she likes to help couples out, and that's something that I like to think is also a motivating factor for her. I think the other one was, she didn't come across as particularly needy or sort of—high maintenance. She really came across as someone with her own life and plan. And she said: "This is what I can do. This is how it can work."

As Raeleen Wilding (2006: 132) notes in the context of maintaining care relationships in transnational families, the use of information communication technologies is critical in "constructing or imagining a connected relationship," and enabling people to overlook their physical separation by time and space. An important part of the relational work these men undertook in establishing their intended fatherhood was e-mail and phone contact with the surrogate and her family. This was critical between the initial visit and the birth, in order to facilitate the men's participation and connection to the pregnancy. Josh and Marty were matched with Patricia. Josh explained that the agency he and partner Marty used went to great lengths to instill what he called "family-like feelings" among all parties and to ensure surrogate and intending parents stayed connected throughout the pregnancy. This included encouraging the men to take an interest in fetal development throughout Patricia's pregnancy, through Skype and e-mail contact, despite living on a different continent. Said Marty, "We are interacting with her on a week-to-week basis. Like we talk to her about things like the babies' kicks and movements and what the scan was like. It all comes back to the hands-on approach, maintaining a personal approach."

Postbirth Relationships with Surrogates

The men whose children had been born had come to, over time, conceptualize the relationship between themselves, the children, and the overseas-resident surrogate using the language of friendship or extended family relationships. None of the men considered the surrogate or egg donor to be the mother of their children, and qualifiers such as "birth mother" also tended not to be used.

For Stephen and Michael, the term "aunty" best encapsulated the degree of relational proximity they believed surrogate Katerina had to their children. In the discussion below, the term aunty connoted a socially distant yet connected relationship that confirmed her status as the person who had assisted the men to have children. The men's choice of words makes it clear that she is not considered part of their immediate family, despite the use of the familial term:

> Stephen: Ah, we see her as like—a bit of an aunty for the kids, not even—maybe not even that close. I suppose we see her the way she sees herself, and that is that she's helped us to have kids, but she has no real social connection with the children. ...
>
> Michael: She has a mild interest in what's happening but she's more interested in her own family than ours, which is perfect.

Ian explained that conceptualizing their surrogate as Aunty Janice had come about after the birth when their baby Toby was about ten days old. A critical relational conversation had occurred when the men were preparing to return to Australia, and were meeting with Janice for the last time before their plane journey:

> Ian: And we said, "Toby, say goodbye to Aunty Janice." And she said, "Yeah, that's right, I'm his aunty from now on." And that's what it's been. I think that was—we'd never really discussed it prior to that, but that was the sort of—a defining moment in all of a sudden knowing where—she stood.

Ongoing communications with surrogates and their families, particularly to announce and celebrate children's milestones such as walking, talking, and birthdays, appeared to be enthusiastically embraced by the men. Since returning to Australia with Toby, who was three years old at the time of the interview, Ian and Sami had maintained regular email contact with Janice, reserving the face-to-face Skype calls for significant occasions such as Christmas and Toby's birthday. Social visits including international travel also featured in the men's stories. For instance, Ian and Sami had recently shared a beach holiday with Janice and her family in Australia and were planning a return visit to the United States for the following year. In the documentaries, *Two Men and a Baby* and *Two Men and Two Babies*, we see surrogate Junoa travel to Australia on several occasions to stay with gay dads Lee and Tony at their Melbourne home and engage in activities while she is there such as bathing and reading to children Alexander and Lucinda, attending parties, enjoying family dinners with the men and their mothers, and accompanying the men and children on sightseeing trips interstate.

This is not to suggest stories of friendship and regular contact between the men and surrogates were ubiquitous. Stephen and Michael described an emotionally and socially distant relationship with their surrogate, Katerina. They attributed this to her relative youth and a lack of shared interests. Yet despite the absence of the friendship and exchanged international visits that other men described, it was also apparent these men put considerable effort into maintaining the connection with Katerina and her family, because they believed there could be potential benefits for their children in the future. They email her regularly, send her photographs of the children, even though they believe she is not very interested in these, and thus ensure they do not lose touch. These men explicitly referred to this communication as work they engaged in for the sake of their children:

> Stephen: We put a lot of work into it. Our relationship with her and her family, if we didn't keep in contact, would die. The relationship will continue because we will continue it.
>
> [*Dempsey*: And what would be the basis for wanting to continue that relationship?]
>
> Michael: For the benefit of our children. So that if our children ever wanted to maintain a relationship or friendship with her, then at least we've still maintained that line of communication.... You don't get much back, because they're young and they're kids basically, mature for their age, but basically they're kids still. So we keep contact for the sake of our children.

Discussion

One important dimension of the relational fatherhood work performed by these men was the effort they invested in in maintaining strong interpersonal ties with surrogates, where possible. The men's preoccupations here were not with a view to providing their children with a social mother or even a close relative; rather they appeared influenced by the view that children born through surrogacy may have a strong interest in knowing more about the woman who gave birth to them because this knowledge is potentially formative for identity. As discussed previously, the social climate in Australia with regard to forced removals of Aboriginal children and the prevailing policy context for ART have done much to gain public purchase for this point of view. The use of technology and visits in order to stay in touch and maintain connections with the surrogates and their families bears many points of resemblance to the processes of maintaining family ties described in research on transnational families separated by migration (e.g., Baldassar et al. 2007; Yeoh et al. 2005).

Given the prevailing biogenetic discourse on relatedness in the developed West, it is somewhat paradoxical that relationships with surrogates more so than egg donors were conceptualized as important to maintain. This minimization of the importance of biogenetic maternal identity by Australian gay men is in sharp contradistinction to Australian lesbian mothers' known interest in identity-release sperm donors (see Dempsey 2005; 2010; McNair et al. 2002). Although this study provides evidence that some gay fathers are keenly interested in selecting identifiable egg donors and wanted to be able to meet them, this appears to be the exception rather than the rule for most men. The men's dependence on commercially sourced donor eggs and the concomitant influence of the clinical culture of egg donation in the United States appear key in this. Jennifer Haylett (2012) notes the extent to which fertility clinics in the United States emphasize a desire to help in their advertising material for egg donors, and have strict vetting policies that reject women with any tendency to view themselves as the mother to the potential child. Although women are given a choice at some clinics about whether or not they are willing to disclose their identity to the children in the future, there is no state-enforced identity registration of donors in the California clinics many Australian gay men utilize, and it seems the message of detached altruism appears, for many women, more consistent with a decision to remain anonymous.

Furthermore, as Charis Thompson (2005) points out, fertility clinics are sites in which "human reproduction is a highly desired, stubbornly difficult, *technical* production goal" (13). As such, fertility specialists were potentially important influences on the men in decisions about oocyte donors, given their power to arbitrate costly "quality control" decisions about obtaining viable and affordable embryos. Youthful "proven" donors were encouraged above other considerations.

Given that most children only have one mother, it could well be that the dispersal of gestational and genetic maternity between two different women allows male couples to justify more easily the fact that there is at least one biological "mother" for the children to access in the future. Emphasizing the gestational, nurturing qualities of the pregnancy as giving rise to the more vital relational connection for their children is indeed the point of view encouraged by clinical staff involved in the recruitment of egg donors (see Haylett 2012). More could be explored about how the clinical cultures of egg donation and surrogacy are influential in the relational fatherhood work men do. The fact that two men, rather than a man and a woman, are the intended parents could also be relevant, in that gestation can be construed as a distinctively female nurturing process, that a child of exclusively male parents might be more interested in knowing about in the future. It would be interesting to know more about how gay male couples as opposed to heterosexual couples value gestational maternal connections as opposed to genetic ones, and how their respective gendered subjectivities as parents play a part in this.

Relational Implications for the Burgeoning Surrogacy Market in India

Until about 2005, California was the main international surrogacy destination for Australian gay men, no doubt due to the wide dissemination of the aforementioned documentary *Two Men and a Baby*. Surrogacy Australia's recent survey indicates that by 2012 more men were traveling to India than to the United States (Stethoscope Research 2012) and that the lower costs of clinical services were a factor in this. For surrogacy in India, intended parents will pay in the vicinity of AUD 70,000 in total for travel and clinical expenses, whereas travel and a comparable range of clinical services in the United States can amount to upward of AUD 150,000.

As Amrita Pande (2011) points out, there are a number of points of similarity between the liberal market models of surrogacy in India and California, in that births are primarily managed by private, commercial agencies that screen, match, and regulate agreements according to their own criteria. However, there are considerable differences between the Indian and Californian contexts for surrogacy that have implications for enacting the relational fatherhood discussed in this chapter. In the first instance, the Indian Council of Medical Research guidelines state that oocyte donation must be anonymous, meaning that identifying information about the women providing their genetic material is not available (Special Broadcasting Service 2011). Given the preference for "white" oocyte donors in order to match the characteristics of Western clients, as noted among the men who took part in this research, oocyte donors to Indian clinics are often obtained through agencies recruiting women from South Africa, Georgia, and the Ukraine, where local laws governing assisted reproduction also favor donor anonymity. Thus for men traveling to India to pursue surrogacy, the oocyte donor and surrogate will most likely live in different countries, meaning there is a vast geographic as well as a genetic and gestational dispersal of maternal connections. Under these conditions, a future "maternal" heritage trail for children is very widely dispersed indeed.

Moreover, it is apparent that opportunities for developing an ongoing relationship with the surrogate and her family are fewer or absent in the Indian context for surrogacy. At a 2012 surrogacy conference held in Melbourne, Australia, at which many Indian surrogacy agencies advertised their services, the clinicians' presentations made it apparent that the processes of bonding and matching surrogates with intended parents described by the men using clinics in the United States simply do not exist in the Indian clinical setting, and it was suggested that this runs counter to cultural expectations. Language barriers often prevent direct communication with the surrogates, and clinicians mediate information sharing about ultrasounds and the progress of the pregnancy (see also DasGupta and DasGupta 2011; Hochschild 2009; Special Broadcasting Service 2011; Vora 2009). While photographs of available surrogates are provided and men may be told the surrogate's name, it appears common for the intended parents to have minimal or no contact with her until close to the birth, meaning there may be negligible difference in India between the process of choosing a surrogate and choosing an oocyte donor, or indeed the ongoing expectations of relatedness. Pande (2010), in ethnographic work conducted at one Indian surrogacy clinic, reports that although intended parents may try to create relationships or ongoing connections with the surrogates, despite the socioeconomic and language barriers, the clinic's rules mandate a rather abrupt termination of the relationship after the baby is delivered.

Arlie Hochschild (2009) comments that in India "a code of detachment" between surrogates and intended parents seems almost necessary in light of the vast socioeconomic divide between the parties. This is not to suggest there is no socioeconomic disparity between surrogates and men traveling to the United States for clinical services. However, the point is that there was also considerable evidence for a relational foundation. This included a common language and shared cultural references such as humor that assist in developing ongoing connections. Kalindi Vora (2009), who has researched surrogacy in India, notes that she heard of intended parents writing to surrogates or sending them photos of children in the first year, but that this tended to wane over time. Vora also found that clients of Indian surrogacy agencies tend to accentuate their own and the child's connections to India rather than to the individual women themselves. There is little to suggest in the current climate for surrogacy in India that a child traveling to that country on reaching adulthood would find a clear heritage trail to follow that could lead to identifying information about a biogenetic or gestational mother, or anything similar to the aunty-like relationship men sought to foster in the U.S. setting. Much more needs to be known about how and whether these different relational opportunities in the two geographic settings are differentiating the gay male and indeed the heterosexual surrogacy market. For instance, is it just the lower costs of surrogacy in India and other Asian countries such as Thailand that make these destinations attractive? Or are some same-sex and heterosexual couples attracted by the relative lack of contact and ongoing energies that seem to be demanded of them with regard to maintaining connections over time with surrogates? Conversely, do intended parents find these relational limitations a problem, and will they in the future lobby for changes to the Indian surrogacy business models? Importantly, how is the relational work gay men traveling to India for surrogacy need to engage in different from that of their peers traveling to the United States due to the different relational constraints in the two vastly different cultural settings?

Conclusion

In enacting relational fatherhood through international surrogacy arrangements, this group of men was engaged in considerable social and emotional work throughout the process of family formation and beyond, in order to make decisions they believed would best facilitate their children's sense of belonging and connectedness to the couple and their extended family. They were also deliberating about how children may feel about their origins in the future, and maintaining relationships with surrogates, and sometimes egg donors, accordingly. Although limitations must be acknowledged given the size of the group, in generalizing to all Australian gay fathers by international surrogacy, there is no reason to believe the range of relational preoccupations and concerns characteristic of this group of men could not be expected in a larger and more diverse population of gay fathers.

With regard to debates within the literature on how same-sex couples enact parenthood, there are areas of both overlap and difference between gay men's and lesbian mothers' attitudes toward use of donor gametes when forming families through ART that warrant further investigation. The short-listing processes displayed by some men when selecting oocyte donors through clinics strongly parallel those applied by some lesbian prospective parents when it comes to the process of choosing a known or unknown sperm provider (see Dempsey 2010). At the same time, this study suggests that lesbian mothers are more concerned about children's entitlements to identity-release gamete donors than gay fathers by surrogacy. The men in this study were prepared to make very pragmatic decisions to opt for what appears to be a much larger number of available anonymous oocyte donors, in some instances when they believed an identity-release donor would be ideal.

In a commercial international surrogacy arrangement all or some of the parties to a child's conception are separated by geographic and potentially ethnic and cultural differences, and relational decision making can seek to accentuate or minimize those differences in the interests of intended family relationships. Gay male couples whose children are conceived through international commercial surrogacy are mandated by their family formation circumstances to participate in an international clinical market deeply predicated on commoditization; yet within the possibilities and limitations of this market, they make reflective choices about the relational consequences of their decisions.

There is now a substantial body of evidence that children born from donor gametes may be interested in knowledge of their biogenetic origins, and the evidence from this study indicates that gay fathers traveling for the purposes of commercial surrogacy are aware of and interested in this principle, yet often prepared to compromise due to the privileging of anonymity for oocyte donors in both U.S. and Indian clinics. At the same time, these two most popular international destinations afford different opportunities for the children regarding access to knowledge about their biogenetic and gestational origins, as well as for future contact with their gestational surrogates and egg donors, and it remains to be seen what children born of these arrangements will make of this in the future. It is highly likely that some children of gay fathers will want to travel overseas to learn about maternal connections and equally likely, given present circumstances, that many will be disappointed in the information available to them.

At a 2011 gay surrogacy forum in Melbourne, the convener of an Australian support group for gay fathers by surrogacy described the relationship between the gay parents and the U.S. resident surrogate as "an important relationship, one that is likely to be lifelong." In doing so, he implicitly contrasted the relational qualities and enduring power of this connection with the customary anonymity of oocyte donors. The men in this study saw important benefits for their children in fostering a geographically distant yet ongoing relationship with the surrogate, whether or not they personally saw friendship or recreational benefits for themselves as adults in maintaining those ties. Although they distinguished the surrogate's connection to the children from their own parental connection, they understood her significance through reference to the language and activities customary of extended family connections, e.g., displaying a photo of her and her family prominently in children's bedrooms, exchanging photographs, birthday cards, and e-mails, and visiting each other on significant occasions. Although it could be argued that there is an instrumental basis for these ongoing ties in the matching processes and meetings facilitated by the agencies in the instrumental interests of having the surrogate fulfill a commercial contract, there is evidence that emotional connectedness and friendship can arise through these processes, giving surrogates, gay fathers, and their children access to new and rewarding transnational possibilities for enacting family relationships.

Postscript

In January 2013, the Indian Ministry of Home Affairs issued new visa guidelines that now prevent Australian gay male couples and many heterosexual couples from traveling to India for the purposes of commercial surrogacy. Only couples who have been married for at least two years can obtain medical visas in order to use commercial surrogacy in India, and only if it is legal in their home countries.

Notes

1. Surrogacy occurs when a woman conceives and gives birth to a child with the intention that another couple or person will raise the child. Commercial surrogacy means the surrogate is recruited through an agency, reimbursed for medical costs, and paid for her gestational services. Commercial surrogacy agencies usually encourage or mandate the use of gestational surrogacy using donor oocytes due to the evidence that surrogates are more likely to feel comfortable relinquishing a child to whom they are not biogenetically related (see Ragoné 1994; Teman 2006; Thompson 2001).
2. In recent years, some Australian states have also sought to create legal impediments to their residents' overseas travel for the purposes of commercial surrogacy. For instance, in 2010, the state of New South Wales passed legislation introducing extra-territorial criminalization of paid surrogacy in the interests of preserving children's entitlements to know their biological heritage and preventing the exploitation of women overseas (see Millbank 2011). The state of Queensland recently followed suit.

References

Almeling, Rene. 2011. *Sex Cells: The Medical Market for Eggs and Sperm.* Berkeley: University of California Press.

Baldassar, Loretta, Cora Baldock, and Raeleen Wilding. 2007. *Families Caring Across Borders: Migration, Ageing and Transnational Caregiving.* Houndmills: Palgrave Macmillan.

Bergman, Kim, R. J. Rubio, R. Green, and E. Padron. 2010. "Gay Men who Become Fathers via Surrogacy: The Transition to Parenthood." *Journal of GLBT Family Studies* 6: 111–41.

Berkowitz, Dana, and William Marsiglio. 2007. "Gay Men: Negotiating Procreative, Father and Family Identities." *Journal of Marriage and the Family* 69: 366–81.

Blyth, Eric. 1994. "'I Wanted to Be Interesting. I Wanted to Be Able to Say I'd Done Something Interesting with My Life': Interviews with Surrogate Mothers in Britain." *Journal of Reproductive and Infant Psychology* 12, no. 3: 189–98.

Carsten, Janet. 2000. "Introduction: Cultures of Relatedness." In *Cultures of Relatedness: New Approaches to the Study of Kinship,* ed. Janet Carsten. Cambridge: Cambridge University Press.

———. 2004. *After Kinship.* Cambridge: Cambridge University Press.

Chavkin, Wendy, and JaneMaree Maher, eds. 2010. *The Globalization of Motherhood: Deconstructions and Reconstructions of Biology and Care.* New York: Routledge.

DasGupta, Sayantani, and Shamita Das DasGupta. 2010. "Motherhood Jeopardized: Reproductive Technologies in Indian Communities." In *The Globalization of Motherhood: Deconstructions and Reconstructions of Biology and Care*, ed. Wendy Chavkin and JaneMaree Maher. New York: Routledge.

Dempsey, Deborah. 2005. "Lesbians' Right-to-Choose, Children's Right-to-Know." In *Sperm Wars: The Rights and Wrongs of Reproduction*, eds. Heather-Grace Jones and Maggie Kirkman. Sydney: ABC Books.

———. 2006. "Beyond Choice: Family and Kinship in the Australian Lesbian and Gay 'Baby Boom.'" PhD thesis, Melbourne, La Trobe University.

———. 2010. "Conceiving and Negotiating Reproductive Relationships: Lesbians and Gay Men Creating Families with Children." *Sociology* 44, no. 6: 1145–62.

———. 2012. "More Like a Donor or More Like a Father? Gay Men's Concepts of Relatedness to Children," *Sexualities* 15, no. 2: 156–74.

———. 2013. "Surrogacy, Gay Male Couples and the Significance of Biogenetic Paternity." *New Genetics and Society* 32, no. 1: 37–53.

Dumit, Joseph, and Robbie Davis-Floyd. 1998. "Introduction—Cyborg Babies: Children of the Third Millennium." In *Cyborg Babies: From Techno-Sex to Techno-Tots*, eds. Robbie Davis-Floyd and Joseph Dumit. New York; London: Routledge.

Edwards, Jeanette. 2000. *Born and Bred: Idioms of Kinship and New Reproductive Technologies in England*. Oxford: Oxford University Press.

Franklin, Sarah. 1997. *Embodied Progress: A Cultural Account of Assisted Conception*. New York; London: Routledge.

Gabb, Jacqui. 2004. "Critical Differentials: Querying the Incongruities within Research on Lesbian Parent Families." *Sexualities* 7, no. 2: 167–82.

Hayden, Corinne. 1995. "Gender, Genetics and Generation: Reformulating Biology in Lesbian Kinship." *Current Anthropology* 10, no. 1: 41–63.

Haylett, Jennifer. 2012. "One Woman Helping Another: Egg Donation as a Case of Relational Work." *Politics & Society* 40, no. 2: 223–47.

Hochschild, Arlie. 2009. "Childbirth at the Global Crossroads." *The American Prospect*. 5 October. http://www.prospect.org/cs/articles?article=child birth_at_the_global_crossroads.

Inhorn, Marcia C., and Zeynep B. Gürtin. 2011. "Cross-Border Reproductive Care: A Future Research Agenda." *Reproductive BioMedicine Online* 23: 665–76.

Jadva, V., C. Murray, E. Lycett, F. MacCallum, and S. Golombok. 2003. "Surrogacy: The Experiences of Surrogate Mothers." *Human Reproduction* 18, no. 10: 2196–2204.

Marshall, Audrey, and Margaret McDonald. 2001. *The Many-Sided Triangle: Adoption in Australia*. Melbourne: Melbourne University Press.

McNair, Ruth, Deborah Dempsey, Sarah Wise, and Amaryll Perlesz. 2002. "Lesbian Parenting: Issues, Strengths and Challenges." *Family Matters* 63: 40–49.

Millbank, Jenni. 2011. "The New Surrogacy Parentage Laws in Australia: Cautious Optimism or '25 Brick Walls.'" *Melbourne University Law Review* 35, no. 1.

Murphy, Dean. 2013. "The Desire for Parenthood: Gay Men Choosing to Become Parents Through Surrogacy." *Journal of Family Issues* 34, no. 8: 1104–24.

Nordqvist, Petra. 2010. "Out of Sight, Out of Mind: Family Resemblances in Lesbian Donor Conception." *Sociology* 44, no. 6: 1128–44.

Pande, Amrita. 2010. "Commercial Surrogacy in India: Manufacturing a Perfect 'Mother-Worker.'" *Signs: Journal of Women in Culture and Society* 35: 969–94.

———. 2011. "Transnational Commercial Surrogacy in India: Gifts for Global Sisters?" *Reproductive BioMedicine Online* 23: 618–25.

Plummer, Ken. 2001. *Documents of Life 2: An Invitation to Critical Humanism.* London: Sage.

Ragoné, Helena. 1994. *Surrogate Motherhood: Conception in the Heart.* Boulder, CO: Westview Press.

Riggs, Damien W. 2008a. "Lesbian Mothers, Gay Sperm Donors and Community: Ensuring the Well-Being of Children and Families." *Health Sociology Review* 17: 226–34.

———. 2008b. "Using Multinomial Logistic Regression Analysis to Develop a Model of Australian Gay and Heterosexual Sperm Donors' Motivations and Beliefs." *International Journal of Emerging Technologies and Society* 6, no. 2: 106–23.

Riggs, Damien W., and Clemence Due. 2010. "Gay Men, Race Privilege and Surrogacy in India." *Outskirts: Feminisms Along the Edge* 22.

Rodino, Iolanda, P. J. Burton, and K. A. Sanders. 2011. "Donor Information Considered Important to Donors, Recipients and Offspring: An Australian Perspective." *Reproductive BioMedicine Online* 22: 303–11.

Rose, Nikolas. 2001. "The Politics of Life Itself." *Theory, Culture and Society* 18, no. 6: 1–30.

Rudrappa, Sharmila. 2012. "India's Reproductive Assembly Line." *Contexts* 11, no. 2: 22–27.

Special Broadcasting Service, Australia. 2011. "Baby Business." Broadcast 22 March.

Stethoscope Research. 2012. "Surrogacy Australia Survey of Intended Parents and Parents by Altruistic and Commercial Surrogacy." Unpublished report available from Surrogacy Australia.

Strathern, Marilyn. 1992a. *After Nature: English Kinship in the Late Twentieth Century.* Cambridge: Cambridge University Press.

———. 1992b. *Reproducing the Future: Anthropology, Kinship, and the New Reproductive Technologies.* New York: Routledge.

Teman, Elly. 2008. "The Social Construction of Surrogacy Research: An Anthropological Critique of the Psychosocial Scholarship on Surrogate Motherhood." *Social Science & Medicine* 67: 1104–12.

———. 2010. *Birthing a Mother: The Surrogate Body and the Pregnant Self.* Berkeley: Univeristy of California Press.

Thompson, Charis. 2005. *Making Parents: The Ontological Choreography of Reproductive Technologies.* Cambridge: The MIT Press.

Tuazon-McCheyne, Jason. 2010. "Two Dads: Gay Male Parenting and its Politicization—A Cooperative Inquiry Action Research Study." *The Australian and New Zealand Journal of Family Therapy* 31, no. 4: 311–23.

van den Akker, O. 2003. "Genetic and Gestational Surrogate Mothers' Experience of Surrogacy." *Journal of Reproductive and Infant Psychology* 21, no. 2: 145–61.

Vora, Kalindi. 2009. "Indian Transnational Surrogacy and the Commodification of Vital Energy." *Subjectivity* 28: 266–78.

Weeks, Jeffrey, Brian Heaphy, and Catherine Donovan. 2001. *Same Sex Intimacies: Families of Choice and Other Life Experiments.* London: Routledge.

Weston, Kath. 1991. *Families We Choose: Lesbians, Gays, Kinship.* New York: Columbia University Press.

Whittaker, Andrea. 2010. "Challenges of Medical Travel to Global Regulation: A Case Study of Reproductive Travel to Asia." *Global Social Policy* 10, no. 3: 396–415.

Wilding, Raeleen. 2006. "'Virtual' Intimacies? Families Communicating Across Transnational Contexts." *Global Networks* 6, no. 2: 125–42.

Yeoh, Brenda S. A., Shirlene Huang, and Theodora Lam. 2005. "Transnationalizing the 'Asian' Family: Imaginaries, Intimacies and Strategic Intents." *Global Networks* 5, no. 4: 307–15.

Zelizer, Viviana. 2005. *The Purchase of Intimacy.* Princeton: Princeton University Press.

Chapter 12

CONCEIVING FATHERHOOD
GAY MEN AND INDIAN SURROGATE MOTHERS

Sharmila Rudrappa

Introduction

For fathers, traditionally, caring for children has orbited around ideals of hegemonic masculinity, such as achievement in the labor market, financial security for the family, parental authority, and involvement with the extraordinary events of childhood, such as attendance at sports or performance events, rather than the everyday tasks of cooking dinner or doing laundry (Coltrane 1996; La Rossa 1997; Lewin 2009; Townsend 2002). Yet, this is not the case in a small but growing number of heteronormative families, and most certainly not in gay families, where two fathers take on both the routine and exceptional tasks involved in raising children (Doucet 2006; Lewin 2009; Risman 1986). In this chapter I examine how gay men in the United States and Australia access and negotiate globalized fatherhood through transnational surrogacy in India.[1]

Various commentators, including intended parents and surrogate mothers, recognize that transnational surrogacy is scarred by exploitation but also that there is immense pleasure, and deep friendship bonds that form among clients and workers (though not necessarily between the two). It is these alternative narratives of transnational reproductive labor that animate my work. My primary focus is on mostly white, American and Australian gay men, who form what I term "caring communities" in order to raise their surrogated, almost always biracial babies who were born halfway across the globe to Third World mothers. The intended fathers perform considerable emotional labor to form nurturing bonds with the fetuses, and then the babies; a large part of such emotive labor is directed toward preparing themselves for fatherhood. Such preparation involves not just an alteration in self-perception of who they are, but also preparing the world around them for the change in their identities from being solely gay men or couples to gay fathers. Such acceptance, the intended fathers recognize, is crucial to the well-being and safety of their children. As a result, they work hard at creating these caring communities around the fetuses and children, which is an essential component to their fathering efforts. In summary, this chapter addresses two questions: How do the intended gay fathers living in Australia and the United States create extended familial ties to the unborn fetuses in India, and subsequently to the newborn babies once they arrive? Second, why do caring communities matter so much for gay fathers? In describing the gay intended fathers' efforts, I demonstrate how these men in the First World sideline the considerable labor efforts of the Third World surrogate mothers, which is so central to the attainment of their fatherhood. The relegation of the mothers' efforts to the margins occurs not because of malintent but because of how the global market in surrogacy is structured and how fatherhood itself is constituted for these gay men. Before describing the gay men's considerable labors at achieving fatherhood, I provide a brief overview of surrogacy in India, followed by my research methodology on how I met with Indian surrogate mothers, and the Australian and American gay men who purchased these women's reproductive labor.

Commercial Surrogacy in India

What is called in the popular press India's "Rent-a-Womb" business exploded when the Indian state commercialized surrogacy in 2002. Compared with close to the $80,000 price tag for a singleton baby in the United States, which is still the leading provider of surrogacy globally (Ikemoto 2009), surrogacy in India costs between $35,000 to $45,000. Surrogacy in India is expected to generate $2.3 billion in gross business profits annually by 2012 (Pande 2009; 2010). Currently, the industry services straight and gay couples and individuals within India, the United States, Canada, the United Kingdom, Australia, Germany, Spain, and Japan, among others. Surrogacy in India is truly a global production phenomenon, with sperm being shipped from the United States or wherever the commissioning couple/individual resides, and eggs being sourced from intended mothers who may be other Indian women, university students in the United States, women from the Republic of Georgia, and even women from South Africa if intended parents desire "white eggs."

It is not uncommon for Indian infertility specialists to contract with two surrogate mothers for each commissioning couple or individual. The two women are each implanted with four embryos, created using sex cells that legally belong to the intended parents. The surrogate mother has no genetic relationship or legally recognized rights to the baby or babies she bears. If all four embryos take, then the doctors selectively reduce fetuses, that is, abort them serially until the surrogate mother is pregnant with the "optimal" number of fetuses.[2] Some of my interviewees had singletons or twins through a single mother; others had "twiblings"—that is, two or three babies sourced from the same egg donor, with each of the two fathers as sperm donor, gestated by two different surrogate mothers, and born within hours to weeks of each other. These are indeed brave new families (Stacey 1998), albeit nuclear families in the United States and Australia, comprised of almost always two fathers and one to three children, all genetically related to each other in some fashion or other; the Indian surrogate mothers and their families, though, are excised from these new family formations.

Because the surrogate mothers have no genetic relationship to their fetuses, they have no legal rights to the babies they bear. The fetuses and babies legally belong to the intended parents who have used their own, or purchased, eggs and sperm in order to procreate. Legally, only those Indian women who have birthed their own children are allowed to become surrogate mothers. The surrogate mother usually delivers the baby through a caesarian section even though all her previous children have been delivered through vaginal births. The caesarians are scheduled to occur between the thirty-sixth and thirty-seventh weeks of pregnancy in order for doctors to have complete control over the birthing process, and to time the arrival of the babies in accordance to the schedules of intended parents who may arrive from international destinations.

Methodology

This chapter is part of a larger project on transnational surrogacy in India, specifically the southern Indian city of Bangalore. Between 2009 and 2011, I interviewed seventy surrogate mothers in Bangalore, ranging from women who were contract mothers almost a decade ago to others who were still being prepped for pregnancies.[3] I spoke with thirty-one egg donors, eight infertility specialists, and two lawyers in Dallas, Bangalore, and Hyderabad. I have also spoken with eight heterosexual and twelve gay individuals/couples availing of infertility services in Mumbai, Anand, and Delhi.[4] All these families reside in the United States, except for four gay couples who live in Australia.

Given this chapter's sole emphasis on gay men, I build from my interviews and ongoing conversations with them and from their online blogs. Upon reading blogs, available as public access documents on the Internet, I contacted intended parents. Most did not reply, but some did. These individuals referred me to others who had been to India for surrogacy purposes. More than half of the straight and gay interviewees (twelve couples) maintain and update their blogs regularly, and I have access to information on how they and their families are doing. Much as family albums that "originated to chronicle the continuity of Victorian bourgeois kin networks" (Petchesky 1987: 283), the intended parents' blogs, replete with fetal images, are a twenty-first-century version of affirming parental lineage, with the assemblage of online images of nurseries, strollers, baby clothes, ultrasounds, and baby photographs visible as self-representations of family. Along with interviews and email exchanges, blogs have been excellent sources of information because parents consciously fashion themselves in ways they want to present themselves to the world. Thus, blogs are a crucial archive of information on surrogacy in India.

I would like to offer a few words on the gay men interviewees. Almost all of them (with the exception of one interviewee who is a single father) are in long-term, monogamous relationships. Three of the men in the United States described themselves as non-white or multiracial (one of the interviewees' partners—not interviewed—is non-white). Three of the interviewees are Jewish. Three others are immigrants to the United States from Europe. Almost all of the men, except for one couple now living in Puerto Rico and another in Melbourne, Australia, are of upper-middle-class origins. All are in their late thirties to mid-late forties, except one couple in Atlanta who are in their late twenties. Four of the American couples had attempted to adopt, but were discouraged by the long waits and by what they felt was homophobia directed against them by adoption agencies. None of the Australians had attempted adoption; in Queensland, Northern Territory, Victoria, and South Australia same-sex couples are not allowed to adopt children, though single parents may adopt children in all but South Australia.[5] In addition, many interviewees said that the costs of surrogacy in India compared favorably to private domestic and international adoption, which led them to the former.

While couples going to India for surrogacy can procure white women's eggs (purchased from the United States, South Africa, or Georgia), all my interviewees had purchased eggs from Indian donors. One couple had sought a South African donor for their first attempt at surrogacy; that did not work, and the second time around they worked with an Indian donor. Almost half the gay men interviewees had worked with two surrogate mothers, each of whom had four embryos implanted in them. All interviewees were familiar with fetal reduction because many of them had dealt with it personally.

One couple had three daughters through surrogacy, all of whom are now three years old; five others had twins or twiblings. Four interviewees had one child each. Two were very early in the stage of surrogated parenthood and were waiting for their surrogated child or children to be born when they spoke with us. While there are differences among gay interviewees, they were overwhelmingly white, and middle-class to upper-middle-class. Almost all spoke in a similar vein about connecting with the fetuses and raising their children.

Forming Bonds with Fetuses: Gay Intended Fathers and the Embodiment of Pregnancy

Jeff said, "I never in my life imagined I could get pregnant. As a gay man, and having been one for so long, I have no interest in experiencing a pregnancy. All I wanted to do was be a parent, not experience pregnancy." Yet, upon receiving news that his and his partner's surrogates in Mumbai both tested positive for pregnancy, Jeff proudly proclaimed—"We're pregnant!" Jeff echoes the other interviewees, almost all of whom talked about "our pregnancy." In fact, Jeff and the other gay men I interviewed are not so different from many heterosexual men who, upon learning about their

women partners' pregnancies, will similarly announce that "we" are
pregnant rather than seeing it as their partner's exclusive condition.
Why do men say they are pregnant, even though they themselves
are not?

A woman's pregnancy, because of her bodily, and often emotional and intellectual involvement with the fetus, allows her a kind
of closeness and experiential knowledge of the forthcoming child
that is simply not available to men. My description of the physical and emotive aspects to experiencing pregnancy is not to privilege women's feelings as more authentic and therefore better than
men's involvement with the fetus. It is simply to explain how men,
through imagination, cognition, and love, can potentially grasp at
pregnancy (Bartky 1997). Not only do men support their partners
in their pregnancies through caring tasks, but they also attempt to
imagine what it might be like to be pregnant. Their female partners
provide thick descriptions of their physical, emotional, and intellectual states as pregnant women, and the empathetic men—through
language but also through seeing, holding, and feeling—comprehend their partners' experiences of pregnancy. As an attestation of
solidarity to their pregnant partners and the forthcoming child, men
proclaim that they too are pregnant.

The problem for the American and Australian gay intended fathers, though, is that they are unable to develop empathetic relationships with the Indian surrogate mothers. Some men went to
tremendous lengths to communicate with the surrogate mothers,
yet language barriers, vast cultural and class differences, and the
organization of the reproduction industry in India hindered them
from developing empathetic ties to the mothers. Bruce and Will
from Perth, Australia, exemplify the conundrum that many couples
face whose interactions with their surrogate mothers are facilitated
by intermediary agents. They met their surrogates for the first time
at the delivery of the two girl babies and were able to talk with them
only ten days after the mothers' caesarian sections. At this meeting,
for the first time ever, each mother held in her arms the baby she
had carried in her body for nine months. Bruce prepared five sentences in Hindi to read to the mothers to express his gratitude for the
gift of fatherhood they had bestowed on them. The translator translated their questions about how the pregnancy went, what it was
like, and how they felt, but Bruce and Will emphasized that in spite
of their best efforts, communication was too late and too hard. They
wanted to send the mothers photos of the girls every year so they
could see how they developed, but were forbidden to correspond

with them directly; they had to send the pictures to the agency that facilitated the arrangement, and the staff there would forward them to the mothers. Thus, in spite of their best efforts, they faced barriers in developing empathetic ties with the mothers. As a result, they could not access the women's bodily or emotional knowledge, and the experiences of pregnancy eluded the intended fathers.

Yet, as demonstrated by Jeff, the men's declarations of being pregnant have nothing to do with experiencing pregnancy. For them, such declarations had to do with establishing a tie, not with the surrogate mother, but with the fetus that grew inside her. In spite of their claims that the pregnancies and the resulting babies were theirs, the intended parents with whom I spoke recognized in silent and unacknowledged ways that the surrogate mother might have a greater moral claim over the baby or babies. After all, the fetus had grown in her body, depending on her nurturance for its growth and survival. What if the newborn and surrogate mother were closer to each other, both physically and emotionally, than the intended parents were to this newly arriving family member? The men's anxieties were palpable; one couple mentioned that they chose India because the surrogate mothers there had few, or no, rights over the baby they gestated. If the mothers changed their minds they would have no legal recourse in claiming that baby as they might in other countries. This couple expressed a fear that many intended parents had, that is, that mothers could change their minds any time over the course of the pregnancy and decide to keep the baby. There was anxiety, too, over breastfeeding. Some men talked about how they want to protect the mothers, guarding against the likelihood of attachment because the women could potentially get closer to the baby if they breastfed them.

Under these circumstances of morally, though not legally enforceable, competing claims, the gay men's anxieties over the establishment of "ownership" of the fetuses was understandable. Therefore, they claimed the surrogate's pregnancy as their own, declaring themselves as being pregnant, imaginatively reassigning the surrogate's labor to their own bodies. In this process of transference the material reality of the surrogate mother disappeared, and all that mattered were the growing fetuses and the gay dads as a familial dyad. The mothers, never having been in a relationship with the men from the start, faded from existence.

In all of this, the opposite happened to the fetus. Not yet an independent person, but one whose existence depends wholly upon the mother, the fetus materialized as a person. The fetus, even when just weeks old, was already a person for the intended fathers. A large part of why they attributed the fetus with such solidity was precisely because it was still immaterial for them, that is, it had not manifested as a full human. But its potential to become one animated the men, who imagined it already as a real child who would enrich their lives in so many different ways.

In addition, the materiality of the fetus seems triply alien for gay men pursuing transnational surrogacy. Not only did they have to experience the fetus vicariously, as all men do; in addition, they were unable, or unwilling, to develop empathetic bonds with surrogate mothers, which hindered their abilities to "know" the fetus. And finally, living halfway across the world in Australia and the United States, these men could only bond with the fetus through ultrasound images provided by the Indian infertility doctors. Thus, the gay intended fathers, in an attempt to feel connected with the fetus, spoke of the pregnancy as their own, and flooded their blogs with ultrasound images and countdowns to delivery dates.

On pregnant women and fetal images, Janelle Taylor (2008: 135) writes that the "ultrasound… makes the fetus available for the pregnant woman herself to possess and enjoy in new ways. An ultrasound examination produces visual imagery and medically authorized information about the fetus—its size, sex, appearance, heart rate, position, activities and so forth—which endow it a sort of objectified existence." In addition to becoming a person, the fetus develops a distinct social identity, enmeshed within kin networks through its image being circulated among family members and posted on blogs. Thus, even before the baby arrived it was a person. And even before the babies' birth, gay intended parents were fathers. Carey and Drew, a Jewish couple living in the American South, noted that they did not want to speak of the baby before she arrived so as not to bring the evil eye upon her. Yet, even they could not resist posting pictures of the fetus on their blogs. Almost all the men we interviewed posted pictures on their blogs of the fetuses, lovingly and with great humor, attributing all sorts of characteristics to them. For example, one gay intended father declares under the picture of the fetus—"I just wanna pinch those little chubby cheeks!!! I think that's his/her little hand in front of his/her mouth. But, I can't help but imagine that he/she is singing a happy tune or whistling the time away. (Now that I look again, maybe it looks like he/she is spitting!)." Quinn and Antonio facetiously write in their blog that one of their twins "looked a bit evil, as if rubbing palms together planning world domination."

For almost all the intended fathers, the fetuses develop into persons within weeks into the pregnancy. This bonding was especially apparent when they talked about how deeply conflicted they felt over the selective reduction of fetuses. Many of their Indian doctors had implanted up to four embryos in the surrogates' bodies. In some cases, when the gay couple worked with two surrogates, they were faced with a scenario of taking eight babies home. Under these circumstances, infertility specialists selectively reduced the number of viable embryos to two or one per surrogate mother. Many gay men felt devastated by selective reduction. The Delhi surrogate mother working for James and Scott from Melbourne faced such a situation, when four embryos implanted in her started to grow into fetuses. The doctor contacted the intended fathers, saying she had to reduce the fetuses to two. They were heartbroken because fetal reduction went against their beliefs, and they mourned what felt like the death of their two babies.

Keith and Richard, a gay couple in Chicago, also had to deal with their surrogate mother undergoing selective reduction. They used two surrogates; in one woman none of the embryos implanted. In the other woman all four took hold, and she had to undergo medical procedures to reduce the number of fetuses to two. Richard said he was fine with it, but "one night, after a few drinks I'm crying about it. I was upset about it. I was really anxious around the time they were doing the reduction... but everything went fine."

Quinn and Antonio had a more complex take on selective reduction than most other interviewees. They hoped the procedure was not too painful or frightening for "the sweet, cheerful-looking woman" who was carrying their children. They believed that it was a woman's right to choose what she does with her body, and if she wanted to carry twins instead of quadruplets, then it was her choice. After all, wasn't "choosing to become a surrogate mother another expression of that freedom?" They claimed it was too early for them to feel too strongly about the fetuses. They also recognized that they had the financial resources for raising two children, not four. Besides, being pregnant with quadruplets increased the risks for surrogate mother and the babies. Selective reduction was their only choice. Yet, Quinn couldn't help thinking that selective reduction would profoundly affect the rest of their lives. He was not sure why the two eliminated embryos were chosen. And he kept thinking, "If that nearly random needle had chosen another, who would they have become? What was lost? And what will we tell our kids if they ever ask, 'What, you mean it could have been me?'" He later

added that the most important thing he'd tell his two children is
that he and Antonio "got exactly the kids we were meant to have."
Thus, Quinn and Antonio expressed ambivalence; they spoke of the
mother's potential anxiety regarding selective reduction, yet they
also spoke of their very real needs as a family. They indicated that
the fetuses were not really people, yet they acknowledged that a
tremendously consequential event had just occurred; perhaps randomly, they had been assigned their children.

The intended fathers' bonds with their future babies were especially palpable in the stories they shared about surrogate mothers'
pregnancy losses, or the death of newborns. Bruce and Will's first attempt at surrogacy in Delhi is one such story. The surrogate mother
had a difficult pregnancy and went into labor prematurely. One
baby boy was stillborn, and the other baby, Ben, was in neonatal
care for five weeks. The fathers kept an agonizing vigil by their son's
bedside for weeks as he struggled to pull through before deciding to
take him off life support at the recommendation of doctors when his
condition deteriorated irreversibly. They presently have two daughters through two Delhi surrogate mothers, but the loss of their twin
sons has stayed with them. They speak as if they have four children.

Baby Stories

Many of the stories the intended fathers related included accounts
involving their labors toward mundane practices, such as nesting,
especially prior to the babies' arrival. The men spoke about converting their homes to make space for babies, anticipating their needs,
imagining what they might enjoy. They moved into bigger homes or
closer to natal families. And almost all the gay intended fathers prepared elaborate nurseries for the imminent arrival of their babies.
They bought new furniture, or refinished secondhand items. They
painted and pasted decals on walls, hung pictures, and prepared
strollers. They bought car seats, clothing, baby carriers, and bottles.
In this process of buying the accoutrements necessary for baby, they
marked for themselves how their lives, their homes, and their relationship with each other and the world around them would change
forever. In addition to building and decorating nurseries, central to
many men's nesting labors were baby showers.[6]

The unborn child became a fully sentient person through the intended fathers' consumption of baby goods and extended kinfolk's
gifting practices. Through buying and gifting for the unborn, they

affirmed their acceptance and love for the yet-to-arrive child as family member. But, along with establishing the fetus's personhood, and the future family's love for it, consumption rituals affirmed to society at large the intended fathers and the newborns as a family unit even before the arrival of the baby. They family existed as a parent-child dyadic unit well before the parents went to India to retrieve the babies.

Stories of consumption became especially important because the pregnant surrogate mothers lived in worlds socially, culturally, and emotionally inaccessible to the intended fathers. Acts of consumption, along with narrating and documenting these acts of consumption, became crucial ways by which to mark their impending entry into fatherhood. However, not all baby stories were solely about consumption. Steve and Steve who live in the United States write in their blog about the first time they went to Mumbai to begin the process of surrogacy. Upon arriving there, they realized there was a gay pride march in the city, in which they participated. They wore a sign in Hindi that said "Hindus, Moslems, Sikhs, Christians, Heteros, Homos, all Brothers." They danced with *hijras* from Tamil Nadu. And they met a mother, whose son lived in Atlanta, carrying a sign that read, "I'm proud of my Gay Son!" They accompanied her because she was alone at the march. Given the cultural taboos against queerness in India, they said the mother "sort of stole [their] hearts."

Once the fathers came back home with the babies, it became much harder to sustain storytelling on blogs. Elbow-deep in household work, they had less time to engage in anything but caring for the babies. Many of the interlocutors in this study came home with two newborn infants, almost always born premature, that needed intensive nurturing; one couple arrived back to the United States with three. As a result, housework and caregiving responsibilities grow exponentially overnight, and the fathers have to make significant work-family adjustments. Both dads shared, some more equally than others, in caregiving tasks such as feeding, bathing, and cleaning. Keith in Chicago, who was a small business owner prior to having twins, is now a stay-at-home dad while his partner, Richard, works as a child psychiatrist. Likewise, Will in Perth plays with the girls for an hour or so in the mornings before beginning work at his own business, and Bruce takes over for the rest of the day. Bruce recently joined a mother's group that meets every Wednesday at a nearby cafe. Scott, in Melbourne, continues as a machine operator, while James became a stay-at-home dad; James joked that with two big dogs and two four-month-old babies, his "full time job was to clean up poop."

As a result, fathers blog less frequently once the babies arrive. New father Mike writes revealingly in his blog: "It has been a while since I have done a 'real' post. The bags under my eyes can attest to this. By the time we get home, we're exhausted... we feed ourselves whilst our girls steal croutons off our plates or beg for chips or chocolates or whatever hits their fancy at the time." Yet, he persisted in writing; Mike continues describing his efforts at potty training in that very same entry: "And while I know it's not supposed to be funny, the first couple of times Rose had an accident you could have sworn the child had gotten stung by a bee. She was in *hysterics* running around trying to figure out what to do as she felt a potential accident coming on. You're trying to get her on the potty, but she still wasn't cotton to that, so she ran around some more like a chicken with its head cut-off while Baba and Daddy tried not to laugh at the flailing child while trying to convince her to go on the potty" (his emphasis). Mike Aki's story of toilet training his daughters are typical on gay fathers' blogs, which light up with updates and photographs over Father's Day, Halloween, and Christmas.

Telling baby stories, especially through maintaining baby books and journaling, is a central activity in middle-class mothering. Mothers preserve documents regarding their babies—the photograph of that first toothless smile, their baby's birth announcement, the first time grandparents met the baby, for example. Yet, what is intriguing in the gay dads' practices of fatherhood is that baby stories are public. That is, blogs are journal-like styles of documentation on how the fathers decided upon surrogacy, what the process felt like, the first time they met their babies, how the babies grow and such, and can be read by anyone who can use the Internet. What is at stake in telling these stories publicly?

The Meanings of Baby Stories

The storytelling serves two purposes: first, these narratives solidified for the men, and to the world around them, their journey to fatherhood.[7] Recounting these stories to real and fictive kin, at media outlets, to researchers, and on blogs affirmed for the gay men their fatherhood. Second, through publicly telling these stories, gay fathers attempted to build caring communities.

Gay fathers recounted delightful stories of their children to build their own poise in fathering and to develop the children's confidence in their place in the family. These baby stories become that much more crucial to children born through international surrogacy because their origins are fuzzy, that is, they have no social or emotional connection to the egg donors or the surrogate mothers. Brian and Adam from Melbourne went to tremendous lengths to contact the surrogate mother and egg donor of their twin girls. They hired an Indian lawyer who went to a village sixty kilometers outside Mumbai, based on the address the two women had provided. However, all their contact information was fabricated, and the women had simply disappeared. The fathers were upset that their daughters were denied the future opportunity, if the need arose, to get in touch with their "mothers."

Many gay fathers recognized that their children will probably have questions about their origins once they reach a certain age—who was the egg donor, and who was the surrogate mother? Because the women are excised from legal memory and from the nuclear family unit, the child has no way of knowing who her mothers are; the women simply vanish into the vastness that is India. To ease the existential anxieties that they feel their children might face when they come of age, the gay men direct tremendous efforts toward documenting as much as possible their personal journeys into surrogacy. They endeavor to capture details that might seem minute and unimportant to fashion an origin story for the child. Thus, spectacular stories of marching in gay pride marches in Mumbai, as well as the more mundane ones regarding potty training, become all that much more crucial for the fathers and the children in building a narrative of familial togetherness.

Building Caring Communities

Extended families' joyous reception of their babies was central to the dads' pleasures in fatherhood. Familial happiness about the babies and the love showered over the new additions provided for the gay men social affirmation and celebrated their entry into fatherhood. For example, when James and Scott returned to Melbourne with their twin neonatal son and daughter born in Delhi, they were delighted to find both their families at the airport rather than meeting them later in their home, as planned. But not all fathers were so fortunate. Richard and Keith in Chicago have two children of the same age. While Richard's family accepted the newborn girls as their grandchildren, Keith's family was ambivalent. Richard was hurt that Keith's family never called to inquire about the pregnancy or how they were coping with fatherhood.

The dilemma gay fathers face—which most middle-class heterosexual couples do not—is the need to find a safe space to raise their children within a society that may disapprove of their lifestyle. Their natal families may ostracize their sexual orientations, or, as many fathers have indicated, some friends criticize their decision to pursue surrogacy in India.[8] Thus, a constitutive element to their fathering was creating caring communities around their children that would accept their little ones without prejudice and relish in their company. Caring communities is a term that I use for the real and fictive kinship networks the fathers create for themselves, and for their children. These communities not only support the fathers in their family-building efforts, but also provide safe spaces outside the home within which the children can securely grow. Fathers recognize that their children may face substantial challenges: their dads are gay, they have no mothers, and many are recognizably biracial in mostly white worlds. Finally, they have resulted from transnational surrogacy, which is ostracized among those on the left and right side of the political spectrum. A focal point of fathering for gay dads, then, is proactively to create caring communities.

I develop the term "caring communities" based on Nancy Naples's (1998; 2002) work on activist mothering, which describes the labors engaged in by African American and Latina mothers who were community workers. Building from mothering practices within homes, these individuals extended the activities of safeguarding the community's children's lives by fighting the "debilitating and demoralizing effects of oppression" (1998: 457) outside their homes. Their anti-racist mothering practices were seen as part of a larger struggle, "namely, doing just what needed to be done to secure economic and social justice for their communities" (2002: 219).

Building caring communities, then, entails a sort of activist fathering practice among gay dads. Their fatherly activities, directed at the world outside their families, do not necessarily aim to secure economic justice, but instead seek recognition and acceptance for gay families and transnational surrogacy and for the children raised in these families. They seek to change the world around them— make society less homophobic—so that their children's well-being may be furthered. As a result, the fathers work hard to create safe spaces for their biracial children in their neighborhoods, schools, and towns. Their globalized fatherhood pursuits necessitate very local efforts in building caring communities. To build caring communities, fathers engage in storytelling through various fora, including blogging, engaging in face-to-face interactions with other parents who have gone to India for surrogacy purposes, agreeing to appear on media outlets, and finally, talking with researchers.

Brian and Adam from Melbourne exemplify activist fathering. Brian thought that gay men tend to be far more contemplative and reflective about their identities than the average person. Growing up in the closet and outside the boundaries of normative sexuality, he believed that this increased awareness translated into effective child-rearing practices, where fathers considered their children's identities and how the adults around them shape their identities. For this reason, he said, he and Adam valued the influence of their friends, family, and other parents of "surro" children as they raise their own three children. The couple hosted regular wine and cheese get-togethers in their home, opening it to other parents with surrogated children, and to those who expressed an interest in having children through transnational surrogacy. By their estimate, they had personally facilitated over 150 people having babies through surrogacy in India. In addition, Brian and Adam also reached out to their neighbors, engaging with them socially and introducing themselves and their surrogated children to them. As a result, their neighbors too felt invested in making their babies feel welcome.

Many of our gay fathers' interlocutors revealed that blogs by other gay men pursuing surrogacy in India were central to their decision to pursue the same path to fatherhood. The success of these blogs encouraged the "converts" to maintain their own, because as one interviewee attested: "Blogs were so helpful for us as we made our way through the planning of India, and I want to be available for the next couples as they plotted their way." A network of fathers, stretching from the United States to Australia, publicized gay fathering stories for all to read. These public stories worked toward normalizing transnational surrogacy for those who might think it is a dangerous practice laden with intrigue and immorality.

The public nature of these stories reveals yet another aspect of gay fathering practices, that is, the open celebration of their love for their children validated them as fathers in a larger, not-so-sympathetic public. In a homophobic society, where gay men are perceived to be promiscuous sexual animals, these stories reveal that these fathers are sexual, yes, but also caring individuals who go to enormous lengths and make tremendous sacrifices not only to beget children, but to love and cherish them, raising them to be ethical human beings. Gay fathers' parenting practices are scrutinized to a far greater degree than are straight parents' caregiving, and any perceived inadequacies at their parenting efforts are judged more harshly than heterosexual parents' shortcomings. If a gay father fails to be a "good father" in any way, his failure stands as proxy for the moral bankruptcy of all gay families, the ostensible constitutive inability of gay men to be caregivers, and finally, the inherent ethical deficiency of transnational surrogacy where supposedly anyone can bring children into the world, regardless of their sexuality, age, health status, or moral virtue. Thus, these blogs are crucial public documents announcing to the world the considerable parenting accomplishments of gay men who pursue transnational surrogacy.

In addition to reaching out to neighbors and blogging extensively, many gay couples agreed to be featured in the media. Participation in television programs, newspaper articles, magazine stories, and radio features is central to activist fathering. The fathers repeatedly explained to the public at large the pains of not having children, what children meant to them, and the fraught but eventually beautiful process of transnational surrogacy. And finally, they spoke with researchers. When my co-researcher and I thanked our interlocutors for agreeing to be interviewed, they interjected that they wanted to assist in building more truthful stories about surrogacy. They said they were tired of being seen as exploiters, baby-snatchers, and self-centered individuals who wanted only to genetically propagate themselves; the list of mean-spirited monikers used to describe them was endless. Thus, gay men expressed that they hoped to see more complicated and sincere descriptions of their fathering efforts.

There was more to these publicizing efforts than building empathy among hostile listeners; these media and academic accounts also documented for the children their fathers' caregiving activities. Many interviewees (straight and gay parents) anticipated that their children would one day read print media that discussed their origins. They hoped that a more dense narrative of their families would emerge. These stories, they feel, would be central to how their children would conceive of themselves. Thus, by blogging, building gay-receptive and surrogacy-friendly networks, and publicizing gay fathers pursuing surrogacy in India, the fathers attempted to build safe spaces in caring communities for their children. They hoped these caring communities would, rather than approach the children with stereotypes and prejudice, be peopled by individuals who would cherish their children in their uniqueness and respect their differences owing to having two fathers, being biracial, and being birthed through surrogacy halfway across the world. For the gay men, constructing caring communities is a central tenet of responsible fathering.

The process of narrating their fathering efforts— even prior to the children's arrival—became a central practice of childrearing. These public stories about caring aid in bolstering the fathers' self-confidence in their capacity for love; the stories affirm for the children their specialness, providing narratives for the development of their own identities; and, finally, the stories help establish caring communities for the children, which were social spaces where children would be cherished, rather than ostracized, for their uniqueness.

Conclusion

My account of globalized gay fathering goes against the grain of current scholarship, where much has been said about the exploitative practices of transnational surrogacy through which First World parents reap benefits through the labor of Third World women (Pande 2009; 2010; Rengachary Smerdon 2008; Vora 2009). While I do not disagree with these perspectives, a central tenet in my work is that transnational surrogacy cannot be isolated from the larger, robust market in babies (Spar 2006). At a fundamental level surrogacy is not different from other production regimes, such as those of garments, coffee, or software. I recognize the difference between products, such as wheat or gasoline, which have different use values, and vastly different meanings, for the people who produce or consume them. My purpose in equating producing babies to producing corn, for example, is to note that both are commodities produced for market exchange. The underlying anxiety is that by moving babies into the market the sacrosanct aspects of life, that is, of family, love, and reproduction, are somehow tainted and made profane. Thus, parents who participate in transnational surrogacy are deemed to be far more exploitative than other kinds of consumers. And workers, in this case surrogate mothers, are believed to be far more exploited than other kinds of Third World workers producing for First World markets.

But just because there is a market exchange—the organization of the reproduction industry in India, the creation of labor markets in surrogate mothers, the creation of consumer markets in India and the global North, and money exchanged for the labors of women in return for babies who travel north—does not mean that exploitation alone characterizes the global reproduction industry. Markets—whether in babies or garments—are marked with profound ambivalence. The laborers and consumers are cognizant of the exploitation in global surrogacy; like any other production system, the participants experience benefits and losses unequally. But also, the surrogate mothers and the intended parents recognize their lives are enriched by these unequal global encounters. It is these alternative chronicles of market encounters that animate my work as a feminist. In my forthcoming work I ask what meanings Indian mothers draw from participating in the reproduction industry as producers of babies. I lay out the ways they structure moral narratives of their decision-making processes.

In this chapter I examine the consumers, the gay men who achieve fatherhood through cross-border reproductive care (Inhorn and Gürtin 2011; Inhorn and Patrizio 2012). Denied access to fatherhood for a plethora of reasons, including the lack of financial resources to pursue surrogacy in their sending countries, discrimination by adoption agencies, and homophobic laws that prevent them from adopting, the men turned to Indian surrogate mothers to achieve fatherhood. Many of the men with whom I spoke attested that their lives were enriched by the presence of children. But also, they recognized the fraught nature of their transnational family-building endeavors. Because of class, race, and gendered and cultural barriers, they had no connection with the surrogate mothers. And, the loving connection they made with the fetuses was through imagination, conjuring up the persons-to-be as whole individuals replete with personalities already apparent in utero. While such a love might seem inauthentic because the intended father conjured her into being, loving her as a concept rather than building love based on real knowledge, such love was also essential to preparing themselves emotionally for the arrival of the little ones. Imagining the babies helped the gay men establish themselves as fathers; they existed as a parent-child dyadic family unit before they went to India to pick the babies up. In all of this, those who risked the most, those Indian surrogate mothers who put their lives and bodies on the line, disappeared. The women had to disappear not just because of the global nature of this reproductive exchange, but also because these women had no place in the men's lives and Western worlds that were structured by ideals of nuclear family and normative parenthood. Structurally and culturally, the mothers had no place in normative families as conceived in the United States and Australia.

Because they are not heterosexual and because they had engaged in transnational surrogacy, these gay intended fathers are seen as doubly deviant. Not only are they perceived as homosexuals, but also, they are perceived as bending the law (in Australia) by engaging in reproductive tourism and exploiting Third World women to further their ends. Thus, the gay intended fathers have real reason to worry about the worlds into which they bring their children. As a result, they attempt to build caring communities through narrating their journey into fatherhood. Prior to becoming fathers, and upon achieving that social distinction of fatherhood, gay intended dads attempt to establish themselves as worthy individuals. Thus, gay men engage in telling public stories about their journey through surrogacy, their love for the not-yet-born babies, and finally, the caring work they do in holding, comforting, cleaning, cooking, and feeding once the children arrive into their Western world. These stories legitimize not just their individual fathering efforts, but are central to their attempts to create caring communities around their surrogated children, that would not just respect the young ones, but also cherish them in their familial and racial uniqueness. For gay men in this study, an essential part of their experience of globalized fatherhood is building caring communities in their localities.

Notes

1. A large number of gay men pursuing surrogacy in India are from the United States, Australia, and Israel.
2. The fetuses selected for termination are injected with potassium chloride. The risk with multiple fetal reductions is that the mother might miscarry all fetuses because of rapid changes in hormonal levels. As a result, fetuses are eliminated serially, with a gap of up to a week or so, over a period of time. This procedure can be highly uncomfortable for the pregnant woman.
3. My sample of surrogate mothers includes women who were traditional surrogates, that is, they are genetically related to the babies they surrogated because they were impregnated through intrauterine insemination. Most of the surrogate mothers I interviewed, though, are gestational surrogates.
4. Six of the interviews with gay couples/individuals were conducted by Caitlyn Collins, a doctoral candidate in sociology at the University of Texas at Austin.
5. I learned this from an interview with Sam Everingham, founder of Surrogacy Australia, a Melbourne-based advocacy group for parents using surrogacy. With his partner, Everingham is the father of two daughters.

6. In so-called normal pregnancies, too, where parents keep the babies they birth, individuals engage in nesting and conduct rituals such as baby showers, which Taylor (2000: 401) calls "consumer rites of American culture." It is not just that patterns of consumption change with impending parenthood but also, the meaning of consumption itself changes. Taylor observes that "consumption is itself invested with new levels of moral significance—consumption is cast as an act of maternal love, and an expression of a woman's character and powers of self-discipline, even as consumption is also seen to literally create the fetal body" (403).

7. I build this part of the chapter based on my reading of Sara Ruddick's (1995) *Maternal Thinking*, in which she observes that narratives are central to parents, and to children's, sense of self.

8. Jeff says that he has lost friends over his and his partner's decision to have daughters through surrogacy in India. These friends felt that the process is exploitative.

References

Bartky, Sandra Lee. 1997. "Sympathy and Solidarity: On a Tightrope with Scheler." In *Feminists Rethink the Self*, ed. Diana Tietjens Meyers. Boulder, CO; Oxford: Westview Press.

Coltrane, Scott. 1996. *Family Man: Fatherhood, Housework, and Gender Equity.* New York: Oxford University Press.

Doucet, Andrea. 2006. *Do Men Mother? Fatherhood, Care, and Domestic Responsibility.* Toronto: University of Toronto Press.

Ikemoto, Lisa. 2009. "Eggs as Capital: Human Egg Procurement in the Fertility Industry and the Stem Cell Research Enterprise." *Signs* 34, no. 4: 763–81.

Inhorn, Marcia C., and Zeynep B. Gürtin. 2011. "Cross-Border Reproductive Care: A Future Research Agenda." *Reproductive BioMedicine Online* 23: 665–76.

Inhorn, Marcia C., and Pasquale Patrizio. 2012. "The Global Landscape of Cross-Border Reproductive Care: Twenty Key Findings for the New Millennium." *Current Opinion in Obstetrics & Gynecology* 24, no. 4: 158–63.

La Rossa, Ralph. 1997. *The Modernization of Fatherhood: A Social and Political History.* Chicago: University of Chicago Press.

Lewin, Ellen. 2009. *Gay Fatherhood: Narratives of Family and Citizenship in America.* Chicago: University of Chicago Press.

Naples, Nancy. 1998. *Community Activism and Feminist Politics: Organizing Across Race, Class, and Gender.* New York: Routledge.

———. 2002. "Activist Mothering and Community Work: Fighting Oppression in Low-Income Neighborhoods." In *Child Care and Inequality: Re-Thinking Carework for Children and Youth*, ed. D. Kurz, F. M. Cancian, A. S. London, R. Reviere, and M. Tuominen. New York: Routledge.

Pande, Amrita. 2009. "It May Be Her Eggs but It Is My Blood: Surrogates and Everyday Forms of Kinship in India." *Qualitative Sociology* 32, no. 4: 379–97.

———. 2010. "Commercial Surrogacy in India: Manufacturing a Perfect Mother-Worker." *Signs* 35, no. 4: 969–92.

Petchesky, Rosalind. 1987. "Fetal Images: The Power of Visual Culture in the Politics of Reproduction." *Feminist Studies* 13, no. 2: 263–92.

Rengachary Smerdon, Usha. 2008. "Crossing Bodies, Crossing Borders: International Surrogacy Between the United States and India." *Cumberland Law Review* 30, no. 1: 15–85.

Risman, Barbara. 1986. "Can Men Mother? Life as a Single Father." *Family Relations* 35, no. 1: 95–102.

Ruddick, Sara. 1995. *Maternal Thinking: Toward a Politics of Peace.* Boston: Beacon Press.

Spar, Deborah. 2006. *The Baby Business: How Science, Money, and Politics Drive the Commerce of Conception.* Boston: Harvard Business School Press.

Spelman, Elizabeth. 1989. *Inessential Woman: Problems of Exclusion in Feminist Thought.* Boston: Beacon Press.

Stacey, Judith. 1998. *Brave New Families: Stories of Domestic Upheaval in Late-Twentieth Century America.* Berkeley: University of California Press.

Taylor, Janelle. 2000. "Of Sonograms and Baby Prams: Fetal Diagnosis, Pregnancy, and Consumption." *Feminist Studies* 26, no. 2: 391–418.

———. 2008. *The Public Life of the Fetal Sonogram: Technology, Consumption, and the Politics of Reproduction.* New Brunswick, NJ: Rutgers University Press.

Townsend, Nicholas. 2002. *The Package Deal: Marriage, Work, and Fatherhood in Men's Lives.* Philadelphia: Temple University Press.

Vora, Kalindi. 2009. "Indian Transnational Surrogacy and the Commodification of Vital Energy." *Subjectivities* 28, no. 1: 266–78.

Part VII

AMBIVALENT FATHERHOOD

Chapter 13

FATHERHOOD, COMPANIONATE MARRIAGE, AND THE CONTRADICTIONS OF MASCULINITY IN NIGERIA

Daniel Jordan Smith

Introduction

In an era of lower fertility, companionate marriage, and changing family structures, Igbo men in southeastern Nigeria are beginning to adopt new approaches to fatherhood. Men are more involved in the daily lives of their children than in the past. They help more with childcare, exhibit greater intimacy with their children, and generally treat them in a less authoritarian manner than fathers in the past. While many Igbo men participate in and support these changes, ambivalence and contradictions abound. For example, messages from ever more popular Pentecostal churches that exhort men to embrace monogamy and fidelity compete with male peer pressure to prove masculinity and economic status by spending money on young mistresses. Further, the emergence of globally influenced ideals of romantic love and marital intimacy—and, to an increasing extent, gender equality—frequently come into conflict with the enduring conviction that a man must be the king of his castle. Pressures to have fewer children and invest in them educationally and emotionally contend with still-salient notions of wealth in people and patriarchal authority.

In anthropology, demography, and other social sciences, the relative dearth of accounts of men's lives and roles in the spheres of family, reproduction, contraception—and, indeed, fatherhood—has been lamented for at least a couple of decades (Connell 1995; Green and Biddlecom 2000; Gutmann 1997; Inhorn et al. 2009). Matthew Gutmann (1996), Nicholas Townsend (2002), and others have drawn attention to the intersection between notions and values of fatherhood and those of masculinity. While the vacuum in the study of masculinity in sub-Saharan Africa has begun to be filled (Lindsay and Miescher 2003; Miescher 2005; Ouzgane and Morrell 2005), relatively little has been written in anthropology about fatherhood in Africa (for South Africa cf. Richter and Morrell 2006). Further, I am aware of no anthropological accounts specifically focused on fatherhood in contemporary Nigeria, Africa's most populous country. In the wake of seemingly more spectacular shifts in the lives of women, related to new patterns in the gendered division of labor and more widely accepted global norms about women's rights, it is easy to overlook the quieter and uneven shifts in how men navigate their status as fathers.

This chapter examines changes in men's experience of fatherhood in Igbo-speaking southeastern Nigeria, a region undergoing rapid and far-reaching social change. I argue that men's ambivalence about modern masculinity and about their changing roles as fathers can be constructively analyzed in relationship to changes in marriage. Specifically, as marriages become more companionate, and as fathers find that the burdens of raising children fall ever more directly on their shoulders, men experience fatherhood as, simultaneously, an essential arena to forge and prove masculinity and a tremendous challenge to their manhood. In the face of changing expectations about marital dynamics and a shifting gendered division of labor, new ideals and practices of fatherhood produce deep anxieties about the weakening of male privilege.

The structure of the chapter is as follows. After briefly describing the research setting and methods, I explain the centrality of fatherhood in Igbo men's experiences of masculinity. The ethnographic evidence includes many elements that point to continuity over time, but also to significant changes. The individualism that characterizes ideals of modern marriage also leads men to question some of the strict cultural expectations that make marriage and parenthood imperative, at the same time as economic circumstances make fulfilling these social duties ever more challenging. Having illustrated the pressures men experience to marry and have children, I next explore some of the interplay between marital relationships and fatherhood, particularly as these connections are affected by powerful and widely shared Christian messages about family and fidelity. I show how these prevalent Christian influences come into conflict with dimensions of male privilege but also reaffirm some aspects of patriarchy. Finally, I look at practices of fatherhood specifically through the lens of men's relationships with their wives, arguing that fathering in contemporary southeastern Nigeria must be understood as part of a larger project of family-making, in which companionate marriage, lower fertility, and an emphasis on investment in children's education have reconfigured masculinity in ways that men find both rewarding and troubling.

Research Setting and Methodological Approach

The findings in this chapter draw on almost twenty years of research in southeastern Nigeria on issues of gender, sexuality, marriage, kinship, and reproduction, but especially on six months of fieldwork in 2004 for a project called "Love, Marriage, and HIV." The study focused on the intersection of changing marriage (particularly the rise of choice, love, and intimacy as aspects of how people in southeastern Nigeria imagine and practice marriage), persistent gender inequality (including pervasive double standards around extramarital sex that tolerate—and even celebrate—male infidelity, while condemning similar behavior by women), and the risk of HIV transmission in marriage (Hirsch et al. 2009; Smith 2007a; 2009). While parenthood was not the focus of the project, interviews with married men and women and participant observation in households uncovered extensive evidence about the evolving arena of fatherhood.

The research was undertaken in two communities in Igbo-speaking southeastern Nigeria. The study areas included the semi-rural community of Ubakala in Abia State and the city of Owerri in Imo State. With very few exceptions, the entire population in both sites is Christian, and most people are regular participants in the activities of the many churches present in the area. Most men and women below the age of fifty have completed at least primary school and are literate, and nearly all parents aspire to have their children achieve degrees in higher education.

I spent June through December of 2004 in Nigeria, living in a household in Ubakala that included a married woman, several children, and a migrant husband. I also lived part-time in Owerri with a young newlywed couple. Local research assistants assisted with interviews in both sites, particularly with women. I undertook participant observation in each setting. Intensive interviews were carried out with twenty couples, fourteen residing in Ubakala and six residing in Owerri. The couples were selected opportunistically with the objective of sampling marriages of different generations and duration, couples with a range of socioeconomic and educational profiles, and, of course, in both rural and urban settings. I have returned to Nigeria for shorter research stints several times since the 2004 study, most recently in 2012, when I explicitly focused on issues of fatherhood in follow-up interviews with many of the men interviewed in the earlier study.

The Pressure to Marry and Have Children

The preeminent Africanist anthropologist Meyer Fortes (1978: 121) noted long ago that it is "parenthood that is the primary value associated with the idea of family in West Africa." "Parenthood," Fortes said, "is regarded as a sine qua non for the attainment of the full development of the complete person to which all aspire" (125). In southeastern Nigeria, even with all the changes in marriage, fertility, and kinship—some of which might lead one to expect that the social importance of parenthood would diminish—Fortes's observation is as true now as ever. Indeed, one might reasonably argue that marriage and parenthood are more valued than ever, in part because they are perceived as ever more difficult and costly to achieve.

Further, in southeastern Nigeria marriage remains the only socially approved arena in which to be a parent. While marriage rates are waning in some parts of Africa, including some dramatic declines in parts of southern Africa (Hosegood et al. 2009; Preston-Whyte 1993), this is not the case in Igbo-speaking Nigeria, where the expectation to marry is almost universal, the overwhelming majority of adults marry, and most children are born to married couples. But while marriage remains both the ideal and a highly prevalent practice, a number of factors make men feel that getting married is more difficult than in the past. This results in constant discussion and palpable anxiety among men between the ages of twenty-five and forty (generally the period when Igbo men are expected to marry). The two cases below exemplify how men experience social pressure to marry, how fatherhood is a marker of competent masculinity, and how at least some men are questioning society's expectations, even as they feel compelled to live up to them.

Silas Ndubuka is the third son of his parents, the fourth child in a family of five.[2] His oldest brother disappeared and almost surely died as a child soldier fighting for Biafra in Nigeria's civil war. Silas's surviving brother and his two sisters—one several years younger than him—were all married more than fifteen years ago. Each has at least three children. Silas's father died more than a decade ago, but to Silas's aging mother's deep disappointment, Silas had passed the age of forty and still was not married. His mother constantly reminded him that he needed to marry, and when he visited Ubakala from Lagos, where he had lived for well over a decade, she often arranged for him to meet young women from around the community whom she hoped he might be persuaded to marry. She also recruited everyone she could—her son and daughters, cousins, neighbors, the pastor in the family's church—to convince Silas he must marry.

Interestingly, the person who expressed the greatest sympathy for Silas's hesitation to marry was his older brother, who himself had been married for twenty years and was the father of four children. When I asked him about Silas's advancing age and his failure to marry, he voiced the same concern that Silas expressed in his discussions with me: Silas was not economically secure enough to marry. Silas would often say—to me, but also to his mother when she hounded him—"How can I marry when I don't have anything doing?" By this he meant that he did not have steady work or a stable income, so how could he afford a wedding ceremony, much less the costs of a family? Silas's elder brother knew the economic burdens of being a husband and a father, and this seemed to influence his sympathy for Silas's reluctance to marry without sufficient means. Silas's brother was also the one, in the absence of their late father, most expected to contribute to help Silas marry, so perhaps economic self-interest also influenced his tolerance of Silas's delay in marrying.

About three years ago Silas finally married. His sisters contributed significantly to the cost of the wedding and his sister-in-law (Silas's brother's wife) was instrumental in finding the bride, who was a relative of hers. I had the impression that Silas may have received a discount in the amount of bridewealth he had to provide because it was the second marriage between these two extended families. Not more than a year after the wedding, Silas and his wife (almost twenty years his junior) had a baby boy. Everyone in Silas's family is extremely happy about the marriage and the child, especially Silas's mother—though she is already hurrying her son and daughter-in-law to have another baby. Silas seems much relieved to have finally procreated. On my last trip to Nigeria in 2012, Silas proudly took me to the daycare center where his son stays when Silas and his wife are working, so that I could take pictures of him and his son.

While marriage and parenthood remain the most imperative and taken-for-granted dimensions of social adulthood in southeastern Nigeria, and while the main reason most men delay the transition to marriage and fatherhood is a worry about the economic burdens entailed rather than because of reluctance to marry and have children in and of itself, I have recently begun to hear unmarried Igbo men question the very institutions of marriage and parenthood. During my last visit to Nigeria I had a long discussion with a younger friend of mine who is a researcher at a local university in Umuahia. Chiwendu Aguh is thirty-five years old, several years past the normative age for men to marry in southeastern Nigeria, but still young enough not to have reached the stigmatized status that Silas experienced before he finally married in his forties. I had noticed Chiwendu spending a lot of time with one particular young woman, and I asked him about the relationship.

He narrated a long story about how they met and became involved, culminating in his sharing that if all continued to go well he would likely marry her. He then explained how much pressure he was under—from his parents, but also seemingly from society at large—to get married. "Everyone is looking at me somehow," he said. "In our society, no one takes you seriously unless you are married and have children. You cannot speak up. Your opinion is dismissed. I am tired of being looked at as a small boy." He then explained some obstacles that remained to marrying the young woman—the principal one being that she belonged to a Pentecostal church and that her pastor and her parents wanted her to marry from within the church. Chiwendu was attending her church and taking classes with the pastor that would enable him to be baptized (and "born again"), thereby allowing him to officially join her church and get the pastor's and the parents' permission to marry.

While he was forging ahead with this plan, he expressed some displeasure at several aspects, including that it was the traditional practice in Igboland for the wife to join the husband's church, not vice versa. Chiwendu also had some apprehension about whether he really liked this church, though one of his friends pointed out that men often attend church with their fiancées, only to eschew regular worship once the marriage is official. Chiwendu's family was Anglican, and he knew his father would not like his leaving their church. But his father had pressured him not to marry a woman a couple of years ago because investigations had uncovered that her family had a "spiritual" problem (in my experience this could mean anything from a history of mental illness in the family to rumors of witchcraft). In that case, Chiwendu relented to his father's wishes. He said his dad was now so eager for him to marry, he would probably overlook his misgivings if Chiwendu had to join his girlfriend's church in order to marry her.

Most interestingly, as Chiwendu narrated his experience with the social pressure to marry and have children he said: "If it weren't required to by society I don't need it. What do I need marriage and children for? All that trouble. I'm OK like this. But I have no choice. I will marry and have a couple of kids and that's it." I suspect Chiwendu's negative attitude about marriage and parenthood was partly a result of the stress from the social pressure he was feeling from his family and peers. But it is unusual in southeastern Nigeria for people to voice any dissent regarding the ubiquitous expectation that a full and proper life requires marriage and parenthood. That said, the notion Chiwendu expressed—that there might be any alternative to marrying and having children—is itself evidence of the influence of dramatic social changes. And yet the fact that men like Silas and Chiwendu, who married late and who articulated the burdens of marriage and fatherhood, ultimately decided to follow convention attests to just how powerful these norms and institutions remain even in the face of significant transformations.

Silas was socially rehabilitated in the eyes of his family and community when he married and had a son. Though somewhat resentful of the pressures to wed and father children, Chiwendu expects the same outcome. It is important to reemphasize that while marriage remains the only socially acceptable space for fatherhood in southeastern Nigeria, marriage without parenthood is almost as calamitous as no marriage at all. While an adequate engagement with the issue of male infertility is outside the scope of this chapter, I include here a few words that connect it to the social importance of fatherhood.

In Nigeria's still highly gender-unequal cultural context, infertility is commonly blamed on women (Cornwall 2001; Hollos 2003; Hollos et al. 2009), but men increasingly acknowledge, at least privately, that they can also be the source of infertility. However, with paternity—and most Nigerians mean biological paternity—being a social imperative, few men will openly acknowledge being sterile or impotent. Instead, in a context where assisted reproductive technologies remain economically out of reach (not to mention ethically problematic) for most people, and where adoption is still uncommon and largely unacceptable, Nigerian men unable to father children are widely known (or at least widely believed) to look the other way so that their wives can get pregnant by another man and have a child for them, the tacit agreement being that paternity will be attributed to the husband. Such stories circulate widely in popular discourse. In Ubakala, I was told of several examples. For a man's wife to have sex with another man is considered an egregious affront to his masculinity. The fact that Nigerian men who are infertile are believed to look the other way so their wives can get pregnant, and the fact that they apparently accept the role of father to the children of such liaisons, is strong evidence for the social importance of fatherhood and its foundational place in the construction of manhood.

Fatherhood, African Manhood, and Christian Families

Although the contradictions and ambivalence that Igbo men experience about marriage, family, and fatherhood must be seen in the context of dramatic demographic and social changes, it is far too simple to characterize men as caught between tradition and modernity. Instead, it is more accurate to describe and try to explain the extant realities that produce different ambitions, desires, obligations, and constraints that pull men—as husbands and fathers, but also as socially positioned actors in their communities, workplaces, and male peer groups—in conflicting directions. In this section, I show how Christian messages, especially those of increasingly popular Pentecostal churches, have contradictory effects on fatherhood and masculinity, at once challenging and reinforcing different aspects of patriarchal privilege.

While the intersection of masculinity and fatherhood includes many dimensions, the contradictions that Igbo men face are tellingly revealed in the tension between widely circulating Christian family values and the ways that men feel pressured to demonstrate both economic success and masculine competence among their male peers. Specifically, as Christianity in southeastern Nigeria is ever-more influenced by Pentecostalism, which preaches the importance of monogamy and fidelity and which emphasizes one's nuclear family as the arena of kinship relations where God's ways can be enacted most faithfully, these expectations come into conflict with other widely prevalent norms that reward married men for demonstrating their economic and masculine prowess through having extramarital relationships.

Elsewhere I have documented how social pressures to demonstrate economic success and social status intersect with powerful norms about sexual privilege (and specifically the notion that a real man should want and have many sexual partners) to produce widely prevalent patterns of men's extramarital sex, particularly among men of relative means (Smith 2002; 2008). While acknowledging that many different motivations for and kinds of extramarital sexual relationships exist, I argue that married men who have sex with women other than their wives (most often younger, unmarried women) are commonly performing for their male peers in an act akin to conspicuous consumption. The intersection of class ambitions, masculine ideals, and persistent gender inequality has produced a virtual epidemic of extramarital sex. The prevalence of men's extramarital sex has been widely acknowledged in the literature, with scholarly attention perhaps especially focused in sub-Saharan Africa because of the concerns created by HIV and AIDS (Kimuna and Djamba 2005; Parikh 2007; Smith 2007a). The dynamics of gender and social class that drive extramarital sex in southeastern Nigeria have been observed and analyzed in other settings (Hunter 2002; 2007; 2010; Luke 2005).

Less acknowledged in the literature, however, is the degree of ambivalence many married men feel about their extramarital exploits, including in relationship to perceived duties regarding family and fatherhood. These perceived duties are perhaps best encapsulated in southeastern Nigeria by the messages of widely popular Pentecostal churches. While it is not possible to do justice here to the array of factors that account for Pentecostal Christianity's spectacular popularity in southeastern Nigeria, much less the multiple (and still unfolding) social consequences of its growth, for my purposes in this chapter, suffice it to say that its messages about economic success and nurturing a good Christian family contribute to the contradictions and anxieties men experience regarding fatherhood and masculinity.

Over the past couple of decades, these churches have become known especially for the promotion of the "prosperity gospel," which asserts (among other things) that eternal salvation is achieved and demonstrated through success achieved in this life (Marshall 2009; Meagher 2009). Further, Pentecostal churches are widely acknowledged to promote monogamy, nuclear family organization, and investment in one's own children. In southeastern Nigeria, many people attribute the particular popularity of Pentecostal churches among women to the fact that they can use Pentecostal teachings, congregational peer pressure, and their pastors' influence to rein in misbehaving husbands. Just as converts in general are made to feel a part of a global community that supersedes allegiances to extended kin and rural villages, men can imagine new projects of fatherhood as something they share with other born-again Christians (Meyer 2004; Robbins 2004). Some argue that one of the effects of Pentecostal conversion, aside from the reconfiguration of family roles, is people's ability to justify reducing their social and economic obligation to the wider extended family, with the prosperity gospel legitimating a more individualistic pursuit and accumulation of wealth (Marshall 2009).

As a testament to the complexity of the contradictory pressures that modern Igbo men face, even the influence of Pentecostal Christianity on the relationship between masculinity and fatherhood is mixed. While most of these churches encourage monogamy, fidelity in marriage, and fatherly investment in the well-being of one's nuclear family, the prosperity gospel also feeds into and reinforces desires for wealth, consumption, and upward class mobility that so preoccupy almost everyone in contemporary Nigeria. Thus, even though Pentecostal pastors preach against adultery and in favor of family-oriented fatherhood, by glorifying the accumulation of wealth and the future salvation supposedly associated with conspicuous consumption in the present, Pentecostal churches are contributing to a wider obsession with money and economic status that helps fuel the rewards of extramarital relationships.

Further, even Pentecostal churches' emphasis on monogamy, fidelity, and family are not completely straightforward in their effects on fatherhood. While Nigerians, as I noted above, often attribute women's attraction to Pentecostal churches to the leverage it can give them with men, in my own observations of Pentecostal church sermons and of families where both husband and wife belong to such churches, it was clear that the Pentecostal message often reinforces a highly gendered household division of the labor that heavily favors men. The notion that the man is head of the family is explicitly emphasized and a woman's obedience to her husband is strongly promoted. Pastors often make the analogy between God the father and the father as the head of the family, emphasizing why wives and children should be obedient. Thus, while Pentecostal churches urge men not to drink, not to cheat on their wives, and to provide well for their wife and children, they also reassert masculine supremacy in the family, with the father being the ultimate authority figure. In many respects, the Pentecostal message amounts to the reassertion of a kind of a patriarchal bargain (Kandiyoti 1988), with the man guaranteed domestic authority in exchange for being a faithful husband, an effective breadwinner, and a good Christian.

Not surprisingly, then, men are pulled in many directions. I remember interviewing Emeka, a 47-year-old civil servant whose government postings often forced him to live away from his family for extended periods of time. Emeka's wife joined a Pentecostal church, and he eventually followed. In one interview he admitted to me having had more than one extramarital relationship. Much of what he explained about the context of his affairs was similar to what I'd heard from other men and observed in the venues—such as bars, restaurants, and nightclubs—where married men typically entertain their unmarried lovers. Men in the company of other men (particularly when alcohol is part of the scene) are especially likely to initiate an extramarital relationship. But like so many men I spoke with, Emeka emphasized that his extramarital relationships did not threaten his commitment to his marriage and his family. As was typical, Emeka's view that his family came first resulted in considerable discretion regarding his infidelity. And interestingly, his duty as a father factored as much or more into his thinking as his role as a husband: "I am a mature man with responsibilities in my community—in the church, in various associations. I hold offices in these organizations. I can't be seen to be running here and there chasing after women. My own son is almost a man now. How can I advise him if I am known for doing this and that?"

Just as Pentecostal Christianity's effect on fatherhood and masculinity is not monolithic, acting as something of a check on men's marital indiscretion even as it also buttresses other aspects of patriarchy, so too the influence of male peer groups proves to be multifaceted. While I collected extensive evidence that male peer groups played a role in encouraging and rewarding men's extramarital sex (Smith 2002; 2007a; 2009), these same peer groups also enforced certain limits on men's behavior that reflect the social importance of marriage and fatherhood. The following case offers an apt example.

Chibuike was a 36-year-old married father of four. He was involved in a sexual relationship with a student at a local university; he brought her to his tennis club, a mostly male social space, almost daily. Chibuike conducted himself, however, in ways that other men found highly inappropriate. While it is acceptable to "show off" girl-friends in male-dominated places like the tennis club, Chibuike paraded around with his girlfriend in fully public and sex-integrated settings, such that his wife and in-laws became aware of his affair. He openly touched and kissed his girlfriend in these public environments (whereas most men restrict physical contact with girlfriends to private venues), and he would sometimes spend several nights away from home, sleeping with his lover. Worst of all from his peers' point of view, he squandered his money on his girlfriend to the extent that he was no longer adequately supporting his family. While Igbo men tolerate—indeed, in some contexts even encourage—extramarital sexual relationships among their peers, as a rule men do not leave their wives for a lover (divorce is highly frowned upon in Igbo society). Further, part of the economic success a man exhibits by having a girlfriend depends on the fact that he still supports his family. Failure to do so undercuts any social rewards men bestow upon their peers for infidelity.

Ultimately, the club members organized themselves and intervened. A group counseled Chibuike to stop the affair, threatened him with suspension from the club, and even visited the wife in solidarity with her predicament, urging her to endure while they acted to rein in her husband. From a Igbo male point of view, competent masculinity allows and even encourages extramarital sex, but not at the expense of neglecting responsibility for one's family. The boundaries that men enforced among themselves were partly in response to their anxieties that unbridled extramarital relationships threaten values associated with marriage and fatherhood.

Fathers, Mothers, Marriage, and Child-Rearing

When I arrived for a planned interview with Ugochukwu Oriaku, he was busy in the kitchen warming *akamu,* a soft semi-liquid pap made from corn flour. Ugochukwu's older son held Ugochukwu's 18-month-old daughter who would consume the food, jiggling her up and down on his knee to ward off the crying that seemed imminent. Ugochukwu immediately apologized that his task would delay the start of our interview. He then explained that his wife had yet to return from the office and his daughter was hungry. Judging from the confidence with which he tested the consistency of the pap to decide whether it was ready, Ugochukwu had obviously done this before, but he also made it clear that, had his wife been home, this would have been her job. When the *akamu* was ready, Ugochukwu handed the bowl and spoon to his son to feed his younger sister. But as Ugochukwu moved away and motioned me to the parlor where we would talk, his daughter cried and pushed away the spoon, spilling pap in her brother's lap. Ugochukwu then took his daughter from her brother, carried her and the food to the parlor, and at the same time asked me if it was okay to begin the interview while he fed his daughter. She ate as we spoke, and eventually she fell asleep in her father's lap.

While it is still more common to see mothers undertake the routine household tasks of parenting—cooking, feeding children, dressing them, washing dishes, laundering clothes, and so on—it is no longer shocking to see some men contributing to this work. In this section, I focus on understanding how the changing dynamics of marriage and family organization are shaping fathering practices, because these are the factors that seemed to influence most directly the more intimate dimensions of being (or having) a father in the communities where I conducted research.

A primary backdrop to changes in practices of fatherhood in southeastern Nigeria is the transformation of marriage. Among younger generations, marriage is widely valued and experienced in much more companionate terms than in earlier times, with the quality of the personal, emotional, and sexual relationship between husband and wife now likely to figure into both men's and women's assessments of whether they have a good marriage. In this respect, marriages in southeastern Nigeria appear to be following a global trend (Ahearn 2001; Hirsch 2003; Hirsch and Wardlow 2006). In modern, companionate marriages, Nigerian couples often think about limiting the number of children they have to three or four, they commonly view educating their children as their highest priority and shared goal, and they often communicate and cooperate with regard to training children such that they will be prepared to be successful in an increasingly urbanized and globalized social and economic environment. As the selection of a spouse has become a more individualized decision, as marriage has become more companionate and an arena of greater personal intimacy between husband and wife, and as lower levels of fertility have unfolded in consonance with greater investments in individual children (especially their education), fathers in southeastern Nigeria have become more directly involved in many aspects of parenting.

Because Ugochukwu's parenting practices struck me as indicative of a changing gendered division of labor, in the interview I asked him about how he and his wife divided domestic labor. What struck me most was how he emphasized the importance of consultation and solidarity between him and his wife regarding their children. While his wife still did most of the household labor associated with parenting, Ugochukwu—and many younger men I interviewed— went out of his way to emphasize that raising a family was a joint project in which he and his wife cooperated closely.

More pronounced than the still-incipient relaxing of a highly gendered domestic division of labor is the dramatic shift in the way mothers and fathers communicate to raise their children. This involves major changes in both fatherhood and motherhood, with the role of parents ascending vis-à-vis other kinship relations as the primary locus for authority and socialization. Parents were not unimportant in the past, but other kin (aunts and uncles, other wives of one's father, older siblings, cousins, etc.) took on a more significant role in caring for, supervising, and disciplining children than is the case now. Marriage as a project of social reproduction is, of course, not new, but the way that couples view themselves—as a couple and as mothers and fathers—as the primary agents in this socialization process is something quite recent. For men, the degree of father involvement is itself a change; for both men and women the focus on providing formal education and other material and symbolic resources in order to train their children to be prepared for a more modern, urban, and individualistic world involves significant shifts from the past.

The rise of formal education and the decline in fertility have gone hand-in-hand in southeastern Nigeria, as in many parts of the world. Igbos have gradually moved from thinking that having lots of children was the best practice, to believing that limiting the number of one's offspring to three or four is the wisest strategy. To put it crudely, people have moved from desiring quantity to desiring quality. While I do not think it is accurate to portray high fertility societies as not valuing "quality" in their children (indeed, I heard many Igbo proverbs promoting high fertility that also suggested the importance of attributes one might label as "quality"), it is nonetheless true that economic investments in children, particularly in formal education, have increased significantly as fertility levels have declined.

In southeastern Nigeria, the notion that it is the father (but, in reality, the father and mother) who is solely responsible for providing for a child's education is new and contrasts strongly with cultural norms of the past. When Victor Uchendu (1965) published his classic account of the Igbo, one of the most striking aspects of Igbo society was the degree to which entire kin groups and communities shared the responsibility for and celebrated the educational achievements of their "sons"—and in that era it was really only sons and not daughters, another feature of society that has changed dramatically. In fact, people still commonly appeal to their wider kin for help in all kinds of endeavors, including paying children's school fees. It is not unusual for a wealthier sibling, uncle, or cousin to contribute to the education of their poorer kin. But it is much less common than in the past. Today's fathers accurately perceive that, increasingly, the duties of parenting fall directly on children's actual parents.

In formal interviews and countless informal interactions, fathers in both Ubakala and Owerri spoke regularly and emphatically about the priority of educating their children. Most men either suggested or explicitly stated that providing for their children's education was their greatest duty as a parent. Implicit in prioritizing education was the assumption that along with money for school fees, school uniforms, books, and so on, a father should be able to provide the basic requirements for raising a child, including food, shelter, security, and a proper social and moral foundation. Further, most men emphasized that educating one's children was, ideally, the responsibility of a child's parents exclusively.

Chuka, a 35-year-old father of four, describing the challenges posed by the costs of formal education, expressed a sentiment I heard from many fathers: "Who else will pay my children's school fees? It is only me. As a father that is my duty." In reality mothers and fathers in modern marriages frequently pool their resources to amass the funds necessary to pay the costs of children's schooling. But even so, it is a widely shared view that fathers ultimately bear this responsibility, and if a family can no longer afford to send a child to school, even though the mother will likely feel just as exasperated as her husband, it is the father who will be seen by kin and community as failing to provide.

This perception that fathers are solely responsible for educating their children represents both continuity and change in the institution of fatherhood in southeastern Nigeria. Lower fertility, more nuclear family organization, neolocal residence formation associated with rural-to-urban migration, ever more prevalent ideals and practices associated with companionate marriage, and wider social and economic changes that have reconfigured the gendered division of labor all place fathers in a more central and more intimate parental role. And yet at the same time, the notion that it is the father

who is carrying the entire economic burden of the family reproduces a patriarchal ideology that does not reflect real contributions
of women—not just in the more traditionally recognized tasks of domestic social reproduction, but in more modern (and ideologically
male) endeavors such as earning an income or cultivating more
public social and political relationships that are vital as families navigate Nigeria's clientelistic political economy (Smith 2001; 2007b).

For women and children, changing ideals and practices of fatherhood have many benefits. Generally, married women in my study
claimed to experience modern marriage as offering them more equal
footing in their relationships with their husbands. The idea that men
increasingly believe that part of what makes a good marriage is the
quality of their personal relationship with their wives seems to provide women welcome leverage. The fact that younger married couples with smaller families and more nuclear household organization
see cooperation in the project of educating their children as one of
the primary goals of their relationship, and also that many men now
see their wives as key and even equal partners in this endeavor, produces and reinforces new configurations of domestic gender dynamics that most women seem to experience positively. Based on my
observations, the most profound costs to women of modern marriage are when they have a "bad" husband—one who is flagrantly
unfaithful, drinks too much, or is physically abusive. The more cou-
ple-centered, nuclear organization of marriage and family makes it
more difficult than in the past for a woman with a bad husband to
call on kin for help, whether it is to rein in a man's bad behavior
or simply to seek economic assistance that her husband is failing to
provide. As I have noted, many women in contemporary Igbo society join Pentecostal churches in part to help manage problematic
relations with their husbands.

For children, too, modern fatherhood seems to have many benefits, but also some costs. In the many families I have come to know
well over the last two decades, the degree to which children feel
dependent on and more emotionally attached to their fathers seems
greater among the current generation than in the past. I do not mean
to suggest that children did not love or feel close to their fathers in
the past (which would be obviously untrue), but the changes in
marriage, family, and fatherhood I have described in this chapter
do seem to entail more communication, greater intimacy, and more
direct dependence on fathers than before. As they become adults,
most children who grew up in these more modern households seem
to value the kind of relationship that modern fatherhood enables—

though they do not necessarily spend much time consciously comparing the current situation to the past. But like for women in their positions as wives and mothers, these changing circumstances mean that children can no longer rely as much on wider kin networks for help navigating the challenges of everyday life in Nigeria. Many intertwining social changes threaten (though by no means fully undermine) the centrality of wider kinship ties for how people succeed in contemporary Nigeria. Children must now rely on their fathers more than ever. The burden on fathers is growing even as the emotional payoffs of fatherhood increase.

Conclusion

As I have tried to illustrate and explain, for Igbo men in southeastern Nigeria, modern fatherhood creates significant contradictions and ambivalence, particularly in relation to the wider context of masculinity, wherein men have many reasons to feel uneasy about change. While many men seem to welcome and enjoy the more intimate relationships with wives and children that characterize contemporary Igbo families, the social and demographic changes that drive or accompany these new ideals and practices of fatherhood threaten certain aspects of patriarchal authority that men benefit from and do not want to relinquish easily. As men and women value spousal cooperation and communication and as parenting becomes more of a joint marital project focused on education and other investments in a smaller number of children, men are sharing domestic authority with women and interacting with their children less distantly. But although patriarchal authority seems to be somewhat less absolute, it has by no means disappeared, as illustrated by the messages of popular Pentecostal churches, which seem to promise and promote men's privileged position in the family in exchange for particular commitments to marriage, parenting, and God.

While being a father has long been and remains the most important aspect of being a man in southeastern Nigeria, fatherhood sometimes comes into conflict with other socially valued aspects of masculinity. In this era of urbanization, economic transformation, and globally influenced desires for status-enhancing consumption, men's perception of what constitutes competent masculinity is deeply tied to aspirations connected to social class—aspirations that are social and symbolic as well as economic. The most poignant example from my research of the contradictions that the intersection

of masculinity and class ambitions poses for fatherhood is the social pressure and rewards men experience in relation to extramarital
sex. Many of the very same men who embrace new ideals and practices of fatherhood are also unfaithful to their wives, seemingly undermining aspects of modern marriage and family-making to which
they simultaneously subscribe.

Given my focus on marital relations as the lens through which to
understand the changing experience of fatherhood in Igbo-speaking
Nigeria, and my argument that the relationship between fatherhood
and masculinity involves many contradictions, it is necessary to conclude with a few words about the seeming conflict between men's
positions as fathers and as unfaithful husbands. Two questions seem
obvious: (1) What has gone wrong with fatherhood such that some
young Igbo women need to resort to having a "sugar daddy" to support themselves? and (2) How do unfaithful husbands reconcile the
fact that the unmarried women with whom they are having extramarital sex are someone's daughters? In response to the first question, I think the answer is that most young unmarried women who
have sex with married men do so primarily for economic reasons in
order to fulfill socially influential economic aspirations. Most often,
young women hide these relationships from their fathers, and to the
extent that there is any failure of fatherhood contributing to prevalence of these relationships, it is related to larger economic struggles
that many fathers and their daughters share, rather than to a moral
failure on the part of fathers (or their daughters). With regard to
the second question, married men seem to resolve this implicit contradiction by having extramarital relations only with the daughters
of men they do not know. It would indeed feel wrong for a man to
have an affair with a young woman whose father he knows. The
contradiction is real and is mitigated by the anonymity offered by
urban life.

Although one might be tempted to see companionate marriage
and invested fatherhood as fundamentally contradicted by infidelity, such a conclusion would mischaracterize Igbo men's experiences. Every man I interviewed who cheated on his wife asserted
that his marriage and his family remained much more important
priorities than anything achieved in extramarital relationships. The
fact that the same male peers who seem to reward infidelity will also
intervene, as in the case of Chibuike, when a man's indiscretions
threaten his duties as a father attests to the collective support for this
view that a man's greatest priority is his family. Many men felt ambivalence about their infidelity, but also about wider social changes

that affect marriage, family, gender dynamics, and male privilege. Ultimately, however, the vast majority of men take being a father to be the most important aspect of being a man.

Notes

1. The "Love, Marriage, and HIV" study was supported by National Institute of Health grant # 1 R01 41724-01A1.
2. All names of individuals are pseudonyms.

References

Ahearn, Laura. 2001. *Invitations to Love: Literacy, Love Letters, and Social Change in Nepal.* Ann Arbor: University of Michigan Press.

Connell, R. W. 1995. *Masculinities.* Berkeley: University of California Press.

Cornwall, Andrea. 2001. "Looking for a Child: Coping with Infertility in Ado-Odo, South-Western Nigeria." In *Managing Reproductive Life: Cross-Cultural Themes in Fertility and Sexuality,* ed. Soraya Termayne. New York; Oxford: Berghahn Books.

Fortes, Meyer. 1978. "Parenthood, Marriage and Fertility in West Africa." *Journal of Development Studies* 14, no. 4: 121–48.

Green, Margaret, and Ann Biddlecom. 2000. "Absent and Problematic Men: Demographic Accounts of Male Reproductive Roles." *Population and Development Review* 26, no. 1: 81–115.

Gutmann, Matthew. 1996. *The Meanings of Macho: Being a Man in Mexico City.* Berkeley: University of California Press.

———. 1997. "Trafficking in Men: the Anthropology of Masculinity." *Annual Review of Anthropology* 25: 385–409.

Hirsch, Jennifer. 2003. *A Courtship After Marriage: Sexuality and Love in Mexican Transnational Families.* Berkeley: University of California Press.

Hirsch, Jennifer, and Holly Wardlow, eds. 2006. *Modern Loves: The Anthropology of Romantic Courtship and Companionate Marriage.* Ann Arbor: University of Michigan Press.

Hirsch, Jennifer, Holly Wardlow, Daniel Jordan Smith, Harriet Phinney, Shanti Parikh, and Constance A. Nathanson. 2009. *The Secret: Love, Marriage, and HIV.* Nashville: Vanderbilt University Press.

Hollos, Marida. 2003. "Profiles of Infertility in Southern Nigeria: Women's Voices from Amakiri." *African Journal of Reproductive Health* 7, no. 2: 46–56.

Hollos, Marida, Ulla Larsen, Oka Obono, and Bruce Whitehouse. 2009. "The Problem of Infertility in High Fertility Populations: Meanings, Consequences and Coping Mechanisms in Two Nigerian Communities." *Social Science & Medicine* 68, no. 11: 2061–68.

Hosegood, Victoria, Nuala McGrath, and Tom Moultrie. 2009. "Dispensing with Marriage: Marital and Partnership Trends in Rural KwaZulu-Natal, South Africa 2000-2006." *Demographic Research* 20, no. 13: 279–312.

Hunter, Mark. 2002. "The Materiality of Everyday Sex: Thinking Beyond 'Prostitution.'" *African Studies* 61, no. 1: 91–120.

———. 2007. "The Changing Political Economy of Sex in South Africa: The Significance of Unemployment and Inequalities to the Scale of the AIDS Pandemic." *Social Science & Medicine* 64, no. 3: 689–700.

———. 2010. *Love in the Time of AIDS: Inequality, Gender, and Rights in South Africa*. Bloomington: Indiana University Press.

Inhorn, Marcia C., Tine Tjornhoj-Thomson, Helene Goldberg, and Maruska la Cour Mosegaard, eds. 2009. *Reconceiving the Second Sex: Men, Masculinity, and Reproduction*. New York; Oxford: Berghahn Books.

Kandiyoti, Deniz. 1988. "Bargaining with Patriarchy." *Gender & Society* 2: 274–90.

Kimuna, Sitawa, and Yanyi Djamba. 2005. "Wealth and Extramarital Sex among Men in Zambia." *International Family Planning Perspectives* 31, no. 2: 83–89.

Lindsay, Lisa, and Stephan Miescher, eds. 2003. *Men and Masculinities in Modern Africa*. Portsmouth, NH: Heinemann.

Luke, Nancy. 2005. "Confronting the 'Sugar Daddy' Stereotype: Age and Economic Asymmetries and Risky Sexual Behavior in Urban Kenya." *International Family Planning Perspectives* 31, no. 1: 6–14.

Marshall, Ruth. 2009. *Political Spiritualities: The Pentecostal Revolution in Nigeria*. Chicago: University of Chicago Press.

Meagher, Kate. 2009. "Trading on Faith: Religious Movements and Informal Economic Governance in Nigeria." *The Journal of Modern African Studies* 47, no. 3: 397–423.

Meyer, Birgit. 2004. "Christianity in Africa: From African Independent to Pentecostal-Charismatic Churches. *Annual Review of Anthropology* 33: 447–74.

Miescher, Stephan. 2005. *Making Men in Ghana*. Bloomington: Indiana University Press.

Ouzgane, Lahoucine, and Robert Morrell, eds. 2005. *African Masculinities*. New York: Palgrave Macmillan.

Parikh, Shanti. 2007. "The Political Economy of Marriage and HIV: The ABC Approach, 'Safe' Infidelity, and Managing Moral Risk in Uganda. *American Journal of Public Health* 97, no. 7: 1198–1208.

Preston-Whyte, Eleanor. 1993. "Women Who Are Not Married: Fertility, 'Illegitimacy,' and the Nature of Households and Domestic Groups among Single African Women in Durban." *South African Journal of Sociology* 24, no. 3: 63–71.

Richter, Linda, and Robert Morrell. 2006. *Baba: Men and Fatherhood in South Africa*. Cape Town: HSRC Press.

Robbins, Joel. 2004. "The Globalization of Pentecostal Christianity." *Annual Review of Anthropology* 33: 117–43.

Smith, Daniel Jordan. 2001. "Kinship and Corruption in Contemporary Nigeria." *Ethnos* 66, no. 3: 344–64.

———. 2002. "'Man No Be Wood': Gender and Extramarital Sex in Contemporary Southeastern Nigeria." *The Ahfad Journal* 19, no. 2: 4–23.

———. 2007a. "Modern Marriage, Men's Extramarital Sex, and HIV Risk in Nigeria." *American Journal of Public Health* 97, no. 6: 997–1005.

———. 2007b. *A Culture of Corruption: Everyday Deception and Popular Discontent in Nigeria.* Princeton: Princeton University Press.

———. 2008. "Intimacy, Infidelity, and Masculinity in Southeastern Nigeria." In *Intimacies: Love and Sex Across Cultures,* ed. William Jankowiak. New York: Columbia University Press.

———. 2009. "Migration, Men's Extramarital Sex and the Risk of HIV Infection in Nigeria." In *Mobility, Sexuality and AIDS,* ed. Felicity Thomas, Mary Haour-Knipe, and Peter Aggleton. New York; London: Routledge.

Townsend, Nicholas. 2002. *The Package Deal: Marriage, Work, and Fatherhood in Men's Lives.* Philadelphia: Temple University Press.

Uchendu, Victor. 1965. *The Igbo of Southeast Nigeria.* Fort Worth, TX: Holt, Reinhart and Winston.

Chapter 14

THE FOUR FACES
OF IRANIAN FATHERHOOD

Soraya Tremayne

Introduction

The impact of globalization on fatherhood in Iran can best be understood in the context of the major social and political changes
that have taken place since the Islamic Revolution of 1979.[1] The
establishment of an Islamic state initially meant the resurgence of
conservative values and norms, which were undermined and threatened by the previous regime's modernizing reforms. Such a revival
and its associated practices became so prominent that they gave the
outside world the impression that Iran was an insular and fanatical
country. On one level, Iran became a closed society, protecting conservative and conformist values and practices and rejecting what it
saw as imported corrupt Western values; but on another level, the
country has never closed its doors to change and has adopted many
innovations offered by globalization with open arms (Tremayne
2006a). However, an assumption that such a dichotomy has resulted in a polarization of the society into the conservative versus
liberal groups, or an attempt to identify and define clear-cut social
and ideological categories, would be misleading and simplistic. The
ongoing intermingling of old norms and values with modernity and

global practices results in the emergence of complex and varied, or even paradoxical, responses among different groups in society. Inevitably, such diversity affects the core values attached to fatherhood and has transformed the relationship between fathers and their globalized children. The question, therefore, is not whether but how and to what extent have the changes brought about by globalization altered the ingrained cultural understanding of what constitutes fatherhood. The fact that global trends, on reaching various cultures, are interpreted by their local recipients to make them fit into their own cultural molds, is by now well-trodden ground and has been addressed by various scholars from different disciplines.[2] This chapter therefore focuses on the specific cultural responses of Iranian fathers in this study, and the strategies they adopt to maintain their position vis-à-vis their children, to realize their vision of fatherhood. I argue that, faced with the threat of losing their position, fathers strive to remain in control of their children and resort to a variety of tactics to secure their authority over them.

This chapter opens with a brief explanation of what fatherhood means in Iranian culture in light of the fact that, historically, controlling the family has been an inextricable part of fathering. Through analysis of the data in this study, I conclude that Iranian fathers, faced with the changes in the behavior of their globalized children, have been forced the give fatherhood new guises in order to remain in control and to avoid losing face for failing to maintain their authority. In examining the global factors as agents of change, I consider the outcome of two areas of reform: population policies and literacy campaigns. These initiatives aimed at modernizing the country and, by implication, improving the relationship within the family; both proved highly successful.

Methodology

The data presented in this chapter include 120 case studies of fathers and their families in three different locations. The study in Tehran includes two groups of fathers: one of highly educated, economically well-off fathers of liberal and secular backgrounds, and another of fathers from predominantly—although not necessarily—religious and/or conservative backgrounds of varying levels of education and income. The second site of study is Yazd in central Iran. Here almost all of the fathers are less educated, with no more than a high school education. They come from low-income, religious, and conservative

homes. The third site is a group of Iranian refugees in the United
Kingdom, which is predominately religious and conservative and
comes from the middle or lower strata of Iranian society. The main
method used in all three sites was that of participant observation
and in-depth interviews, conducted in Persian. In addition, the findings of this study rely on data from two separate studies (Tremayne
2006b; 2009), as well as on research on runaway and street children
carried out from 2000 to 2004.

Fatherhood and Patriarchy

Iranian culture is predominantly patriarchal, and although modernity and globalization visibly affect the role and position of fathers
vis-à-vis their families, their impact is not yet profound enough to
dislodge the deep-seated values attached to fatherhood. The rein-
forcement of the *sharia,* which has been the basis for the country's
legal code since the 1979 Islamic Revolution, further supports and
lends legitimacy to patriarchal practices. According to *sharia,* the father owns the child, and the mother is considered a caretaker, not
an owner (Ebadi 2002; Mir-Hosseini 1993).[3] Fatherhood, therefore,
symbolizes an overall figure of control and authority, whose powers over his family are unlimited and assumed. However, the social,
cultural, and legal recognition of fathers' overall authority and right
to control should not be interpreted only as legitimizing the use of
physical force and violence. Instead, such authority can be exercised
and demonstrated in a variety of ways, including through the expression of genuine love and affection, and when necessary through
violence and aggression. "Patriarchal connectivity," a term coined
by Suad Joseph (1999) to define the structure of the Arab family,
provides the key to understanding the subtle and often invisible aspects of the multifaceted and complex relationships that underlie
the patriarchal systems of Arab—and Persian—societies. As Joseph
explains, the relationships in patriarchal systems are not just about
control, authority, and violence; they also include emotions, affection, tolerance, and many other forms of articulating connections,
which are called upon to ensure the survival of the system. In Joseph's (1999: 11–13) words, "By connectivity I mean relationships
in which persons' boundaries are relatively fluid so that persons feel
a part of significant others. Persons do not experience themselves as
bounded, separate, or autonomous." Such connectivity means that
the children are considered inseparable parts of the father and that

their actions reflect that of the father. A child's deviation is, therefore, interpreted as that of the father's, and this is what gives meaning to and justifies the exercise of control of children by the patriarch. Following Joseph's work, Marcia C. Inhorn (2012), in her study on "the new Arab man," also offers a new understanding of patriarchy in its globalized context by challenging the stereotypes of Arab men in patriarchal societies as controlling, aggressive, and brutal and as oppressors of women and children (see also Inhorn in this volume). Inhorn's (2012) new Arab man is "self-consciously rethinking the patriarchal masculinity of his forefathers and unseating received wisdom." In Inhorn's words, "he is loving, caring and committed" and he is "seriously re-thinking marriage, family life, and what it means to be a man in the twenty-first century" (158). Both Joseph's and Inhorn's groundbreaking work on the Arab world strikes chords with evolving forms of patriarchal practices in Iran. Research on the modern Iranian family demonstrates that it is closely knit and that the relationship between its members remains unaffected, in spite of the considerable changes in its structure. For example, in his article on love for children, Mohammad Taghi Sheykhi (2009) argues that children are a source of happiness in Iranian culture. Massoume Price (2006) and Elton L. Daniel and Ali Akbar Mahdi (2006) emphasize the persistence of warmth and affection between family members. However, such warmth and closeness, or any other forms of connectivity fathers may have with their children, are increasingly affected by modernity and globalization, and the fathers' perceptions of the real or imaginary threats posed by globalization, are forcing them to rethink their relationships with their children and to reposition themselves to counteract such threats, as demonstrated in the following examples.

Massoud is a successful surgeon and a gentle and mild-mannered man. He is devoted to his family, and his love for and closeness to his four children are exemplary. Massoud's children were educated in the West and, despite the freedom of choice and the financial ability to remain abroad, they were tempted to return to Iran by their father's promise to provide them with the familiar and generous comforts of home. However, even within such a harmonious and happy family, the father's authority remains incontestable. The mother presents the important decisions as that of "your father thinks" to the children, who would not even conceive the idea of going against their father's will. During one of his more relaxed moments, Massoud confided in me: "Frankly, there are times when I grind my teeth and stop myself from shouting and asking the children to move away and have their own independent lives. But, I know that unless I keep my smile and continue to be generous with them, I shall lose my authority over them. I will no longer know what they are doing and who their friends are, whereas by letting them think that they are welcome at home, I can keep better control over them." Although Massoud loves his children, he worries about losing control over them. This separation of emotions from authority is confirmed by various other studies. For example, in her study of Iranian mothers, Mahnaz Kousha (2002) shows that even the most sensible and gentle fathers behave irrationally when their children challenge their authority. In one case when the husband lost his temper with his children, the mother explained, "My husband is a good man and makes rational choices but when it comes to children and their emotional matters he is at a loss" (211). Another study by Behnaz Jalali (2005) describes how mothers mediated between fathers and their children, especially their sons. She argues that the relationship between fathers and sons is more difficult and that mothers constantly act as go-betweens to establish peace between the two sides. "Wait till your father comes home," was one of the most frequently heard sentences in many households and was meant as a threat by mothers, who were unable to control the children, especially the boys. In such cases it was not just the father's physical presence that made the children comply, but the awesome force of his omnipresence, which created an aura of self-control and haunted the children long into adulthood, if not for the rest of their lives.

Marjan is an architect and a Western-educated woman whose husband is infertile. When they decided to use donor sperm to have a baby, Marjan's only and real concern was that this should be kept a secret from her father. She said: "If my father finds out, all hell will break loose and the world will come to an end as far as he is concerned. For him, using another man's sperm means that I have committed adultery. The thought of his son-in-law being infertile and his grandchild being a 'bastard' is a complete blow to his manhood and too shameful to be able to face."

In general, the fathers' treatment of their children is guided more often by their concern to protect and reinforce their status as worthy fathers. The loss of authority and control of their children means a loss of "face," in all its social implications, for fathers. As I have discussed elsewhere, one of the manifestations of the deep-rooted values that determine the form and extent of acceptance of modernity is the consideration of one's "face" (*aberu* in Persian) in public (Tremayne 2006a). Face acts as a regulating agent directing the choices people make vis-à-vis societal change. In a society such as that of Iran, which is constantly in flux, people do not remain passive. In making decisions about where and how to adapt to change, face plays an important part in checking and shaping cultural responses. Face is one of the manifestations of Iranian culture that has not been weakened by the challenges of modernity and the introduction of new elements in society. Whereas the concept and definition of face exists in every culture, its meaning can be more critical and extensive in some cultures than others. While the loss of face in Western cultures may mean embarrassment, it often means much more than this in Middle Eastern cultures. There, the loss of face implies a failure to meet expectations and often causes loss of honor and a deep humiliation, which in turn can lead to loss of credibility and entail other social and economic consequences. In extreme cases, it can provoke strong reactions, violence, and even blood feud. Awareness of one's social position and of appropriate related behavior is imperative in all social interactions. Therefore, any decision must consider these social consequences, as far as the status and respectability of the family are concerned. Face controls the actions and decisions taken by individuals in the public aspects of their lives, regardless of class, age, ethnicity, or gender. It follows that loss of control over one's children is not an option for fathers, and the underlying reason for their willingness to make unexpected and surprising compromises is to control, or to be seen to control, their children, as the following case illustrates.

Karim is a money exchanger who runs a profitable business in Tehran. When his 12-year-old son started secondary school and became involved in an unsavory social circle, he became unruly and no longer obeyed Karim. No amount of counseling by other relatives had any effect on him, and the inevitable involvement of relatives meant that rumors began to circulate about Karim's inability to bring this young boy under control. Karim said, "To regain control of my son and save face, I was left with no choice but to uproot the family and start a new life in a different country, Dubai, where I have opened a new branch of my business, and hope that my son will behave better there." Since moving to Dubai, Karim's esteem among his relatives has risen, and his brother-in-law proudly announced, "Karim has proved that he is a real man and a very good father, who does not easily give into his children's unruly behavior." The drive to control one's children is also shown in the example of fathers from Yazd, whose daughters had been admitted to university in Tehran. Not wishing to deny their daughters the benefits of higher education, fathers asked their wives to move to Tehran to stay with them for the duration of their studies. Such upheavals seem a small sacrifice on the part of fathers in exchange for making sure that their children behave as the fathers think fit.

The Small-Sized Family and the Value of Children

Karim's situation, similar to those of other Iranian fathers, is largely the inevitable consequence of two major policies that have altered the structure of the Iranian family and the gender and intergenerational relationships in society. Beginning in 1986, Iran initiated a public awareness campaign to educate people about the advantages of having smaller families, arguing that having fewer children would result in more responsible parenthood, better health, better education, and better life conditions for their children. The policies assumed that having fewer children meant that the children would be more cherished and valued by their parents. These policies were so successful that the rate of population growth dropped from 3.8 percent per annum in 1986 to around 2 percent in 1996 and 1.3 percent in 2011, with variations among the rural and urban areas (United Nations Population Fund 2011). This outstanding achievement, which won Iran the United Nations Award for Population Policies in 1999, led to a major reduction in family size at the national level. However, this attempt to improve the status of children in smaller families was not universally successful. Educated and more secular layers in society, who lived in urban areas and had started reducing their family size before the policies were introduced, were familiar with these arguments. They treated their children with more care and valued them already, to the point that some researchers argued that the Iranian society had become a child-centered society and that the patriarchal values had weakened (Kian-Thiébault 2005: 52).[4] A study by Marie Ladier-Fouladi (2002) also points out that the relationship between members of the smaller families has been altered and that "[the] Iranian urban family is now nuclear, relationships are more egalitarian, and family solidarity is based on emotional affinities."

While these studies reflect some of the changes among certain groups in society, they do not address the widespread violence inflicted on children by parents who refuse to adapt to modernity. As evidence shows, a reduction in the size of the family or an increase in the level of education of children bears little relation to the behavior of fathers and the traditional values attached to fatherhood.

For example, a recent article by Rob Stephenson et al. (2006), on the maltreatment of school children in Kurdistan in western Iran, reports on the extent of both physical and psychological violence inflicted on children, as do regular reports by international agencies. Similar behavior can be seen in cases of refugee children or young people who have run away from parental physical and/or psychological abuse and violence. Even then, those cases that come to public attention are only the tip of the iceberg; the majority of cases go unreported or are ignored by the authorities, who reckon that such matters are for the family and do not require police involvement. The following examples illustrate the extent of the Iranian father's power and authority, which is exercised through persistent physical and psychological violence, or the threat of it.

Mina is a 35-year-old woman from Yazd who had been forced to marry her husband at the age of fifteen. When the Welfare Organization opened an office in Yazd, she went to its director for help and told him, "I hated my husband from the first day of marriage and wanted to divorce him. I cringe at the thought of him approaching me. But I am afraid of my father and the likelihood that he will harm me because I have put him to shame by going over his decision of having chosen this man for me." The Welfare Office summoned Mina's father and asked him about his views on his son-in-law. He said that he found him quite revolting and could not stand him, but, he added, "My daughter is not allowed to divorce him, or I shall kill her." Mina remains married to her husband to date.

Unlike Mina, Fatemeh, who is in her late twenties, had secretly entered into temporary marriage with a married man, whom she had met on the Internet, and had a child by him. When her father found out, he asked her not to renew her marriage contract, but she refused.[5] The father then called his two sons from another town, and together they locked Fatemeh up in the basement for days and beat her until she conceded to break up her marriage. While imprisoned, her temporary marriage had expired, and the husband did not renew it. Fatemeh's marriage without her father's permission was bad enough to make the father lose face among his equals. Having his daughter being married as a temporary wife and to a married man was even more insulting. Because no respectable girl would enter into temporary marriage, this meant that Fatemeh was unfit to be married as a permanent wife. Fatemeh's actions proved too humiliating for the father to bear and, with the mother's intervention, she was allowed to stay at home, but neither she nor her child are accepted as equals at home or among her wide network of relatives.

She has to endure this shame, which will not abate as long as she lives in the same town.

Amir is a 25-year-old man who has finished secondary school and lives with his illiterate parents. When he met and fell in love with a young woman and wanted to marry her, he was told by his father that he was not allowed to do so because the father had decided already who Amir's wife should be. Amir's father forbade him the marriage of his choice. When Amir protested, his father, with help from his brothers and other sons, tied Amir up, locked him in the basement, whipped him twice per day, and denied him food until he submitted to his father's will.

Not all fathers exercise such violence, and any generalization about fathers, the family, and the relationship between family members could be misleading. As Sheykhi (2009: 1) explains: "[L]iving in harmony within family depends on the quality and quantity of children in Iran as in any other developing country. It is argued that we need to consider the family as a controversial issue because of the differences between ideology of the family and the reality of the variety of various ways in which men, women, boys and girls, live together and interact." However, what is viewed as a weakening of patriarchy can be a misinterpretation of what are often conciliatory and negotiating tactics, used by fathers to ensure their connectivity with their children. Such a soft approach does not necessarily imply an absence of authority and control and is likely to be more of a veneer than a profound uprooting of their cultural norms and values, as the following cases show.

Ahmad lives in Yazd and is a clerk in a brick distribution business. He has a modest income and a lower secondary-level education. He is moderately religious but is conservative to the extreme. He has two daughters ages ten and fourteen and keeps the women in his household under strict control. They are not allowed to go out of the house without a man accompanying them. Although the family struggles financially, it has a satellite television and a computer and all the family members have mobile phones. Most evenings, Ahmad puts his 10-year-old daughter on his knees, and the entire family watches a variety of television shows, indiscriminately. These range from the erotic, touching on pornography, to horror or violent shows, to soccer matches. They can be Western, Indian, or Turkish films. Ahmad sees nothing wrong with letting his women watch these potentially inappropriate films, because "My women are completely free to do what they like, as long as this takes place in the house and under my watch." While there were only two books in the house, the Quran and another religious book, the family had stacks of videos and other audiovisual gadgets. When I gave the 10-year-old girl a translated copy of *Harry Potter,* a popular book for children in the West, she said that her father had bought her the DVD and that she does not need to read the book. Ahmad's two daughters are confused as to which values are the right ones to follow because, although they were allowed to watch television and use the Internet, their father forbade them to mention the television at school or discuss it outside the house. Ahmad's brother, who also has a satellite television, is stricter with his children. He mentioned that he would never allow his child to marry someone from families who have a satellite television. Both brothers allow their daughters the use of the latest global technologies but under strict control.

Similar to Ahmad, Ali lives in Tehran and is illiterate and highly conservative, with limited religious beliefs. For most of his life he has treated his five children in an autocratic and loveless manner. Four of the children, now adults, live with their parents and earn good salaries, but none of them contributes to the housekeeping. Ali, in his mid sixties, continues to work until late at night to provide for his family. Ali has no authority over his children and even receives some criticism from them. He could throw them out of his home but refrains from doing so. Ali is only too aware that there is a price to be paid for such an act and that is his loss of face for being defeated by his children. By letting them stay, Ali claims that his children still need him and are dependent on him. Oblivious to his harsh treatment at the hands of his children, the outside world views him as a devoted father. He has gained the admiration of his relatives and has become a greatly respected public figure in his neighborhood.

As discussed earlier, traditionally, obedience, fear, and respect have been some of the most effective pillars of patriarchal structures in upholding the paternal authority. However, while these factors seem to have weakened, respect, bashfulness, and modesty have not, and they remain determining factors cementing the relationship between fathers and their children and preventing children from serious confrontation with their fathers. However, even asking for the children's respect, as witnessed in Ali's case, parents have to make compromises. Mothers in Ladier-Fouladi's (2002) interviews mentioned, "In the majority of the cases women thought that children should respect their parents as long as parents' demands were reasonable."[6]

Education

One of the main factors responsible for the gradual weakening of obedience and fear of fathers is the literacy campaign. On implementing the literacy campaign, the policy makers argued that by having a well-educated young generation as potential future parents, the nation will be better equipped to cope with raising children to succeed in a modern and globalized world. Soon after the Islamic Revolution of 1979, massive resources were allocated to the literacy campaign, which proved greatly successful. One significant factor in this success was the introduction of sex segregation at schools, which led to the conservative parents' approval to send their daughters to school.[7] By 2010, the literacy rate stood at 90.5 for men and 87.5 for women,[8] and research shows that not only do fathers no longer object to their daughters going to school, but they insist on their daughters completing their secondary education, too.[9] However, a series of research projects carried out in earlier decades of the literacy campaign showed that the impact of education on the relationship between the generation of parents and their children had not yielded the anticipated results. For example, a study carried out by the Family Planning Association of the Islamic Republic of Iran (1998), which included a substantial qualitative survey and focus group discussion on reproductive health of 12- to 19-year-old adolescent boys, concluded that: "The knowledge of 15–19 years old boys—the future fathers—in the city of Tehran on matters of puberty, marriage, family planning, and venereal disease is very low. In most cases half of the group is totally ignorant... considering that their present attitude and future practice will be a direct consequence of their knowledge and that their knowledge is relatively better than that of the corresponding age/sex group in other cities, it seems there exists a real problem." Follow-up surveys in 2006 and 2007 confirmed that little had changed during this decade and concluded that the relationship between the fathers and their children remains by and large unchanged, and communication and relationships between fathers and their children remains poor, in general.[10] But, as more recent studies indicate, with the generation of the more educated postrevolutionary men becoming fathers, and with the spread of global media technologies, relationships between the educated children and their less educated fathers are changing, as Ladier-Fouladi's (2002) study confirms. As a result, the one-way pattern of respect for the older generation is also undergoing changes and, in some instances, young people's high level of education and knowledge of modern means of communication have gained them a special place among their elders' kin group and their community. This is especially true in the rural areas, where few people have the knowledge of or access to media technologies. However, this reversal is thus limited and is true of only certain groups in society, with particular levels of education and lifestyles.

Global Technologies and Fatherhood

Beyond the consequences of the demographic changes and the rise in literacy, other global factors, such as the prevalence of satellite television, mobile phones, and the Internet, have had an unanticipated impact on the relationship between fathers and their children. While fathers neither wish to nor are able to prevent their children from accessing these technologies, they remain anxious to retain some control over their children's use of them. To do so, some educated fathers have developed a closer relationship with their children, trying to familiarize themselves with these technologies, with help from their children. Even in such cases, these liberal fathers check their children's computers regularly and secretly to monitor their activity.[11] Other fathers, who are unable to master these technologies, especially the Internet, have become alienated from their children; their frustration is shown in either withdrawing from all activities within the family, or adopting an even more controlling attitude toward their children.

Moving beyond these cases, there are also examples of fathers in their most modern and accommodating, but, in fact, most controlling guise. For example, a few years ago, fathers from Yazd raised funds and built a boarding house in Tehran for their daughters who had been admitted to the university there so that the girls' movements could be controlled. Eric Hoogland's (2007) longitudinal studies of some villages in Fars Province in the central south of Iran refer to fathers who insist on their daughters completing their secondary education, which was initially interpreted as a sign of fathers being modern and enlightened. However, findings of this research show a different side to such fathers' liberal decisions, revealing that it is the fathers' wish to improve their daughters' chances of marriage that drive these decisions. Literature is abundant on how every aspect of both young girls and boys' lives are controlled by their fathers, regardless of the young people's degree of education.

Finally, any attempt to define fatherhood by situating fathers into well-defined categories could lead to confusion, contradiction, and misrepresentation. As is the case elsewhere, Iranian fathers come from a variety of social and cultural backgrounds and are not unanimous in their responses to change. The case studies presented in this chapter illustrate how the fathers' reactions to globalization often turn out to be the opposite of what one might expect of men of their particular backgrounds. For example, the two following cases, of two highly educated fathers from very different social and economic backgrounds, are surprisingly similar.

Mansour is seventy years old and is highly religious, to the point of being fanatical. He has a PhD in economics from a university in the United States and has held high office in the government since the revolution in 1979. His two sons and one daughter were brought up according to the strictest Islamic values and practices until they went to university. Once they graduated from college, they rebelled and started breaking every rule set by their father, by going out with girls, drinking, breaking their religious fast, and gambling. They became contemptuous of their father's "backwards" ideas and called him "moron" behind his back. The daughter took to blogging and found new friends on the Internet, much to her father's horror. When Mansour realized that they were a lost cause and were unlikely to revert to their original upbringing, he first asked them to leave the house, which they refused to do. Like Ali, Mansour was aware that throwing his children out was not a real option, as this would mean a total loss of face and admission to failure as a father. To everyone's surprise, he did not use violence to impose his will on his children. Instead, he let them stay and live the life they wanted but withdrew from any communication with his family and lived a solitary life. He even refused to attend his son's wedding. He is totally alienated and has lost all connectivity with his family. What is left for him is that, to the outside world, he is still seen as the head of his family.

Mohsen shares Mansour's alienation, albeit in a different way and to a different degree. Mohsen is a secular man from a liberal family. He possesses a degree in engineering and is self-employed and financially successful. Soon after the Islamic revolution, Mohsen brought his young children to America because he could not tolerate the "controlling" and "suffocating" atmosphere created by the regime. When his daughter grew up and chose to go to a university outside the town where they lived, Mohsen objected and refused to pay for her education. The mother sided with her daughter and eventually the fights became so intolerable that the family broke up, and his wife and daughter left him. He returned to Iran feeling humiliated and disconnected, until his son, who is a mild-mannered young man, joined him to work under his supervision. Even though Mohsen feels that his status as a father has been restored once more, he has withdrawn from socializing with his large group of relatives as he has not recovered from the humiliation and loss of face he suffered due to his own lack of ability to control his daughter.

The Four Faces of Controlling Fathers

Fathers in this study can be classified into four broad categories. The first category is comprised of resourceful fathers, who foresee and preempt potential disobedience from their children or who, faced with it, go to any length to diffuse the children's rebellion by seeking new solutions. Both Massoud and Karim fall into this group: Massoud pampered his children and bought their respect and compliance through love and affection. Karim realized that the use of force against his disobedient son would only make matters worse; ultimately he changed his life altogether and left Iran.

The second category includes resilient fathers, whose authority is challenged by globalization but who show flexibility and adjust their approaches to retain a degree of control and to ensure their connectivity with their children. Ahmad and Ali are examples of resilient fathers: Ali has no authority over his children but is still able to retain his position as the father figure. Ahmad yields to his children's demands and goes as far as allowing his daughters unlimited access to modern technologies, as long as he can maintain control of the situation. There are similar examples among other patriarchal cultures, whereby fathers, in order to impose their decisions, make surprising compromises. An interesting case was recounted by two British Pakistani men, who were critical of Pakistani fathers' authority and control, on the topic of forced marriage among the Pakistani community in the United Kingdom. They reported that a Pakistani family, in trying to force their son to marry a girl from Pakistan and faced with his objection, made a deal with him that if he agreed to marry the girl they wanted, they would let him marry the girl he wanted, as his second wife.[12]

The third category is comprised of alienated fathers, who refuse to accept their children's aspirations to modernity but do not resort to violence. These fathers become isolated and lose all connectivity with their families, even though some continue to live with their families in the same house. Mansour and Mohsen are two such examples.

Finally, the fourth category comprises violent fathers, for whom physical violence is the only way to counteract any form of disobedience. Mina's, Fatemeh's, and Amir's fathers fall into this category. These cases are not extreme in comparison to tens of others, whose stories are reported regularly by the media, by the authorities themselves, and through the work of charitable organizations. Faced with extreme paternal violence, the children are left with no choice but to run away from home and live in the street, a life that some believe to be better than what they experience back at home. Their stories are echoed in Rachel Baker and Catherine Panter-Brick's (2000) study of street children and the hardship and occasional abuse they encounter while living on the streets, which nevertheless proves safer than living at home and being exposed to systematic abuse by family members. A visit to various charities' web sites in Iran also reveals the extent of violence some families inflict on their children.[13] The following examples are typical of the violence that Iranian fathers inflict on their disobedient children and represent a widespread problem. In one case, described in a confidential report by one of the child protection agencies, a runaway boy was so frightened of his father after having been late attending school that he left home. In another case, a girl fled a forced marriage, ended up in prostitution, and was eventually murdered. During the court trials the father accepted the blood money offered by the murderer and forgave him. But, as he was leaving the court, the judge mentioned that the girl had been raped before being murdered. The loss of his honor proved such a serious blow that the father changed his decision and asked the judge to sentence the man to death. Finally, there is the case of a girl who ran away from domestic violence and took refuge in one of the shelters in Tehran. When the police contacted her father and asked him to collect his daughter, he turned up with a butcher's knife to "wash this stain of shame" for dishonoring the family.

Conclusion

To examine the impact of globalization on fatherhood in Iran's predominantly patriarchal culture, an in-depth study of fathers in three locations was carried out. The findings of the study show that, for men, fatherhood remains the culmination of their personhood and identity, from manhood to masculinity and sexuality (Inhorn 2012; Inhorn et al. 2009; Inhorn, this volume). The findings also reveal that globalization has not dislodged these core cultural values attached to fatherhood and that men's lives are shaped by and become meaningful in their role as fathers and as the custodians of the family and its honor. Losing control over one's children is therefore is not an option and equals a total failure for fathers. Furthermore, faced with globalization, fathers are shown not to be adverse to what modernity has to offer, as long as this does not pose a threat to their authority or disrupt their connectivity with their children. To this end, fathers adopt new strategies to diffuse any potential threats and adjust their behavior toward their children in a variety of ways. However, a close examination of these changes shows that they are not fundamental transformations of the ideals of fatherhood, but mere strategic adjustments, carried out in self-preservation. Furthermore, in spite of these variations and against their diverse sociocultural, political, educational, and religious backgrounds, these fathers share a fundamental interest in retaining control over their children.

In trying to meet their children's aspiration for modernity, fathers respond in unconventional and unexpected ways that do not fit certain stereotypes, such as conservative fathers resisting change and liberal fathers embracing it. In some cases, the religious and/or conservative fathers show incredible tolerance in meeting the aspirations of their children, and the secular and educated ones lack flexibility, resisting their children's most basic demands. The responses of fathers fall into four categories: the resourceful father finds new solutions to ensure his authority; the resilient father accommodates his children's demands to a certain extent; the alienated father lacks flexibility, saving face but losing connectivity with his children; finally, violent fathers resist change completely and resort to physical abuse. Furthermore, fathers who accommodate their children's demands are shown to retain control more successfully than those who refuse to adjust. For these inflexible fathers, isolation is the price to pay for saving face, and fatherhood for them is just an empty shell. Regardless, the father figure remains an omnipresent force for the children. Although the fear and obedience that fathers commanded, traditionally, are gradually receding, children's respect for their fathers remains intact and prevents children from confronting their fathers.

However, as young people's aspirations continue to move toward a more globalized lifestyle, the boundaries of the relationship between fathers and their children are likely to shift and require renegotiation. Further research is needed to discover whether the future generation of fathers will be fundamentally different and will forgo this strong desire to control and exercise authority over their children.

Notes

1. For more details see Abbasi-Shavazi (2001) and Tremayne (2004).
2. For example see Miller (2006) on digital and mobile technologies, Unnithan-Kumar (2010) and Tremayne (2012) on reproductive technologies, and Parkin (2012).
3. As Ebadi (2004: 79) explains, if a father or paternal grandfather kills his child, he can only pay the blood money. The mother has no right to take him to court and must be content with this blood money. This biased law applies only to the father and grandfather but not the mother. If the mother kills her child, the father can request her death sentence. Ziba Mir-Hosseini (1993) also discusses the fact that in Shia Islam, although a child takes his filiation and parentage from both the father and mother, it is the paternal side that has ascendancy over the maternal. The father is, therefore, the central figure and the children are considered his property. In Mir-Hosseini's words, "In all schools of Islamic law the primary significance of filiation and parentage is that of paternity, closely tied to legitimacy, through which a child acquires its legal identity and its religion" (136). The Iranian Civil Code (Article 1170) further confirms that mothers' access to children in the case of divorce and custody is severely restricted. The following website also highlights fathers' uncontested rights over their children, through the lens of runaway children: http://childrenofiran.wordpress.com/about/orphans-vulnerable-children/. However, despite Iran's being a signatory to the Convention on the Rights of the Child, children do not in reality have any rights in Iran: the rights of a child are given to his or her parents. If a child is being abused by anyone, it is rare to get attention unless the parents claim that someone is abusing the child. If a parent is abusive, there are simply no laws to protect the child against the parent. Many children die each year in Iran because of the abuse of their parents. What makes the situation worse is the fact that women do not have any rights to defend their children nor themselves against abusive fathers and in many cases against other abusers.
4. However, in one of her more recent studies, Azadeh Kian-Thiébault (2012) revised her statements about the weakening of patriarchy.
5. Temporary marriage bears a time limit; when this time expires, the marriage automatically becomes null.
6. The importance of respect was also emphasized by anthropologist Soheila Shahshahani during a recent conversation in September 2012.

7. For more details of the education campaign, see Golnar Mehran (2003) and Amir Mehryar (1998).
8. The exact literacy rate varies depending on how it is measured, but these are general figures according to United Nations Educational, Scientific, and Cultural Organization records: http://www.accu.or.jp/litd base/policy/irn/index.htm.
9. See, for example, Hoogland (2007).
10. See, for example, the reports available at: http://www.who.int/repro ductivehealth/publications/adolescence/boys_iran.pdf and http://www .prb.org/pdf07/menayouthreproductivehealth.pdf.
11. A lecture given by Nadia Aghtai, at Women's Rights in the Middle East Seminars, St. Antony's College, University of Oxford, in February 2012, confirmed similar reactions by husbands in Iran, who secretly check their wives' computers to find out who they are in touch with via the Internet.
12. Interview with a Pakistani lawyer with BBC's Radio 4, 13 August 2012.
13. For example, among tens of similar charities, see Omid-Mehr's, a charity that houses tens of runaway girls, most of whom fled abuse from family members, predominantly fathers: http://www.omid-e-mehr.org/.

References

Abbasi-Shavazi, Mohammad Jalal. 2001. "'La fécondité en Iran: l'autre revolution' *Population et société* : 373, 1–4. Also http://www.un.org/esa/ population/publications/completingfertility/2RevisedABBASIpaper.

Baker, Rachel, and Catherine Panter-Brick. 2000. "A Comparative Perspective on Children's 'Careers' and Abandonment in Nepal." In *Abandoned Children*, ed. Catherine Panter-Brick and Malcolm T. Smith. Cambridge: Cambridge University Press.

Daniel, Elton L., and Ali Akbar Mahdi. 2006. *Culture and Customs of Iran.* Westport, CT; London: Greenwood Press

Ebadi, Shirin. 2002. "Serious Steps Taken to Enforce Children's Rights Convention." Iranian News Agency. 26 May.

———. 2004. *History and Documentation of Human Rights in Iran.* Tehran: Roshangaran and Women's Studies Publishing.

Family Planning Association of the Islamic Republic of Iran. 1998. "Reproductive Health Needs Assessment of Adolescent Boys." 23.

Hoogland, Eric. 2007. "Changes in an Iranian Village, Aliabad." Lecture delivered at conference on *Iran on the Move*, Leiden University.

Inhorn, Marcia C. 2012. *The New Arab Man: Emergent Masculinities, Technologies, and Islam in the Middle East.* Princeton: Princeton University Press.

Inhorn, Marcia C., Tine Tjørnhøj-Thomsen, Helene Goldberg, and Maruska la Cour Mosegaard, eds. 2009. *Reconceiving the Second Sex: Men, Masculinity, and Reproduction.* New York; Oxford: Berghahn Books.

Jalali, Behnaz. 2005. "Iranian Families." In *Ethnicity & Family Therapy*, ed. Monica McGoldrick, Joe Giordano, and Nydia Garcia-Preto. New York: Guilford Press.

Joseph, Suad, ed. 1999. *Intimate Selving in Arab Families: Gender, Self and Identity*. Syracuse, NY: Syracuse University Press.

Kian-Thiébault, Azadeh. 2005. "From Motherhood to Equal Rights Advocates: The Weakening of Patriarchal Order." *Iranian Studies* 38, no. 1: 45–66.

———. 2012. "Gendered Citizenship and the Women's Movement in Iran." In *Iran: A Revolutionary Republic in Transition*, ed. Farideh Farhi, Azadeh Kian, Rouzbeh Parsi, Evaleila Pesaran, and Paola Rivetti. European Union Institute for Security Studies, February.

Kousha, Mahnaz. 2002. *Voices from Iran: The Changing Lives of Iranian Women*. Syracuse, NY: Syracuse University Press.

Ladier-Fouladi, Marie. 2002. "Iranian Families between Demographic Change and the Birth of the Welfare State." *Population* 57, no. 2: 361–70.

Mehran, Golnar. 2003. "Gender and Education in Iran." Paper commissioned for the EFA Global Monitoring Report 2003/4, The Leap to Equality.

Mehryar, Amir. 1998. "Draft Country Population Assessment Report." Plan Organization of Iran, unpublished and with limited circulation.

Miller, Danny, and Heather Horst. 2006. *The Cell Phone: An Anthropology of Communication*. Berg: Oxford.

Mir-Hosseini, Ziba. 1993. *Marriage on Trial: A Study of Islamic Family Law*. London: I. B. Tauris.

Parkin, Robert, and James Wilker, eds. 2012. *Modalities of Change: The Interface of Tradition and Modernity in East Asia*. New York; Oxford: Berghahn Books.

Price, Massoume. 2006. "Patriarchy and Parental Control in Iran." Iran Chamber Society.

Sheykhi, Mohammad Taghi. 2009. "Children as a Source of Happiness within the Iranian Families: Profiles and Challenges." *African Journal of Political Science and International Relations* 3, no. 11: 526–31.

Stephenson, Rob, Payam Sheikhattari, Nazilla Assasi, Hassan Eftekhar, Qasem Zamani, Bahram Maleki, and Hamid Kiabayan. 2006. "Child Maltreatment among School Children in the Kurdistan Province, Iran." *Child Abuse & Neglect* 30, no. 3: 231–45.

Tremayne, Soraya. 2004. "And Never the Twain Shall Meet: Reproductive Health Policies of the Islamic Republic of Iran." In *Reproductive Agency, Medicine and the State: Cultural Transformations in Childbearing*, ed. Maya Unnithan-Kumar. New York; Oxford: Berghahn Books.

———. 2006a. "Change and 'Face' in Modern Iran." *Journal of the Anthropology of the Middle East* 1, no. 1: 25–41.

———. 2006b. "Modernity and Early Marriage in Iran: A View From Within." *Journal of Middle East Women Studies* 2, no. 1: 65–95.

———. 2009. "Law, Ethics and Donor Technologies in Shia Iran." In *Assisting Reproduction, Testing Genes: Global Encounters with New Biotechnologies*, ed. Daphna Birenbaum-Carmeli and Marcia C. Inhorn. New York; Oxford: Berghahn Books.

———. 2012. "The 'Down Side' of Gamete Donation: Challenging 'Happy Family' Rhetoric in Iran." In *Islam and Assisted Reproductive Technologies: Sunni and Shia Perspectives,* ed. Marcia C. Inhorn and Soraya Tremayne. New York; Oxford: Berghahn Books.

United Nations Population Fund. 2011. "Country Report."

Unnithan-Kumar, Maya, ed. 2004. *Reproductive Agency, Medicine and the State: Cultural Transformations in Childbearing.* New York; Oxford: Berghahn Books.

———. 2012. "Learning from Infertility: Gender, Health Inequities and Faith Healers in Women's Experiences of Disrupted Reproduction in Rajasthan." *South Asian History and Culture* 1 (2): 315–267.

Part VIII

IMPERILED FATHERHOOD

Chapter 15

"BARE STICKS" AND OTHER DANGERS TO THE SOCIAL BODY

ASSEMBLING FATHERHOOD IN CHINA

Susan Greenhalgh

Introduction

For a culture that loves numerology, the date 11/11/11—six lonely ones—was made in heaven. A major pop culture holiday, 11 November 2011, was billed as the biggest *guanggun jie* ("bare sticks" day) of the century. Created in the early 1990s by college students to mark the plight of men who cannot find a spouse (known in Chinese as *guanggun,* or bare branches, because they have not married and produced offshoots), the holiday was the occasion for aggressive marketing, online advertising of profiles, and the appearance of vertical "sticks" on the landscape of major cities around the country. In a country where potential grooms greatly outnumber potential brides, marriage costs (especially for the groom) have skyrocketed, and young people are on the move spatially and economically, the holiday is but one part of a larger, urban-centered culture that seems to be obsessed with mate-finding. For the marriage-anxious, there are huge matchmaking fairs, television dating shows, dating coaches, and countless online dating web sites to consult.

Chinese men's (and their parents') obsession with mate-finding reflects an increasingly male-heavy gender imbalance due in large part to three decades of the one-child policy enforced in the masculinist culture of a globalizing China. Because many rural parents have aborted or otherwise disposed of their daughters, in China today there are 118 boys for every 100 girls born, the highest sex ratio at birth of any major country. Experts estimate that 10.4 percent of men who should marry between 2005 and 2025 will not be able to marry in the conventional way. If the marriage problems of older urban men are serious, those of older rural men, especially in the poorer regions of the country, are dire. Rural men face two almost insuperable additional problems: the massive, usually long-term out-migration of rural women to the cities, and the huge urban-rural income gap, which gives urban men an advantage in meeting the often heavy demands of brides' families (these days, for a house, a car, and a good-paying job). (Some, of course, migrate to the cities themselves, but many must remain in the villages to meet family obligations.) Older rural men are the barest of bare sticks. They remain culturally invisible. As far as I can tell, no retailer is marketing to them. And no one plants sticks in their yards on *guanggun* day.

Although small numbers of urban Chinese are now opting to remain childless, marriage and fatherhood are still essential to being a "real Chinese man." This is undoubtedly especially true in the countryside. The limited literature on masculinities in China suggests that, despite the growing preoccupation since the 1990s with sexuality, the traditional arenas of marriage and family remain central to the construction of men's gender identities (Brownell and Wasserstrom 2002). Despite the rise in divorce, for men, marrying and perpetuating the family line remains a social imperative. By definition, men who do not marry and rear children cannot be "good men." Although the situation is in flux, in the countryside, having a wife and (at least one) child remains essential for social and even physical survival. Most critically, wives and children are crucial parts of the farm family labor force. Children provide crucial support in old age.

This volume is about fatherhood, but my chapter necessarily focuses on the prior question of the conditions of possibility of fatherhood, especially for China's rural men. For a number of reasons—including the continued sensitivity of the one-child policy, and the Chinese Communist Party's practice of not addressing social issues until they reach urgent level—there is as yet no official framing of the *guanggun* issue or state policy on the matter. A late 2013 interview with China's top birth planning official suggests that this is unlikely to change soon. The reality of men's lives, as well as the official, scholarly, and popular perceptions, can be perceived only dimly, at best. Even the name for this problem is not settled. One never hears talk of a "fathering crisis"; instead, one reads of the problem of the "men who cannot find brides," the "bare sticks," and, in academic work, the "involuntary bachelors." Though the naming and framing are in flux, what seems to be a problem—at least for those with a public voice—is not the quality of fathering but whether a man is able to rear a child. In this chapter I draw on media items, official sources, leader speeches, scientific research, and my own interviews in China, to sketch the outlines of the emergent field of thought and practice surrounding the *guanggun*. This inquiry helps us understand the troubling reality that, despite the dire conditions these older rural men face, their problems scarcely register in the public and official consciousness in China.

In this chapter I examine how this problem-space of excess masculinity (or potential non-fatherhood) is coming together in China. Since the economist Amartya Sen (1989; 1990) published his pathbreaking work on "the missing women" of Asia two decades ago, the distorted sex ratio at birth has become a globally recognized problem, with many experts and policymakers—especially in the international development community—reflecting on and responding to it. Not only in China, but across Asia, the masculinization of sex ratios has been proceeding at a pace unprecedented in recorded history. Male-heavy sex ratios are rising throughout the region, reaching levels ranging from 112 boys per 100 girls in India, Pakistan, and Vietnam, to 120 to 121 in tiny Azerbaijan and Armenia (the international average is 105 to 106) (Guilmoto 2009).[1] Far from mere social or demographic "facts," in each region, the numbers are framed or problematized (and even collected) in particular ways that reflect local histories, cultures, sciences, and politics. Put another way, in each area, the numbers combine with local histories into distinctive assemblages, out of which the problem is articulated by actors in technoscientific, political, and cultural discourse. By articulated I mean they are problematized—that is, reflected upon and intervened in in particular ways (cf. Ong and Collier 2005). My interest here then lies not in the messy social world of the "surplus men"; it lies instead in how that world is being understood and acted upon by actors with the power to shape dominant societal discourses and policies toward them.

As Bruno Latour (2005), among others, has argued, the notion of assemblage captures the real-world contingency, heterogeneity, and instability of the things that actually go into the making of problematizations and social life. More formally, by "assemblage," I mean the loose collection of heterogeneous, often incommensurate elements that come together for a period of time, sometimes quite fleeting, to produce a particular articulation of a social problem.

Studying assemblages requires a distinctive methodology and benefits from a particular expository structure. Conventionally, scholars doing qualitative research employ narrative modes of explanation and craft social scientific accounts that tell a particular story about the world they study. The story is often historically arranged, with a beginning, middle, and end. In studying an assemblage one instead brings together diverse, often incommensurate, and apparently unconnected elements of social life, with the intention of showing how a particular problem-space has been raggedly constituted. Both theoretical literatures and my prior work on China's population policy (Greenhalgh 2008) suggest that the most important clusters of elements are particular cultures, politics, and technosciences.

In this chapter, I bring together some of the diverse histories, cultures, politics, and technosciences that form the assemblage that is shaping how the problem is being framed in China. Instead of relating a straightforward story or history, I introduce each element in a separate section, suggesting its impact on an emerging problem-space, and then bring together the intersections of all the elements in the conclusion. What I can offer, of course, is but a partial accounting of some of the most important elements of the assemblage forming around the bare sticks today. I ask two sets of questions: First, which specific histories, cultures, and so on are coming together to form the assemblage around the bare sticks? Second, how is the problem being defined, reflected on, and intervened in within technoscientific and political discourse?[2] These reflections and interventions are highly consequential, helping to constitute the very field that is emerging. Such an analysis, and the notion of assemblage that underlies it, not only help us see the outlines of a sociopolitical field in the making, they also move us beyond the dominant approaches to this issue today—the demography of the sex ratio and the feminist analysis of gendered inequalities—to see the larger, multidimensional constellation of forces that is at work in the making of Chinese men's lives, and the contingency of their interactions and effects. Equally important, it illuminates what is at stake in how this issue is being articulated, including the reproductive prospects of rural men. Fatherhood is not normally discussed in these terms, but I hope to show that they are highly productive, bringing out the role of technosciences and elite politics in the construction of official framings and interventions that shape identities and practices on the ground.

A "Modern Population": Global Aspirations

The roots of today's "*guanggun* problem" (for lack of a better name) can be traced to the early reform years (the late 1970s to early 1980s), when the new modernizing regime of Deng Xiaoping sought to transform China's "backward," largely rural population into a modern populace suitable to a global power. In Deng's scheme, that modern population would both foster, and in turn reflect, China's status as a rich, globally prominent nation. It was Michel Foucault (1978), of course, who first illuminated the centrality of a biopolitics of the population to the making of power and governance in the modern era, when, he argued, life itself has become a central object of power. Elsewhere I have argued that post-Mao China, with its still-strong state and its ambitious, globalizing agenda, provides the world's most striking case of the rapid "governmentalization" of population and the emergence of a vast biopolitical field aimed at administering and optimizing the vital attributes of human life at the collective level (Greenhalgh and Winckler 2005).

Though generally treated as a naturalized object, a biological entity of no particular interest to human scientists, "population" is a technophenomenon, the product of technologies of science and governance created by situated human actors (Lock and Nguyen 2010). In China's case, the type of population sought was a deliberate product of human design—indeed, the term social engineering is not too strong—created in a particular historical context by specific scientific and political, human (and non-human) actors. Mao Zedong's Cultural Revolution (1966–76) had taken China to the brink of disaster. In the late 1970s, an ambitious new Deng party eager to overcome Mao's ideological legacy turned to what it deemed the opposite, Western science and technology, as the basis for its modernization agenda. Science would be the source of the party's truth claims and the basis for the Deng party's right to rule in the new era. Ultimately, the problem of the childless men stems from the scientific history of the new, Deng-era policy on population.

The work of mapping out a new, modern population fell to a group of newly designated population scientists in the social sciences, mostly statisticians and economists. As China's goal was to take its place among the advanced industrial nations, it is not surprising that the new specialists took the populations of Western nations such as the United States, Great Britain, France, and Japan as the global norm and the model for China. Using United Nations publications and other statistical materials and textbooks that flooded into the

country after a long data drought under Mao, they determined that
a modern population was one with low growth and fertility rates,
low death and infant mortality rates, a balanced age structure, and
an urban distribution. The special (in the sense of peculiar) characteristics (*tedian*) of China's population—the things that marked it
as "backward" and were thus targeted for change—were its rapid
growth, its gargantuan size, its peasant character, and its young,
double-peaked age structure. Although the new population experts
calculated age-sex structures, in establishing the goals for the new
population, they emphasized the age structure. This was deemed
important because the age distribution had been greatly distorted by
the Great Leap Forward and Cultural Revolution; if left unchanged,
the lumpy age structure would cause distortions in labor force and
dependency ratio (of workers to dependents) for decades to come,
slowing the nation's modernization.

By contrast, according to interviews and literature produced at
the time, the sex structure of the population was little discussed.
The sex ratio at birth was not a norm at all. Whether because the sex
ratio among infants was not a measure of demographic modernity
in international demography, because China's ratio appeared to be
relatively normal at the time, or because the possibility of female infanticide was far too politically sensitive to air, in planning the population that would be the target of state policy, the framers of China's
"modern population" did not establish a normative sex ratio at birth.
This meant, among other things, that the sex ratio at birth would not
be measured, at least for over a decade; in a very literal sense, *it did
not count*. It meant too that the sex ratio among infants would not be
deliberately engineered; instead, it would be a political and cultural
byproduct of the engineering of other population characteristics.

"No Other Choice": The One-Child Policy

In China and around the world, it is widely believed that the one-
child policy was China's demographic destiny—that because of rapid
population growth under Mao, the nation's post-Mao leaders had
no alternative but to limit all couples to one child. Yet far from de-
mographically determined, both the policy that was adopted and its
framing in political and scientific discourse were products of particular scientific logics and political choices. I can sketch only the
barest outlines of those connections here. If social scientists created
a map of the ideal population, it was a group of natural scientists,

missile experts with expertise in cybernetics and connections to the top leadership, who fashioned the core policy on population. Drawing on the population alarmist writings of the Club of Rome (think Paul Ehrlich [1968] and the "population bomb"), the scientists created a narrative of "population crisis," in which China was drowning in human numbers. Using cybernetic techniques and population numbers that were mere estimates, they argued that the nation's economic prosperity, global rise, and very survival were threatened by a demographic time bomb. Such a crisis, they argued, could only be averted by a drastic policy placing sharp limits on all couples. The state would take charge of population countrywide, creating a program in which not only material production, but also human reproduction, would come within the purview of state planning.

That policy—also a product of cybernetic equations—called for drastically reducing population growth by limiting all couples to one child, beginning immediately. In a protracted process of political debate and scientific struggle that lasted about six months in 1979–80, there were protests from many quarters. Many declared the one-child rule unenforceable in the countryside. Others insisted that the peasants would be ruined if their family labor and old-age security systems were undermined by such a radical policy. To overcome widespread doubts, the scientists developed a powerful framing in which the one-child policy was not a "good policy," but given the economic and demographic crises facing the nation, it was China's "only choice." Advocacy of single children was officially adopted in late 1980, and in 1982 it was designated one of a handful of "basic state policies," off limits to criticism from anyone.

The policy was to be phased in gradually. In 1981 and 1982 it would be implemented in the cities, where fertility was already low. Then in 1983 it would be carried out across the vast countryside, where childbearing and fertility desires were much higher. The vehicle would be a nationwide mass-mobilizational campaign aimed at sterilizing one member of all couples with two or more children, putting IUDs in women with one child, and aborting all unauthorized pregnancies. The rural campaign, which relied on physical coercion, backfired, as rural couples desperate to have a son began attacking rural birth planning cadres and disposing of their baby girls. To save the lives of little girls and to rescue its own legitimacy, the party-state quietly modified the policy to allow rural couples whose first child was a girl to have a second. This "1.5-child policy" was adopted on a trial basis in 1984, and in 1988 it was extended countrywide. Official "advocacy" of single-child families was encoded in the National Population and Birth Planning Law of 2001–02 and remains in place today.

From the beginning, there were many, especially in the social science community, who abhorred the policy, decrying its effects on rural women, families, and livelihoods. These voices were publicly silenced for decades, emerging only during short periods when debate was allowed. Since the turn of the century, as the sex and age structures have become ever more distorted by the rapid fertility decline (see below), many voices have been arguing, increasingly openly, that the social and economic costs of the one-child-with-exceptions policy are so severe that the state should move to a two-child policy as soon as possible (F. Wang 2005; 2011; Zeng 2007).

For a regime that has asked generations of Chinese to sacrifice fundamental family-building aspirations for the greater good of the nation, and taught them that China had "no other choice," a wholesale change in the policy would carry substantial political risks. Despite growing calls for change, the regime has held fast to the one-child-with-exceptions policy, while expanding the exceptions. In October 2011, Population Minister Li Bin announced that China would stick to the existing policy while working to advance population quality (improve gender and age structure, as well as reduce infant birth defects) (Xinhua 2011c). In the meantime, however, there has been a quiet shift underway to a two-child policy for certain couples (a change seen as conforming to the one-child-with-exceptions policy). By late 2011, all thirty-one provincial-level units allowed couples composed of two single children to have two children of their own (Xinhua 2011b). In late 2013, the state announced that couples in which just one parent was an only child would be allowed a second child. This was an important policy shift, but it is expected to have only a modest impact on the birth rate. For many couples, the high costs of child rearing in China today make having two financially impossible (Levin 2014). Both this "only choice" framing of the one-child policy and its political sensitivity have meant that talk of its adverse effects was not especially welcome. Only some unwanted effects would get constituted as problems worth attention. The "surplus men" would not be framed as a problem until a very late date.

"Surplus Men": The Numbers

The notion that China has a "surplus of men" is the product of China's socialist development-planning model, which assumes near-equality of the sexes and requires planning by the state to remediate any "imbalances." The problems of the gender gap and male marriage deficit are also a product of particular scientific counting schemes and bodily technologies (discussed just below). Following the international scientific norm, the core measure is the sex ratio at birth, which gives the number of boys born per 100 girls born, uncontrolled for behavioral factors such as the conventional age gap between husband and wife. Since the introduction of the one-child policy in 1979–80, that number has been steadily rising, climbing from 108.5 boys per 100 girls in 1982 to 118 in 2011, far outstripping the international average of 105 to 106. The China-wide average, worrying though it is, understates the extent of the problem in some areas, especially poor, rural ones. A county-level analysis of the ratio among children aged zero to four reveals a national average of 120.2, but spatial clusters of counties in which the ratio ranges from 150 to 197.2 to 100. In those areas, scattered around the poorer regions of east, central, and south China, there are now three or four boys for every two girls (Cai and Lavely 2007).

Although the fundamental cause of the growing gap between the genders remains little changed—a male-centered culture and political economy—the immediate behavioral factors underlying the imbalance have changed over time. In the very early years, infanticide and the short-term concealment of girls were important; since the mid-to-late 1980s the major "proximate cause" of the distorted sex ratio has been prenatal sex determination followed by sex-selective abortion (Chu 2001). The key technology in this new techno-phenomenon is the ultrasound scanner, available throughout the countryside since the mid 1980s, which allows identification of the sex of the fetus by around the fourth month. In areas of the country where fieldwork has been done, the scanning of fetuses, especially of second children, has become a routine part of the culture of family formation (Chu 2001).

The disappearance of girls from China's male-centered society, coupled with the rapid rise in marriage costs, has led to a growing crisis for men unable to find brides. Demographic research indicates that, of the cohorts born between 1980 and 2000—those expected to marry between 2005 and 2025—there is an excess of 22 million men, meaning that 10.4 percent of all men will fail to marry in the traditional way. Those affected appear to be mainly poor, ill-educated men from the rural areas. These "surplus men," as they are called in state planning speak, are overwhelmingly poor, illiterate, and rural. For these men, and perhaps for the nation, these numbers portend a real-world social crisis of monumental proportion.

One interesting aspect of these numbers is the state's public silence about them. The rise in the sex ratio at birth was not even acknowledged by the population establishment until around 1993, when the fertility rate fell to below replacement level, allowing the regime to address some of the adverse consequences of rapid fertility decline. Today, the media are constantly flooded with social and economic statistics demonstrating the nation's modernization and global advance, yet, with the exception of a short period around 2007, statistics on the sex ratio and number of older rural bachelors have rarely been publicized. Until very recently, when the campaigns against sex-selective abortion and human trafficking (described below) have picked up, the numbers were surrounded by a stark silence.

Guanggun: Cultural Histories

The term *"guanggun"* may have been appropriated recently for commercial purposes, but it holds much deeper, historically rooted cultural meanings. The "bare stick" was one of the most pitiable figures on the social landscape of pre-Communist China. Poor and ill educated, village men who had no wife, no children, and no way to fulfill their filial duties had no place in the social order. In the eyes of most Chinese, an unmarried and sonless man was consigned to being a perpetual adolescent, unable to become a true adult or a man (R. Watson 1986). In the early years of the People's Republic, such people-out-of-place largely disappeared, only to reappear after Mao's death.

"Guanggun" meant not only unattached, but also outcast and vaguely if not explicitly threatening to public order. Throughout late imperial and Republican-era Chinese history, the bare sticks were widely disparaged and even feared. That is because marriage and family tied men to their village community; those without family connections were seen as itinerant, unsettled, untrustworthy, and threatening to the social order. Work on bandits and rebels suggests that unattached men on the margins of lineage and village life, and unable to fulfill gender expectations, often engaged in petty violence and took on the role of village bullies. Sometimes they formed heterodox groupings such as rebel bands and secret societies (Ownby 1996; 2002). At other times they formed fraternal associations, that, according to the work of historians and anthropologists, involved people banding together for mutual aid and protection, rather than

gangs of criminals or rebel bands challenging authority (J. Watson 1989). Although these groups appear to have been at least as much about mutual support as about petty to serious violence, in popular lore the *guanggun* were known as bullies, bandits, and rebels. Informal conversations with colleagues in China suggest that these associations linger, subtly shaping cultural and political constructions of the *guanggun* as a contemporary problem.

"Women": State Logics and Practices of Gender

After over a decade of silence, in the early 1990s, the party-state began quietly addressing the growing gender gap; a decade later, it put the sex ratio at birth on the public policy agenda. This pattern of state care has a certain logic. As noted above, in the early reform years, the party-state took charge of the Chinese population, taking upon itself for the first time responsibility for using science to foster a biologically optimal population. Following a Foucauldian logic, if only implicitly, the goal operated at two biopolitical poles—improving the welfare of the Chinese people (an anatamo-politics of the body) and boosting the nation's place on world stage (the field of biopolitics proper). Drawing on a series of Western population sciences, the state set its initial bio-goal as solving the crisis of "too rapid population growth" (the quantity problem). As rapid fertility decline in the 1980s and early 1990s led to not only below-replacement fertility but also a widening gender gap and accelerated aging, the state added a second bio-commitment: ensuring a reasonable age-sex structure of the population. A distorted age-sex structure would create havoc in state development planning and in people's lives as they sought to marry, raise one or two children, and create a good life for themselves. A distorted sex structure in the reproductive age group would mean some would be unable to marry—a disaster for the regime as much as for the individuals involved.

The commitment to fostering a "quality" population structure was also part of China's responsibility to the world at large. China takes its international reputation with utmost seriousness; in a world in which major transnational development agencies, such as the United Nations Children's Fund, the United Nations Population Fund, and the World Bank, are constantly stressing gender equity and the "missing girls," righting the sex structure is a crucial piece of China's emergence as a responsible member of the world community of nations. State legitimacy, then—in the eyes of the people and of the transnational social policy community—now hinges in part on righting the gender imbalance and so bringing the population into quality state.

How, then, would the party-state tackle this thorny problem? After years of public denial, around 2000 China's government finally began to openly acknowledge the gender imbalance problem and place it on the policy agenda. The socially oriented administration of Hu Jintao and Wen Jiabao (2003–12) made arresting the rise in the sex ratio at birth a top priority and, drawing on the work of expert advisors, introduced numerous laws, policies, and programs to enhance the well-being of young girls and women (Greenhalgh and Winckler 2005; Shen 2008). Given China's longstanding commitment to making women equal to men, it is perhaps not surprising that the issue of the sex ratio at birth was fitted into preexisting Marxian framings of the woman question. Following well-established constructions of "women's subordination," in the official and scientific framing, the missing girls problem is attributed most basically to feudal culture (*zhongnan qingnu*, "valuing males, devaluing females"); the solution is for the party-state to promote advanced gender-equitable culture, support women's continued liberation, and protect women, guaranteeing their constitutional equality with men. In support of this agenda, in 1995 "male-female equality" was made one of only a handful of top-priority "basic state policies" (Zhao and Qiu 2008).

Formalizing the approach, an important 2007 decision on population set out a wide range of educational, social, economic, and legal responses to "comprehensively address the abnormal sex ratio at birth" (China 2007). The birth establishment has initiated a broad set of activities designed to eliminate discrimination against girls and women and improve their status in the family and society. These include a massive propaganda effort aimed at reducing son preference and promoting gender equality, wide-ranging programs to improve job and other opportunities for women, and a much-publicized Action to Foster (or Care for) Girls designed to boost their well-being through preferential treatment for rural girl-child families that have accepted birth planning. On the legal front, the state has worked hard to popularize legal knowledge about the protection of the legitimate rights and interests of women and children.

Beyond these two approaches—involving cultural change and socioeconomic incentives—since the early 1990s, the state has also relied on law-and-order measures to crack down on medical workers who engage in illegal sex determination and sex-selective abortion for non-medical reasons. In August 2011, the Population Commission, together with the Ministries of Health and Public Security, launched an eight-month nationwide campaign to reduce the incidence of these "two illegals" (*China Daily* 2012). As of May 2012, according to the Minister of Population, authorities had investigated fifteen thousand cases and punished thirteen thousand people for violating the law (Xinhua 2012b). These numbers are likely to represent a small fraction of the total number of cases of illegal gender manipulation. Officials were clearly not satisfied with the results, for the campaign was extended (*China Daily* 2012; Xinhua 2012b). With legislators in the National People's Congress calling for harsher methods—including crippling fines and multiyear jail terms (Xinhua 2012a)—this law-and-order approach, which relies on criminalizing gender-biased medical practices, is likely to remain a major plank in the state's approach to the problem for some time to come.

In addition to these measures, the state has introduced two other important measures designed in part to normalize the sex ratio among infants (and reduce rural fertility). First, it has greatly improved the rural social security system (including old-age pensions), hoping to discourage parents' preference for boys to support them in old age. And second, it has quietly softened the birth policy to allow couples made up of two single children or, more recently, containing one single child, to have two offspring of their own.

In the mid 2010s, the distorted gender structure is a growing concern, as the number of men unable to find brides rises year by year and the social problems they face—and cause—become more visible. Today the gender gap is one of "five major population problems" the population establishment is addressing (Xinhua 2011a). Reflecting concern that the state will not achieve its goal of lowering the sex ratio at birth to 115 by 2015, 2012 was designated the Year of Focused Management of the Sex Ratio at Birth (Y. Wang 2012). With state support, many foreign and Chinese non-governmental organizations have flooded into the field of girl-care. How effective these efforts have been or will be remains unclear. Although the officially measured ratio has fallen recently—from a high of 120.56 in 2008 to 117.78 in 2011—it is not clear if this decline is real or an artifact of measurement procedures (Xinhua 2012b). What one can say with certainty is that, in a larger culture and political economy that in many ways encourage discrimination against girls and women, restoring the sex ratio to normal is likely to be a long-term prospect indeed.

Effectiveness aside, two things are striking about these measures. First, virtually all of them aim to normalize the sex ratio at birth in the future. None addresses the gender gap among children or young adults today. Second, following dominant party framings, all are addressed to helping women and girls; none is aimed at alleviating the problems of men, in particular, the men who cannot find brides. These efforts—which are part of a much larger package of policies, programs, and ten-year development plans for women—are critical to the legitimacy of a party-state that has made "male-female equality" part of its foundational charter. Men are the unmarked, presumably advantaged, comparison group. This difference in official attention is rooted in part in Chinese Marxism, in which gender equates with women, and gender policies with helping women (and girls). Men (or "patriarchy" or "son preference") are positioned as the problem, the object of party and state ire. In practice—if not in official policy—men are treated as much less worthy of humanitarian care or support and concern.

The rural men who cannot find brides suffer not only from their maleness, but also, and equally importantly, from their peasantness. Although there is not space to elaborate here, in the reform decades, rural people have been positioned as "backward" in the Chinese scheme of things, hindrances to the nation's modernization and upward mobility. As the divide between rural and urban has widened, rural people, and especially poor, ill-educated villagers, are seen not as treasured resources who might contribute to the nation's goals, but as problems to be dispensed with as quickly as possible (Cohen 1993; Gaetano and Jacka 2004; Kelliher 1994; Whyte et al. 2010). Far from deserving official support, they are viewed as deeply unworthy of much consideration or care. For the rural bachelors, gender differences have interacted with rural/urban inequalities to place them apparently beyond care and support.

"Social Stability": Western Science and Party Priorities

Given the centrality of marriage and family in Chinese society, the inability of growing numbers of men to form families has worrying implications for China's future. Just as scientific logics shaped the one-child policy, they have also shaped official thinking about which of those implications should matter for politics and state policy. For many years, Chinese social scientists have been hampered by state restrictions on this sensitive topic, but Western scholars in security studies, demography, and public health have plunged into the issue, creating a narrative in which growing numbers of bachelors will form a mobile army of violent males that will threaten China's sociopolitical stability and perhaps make it more bellicose abroad. In the absence of concrete data on how the surplus men are coping on the ground, the scholarly literature has drawn on theoretical insights, historical precedents, scattered journalistic reports, and survey data on other groups to assess the implications. In their influential book, *Bare Branches: The Security Implications of Asia's Surplus Male Population,* security scholars Valerie M. Hudson and Andrea M. Den Boer (2004) foresee the spread of violent crime—from smuggling and prostitution to robbery, rape, and murder—and the export of violence to neighboring countries (see also Ebenstein and Jennings 2009; Edlund et al. 2007). Public health researchers and demographers warn of the potential for an HIV/AIDS epidemic of previously unimagined scale, as the surplus men migrate to cities to have sex with commercial sex workers, risking contracting HIV and becoming a bridge population from high- to low-risk individuals (Ebenstein and Jennings 2009; Poston and Zhang 2009; Tucker et al. 2005).

The scientific figure of the sex-starved, violence-prone rural bachelor accords with the Chinese Communist Party's own rural imaginary, at least the one that became public for a short time a few years ago. In January 2007, the party's Central Committee and the governmental State Council issued a report saying that the gender ratio imbalance amounted to a "hidden danger" for society that "will affect social stability" (*China Daily* 2007), an obsession of the ruling party. Reflecting the top leadership's official security framing, in 2007 and 2008 the population establishment began articulating a narrative of impending demographic crisis in which a large mass of potentially violent unmarried men constitutes a "social time bomb" (*China Daily* 2007) that threatens the regime's cherished goals of creating a "harmonious society" and fostering China's "peaceful rise" in the world. Commissioned by the government, some universities began studying the matter, labeling the topic "surplus men and social stability" (Xinhua 2007).

Although this rural bachelor–threat framing seems to have been short-lived, at least in public utterances, social stability remains a predominant concern of the party, especially given the recent leadership transition in late 2012. In a mid-2012 statement, Population Minister Wang Xia expressed concern about the sex imbalance because it causes a "series of social problems," including sex crimes and trafficking in women (Xinhua 2012b). The scientific and, in turn, official framing of the problem is critically important because it will shape the policy measures adopted, and, in turn, the kinds of subject positions, forms of citizenship, and solutions to their life problems available to these men. Although no policy directed toward the men specifically has been articulated, a threat framing implies harsh, authoritarian measures, quite the opposite of the supportive measures directed toward rural women and girls.

Official and scientific framings aside, what is happening at the village level? The very limited research on the rural bachelors suggests a plight not that different from the one the *guanggun* faced in earlier centuries. Some, of course, have migrated to the cities in search of work and wives. Yet for many, obligations in the villages foreclose that option. In one small-scale study in the northern province of Hebei, bachelors were allotted poor-quality land and housing at family division. As the last in their families to find wives, they were responsible for the support of the parents. Unable to take jobs outside the village, they were often forced to work for others, leading to a loss of face. Lacking support from their families and their communities, the bachelors faced lives of severe social discrimination and economic destitution. Another study—in the east-central province of Anhui—paints a picture of extreme privation in which involuntary bachelors experience lower socioeconomic status, weaker social support systems, and more fragile psychological states than married men (Huang 2007; Li et al. n.d.) Whether some are turning to violence to right these social wrongs, we simply do not know.

"Crime": Party Crackdown

Given the personal stakes, older rural men seem to be trying every means conceivable—legal and illegal—to secure a bride or, failing that, simply a child. Informal discussions with Chinese researchers over the last few years suggest that men in different areas are dealing with the bride shortage in different ways. In the border areas of the northeast and southwest, the dearth of local brides has been met by importing women from North Korea, Vietnam, and Myanmar, and, more recently, also from Laos, Thailand, Cambodia, and Mongolia. (Xinhua 2011d). Men in border provinces sometimes travel abroad to select their bride personally; in other cases, they work through middlemen to acquire "mail-order brides." Both ethnographic research and some press reports suggest that many women from these countries are eager to marry men they perceive as wealthier than men in their home countries (Belanger et al. 2010). In poor interior provinces, interviews suggest, the scarcity of marriageable women has given rise to culturally non-preferred forms of union, including polyandrous unions (*yiqi duofu*) in which the wife of one man informally services several others.

Increasingly since the late 1980s, the urgent need of poor peasant men for brides has been met by the development of clandestine smuggling networks involved in the long-distance buying and selling of young women (*maimai hunyin*) (Chao 2005; Han and Eades 1995; Zhuang 1993). In the most common pattern, girls are purchased or kidnapped from their families in poverty-stricken areas of the southwest, often promised jobs, and then transported long distances to villages in the northeast, where they are bought by poor villagers desperate for a wife and family (Fan and Huang 1998). To pay the high bride prices, men often save for years and borrow from family members. These arrangements have sometimes proven disastrous, with brides absconding with the bride payments, to the great distress of the grooms and their families (Fong 2009; He 2010). In central China, some men unable to marry are adopting daughters to provide future support.[4] Those unable to find brides in these or other ways may have no marriage prospects at all. These men may live together in bachelor communities, where they join forces to manage life's problems, or form a spatially dispersed bachelor underclass (for reports from the Guangxi and Guizhou regions, see He 2010).

Reflecting the official construction of the men as violent threats to social stability and public security, the party has responded by criminalizing the trafficking in women and children. Although police efforts to crack down on smuggling networks and *maimai hunyin* (marriage by purchase) started as early as the 1980s, as the number of men who cannot find brides has grown in recent years, these efforts have become increasingly public and strident. Frequent media reports announce how many kidnapped women and children have been rescued and returned to their homes by the police (e.g., forty-two thousand between 2001 and 2003). Between April 2009 and December 2011 a special campaign reportedly broke up 7,025 human trafficking groups with 18,518 children and 34,813 women rescued (Xinhua 2011e). In July 2011, the party announced a "people's war" against infant traffickers, who are now targeting rural transients in the cities who are too busy to watch their young children. Of course, there is no way to verify these numbers or put them in larger context. Nor is there any way to know how many of the women did not want to be "saved," but rather willingly left their home counties or countries in an effort to escape poverty. What does seem clear is that, at least in official discourse on this issue, the unmarried rural men are being framed as violent, anti-state, quasi-criminal elements, while the party appears as the heroic rescuer of vulnerable women and children.

Conclusion: The Problem of the *Guanggun*— Reflections and Interventions

How then is the problem of the *guanggun* being articulated? Let us begin with how it is being framed. As the notion of assemblage suggests, the official framing of the issue is highly contingent, reflecting local cultures, sciences, and politics. Echoing a culture in which *guanggun* means threatening to the social order and gender often means women and children needing rescue from feudal patriarchal culture, a constellation of sciences in which the Western nations are the norm and the one-child policy is China's "only choice," and a politics in which the one-child policy is a key to transforming China into a global power under the Chinese Communist Party, the *guanggun* problem is being largely subsumed under the master problem of the sex ratio imbalance. Surrounded mostly in a shroud of silence, the rural bachelors appear in public discourse not as sympathetic figures to be helped, but primarily as threats to the sociopolitical order to be contained by a firm criminal justice system and an able police force, which courageously uncovers criminal smuggling networks and rescues vulnerable women and children.

As for interventions, the dominant one is a cluster of cultural and socioeconomic (and legal) measures aimed at helping women become equal to men. As the open discussion of the rural men as "threats to sociopolitical stability" of 2007 and 2008 makes clear, the leadership is concerned about the unmarriageability of China's older rural men, taking quiet measures to alleviate the situation for future generations. These include a gradual relaxation of the one-child policy (dubbed an "extension of the one-child-with-exceptions policy") and a strengthening of the rural social security system, as well as continued education to teach the populace that "women are the equal of men." What is striking is how few measures are directed at helping the older men now in the population resolve their marriage and fatherhood problems. Although rural local officials in some areas are reportedly breaking the law to assist some of the men in their villages secure families and in that way become stable forces in the village, at the level of the political center, little that is visible is being done. The most visible central-level measure is to criminalize men's efforts to purchase brides (and sometimes children) from intermediaries, making unavailable one of the only ways open to many to secure a family and ensure themselves a life that accords with the conventions of Chinese culture.

Clearly, much is at stake in how this problem is articulated, not only for the rural men—many of whom seem to face dim prospects of ever marrying and having a child—but also for the leadership, whose promises to ensure sociopolitical stability are fundamental to its continued legitimacy. As an assemblage of changeable, historically fluctuating elements, the problem-space of the older bachelors remains unstable, so the framing could shift in response to any number of changes. Certainly, as the number of *guanggun* rises—and it will, given the demography of the one-child policy—this issue will become more prominent on the political agenda, whether quietly or publicly. The state may be forced to address the issue, if not by helping men find brides or children, then by essentially taking them out of the reproductive population by providing long-term jobs in national construction, say, or the military. Yet as long as the cultural presumptions about gender (among others) remain in place, whatever the measures directed at them, China's rural men are unlikely to be the objects of compassion and care. Facing the dual burden of manhood (and thus not needing help) and peasanthood (thus inherently "backward" in the grand scheme of Chinese modernity), they seem to be just one of the barely mentionable social costs of the one-child policy.

Notes

1. See Attane and Guilmoto (2007) for a deeper analysis.
2. The emergence of the "bare sticks" also poses many ethical problems, but ethical reflections remain publicly indecipherable so I do not pursue them here.
3. Indeed, given the "low quality" of the rural bachelors, evidenced by their poverty, farm status, and low levels of education, the state may quietly prefer that they not reproduce, since their reproduction would likely lower the overall quality of the population. Such logic is consistent with calls over the years for well-educated urban professionals to be allowed more than one child.
4. Based on conversations with Kay Ann Johnson, a professor of Asian Studies and Politics at Hampshire College; for more on this see Johnson (2004).

References

Attane, Isabelle, and Christophe Z. Guimoto, eds. 2007. *Watering the Neighbor's Garden: The Growing Demographic Female Deficit in Asia*. Paris: Committee for International Cooperation in National Research in Demography.

Belanger, Daniele, Hye-Kyung Lee, and Hong-Zen Wang. 2010. "Ethnic Diversity and Statistics in East Asia: 'Foreign Brides' Surveys in Taiwan and South Korea." *Ethnic and Racial Studies* 33, no. 6: 1108–30.

Brownell, Susan, and Jeffrey N. Wasserstrom, eds. 2002. *Chinese Femininities, Chinese Masculinities*. Berkeley: University of California Press.

Cai, Yong, and William Lavely. 2007. "Child Sex Ratios and Their Regional Variation." In *Transition and Challenge: China's Population at the Beginning of the 21st Century*, ed. Zhao Zhongwei and Guo Fei. Oxford: Oxford University Press.

Central Committee of the Chinese Communist Party and the State Council. 2007. "Decision of the Central Committee of the Communist Party of China and the State Council on Fully Enhancing the Population and Family Planning Program and Comprehensively Addressing Population Issues," http://www.npfpc.gov/cn/en/en2007-01/news20070124.htm. 22 January.

Chao, Emily. 2005. "Cautionary Tales: Marriage Strategies, State Discourse, and Women's Agency in a Naxi Village in Southwestern China." In *Cross-Border Marriages: Gender and Mobility in Transnational Asia*, ed. Nicole Constable. Philadelphia: University of Pennsylvania Press.

China. 2007. "Decision of the Central Committee of the Communist Party of China and the State Council on Fully Enhancing the Population and Family Planning Program and Comprehensively Addressing Population Issues." 22 January. http://npfpc.gov.cn.

China Daily. 2007. "Rising Sex-Ratio Imbalance a 'Danger.'" 23 January. http://www.chinadaily.com.cn/china/2007-01/23/content_789821.htm.

———. 2012. "Gender Imbalance Set to Ease." 31 March. http://npfpc.gov.cn/news/central.

Chu, Junhong. 2001. "Prenatal Sex Determination and Sex-Selective Abortion in Rural Central China." *Population and Development Review* 27, no. 2: 259–81.

Cohen, Myron L. 1993. "Cultural and Political Inventions in Modern China: The Case of the Chinese 'Peasant.'" *Daedalus* 122, no. 2: 151–70.

Ebenstein, Avraham Y., and Ethan Jennings. 2009. "Bare Branches, Prostitution, and HIV in China: A Demographic Analysis." In *Gender Policy and HIV in China: Catalyzing Policy Change*, ed. Joseph Tucker and Dudley L. Poston. New York: Springer.

Edlund, Lena, Li Hongbin, Junjian Yi, and Junsen Zhang. 2007. "More Men, More Crime: Evidence from China's One-Child Policy." Bonn, Germany: Institute for the Study of Labor, discussion paper no. 3214.

Ehrlich, Paul R. 1968. *The Population Bomb*. New York: Ballantine Books.

Fan, Cindy C., and Youqin Huang. 1998. "Waves of Rural Brides: Female Marriage Migration in China." *Annals of the Association of American Geographers* 88, no. 2: 227–51.

Fong, Mei. 2009. "It's Cold Cash, Not Cold Feet: Motivating Runaway Brides in China." *Wall Street Journal.* 5 June.

Foucault, Michel. 1978. *The History of Sexuality. Volume 1.* New York: Random House.

Gaetano, Arianne M., and Tamara Jacka, eds. 2004. *On the Move: Women in Rural-to-Urban Migration in Contemporary China.* New York: Columbia University Press.

Greenhalgh, Susan. 2008. *Just One Child: Science and Policy in Deng's China.* Berkeley: University of California Press.

Greenhalgh, Susan, and Edwin A. Winckler. 2005. *Governing China's Population: From Leninist to Neoliberal Biopolitics.* Stanford, CA: Stanford University Press.

Guilmoto, Christophe Z. 2009. "The Sex Ratio Transition in Asia." *Population and Development Review* 35, no. 3: 519–49.

Han, Min, and J. S. Eades. 1995. "Brides, Bachelors and Brokers: The Marriage Market in Rural Anhui in an Era of Economic Reform." *Modern Asian Studies* 29, no. 4: 841–69.

He, Na. 2010. "Brides and Prejudice in China." http://www.chinadaily.com.cn/china/2010-08/23/content_11186841.htm. 23 August.

Huang, Xiyi. 2007. *Power, Entitlement and Social Practice: Resource Distribution in North China Villages.* Hong Kong: Chinese University Press.

Hudson, Valerie M., and Andrea M. Den Boer. 2004. *Bare Branches: The Security Implications of Asia's Surplus Male Population.* Cambridge: MIT Press.

Johnson, Kay Ann. 2004. *Wanting a Daughter, Needing a Son: Abandonment, Adoption, and Orphanage Care in China.* St. Paul, MN: Yeong and Yeong.

Kelliher, Daniel. 1994. "Chinese Communist Political Theory and the Rediscovery of the Peasantry." *Modern China* 20, no. 4: 387–415.

Latour, Bruno. 2005. *Reassembling the Social: An Introduction to Actor-Network-Theory.* Oxford: Oxford University Press.

Li Yan, Li Shuzhuo, and Peng Yong. n.d. "Nongcun daling weihun nanxing yu yihun nanxing xinli fuli de bijiao yanjiu" [A Comparison of psychological well-being between forced bachelors and married men]. Xi'an, Shaanxi, China: Xi'an Jiaotong University, unpublished manuscript.

Lock, Margaret, and Vinh-Kim Nguyen. 2010. *An Anthropology of Biomedicine.* Malden, MA: Wiley-Blackwell.

Ong, Aihwa, and Stephen J. Collier, eds. 2005. *Global Assemblages: Technology, Politics, and Ethics as Anthropological Problems.* Malden, MA: Blackwell.

Ownby, David. 1996. *Brotherhoods and Secret Societies in Early and Mid-Qing China: The Formation of a Tradition.* Stanford, CA: Stanford University Press.

———. 2002. "Approximations of Chinese Bandits: Perverse Rebels, Romantic Heroes, or Frustrated Bachelors?" In *Chinese Femininities/Chinese*

Masculinities, ed. Susan Brownell and Jeffrey N. Wasserstrom. Berkeley: University of California Press.

Poston, Dudley L., and Li Zhang. 2009. "China's Unbalanced Sex Ratio at Birth: How Many Surplus Boys Have Been Born in China Since the 1980s?" In *Gender Policy and HIV in China: Catalyzing Policy Change*, ed. Joseph Tucker and Dudley L. Poston. New York: Springer.

Sen, Amartya. 1989. "Women's Survival as a Development Problem." *Bulletin of the American Academy of Arts and Sciences* 43, no. 2: 14–29.

———. 1990. "More than 100 Million Women Are Missing." *New York Review of Books* 37, no. 20. 20 December.

Shen, Yifei. 2008. *Study on Gender Mainstreaming in the Specific Policy Contexts of China: Political Participation, Legal Status and Social Security*. Shanghai: Shanghai Academy of Social Sciences Press.

Tucker, Joseph D., Gail E. Henderson, Tian F. Wang, Ying Y. Huang, William Parish, Sui M. Pan, Xiang S. Chen, Myron S. Cohen. 2005. "Surplus Men, Sex Work, and the Spread of HIV in China." *AIDS* 19, no. 6: 539–47.

Wang, Feng. 2005. "Can China Afford to Continue its One-Child Policy?" *Asia Pacific Issues* 17. Honolulu: East-West Center.

———. 2011. "Future of the Demographic Overachiever: Long-Term Implications of the Demographic Transition in China." *Population and Development Review* 37, Supplement 1: 173–90.

Wang, Yang. 2012. "National Forum on Population and Family Planning Work Convened in Beijing." 13 February. http://NPFPC.gov.cn/news/central.

Watson, James L. 1989. "Self-Defense Corps, Violence and the Bachelor Sub-culture in South China: Two Case Studies." In *Proceedings of the 2nd International Conference on Sinology, Section on Folklore and Culture*. Taipei: Academia Sinica.

Watson, Rubie S. 1986. "The Named and the Nameless: Gender and Person in Chinese Society." *American Ethnologist* 13: 619–31.

Whyte, Martin King, Jennifer Adams, Arianne Gaetano, and Lei Guang, eds. 2010. *One Country, Two Societies: Rural-Urban Inequality in Contemporary China*. Cambridge: Harvard University Press.

Xinhua. 2007. "Number of Young Unmarrieds in China Increases." 11 December.

———. 2011a. "400 Million Births Prevented by Family Planning Policy." 28 October.

———. 2011b. "Grandparents Embrace China's Loosening of Family Planning Rules, but Parents Take Cautious Approach." 30 November.

———. 2011c. "China to Maintain Its Family Planning Policy: Official." 31 October.

———. 2011d. "Hundreds of Foreign Mail-Order Brides Rescued." 3 November.

———. 2011e. "Police Rescue 178 in Child Trafficking Cases." 7 December.

———. 2012a. "Lawmaker Calls for Tougher Penalties for Illegal Gender Testing." 14 March.

———. 2012b. "Official Vows China Will Correct Gender Imbalance." 30 May.

Zeng, Yi. 2007. "Options for Fertility Policy Transition in China." *Population and Development Review* 33, no. 2: 235–46.

Zhao, Jinfang, and Sulan Qiu, eds. 2008. *Nannu pingdeng jiben guoce jianming duben* [Concise reader on the basic state policy of male-female equality]. Beijing: Peking University Press.

Zhuang, Ping. 1993. "On the Social Phenomenon of Trafficking in Women in China." *Chinese Education and Society* 26, no. 3: 33–50.

Chapter 16

PATERNITY POISONED

THE IMPACT OF GULF WAR SYNDROME ON FATHERHOOD

Susie Kilshaw

Introduction

During my research into Gulf War Syndrome (GWS), one Scottish veteran expressed concern about how the illness might impact his reproductive life: "We can't have kids now, and I wonder if that is because of me. Before me [my wife] had a healthy pregnancy, no problems. And I had a child before [the war] who was perfectly healthy. [*Kilshaw*: Was there a concern when you tried to get pregnant?] Aye. Miscarried. We had fertility treatment. Sometimes it's a relief because one of my friends, his child was born with webbed feet and webbed hands, another was born with heart problems, and my friend, his kid's got behavioral problems."

GWS is a cluster of symptoms and illnesses affecting some of the soldiers and civilian workers who participated in the 1991 Gulf War. It is generally characterized by fatigue, headaches, muscle pain, joint pain, rashes, cognitive problems, diarrhea, and respiratory disorders, although I found that sufferers credited almost any symptom to the illness. GWS is attributed to reactions to prophylactic drugs and vaccines or exposure to pesticides and other chemicals, radiation, and oil fires. Elsewhere I explore the way masculinity is at the heart of GWS (Kilshaw 2006; 2007; 2009), but in this chapter I focus the intersection of GWS and one particular feature of the life of men: fatherhood. My encounter described above reflects many Gulf War veterans' concerns about having children. Masculinity is the social elaboration of the biological function of fatherhood (Connell 1995), and sufferers report difficulties in enacting this form of masculinity. Whether through experiences of difficulty in conceiving, concerns about having "damaged" children because of what they allude to and I characterize as "toxic semen," or anxiety about the illness's impact on their role as fathers, veterans express experiences of impeded and poisoned fatherhood. Bodily notions of toxicity expressed were extended to experiences of fatherhood. The construct of "toxic fatherhood" includes fears of contagion: that the sufferer will pass on the disability or illness to his offspring. This form of fatherhood can also be termed toxic as a result of the way the illness impacts family life as a whole.

The Study

Data for this chapter is derived from my fieldwork among members of the U.K. GWS community. Using the theories and methods of anthropology, the project investigates the emergence of GWS. During a fourteen-month period between September 2001 and November 2002, I immersed myself as best as possible in the GWS community: through spending time with the veterans' associations, participating in meetings, attending pension tribunals, and observing clinical encounters, data were collected from media files and other relevant documentation, including transcribed interviews with sufferers, family members, advocates, practitioners, scientists, and researchers. A total of ninety-three interviews were conducted, sixty-seven of which were with U.K. Gulf veterans, the majority of whom believed themselves to be ill with GWS. Most interviews were conducted in the home of participants; an interview schedule was used, but questions remained broad. Interviews focused on experience with GWS, health beliefs, and experiences, as well as military and employment background. Interviews ranged from two to four hours and were recorded and transcribed at a later date. I met with some participants several times and remained in contact with them, seeing them at subsequent meetings. To further explore the biomedical discourse surrounding GWS and the way this was negotiated by sufferers, I spoke to scientists and doctors involved in the GWS debate. The way sufferers represented their illness was the primary focus.

My research set out to provide an ethnography of GWS. It became clear that sufferers considered themselves to be poisoned by their exposure to chemicals during their service in the Gulf, including depleted uranium (DU), chemical weapons, and/or smoke from oil fires. Prior to and during the war a number of medical countermeasures were used to protect troops from potential nuclear, biological, and chemical attack, and it is these prophylactic measures that have garnered the most attention as the possible cause of the condition. Such measures include multiple vaccines against biological warfare attacks, in addition to numerous additional routine vaccines: Nerve Agent Pre-treatment (NAPS) tablets, containing pyridostigmine bromide (PB), given to protect against exposure to chemical weapons; and organophosphates (OPs), pesticides and insect repellents that were used to minimize pest-borne disease. Veterans spoke about their bodies being penetrated or corrupted, and thus, irrevocably damaged. Sufferers often referred to immune systems in discussion of the illness. They see their body as being attacked, resulting in overwhelmed, vulnerable immune systems. They considered their body fluids as polluted, with blood and semen being particularly toxic. One of the unique aspects of GWS is that the veterans see it as contagious and able to be passed by sexual contact, reproduction, or living in close proximity with a sufferer.

Many sufferers maintain that they were experimented upon and blame the government for their illnesses. This can be seen as part of a larger trend of loss of confidence in authority. We find ourselves in a risk culture: the concept of risk is fundamental to the way lay actors and technical specialists organize the world (Giddens 1991). More and more social problems have begun to be examined through the prism of risk. Risk has become reflexive: humanity now has to deal with new "manufactured" risks of its own creation (Beck 1992, Giddens 1991). This rings true in the case of Gulf War toxins, where the perils are manmade and emerge largely from one's own side. Linked to this is an erosion of faith in science. The post-9/11 climate only reinforces what it means to live in a risk society where uncertainty prevails and the boundaries between friend/foe and civilian/military continue to erode. GWS risks can be seen as an example of Beck's (1992) notion of circulation of bads: in a risk society dangers come from goods that are converted into bads. Similarly, Hochschild's emotional aquifer[1] resonates here: human emotion is contagious. We all draw from an emotional aquifer that, unbeknown to us, connects us; when it is polluted by war or violence we all suffer.

Distinguishing something as a risk is a means of making sense of the world. Given the moral component of the causation of GWS, Mary Douglas's (1966) work influences my reading of the condition, particularly her introduction of morality in understanding risk and danger and her focus on the differences in risk perception. When GWS began to appear and before an organized movement had developed, the sufferers, who were seeking meaning for their suffering, were already focusing on the confusion of categories that previously defined friend and foe (Cohn et al. 2008). One of the main tropes in GWS discussion is the way the illness is a form of "friendly fire." In the United States, the phrase "friendly fire" refers to inadvertent firing toward one's own or otherwise friendly forces while attempting to engage enemy forces, particularly where this results in injury or death. Such incidents are more commonly referred to as "blue on blue" by NATO militaries. A consequence of all wars, friendly fire came to have significant meaning during the Gulf because it was: "reconfigured in the experience of the soldiers as a betrayal of the highly advanced technology of the conflict. Here, the inevitability of human error is reconfigured in their accounts of what happened as a story about newly manufactured risk and the role of novel weaponry, areas of uncertainty during conflict, and the erosion of a soldier's traditional role" (2008: 1644).

Veterans commonly expanded upon the metaphor of friendly fire, often employing the U.S. terminology, to describe not only the way they see the illness as caused by their government, but also the way they believe it behaves like an autoimmune disorder: the body turning on itself. Importantly, the metaphor was extended to represent the way the illness affected members of the victims' families through contagion and contamination. Moreover, friendly fire incidents not only provided a general metaphor, but a "conceptual ground for those who came to suffer from GWS in that they had been wounded by the medical counter measures they received. The enormous moral and psychological requirements to make sense of illness, especially one that was unknown and unaccounted, were for many enough to overturn the division that normally provides a moral certainty about who the enemy is and where it is located" (Cohn et al. 2008: 1647).

When exploring GWS I am not asking the questions, "Is it real?" or "Does it exist?"—which were often the focus of inquiries about my research. For the purpose of this analysis, the objective truth of whether or not this illness is indeed either "real" or psychosomatic is irrelevant; instead, I maintain that GWS is at the very least subjectively real in that veterans are suffering and they are convinced that they have been negatively affected, indeed, poisoned, by their time in the Gulf and that their experience of fatherhood is influenced by it. Here I focus on the perception of the sufferers and in this case I am not intending to endorse nor refute the position of these beliefs in relation to mainstream scientific and epidemiological approaches; instead, I strive to transcend the conventional boundaries of modern biomedicine, which establishes a dichotomy in respect to the nature of illness, contending that it must either be physical or psychological. In taking this approach, I am more effectively able to explore the way in which veterans subjectively experience GWS, particularly as it relates to their perceived ability to engage the role of fatherhood.

Sexuality and GWS

Men, or, more specifically, military men, are the focus of my work on GWS. As Dudgeon and Inhorn (2009:80) note, "[Only] recently have men as men—that is, as gendered agents, with beliefs, behaviors, and characteristics associated with but not dependent on biological sex—become subjects of theory and empirical investigation within the social sciences (Connell 1987; 1995; Seidler 1994), including in anthropology (Bourgois 1995; Gutmann 1997; Lancaster 1992)." They continue: "Recently, theorists have stressed that individual men do not simply fill static roles and identities; rather, they must perform masculinity as an ongoing process drawing on existing sets of behaviors and ideas while allowing for innovation and change over time" (Dudgeon and Inhorn 2009: 80). Gilmore (1990) argues that masculine identities and roles are more tenuous than feminine identities and roles, thus they must be performed more vigorously. Masculinity is not considered permanent and must be continually reconfirmed. This is particularly the case in military culture where both formal and informal performances of masculinity abound. Military culture creates structure and routines that call for continual testing of such qualities. Barrett (1996: 131) describes the U.S. Navy as a "culture that chronically creates trials that separates the 'weak' from the rest. From the first day of training, the culture creates a testing ground that creates boundaries of inclusion around those who exhibit strength, endurance and competence."

Masculinity is characterized as a plural set of gender identities or masculinities (Connell 1995) that are related to, but not determined by, biological sex. However, masculinity is almost always thought to proceed from men's bodies, be inherent in a male body, or express something about a male body (Connell 1995). The phrase "hegemonic masculinity" is used to describe ideal types of male behavior. There is a hierarchy of masculine behavior and most societies encourage men to embody a dominant version of masculinity. Conversely, "subordinate masculinities" embody some of the opposites of these ideal attributes. The military plays a primary role in shaping images of both hegemonic and subordinate masculinity to the larger society (Connell 1992; Morgan 1994). Military masculinity emphasizes stamina, strength, and vigor, and exerts pressure on soldiers to live up to these ideals: participants focused on a physical form of masculinity comprised of fitness, strength, endurance, and muscle bulk. Soldiers are defined as an embodiment of male sex role behaviors (Barrett 1996). Models of hegemonic masculinity, or ideal masculine behavior and identity, may distress men unable to achieve these ideals. The sufferers I met aspired to, but ultimately fell short of, the ideal form of military masculinity: a hypermasculinity. Illness in general may be characterized as unmasculine, and some disorders, such as infertility and erectile dysfunction, are seen as particularly emasculating (Inhorn 2002; 2003; Webb and Daniluk 1999). Will H. Courtenay (2000) argues that there is a reciprocal relationship between masculinity and health, stressing that men's health problems are often produced by men's enactment of masculinity and that cultural norms and expectations reinforce these enactments (Dudgeon and Inhorn 2009: 83). In the case of military men, weakness and illness particularly are framed as unmasculine. These ailments contribute to GWS being constructed as a loss of masculinity or even a feminizing condition (Kilshaw 2009).

The experience of the Gulf War and of having GWS seems to touch on the very notion of what it means to be a man. Veterans and those around them focused on the loss of physical strength and vigor and described a state of eroded masculinity. They spoke about becoming weak, lacking fitness and muscle, and being old before their time and "like women." Symptoms included problems with reproduction and sexuality, which were mirrored in the wider world in which they lived. As Lisa Moore (2009: 56) comments, there are "interesting parallels to consider between reports of the global declines in sperm production and global masculinity 'under threat.'" Concern about reproduction among GWS sufferers makes sense given the central place it holds in the demonstration of masculinity. If sufferers experience their illness as eroded masculinity, it is not surprising that they would see their biological function of masculinity as impeded. I have interpreted this as the expression of anxiety about gender and identity, particularly in light of a life and a military in flux (Kilshaw 2009).

Common symptoms of GWS are impotence and low libido, which makes the opportunity of conceiving a child less likely. But veterans also spoke about impediments to producing children and "ideal" children in that they reported that their semen was toxic and damaged and that, as a result, fetal death and birth defects were likely. Narratives of GWS take an ambivalent approach to semen (Kilshaw 2007). Semen serves as a potent symbol of identity, and a focus on semen among sufferers expresses an anxiety about identity, or, more specifically, about masculinity. When veterans discuss their damaged bodies and their damaged semen, they are communicating experiences of impaired masculinity.

Helene Goldberg (2009) and others illustrate the conceptual connection between impotency and infertility. However, with GWS, sufferers emphasize impotence and low libido but do not conflate this with infertility. Impotence and low libido are, however, conceptually linked. For example, sufferers and their partners sometimes suggest the need for Viagra to remedy low libido, when in fact Viagra is a treatment for impotence and not low libido. Militaries emphasize a hypersexuality, a trait central to masculinity. Cultural constructions of sexual behavior and sexual disorders shape the ways individual men experience their own masculinity. With heterosexuality and hypersexuality as a characteristic of military masculinity, one must question what is considered low libido in this context. It may be that veterans were interpreting their own sex drive as impaired in light of the discourse of hypersexual desire common in military circles.

Infertility and GWS

Despite concern about reproduction and adverse outcomes of pregnancy following service in the Gulf War, there have been relatively few studies on the topic compared to the multitude of studies on Gulf War illness (Doyle et al. 2006). This is particularly surprising given the centrality of the concern for the people at the heart of my research. The research into a possible link between Gulf service and infertility is unclear mainly due to low response rates and the possibility of selective participation (Maconochie et al. 2004). Three epidemiological studies (Ishoy et al. 2001; Maconochie et al. 2004; Sim et al. 2003) have specifically examined fertility in relation to

Gulf War service in general. The first was an interview-based study that took blood samples to test reproductive markers. The second used a postal questionnaire to examine self-reported fertility status among Australian veterans. The final, largest study was a U.K. study (Maconochie et al. 2004), which used a self-administered postal questionnaire; but unlike other studies, an attempt was made to verify and obtain more information on reported fertility problems. Differential recall of infertility by the Gulf veterans or the comparison group is also a possibility, particularly as some evidence exists that miscarriage, particularly early miscarriage, is under-reported by male non-Gulf veterans in this dataset (Doyle et al. 2004). It is possible that "Gulf veterans had more incentive to report infertility if they perceived that it might be related to their Gulf war service" (Maconochie 2004: 5). The analyses of Doyle et al. (2006) revealed little or no evidence of increased risk of infertility in relation to any specific exposure. The authors' concerns about bias resonate with my findings: the way in which concerns about the Gulf War may impact symptom perception and reporting.

Anxiety about the connection between war, virility, and reproduction exists throughout history (Bourke 1996; 1999; Showalter 1997), but in the case of GWS it has come to be associated with notions of purity and infection since early in the emergence of the condition (Cohn et al. 2008). Although concern about infertility is contained in the popular discourse of GWS, it was primarily a worry of veterans who were not (or not yet) ill. Many well veterans expressed a fear that they might become ill in the future; infertility was a dominant concern. This perhaps relates to a more widespread apprehension about infertility in the United Kingdom, tapping into cultural anxieties as evidenced in the media. With subsequent military deployment to Iraq more than ten years later, concerns about fertility and semen quality were of high enough interest to prompt some U.S. military men to cryopreserve their sperm prior to deployment (Kelly 2003). In the United Kingdom, *The Observer* reported:

> Scores of British servicemen heading to the Gulf are visiting sperm banks so their partners can still have their children if they are killed or rendered infertile by chemical or biological weapons... Veterans' groups say they have had many inquiries from servicemen concerned at the possible effects of vaccines administered by the Ministry of Defence, apart from the danger of being killed or rendered infertile during fighting. The cocktail of chemicals, similar to that given out before the first Gulf war in 1991, is meant to guard against insect bites and Iraqi chemical and biological weapons. The MoD insists it is safe,

but some veterans say it has been linked to problems of fertility in soldiers returning from conflict. (Harris 2003)

The article links soldiers' concerns about fertility to other issues about GWS; we can see that infertility remains part of the public discourse. NAPS tablets were cited most commonly as the cause of low libido, infertility, and impotence, while vaccinations were also considered to be linked with these symptoms. Gulf veterans' concerns about particular exposures being linked specifically to fertility problems resonates with popular cultural beliefs. Indeed there is evidence revealing that exposure to pesticides, chemotherapy, and ulcer and blood pressure medications, as well as to alcohol, marijuana, and anabolic steroids, has been demonstrated to lower sperm counts (Moore 2009: 56). There is an ongoing debate in the fields of epidemiology, toxicology, and infertility regarding the increased rate of men's infertility, and men exposed to environmental and occupational toxins have reported consistently higher rates of infertility (Schrader, Turner, and Simon 1991; Whorton et al. 1977; Wyrobek et al. 1983). Furthermore, scientific findings based on research from sixty-one studies indicate that lower sperm counts are prevalent in our global environment (Swan and Elkin 1999).

Moore (2009) demonstrates the ways popular accounts conflate male infertility with impotence, where low sperm count is conflated with a lack of sexual potency. However, this does not seem to be the case with GWS sufferers. In fact, Gulf War veterans spoke a great deal about infertility, but GWS sufferers did not focus on this concern. Infertility seemed to be a projection upon the future, whereas sufferers were focused on the reality and the present existence of their illness. The sufferers I met were looking more to the past than to the future. Why is this? Is this an issue of age? Is it that the well veterans I met had not begun to attempt to father children? What is the absence of anxiety about infertility among the GWS cohort saying? There seems to be an emphasis on loss of sexuality, loss of masculinity, and damaged reproduction, but not necessarily on a loss of reproduction. Instead, we again see this elaboration of toxicity to fatherhood, that the illness is impacting, but not impeding, fatherhood.

Fetal Death and GWS

Part of my fieldwork was spent at the Gulf Veteran's Medical Assessment Programme at St. Thomas' Hospital, London. One day a

veteran came in and described how his wife had experienced a miscarriage a few weeks previously. The consultant outlined his belief
that this veteran's problems were not caused by, and that his lon-
gevity would not be affected by, the Gulf War. He then said that the
veteran's wife should feel reassured that her recent miscarriage was
not the result of his Gulf service. The veteran reported that he felt
reassured. Others, however, were not reassured by evidence and
remain convinced of a link between fetal death and Gulf War exposures. One prominent sufferer said, "You've got many, many, many
cases where wives and female veterans have actually lost children."
There have been seven studies of fetal death in the offspring of Gulf
veterans. None of these studies found an association between service in the Gulf and increased risk of stillbirth in pregnancies conceived after deployment (Doyle et al. 2006). Studies on miscarriage
rates are more problematic, with conflicting findings. Two studies
(Doyle et al. 2004; Kang et al. 2001) found statistically significant
increases in miscarriage reported by male Gulf veterans as compared
to a control group. For miscarriage, there is some evidence of small
increased risks associated with service, but the role of bias is likely
to be strong (Doyle et al. 2006), with the authors pointing to the
unusually low rates reported by non-Gulf War veterans. In both of
these studies the miscarriage rates in comparison to the non-Gulf
control group were unusually low, rather than the rates of the Gulf
veterans' miscarriages being particularly high (2006).

Ed and his wife tried for a year to conceive, but unfortunately
their pregnancy ended in a miscarriage. Ed felt there were strange
and unusual circumstances surrounding the loss of the pregnancy.
He explained that he was told that his sperm had attacked his wife's
egg: "Yeah, it was the chromosomes; I had double the chromosomes.
I mean I think you are supposed to have thirty-six or thirty-seven
chromosomes for male, but I had seventy-something. I had double
the chromosomes. And they were attacking the egg, the fetus; they
were fighting each other. And they put it down to a, what's called
a blighted ovum. Ummm and they, I mentioned the Gulf War because I was pretty upset because I was almost 100 percent sure that
it was down to that." Ed's story reflects a common theme of hostile
sperm and is further elaborated in that he also reported that his
wife suffered from burning semen syndrome. The sufferers I met
strongly felt the toxins and chemicals to which they were exposed
in the Gulf War had affected their bodies. Anxieties about toxic body
fluids (particularly blood and semen) are associated with reproduction and fertility problems, "linking the notion of possessing a future

hazard in body fluids with ideas of strength with masculinity, and with the fear that even if the illness doesn't surface in their own body, perhaps it does in someone more defenceless" (Cohn et al. 2008: 1644). They perceive that toxic fatherhood poisons their bodies and affects those around them. Furthermore, they see this effect as permanent: their bodies had been permanently altered and damaged, which could then affect those around them.

Gulf Babies and GWS

Blame and guilt are central to veterans' discussions as they worry about infecting their partners or children. For those veterans who have had ill or disabled children after the Gulf War, there is a further desperate anxiety that they are to blame. Veterans both well and unwell expressed anxiety about transmitting the condition to their offspring. I asked Chris, a veteran, if he was concerned about having children, and he replied:

> Um, yeah I was when I came back because you heard all these deformities and that… my wife said she wanted kids and I said no and she thought I had gone off her… You see on TV that children are born with one arm and one leg. They love them as much as their normal children, but I don't think I could have coped. We opted not to do nothing for about a year or so. When I was getting reviewed you wondered if there was something wrong, and they're not telling you… If something did happen and we did lose a child would it be down to my wife? Would it be down to what I had? We just didn't know. The medical staff just really didn't want to know: they didn't want to advise you, they didn't want to help you out. You just basically had to go and speak to your friends, but you have to be very careful who you speak to.

Although he continued to be worried about the possibility of having a "damaged" child, they did choose to proceed, mainly because he felt it was the only way to reassure his wife that there was nothing wrong with him and to prove his devotion to her. He explained his relief at having a healthy daughter. As they considered expanding their family, they continued to speak to friends and relatives about their concerns, including a family member who was a nurse. She told them to go ahead with their plans as a scan would pick up any abnormalities and they could then decide to abort the pregnancy.

The possibility of having children with birth defects seems to be an overriding concern of well veterans. Thus, although they remain symptom-free and healthy, they fear that something remaining in their body could affect their children (Kilshaw 2009: 168). The illness may not have affected them, but it may lie within the body and affect offspring. The invisibility of the condition is a common theme—the invisible illness in the asymptomatic veteran made visible in children.

One well officer said that if he had a child in the future and if that child were born with problems, he would question whether the Gulf War was responsible. Until that point he was not concerned about the illness, however. James, another well veteran, pondered over the reality of GWS and said:

> Whether it is GWS or something else, I don't know. I am fine. There possibly is something, but I am fine, but if I were to have a child who was born with birth defects then I would blame it on the Gulf. [*Kilshaw*: Why is that?] Because there is no family history of anything like that either on my side or my wife's. The Gulf is the only thing I could blame it on. I suppose it could just happen, but there is something that I have in my past that would explain it. It's like if I found out I was infertile. I know I was fertile because I got a girl pregnant, and she had an abortion. So if I found out I was infertile I would then investigate and come back to GWS and I think I would have the right to do so.

During a follow-up interview James said: "If I got cancer I would not blame it on the Gulf. It would have be something unusual; if I had a three-armed baby I would blame it on the Gulf. That's not a normal birth defect... Or if I were told I was infertile..." Interestingly, it emerged that he had different explanatory models based on the perceived hierarchy of the seriousness of the condition. A "serious" disorder, such as Down syndrome, he explained, would be attributable to his participation in the Gulf War, but a minor condition would not.

Josh, an officer who was not suffering from GWS but had been injured during his service in the Gulf, expressed his concerns about having children:

> It is a worry because you meet people at the [association's annual meeting], some of who have three damaged kids. It puts me off. It has done. I have some friends who have had children who are fine, but you wonder. I definitely have the feeling that I've been contaminated. Toxic war. Ties into the contamination thing. I don't feel I'm contaminating you by sitting here, but contaminating relationships... that their futures may not be as bright because of what I've been party to,

what I've done, inhaled, injected with... to do with reproduction...
It clouds my future and progeny's future. We've been exposed to so
many chemicals. The chances of birth defects are vastly increased. It
may not be noticeable in great scheme of thing, but for my family it's
bloody important. The government is losing hold on our bodies... We
are meant to be in charge of our own bodies. We weren't in control
of our own bodies... My children might not be fit enough to survive
because of what happened to me. Every chemical has an impact on
our cells either the way they reproduce or the nucleus...will change
in your body... The chemical we had: we are going to have defects.

Josh expressed concern about having children and his belief that it
is likely that the exposures in the Gulf will cause problems in any
future children. But he also spoke about contamination and toxicity
that is both literal—veterans' bodies are toxic and this can be passed
on to loved ones—and more conceptual—experiences of war, the
military, and the illness contaminate relationships and make them
toxic.

This extension of the friendly-fire metaphor was used in the case
of birth defects, as Lee describes his family situation:

I was having mood swings, drinking. That progressed. My wife moved
back to the UK with our daughter, who is eight. I had problems seeing
my daughter. She has heart and lung problems. That was the main
thing that got me on the Gulf War program, I signed on the dotted
line. I'm big enough and ugly enough to handle it... but my daughter... that is like friendly fire and if I have another child... I couldn't
handle a disabled child.

Kerry, the wife of a sufferer, spoke of her experience with birth
defects in her daughter:

Emily had a birth defect when she was born, so Stan was guilt-rid-
den... Stan blames it on the Gulf, but I know lots of children born
with birth defects: I was born with a kidney defect; that's a birth defect too. I think it's genetic, a birth defect. I want him to think that,
for my own sanity. I'm not going to drag my daughter through the
courts. I don't want my daughter growing up as a Gulf baby. I want
her to have a normal life.

Kerry's remarks reflect ambivalence around the cause of birth defects:
causation is often unclear and uncertain. It is not only causation, but
also the disabilities themselves, that remain uncertain. There is no
consistent evidence of a strong association between Gulf War deployment of servicemen and the appearance of major, clearly de-

fined, birth defects among infants conceived after the war (Doyle et al. 2004; 2006; Kang et al. 2001). However, despite these findings, birth defects are seen as a central fact of GWS, with veterans and advocates commonly reporting increased rates of birth defects among their children. It is important to note the difference between biomedicine, which may have clear markers of birth defects, and the interpretation of veterans and those around them, who see a range of conditions as "birth defects." The ambiguity of GWS birth defects further continues when one considers minor and more ambiguously defined birth defects, such as anomalies of the musculoskeletal system. For "such conditions there is an element of judgment and what one person considers a birth defect another might consider a normal variant of structure" (Doyle et al. 2006: 582). I witnessed this when I met with one family who was referred to me because it had a number of children with birth defects related to GWS. The children suffered from a range of symptoms and conditions, but when I met with them the nature of their "defects" was unclear: I was uncertain whether they would be classified as birth defects by external (medical) observers. Men, families, and advocates were attributing a wide variety of difficulties with children to GWS exposure-related birth defects. One sufferer explained how his son's birth defect was the result of his own GWS: "Through my genes? If it was transmitted in any other way, like a communicable disease, then it would have affected the others as well and my wife...Are we carrying around these chemicals in our body and you know, are they still there? Are they going into every sort of facet of our body? Sperm has blood and everything in it and you're carrying other chemicals around in your body, then that's creating a chemical imbalance or something like that. Who knows what it could be doing?" Sufferers believe that Gulf exposures are concentrated in their semen: it has become toxic and contaminated and this can then be passed on through sexual contact and reproduction. The combat zone is no longer a remote place; it returns in the bodies of soldiers who then contaminate others, such as innocent family members.

Harry, a GWS sufferer who has a disabled son, outlined a number of key themes that emerge in GWS discussions of biological aspects of fatherhood as it pertains to the illness:

> As I say, my son Thomas has got brain damage [seen on] an early CT scan and what's now on, what's now I'm thinking I may have passed it on genetically from the way I am. So that's the next thing we will be looking at is having a chromosome test for me and my son to see

if there is any link. I mean, my daughter Jade's OK and it's the male that passes it on to the son. So I think we just want to find out if there is a connection and if there is anything that can be done to improve his quality of life... Thomas is a Gulf war baby; he was conceived, you know, not long after the Gulf war, you know. And he was a boy. A lot of other veterans who have children with the same problem they are all boys. So that's why the question is because they did actually did pass on via the cells the father's like.

I was told that children born soon after the war were at greater risk than those born at a chronological distance from the war. Some veterans see their bodies as more hazardous soon after the war, with the possibility of contamination wearing off with time. The theory also suggests that the illness becomes concentrated in maleness. Men pass on the illness to their male children.

Families would commonly refer to an affected child born to a veteran after Gulf service as a "Gulf baby," as Harry does above. Thus the children become labeled: their identities are linked to their fathers' service and subsequent illness. Gulf babies are considered to be the most at-risk because toxicity is contained in the body of their GWS sufferer parent. Interestingly, Kerry states that she does not want her daughter to be considered a Gulf baby: she says that such a label would prevent her from having a normal life. However, for others, emphasizing the child's identity as a "Gulf baby" is being a good father. This may be tied to claiming an identity for the child as being the offspring of someone who fought for the country and therefore worthy of state and medical support. Emphasizing the child's identity in this way may help to define these advocates as fathers, seeking help and protection for their child. It also uniquely binds the child to the man and emphasizes the physicality of paternity.

Gulf veterans are not merely concerned with potential birth defects in regard to their children; they also see their children as more at risk, generally. The express fear that their children suffered from diminished immune systems and, as a result, were more susceptible to environmental hazards. They suggested their children were more vulnerable to immunizations and injections. GWS is seen as contagious and so all children and those living in close proximity are considered to be at risk. Children can also be affected in other ways; such was the case when two veterans reported that their children had become unwell as the result of souvenirs of war in the family home. The suggestion here is that the toxins, likely DU, had infected the house by way of these objects.

In GWS narratives, DU is the exposure most often cited as linked to reproductive problems and is conceptually and lexically linked with radiation and the Chernobyl nuclear accident of 1986. Adriana Petryna's (2002) work exploring how Ukrainians become biological citizens, forgoing other identities in order to get treatment for the effects of Chernobyl, is similar to the way GWS sufferers produce an identity around the illness. However, for U.K. veterans there is a difference in that, because of the National Health Service, it is not a battle for care and treatment, but one for recognition. Importantly, just as the people at the center of Petryna's work fought for ties to Chernobyl for their children in order to assert claims to benefits and care, so are veterans negotiating identities for their children linked to the illness. Being a good father means providing and protecting and, in some cases, this is seen in a father's battle to have his child labeled as a Gulf baby, affected by his exposure to Gulf toxins.

Fatherhood and GWS

It is well documented that aspects of military lifestyle, especially separations caused by deployments, can have a negative impact on the personal relationships of military personnel (Barker and Berry 2009; Barnes et al. 2007; Gorman et al. 2010).[2] Older children who had a father return from the Gulf War faced the usual stressors: the absence of a parent, disruption of family roles and responsibilities, and the reintegration of the parent into the family structure. Sufferers are overwhelmingly ex-military who left service soon after the war. The children at the heart of GWS were born primarily after the war, and sufferers are overwhelmingly those who left service soon after the war. Thus, the impact of military life on the child is not the primary concern; it is the social impact of being a child of an ex-soldier and an ill father that is of central importance.

Parents are concerned about the social and psychological impact on the children being raised in toxic environments, resulting from the illness. Kerry said her husband's behavior affected their children: "I know these things happen in other families, but this is different. The kids shouldn't have to get used to it. He snaps at the kids all the time." A common theme is that the illness makes the father irritable and angry. One of Ryan's main concerns was the effect of his illness on his children: "Because my lifestyle isn't as it should be, not as jolly as it should be. I'm bringing up my children the way I am. They are growing up with anger and no motivation. Whether its PTSD or nerve agent we heard about whatever it is I have to blame the army. They put me in a position that I couldn't refuse. I was made like I am and passed on to children and wife... oldest son going through what I'm going through. Very angry. There is something missing." His wife adds: "[Our daughter] stands out like a sore thumb. All her friends are gently. She and her brother go in fists first... I have to say, 'Please don't be like your dad.' She is getting angrier as she gets older. She says she's stressed up, says, 'You are stressing me out.' [Our son] wants to know why we don't work." Children were described as having difficulty in their social lives. Children are seen as potentially contagious and are ostracized by their peers; others were teased for having sick fathers. One family who has a son with behavioral problems and dyslexia, which they felt was due to GWS, said: "Our son doesn't have many friends. He was having a hard time at school because the other kids say they are scared they will catch something from him." This same family also reported that their son was told by a classmate that the classmate's father had said the father did not need a walking stick, that he was not as ill as it seemed.

Early in my research I met with two veterans who had come to London to take part in the Armistice Day activities. As we spoke, they drank whiskey and told me about the impact of the war on soldier's lives: "Men, it's a cultural thing that you don't show your emotions. They are supposed to be the breadwinner and the father figure. These things are taken away from them because they are ill." Sufferers and their partners often spoke of the detrimental impact of the illness on family life. The illness prevents them from performing certain activities and functions of hegemonic masculinity related to fatherhood. Territorial Army (TA) soldiers are over-represented among those suffering from the illness and, thus, are a primary concern of the association. The TA is the spare volunteer force of the British Army; it forms a quarter of the army's overall manpower. Although TA soldiers are supposed to have their jobs left open for them, many reported difficulty returning to work: "People come back, and their jobs aren't there for them. When they are, the co-workers are angry because you haven't kept up." Others, who had been "regulars," often left the military soon after the war and also found it difficult to find employment. Most of the sufferers I met did not work. They explained that their illness made them incapable of fulfilling their role as provider. Many participants receive some form of benefit from the state, usually in the form of a war pension.

Sufferers described lives dominated by fatigue, illness, and inability to participate in family activities. Some explained that their children questioned why they did not work like other fathers. As Harry explains, "It's role reversal at home. My wife works now and I'm doing the chores and that takes some getting used to... I'm a househusband and that. You have to know your limitations. And I know my limitations. I can't do DIY and that.... I have to admit I felt a bit inadequate." He is unable to do "DIY" (Do-It-Yourself): repairs, modifications, or building works that are seen traditionally as masculine pursuits in the United Kingdom.

Many sufferers said that GWS prevented them from playing with, "running around" with, or "kicking a football" with their children. It was often the physicality of fatherhood that was central and deemed missing because of the effects of the illness. Kerry, introduced above, described her husband as selfish: "He won't go near sand, so he won't go near a beach. I hate him for that because kids can't go on a beach. He can't play football with our son. He has been cut down in his prime. But he's had it for ten years, so you would think he would get used to it."

The performance of fatherhood is often described through participation in particular activities. Among my peer group in the United Kingdom, men express a desire to have a son to "kick a football with" and share an interest in sport and other "masculine" hobbies; I am often surprised by this rigid expression of gender. It is not surprising that GWS sufferers focus on their inability to play and be active with their children and that this seems to be more acute with sons. Indeed, this notion of damaged fatherhood was particularly emphasized in the relationship between fathers and sons, which parallels the theory of contagion described above.

Conclusion

Each modern war produces its own postcombat syndrome, and while different wars share similar features, each ensuing malady bears unique characteristics. Although I focus on Gulf War veterans, my research is timely given that the United Kingdom, Canada, and the United States, among other states, continue to engage in military campaigns likely to produce veterans who harbor a variety of illnesses and conditions. Soldiers continue to return home, many affected by their time in combat zones. We continue to have an epidemic of wounded warriors. However, so far evidence does not support an "Iraq war syndrome" despite the use of OPs, NAPS, and DU (Cohn et al. 2008; Horn et al. 2006; Wessely et al. 2009). The Gulf veterans I met sometimes referred to Iraqi birth defects, suggesting a link between the condition and adverse exposure, largely to DU munitions. In recent years there has been significant international concern, which has been generated over reports from medical staff in cities such as Fallujah and Baghdad of spiraling rates of congenital birth defects. Fallujah is particularly notorious, and medical staff and civil society organizations argue that the increases are linked to environmental contamination from the U.S.-led attacks on the city in 2004. The World Health Organization and the Iraqi Ministry of Health have now launched an assessment of congenital birth defects. We await the findings of this research, which will hopefully indicate whether there is a rise in birth defects and, if so, whether DU is the likely cause or whether other factors play a role. We must remember, for example, that there is an ongoing concern in Iraq and the rest of the Gulf region about the relationship between consanguinity and reproductive problems, so we await robust findings to help make sense of the situation.

Participation in the military impacts families and family life in numerous ways, but in the case of Gulf War veterans this assumes an added dimension: fatherhood itself is considered to be potentially toxic. Their ability to become fathers is seen to be impaired by the substances to which they were exposed. If they are able to conceive, these veterans fear their children will be born with birth defects as the result of Gulf War exposures. They see their bodies as weakened, ill, and toxic and believe that this toxicity can then be passed on to children. But GWS impacts fatherhood in other ways: children are being raised in toxic environments where they are physically and psychologically impacted by the war's residue. Their bodies, home environments, and social worlds all may be affected by their fathers' service in the Gulf War. GWS fathers are unable to enact key roles of fatherhood, including serving as the family's breadwinner and playing with their children. Their irritability and frustration creates a toxic home environment. Furthermore, it is not only the illness that impacts the family, but also the fight for its recognition by society. The veterans continually had to prove their illness, and this continuous enactment becomes a source of suffering. This fight for recognition means that they must constantly be performing the sick role. GWS affects the very core of masculinity, and one of the main elaborations of this is damaged and toxic fatherhood.

Notes

1. I am grateful to Scott North for alerting me to this concept.
2. Most studies, such as the ongoing large-scale study by the King's Center for Military Health Research, focus on the cycle of separation and reintegration that is a key feature of current deployments.

References

Barker, Lisa H., and Kathy D. Berry. 2009. "Developmental Issues Impacting Military Families with Young Children during Single and Multiple Deployments." *Military Medicine* 174: 1033–40.

Barnes, Vernon A., Harry Davis, and Frank A. Treiber. 2007. "Perceived Stress, Heart Rate, and Blood Pressure among Adolescents with Family Members Deployed in Operation Iraqi Freedom." *Military Medicine* 172: 40–43.

Barrett, Frank J. 1996. "The Organizational Construction of Hegemonic Masculinity: The Case of the U.S. Navy." *Gender, Work and Organization* 3, no. 3: 129–42.

Beck, Ulrick. 1992. *Risk Society.* London: Sage.

Bourgois, Phillipe. 1995. *In Search of Respect: Selling Crack in El Barrio.* Cambridge: Cambridge University Press.

Bourke, Joanna. 1996. *Dismembering the Male: Men's Bodies, Britain and the Great War.* London: Reaktion Books.

———. 1999. *An Intimate History of Killing: Face to Face Killing in Twentieth Century Warfare.* London: Granata Books.

Cohn, Simon, Clare Dyson, and Simon Wessely. 2008. "Early Accounts of Gulf War Illness and the Construction of Narratives in UK Service Personnel." *Social Science & Medicine* 67: 1641–49.

Connell, R. W. 1987. *Gender and Power: Society, the Person, and Sexual Politics.* Stanford, CA: Stanford University Press.

———. 1992. "Masculinity, Violence, and War." In *Men's Lives,* ed. Michael S. Kimmel and Michael A. Messner. New York: Macmillan.

———. 1995. *Masculinities.* Berkeley: University of California Press.

Courtenay, Will H. 2000. "Constructions of Masculinity and Their Influence on Men's Well-Being: A Theory of Gender and Health." *Social Science and Medicine* 50: 1385–1401.

Douglas, Mary. 1966. *Purity and Danger: An Analysis of the Concepts of Pollution and Taboo.* London: Routledge.

Doyle, Patricia, Noreen Maconochie, Graham Davies, Ian Maconochie, Margot Pelerin, Sue Prior, and Samantha Lewis. 2004. "Miscarriage, Stillbirth and Congenital Malformation in the Offspring of UK Veterans of the First Gulf War." *International Journal of Epidemiology* 33: 74–86.

Doyle, Patricia, Noreen Maconochie, and Margaret Ryan. 2006. "Reproductive Health of Gulf War Veterans." *Philosophical Transactions of the Royal Society* 361, no. 1468: 571–84.

Dudgeon, Matthew, and Marcia C. Inhorn. 2009. "Gender, Masculinity, and Reproduction: Anthropological Perspectives." In *Reconceiving the Second Sex: Men, Masculinity, and Reproduction,* ed. Marcia C. Inhorn, Tine Tjørnhøj-Thomsen, Helene Goldberg, and Maruska la Cour Mosegaard. New York; Oxford: Berghahn Books.

Giddens, Anthony. 1991. *Modernity and Self Identity.* Cambridge: Polity Press.

Gilmore, David. 1990. *Manhood in the Making: Cultural Concepts of Masculinity.* New Haven, CT: Yale University Press.

Goldberg, Helene. 2009. "The Sex and the Sperm: Male Infertility and Its Challenges to Masculinity in an Israeli-Jewish Context." In *Reconceiving the Second Sex: Men, Masculinity, and Reproduction,* ed. Marcia C. Inhorn, Tine Tjørnhøj-Thomsen, Helene Goldberg, and Maruska la Cour Mosegaard. New York; Oxford: Berghahn Books.

Gorman, Greg H., Matilda Eide, and Elizabeth Hisle-Gorman. 2010. "Wartime Military Deployment and Increased Pediatric Mental and Behavioral Health Complaints." *Pediatrics* 126: 1058–66.

Gutmann, Matthew C. 1997. "Trafficking in Men: The Anthropology of Masculinity." *Annual Review of Anthropology* 26: 385–409.

Harris, Paul. 2003. "Soldiers Line Up to Bank Sperm." *The Observer.* 9 February. http://observer.guardian.co.uk/iraq/story/0,892104,00.html.

Horn, Oded, Lisa Hull, Margaret Jones, Dominic Murphy, Tess Browne, Nicola T. Fear, Matthew Hotopf, Roberta J. Rona, and Simon Wessely. 2006. "Is there an Iraq War Syndrome? Comparison of the Health of UK Service Personnel after the Gulf and Iraq Wars." *The Lancet* 367, no. 9524: 1742–46.

Inhorn, Marcia C. 2002. "Sexuality, Masculinity, and Infertility in Egypt: Potent Troubles in the Marital and Medical Encounters." *Journal of Men's Studies* 10, no. 3: 343–59.

———. 2003. "'The Worms are Weak': Male Infertility and Patriarchal Paradoxes in Egypt." *Men and Masculinities* 5, no. 3: 236–56.

Ishoy, Torbin, Anna Maria Andersson, Poul Suadicani, Guldager Berndette, Merete Appleyard, F. Gyntelberg, and N. E. Skakkebaek. 2001. "Major Reproductive Health Characteristics in Male Gulf Veterans." *Danish Medical Bulletin* 48: 29–32.

Kang, Han, Carol Magee, Claire Mahan, Kyung Lee, Frances Murphy, Leila Jackson, and Genevieve Matanoski. 2001. "Pregnancy Outcomes among US Gulf War Veterans: A Population-Based Survey of 30,000 Veterans." *Annals of Epidemiology* 11: 504–11.

Kelly, John F. 2003. "Deploying Soldiers Put Family Plans on Ice." *Washington Post.* 4 February: B1, B2.

Kilshaw, Susie. 2006. "On Being a Gulf Veteran: An Anthropological Perspective." *Philosophical Transactions of the Royal Society* 361, no. 1468: 697–706.

————. 2007. "Toxic Emissions: The Role of Semen in Gulf War Syndrome Illness Narratives." *Anthropology and Medicine* 14, no. 3: 251–58.

————. 2009. *Impotent Warriors: Gulf War Syndrome, Vulnerability and Masculinity.* New York; Oxford: Berghahn Books.

Maconochie, Noreen, Pat Doyle, and Claire Carson. 2004. "Infertility among Male UK Veterans of the 1990-1 Gulf War: Reproductive Cohort Study." *BMJ* 329: 196.

Moore, Lisa. 2009. "Killer Sperm: Masculinity and the Essence of Male Hierarchies." In *Reconceiving the Second Sex: Men, Masculinity, and Reproduction,* ed. Marcia C. Inhorn, Tine Tjørnhøj-Thomsen, Helene Goldberg, and Maruska la Cour Mosegaard. New York; Oxford: Berghahn Books.

Morgan, David. 1994. "Theater of War: Combat, the Military and Masculinity." In *Theorizing Masculinities,* ed. Harry Brod and Michael Kaufman. London: Sage.

Petryna, Adriana. 2002. *Life Exposed: Biological Citizens after Chernobyl.* Princeton: Princeton University Press.

Schrader, Steven M., Terry W. Turner, and Stephen D. Simon. 1991. "Longitudinal Study of Semen Quality of Unexposed Workers: Sperm Motility Characteristics." *Journal of Andrology* 12, no. 1: 126–31.

Seidler, Victor J. 1994. *Unreasonable Men: Masculinity and Social Theory.* London: Routledge.

Showalter, Elaine. 1997. *Hystories: Hysterical Epidemics and Modern Culture.* New York: Columbia University Press.

Sim, Malcolm, Michael Abramson, Andrew Forbes, Deborah Glass, Jill Ikin, and Peter Ittak. 2003. "Australian Gulf Veterans' Health Study 2003." Vol. 2. Commonwealth Department of Veterans' Affairs. http://www.dva .gov.au/media/publicat/2003/gulfwarhs.

Swan, Shanna, and Eric Elkin. 1999. "Declining Semen Quality: Can the Past Inform the Present?" *Bioessays* 21, no. 7: 614–22.

Webb, Russell E., and Judith C. Daniluk. 1999. "The End of the Line: Infertile Men's Experiences of Being Unable to Produce a Child." *Men and Masculinities* 2: 6–25.

Wessely, Simon, Neil Greenberg, Charlotte Woodhead, and Nicola T. Fear. 2009. "Letter to the Editor: Gulf War Illness." *The Lancet* 373, no. 9662: 462.

Whorton, Donald, Ronald M. Krauss, Sumner Marshall, and Thomas H. Milby. 1977. "Infertility in Male Pesticide Workers." *Lancet* 310, no. 8051: 1259–61.

Wyrobek, Andrew J., Laurie A. Gordon, James G. Burkhart, Mary W. Francis, Robert W. Kapp, Gideon Letz, Heinrich V. Malling, John C. Topham, and M. Donald Whorton. 1983. "An Evaluation of Human Sperm as Indicators of Chemically Induced Alterations to Spermatogenic Function." *Mutation Research* 115, no. 4: 3–148.

CONTRIBUTORS

Maram Abu Yaman is a graduate student in the Department of Nursing at the University of Haifa, Israel. Abu Yaman works as a registered nurse in the hemato-oncology ward at Tel Aviv Medical Center, where she currently also serves as a bone marrow donation coordinator. During her studies, Abu Yaman participated in several research studies on pain and hospital nursing. She has volunteered extensively in various frameworks of support and empowerment for disadvantaged youth and elderly minority populations.

Daphna Birenbaum-Carmeli is Associate Professor in the Faculty of Social Welfare and Health Sciences at the University of Haifa, Israel. As a medical anthropologist, her research interest is the intersection between politics and health. In the domain of women's health, she focuses on the application of assisted reproductive technologies in the Israeli political context. In the broader Mediterranean setting, she is interested in the interface of health care and international state politics, primarily in its repercussions on various Palestinian populations. Birenbaum-Carmeli has published extensively in books and professional journals, including *Social Science and Medicine, Annual Review of Anthropology,* and *The Sociology of Health and Illness.* She is the author of *Tel Aviv North: The Making of a New Israeli Middle Class* (Hebrew University Press) and the co-editor of *Assisting Reproduction, Testing Genes: Global Encounters with New Biotechnologies* (with Marcia C. Inhorn) and *Kin, Gene, Community: Reproductive Technology among Jewish Israelis* (with Yoram S. Carmeli), both published by Berghahn Books.

Jude Browne is the Jessica and Peter Frankopan Director of the University of Cambridge Centre for Gender Studies and Fellow of

King's College, Cambridge. Her research is focused on gender, public policy, human, social, and economic rights, structural injustice, and political theories of equality and justice.

Wendy Chavkin is Professor of Public Health and Obstetrics and Gynecology at the Columbia University Mailman School of Public Health in New York City. She has served as the Director of the NYC Department of Health's Bureau of Maternity Services and Family Planning, the Editor-in-Chief of the *Journal of the American Medical Women's Association,* and Associate Editor for Women's Health of the *American Journal of Public Health.* She has conducted numerous studies on reproductive health policies and outcomes. She is a founding member of Physicians for Reproductive Choice and Health and former Board Chair. Her numerous honors include the Allan Rosenfield Award for Social Justice from the Public Health Association of NYC, Felicia Stewart Award for Advocacy from the American Public Health Association, a Fulbright New Century Scholarship, and the Bertha Van Hoosen Award and President's Award from the American Medical Women's Association. Chavkin is co-editor of *The Globalization of Motherhood: Deconstructions and Reconstructions of Biology and Care* (with JaneMaree Maher). She helped launch Global Doctors for Choice in 2007 and is a member of its Global Steering Committee.

Deborah Dempsey is Senior Lecturer in Sociology in the Faculty of Health, Arts and Design at Swinburne University of Technology, Melbourne, Australia. Her research interests are in the sociology of families, relationships, and sexuality and include: fatherhood and fathering; sociolegal aspects of assisted reproductive technologies (ARTs) and same-sex relationships; kinship and relatedness in the ART era; and cross-border reproductive care. Recent publications include *Families, Relationships and Intimate Life* (with Jo Lindsay), published by Oxford University Press, and articles on lesbian and gay family formation in *Sociology, Sexualities, and New Genetics and Society.*

Yana Diamand is a registered nurse in the pediatric oncology ward at the Rambam Medical Center in Haifa, Israel. Diamand works with children aged zero to twenty who suffer from a wide range of malignancies. She is also currently completing her MA in nursing at the University of Haifa.

Susan Greenhalgh is Professor of Anthropology and John King and Wilma Cannon Fairbank Professor of Chinese Society at Harvard University. Her research lies at the intersection of science and technology studies, gender studies, the anthropology of public policy, and the politics of life itself, a broad field that includes the politics of population and reproduction. A specialist on contemporary China, she is author of *Just One Child: Science and Policy in Deng's China* (2008) and *Cultivating Global Citizens: Population in the Rise of China* (2010), and co-author of *Governing China's Population: From Leninist to Neoliberal Biopolitics* (2005). *Just One Child* was awarded the 2010 Joseph Levenson Book Prize of the Association for Asian Studies and the 2010 Rachel Carson Book Prize of the Society for the Social Study of Science. In 2011 it received honorable mention in the Senior Book Prize competition of the American Ethnological Society. More recently, her research has focused on the biopolitics of the U.S. and global "obesity epidemic." Her book, *Making War on Fat: The Human Story of America's Anti-Obesity Campaign,* is expected in 2015.

Zeynep B. Gürtin is a Research Associate in the Sociology Department at the University of Cambridge and Founding Convener of the Cambridge Interdisciplinary Reproduction Forum. Her academic interests are in the social, psychological, and bioethical questions surrounding the use of assisted reproductive technologies (ARTs), particularly the ways in which they impact gender relations, family relationships, embodiment, and bodily experiences. Gürtin's research focuses on the empirical study and ethical analysis of gamete donation, particularly egg-sharing, cross-border reproductive care, and ARTs in Turkey. She lectures for various departments and faculties within the University of Cambridge, including on bioethics and assisted reproduction, globalization and reproduction, and gender studies.

Marcia C. Inhorn is the William K. Lanman Jr. Professor of Anthropology and International Affairs at Yale University. A specialist on Middle Eastern gender and health issues, Inhorn has conducted research on the social impact of infertility and assisted reproductive technologies in Egypt, Lebanon, the United Arab Emirates, and Arab America over the past twenty-five years. She is (co)editor of eight volumes and author of four award-winning books on the subject, including her most recent, *The New Arab Man: Emergent Masculinities, Technologies, and Islam in the Middle East* (Princeton University Press, 2012). Her fifth book, *Cosmopolitan Conceptions: IVF Sojourns in Global Dubai,* will be published by Duke University Press. Inhorn is the founding editor of the *Journal of Middle East Women's Studies* (*JMEWS*) and co-editor (with Soraya Tremayne) of Berghahn Books' "Fertility, Reproduction, and Sexuality" series. Inhorn has directed Yale's Council on Middle East Studies and the Center for Middle Eastern and North African Studies at the University of Michigan. She has served on the Board of Directors of the Middle East Studies Association, and was President of the Society for Medical Anthropology of the American Anthropological Association (AAA). In fall 2010, Inhorn was the first Diane Middlebrook and Carl Djerassi Visiting Professor at the Centre for Gender Studies, directed by Jude Browne at the University of Cambridge. In 2013, she received the Middle East Distinguished Scholar Award from the AAA's Middle East Section, and the Graduate Student Mentor Award from the AAA's Society for Medical Anthropology.

Linda G. Kahn is a doctoral candidate in the Department of Epidemiology at the Mailman School of Public Health at Columbia University. Her current research focuses on the effects of stress and environmental exposures on human fertility, as well as maternal and child health outcomes of assisted reproduction. In her prior career in publishing, she co-authored several trade books on diet, health, pregnancy, and childcare.

Susie Kilshaw is a Principal Research Fellow at the Department of Anthropology, University College London. She has two ongoing research projects in Qatar, both funded by the Qatar National Research Fund. The first investigates popular understandings of genetic risk and social implications of genetic knowledge in Qatar. The second is a cross-cultural exploration (United Kingdom and Qatar) of the experience of pregnancy and miscarriage. She was a teaching fellow in Medical Anthropology and Applied Studies at University College London (2004–10). Her previous work focused on the emergence of Gulf War Syndrome in the United Kingdom, and her book on the subject, *Impotent Warriors: Gulf War Syndrome, Vulnerability and Masculinity,* was published by Berghahn Books in 2009. She is also the deputy editor of *Anthropology and Medicine,* an interdisciplinary journal.

Theodora Lam is Research Associate in the Asian MetaCentre for Population and Sustainable Development Analysis and a PhD candidate in the Department of Geography, National University of Singapore. She is also the Research Assistant for the project titled Child Health and Migrant Parents in Southeast Asia (CHAMPSEA), analyzing the impact of parental absence due to migration on the health and well-being of left-behind children. Her research interests cover transnational migration, children's geographies, and gender studies. She has co-edited two special journal issues, "Asian Transnational Families in Transition: The Liminality of Simultaneity in International Migration" (2008, with Shirlena Huang and Brenda Yeoh) and "Asian Transnational Families in Global Networks" (2005, with Brenda Yeoh and Shirlena Huang), and is also the co-author of several book chapters and articles published in journals such as *Asia Pacific Viewpoint, Children's Geographies, Environment and Planning A,* and *International Development Planning Review.*

Jessaca Leinaweaver is Associate Professor of Anthropology at Brown University. Her research and teaching interests include kinship, childhood, migration, and anthropological demography, with a focus on Latin America. She is the winner of the Margaret Mead Award for her first book, *The Circulation of Children: Kinship, Adoption, and Morality in Andean Peru* (Duke University Press, 2008). The book has also been published in Spanish as *Los niños ayacuchanos: una antropología de la adopción y la construcción familiar en el Perú* (Instituto de Estudios Peruanos, 2009). Her most recent book, *Adoptive Migration: Raising Latinos in Spain* (Duke University Press, 2013), is based on research in Spain on the international adoption and migration of Peruvians. Leinaweaver is currently working on a project on aging and family caregiving in Peru.

José-Alberto Navarro is an MSc student at HEC Paris. His most recent work examines processes of fragmentation, objectification, and body commodification within invisible and illicit economies created through social-networking applications. Navarro's research focuses on exploring the intersections of economics, finance, and anthropology.

Scott North is Professor of Sociology in the Graduate School of Human Sciences at Osaka University. His recent publications about Japanese society include book chapters and journal articles in Japanese and English on work hours, death from overwork (*karoshi*), the gendered division of labor in dual-income households, corporate labor welfare regimes, strategies of leisure, and fatherhood. His current projects are a study of work-life conflict in Japan and participant observation in social movements that use litigation to promote worker health and well-being.

Sharmila Rudrappa is Associate Professor in the Department of Sociology, the Center for Asian American Studies, and the Center for Women and Gender Studies at the University of Texas at Austin. Her larger research interests are immigration, race, and ethnicity in the United States, gender and sexuality, and labor. She is currently working on two projects, both of which focus on fertility and infertility. The first project examines the cultural politics of assisted reproductive technologies in India, and the second project is on transnational surrogacy, where India is an emerging market in surrogate mothers.

Daniel Jordan Smith is Professor and Chair of the Department of Anthropology at Brown University. He conducts research in medical anthropology, anthropology and population, and political anthropology in sub-Saharan Africa, with a specific focus on Nigeria. He is the author of *A Culture of Corruption: Everyday Deception and Popular Discontent in Nigeria* (Princeton University Press, 2007), for which he received the 2008 Margaret Mead Award, and a co-author of *The Secret: Love, Marriage, and HIV* (Vanderbilt University Press, 2009). Smith's newest book is *AIDS Doesn't Show Its Face: Inequality, Morality, and Social Change in Nigeria* (University of Chicago Press, 2014). His current research project examines the social impact of popular evangelical and Pentecostal churches in southeastern Nigeria.

Vu Thi Thao is a research associate at Nordic Institute of Asian Studies, University of Copenhagen, Denmark. Her research interests focus on the ways in which feminization of labor migration is reshaping gender, family, and development in Vietnam. Thao is currently working on a project studying cultural encounters among Asian immigrant communities in Nordic countries. Her work has been published in *Geoforum*; *Population, Space and Place*; and *Asian Population Studies*.

Soraya Tremayne is a social anthropologist and the Founding Director of the Fertility and Reproduction Studies Group at the Institute of Social and Cultural Anthropology, University of Oxford. She has carried out research in Iran, the United Kingdom, Malaysia, and Hong Kong. Her current research focuses on the politics of reproduction in Iran, more specifically on assisted reproductive technologies. She is the founding co-editor of the Fertility, Reproduction and Sexuality Series with Berghahn Books.

Emily Wentzell is an Assistant Professor in the Department of Anthropology, University of Iowa. Her research combines approaches from medical anthropology, gender studies, and science and technology studies to examine sexual health interventions' gendered social consequences. She is currently researching the construction of gendered selfhood among Mexican married couples participating in a longitudinal study of HPV transmission, and is author of *Maturing Masculinities: Aging, Chronic Illness, and Viagra in Mexico* (Duke University Press, 2013).

Brenda S. A. Yeoh is Professor (Provost's Chair) of the Department of Geography and Dean of the Faculty of Arts and Social Sciences, both at the National University of Singapore (NUS). She is also the Research Leader of the Asian Migration Cluster at the Asia Research Institute, NUS. Her research interests include the politics of space in colonial and postcolonial cities, along with a wide range of migration research themes in Asia, such as cosmopolitanism and talent migration; gender, social reproduction, and care migration; migration, national identity, and citizenship issues; globalizing universities and student mobilities; and cultural politics, family dynamics, and international marriage migrants. Her latest books include *The Cultural Politics of Talent Migration in East Asia* (Routledge 2012, with Shirlena Huang), *Migration and Diversity in Asian Contexts* (ISEAS press, 2012, with Lai Ah Eng and Francis Collins), and *Return: Nationalizing Transnational Mobility in Asia* (Duke University Press, 2013, with Xiang Biao and Mika Toyota).

INDEX